The UAW and the Heyday
of American Liberalism

KEVIN BOYLE

THE UAW AND THE HEYDAY OF AMERICAN LIBERALISM 1945-1968

CORNELL UNIVERSITY PRESS

ITHACA AND LONDON

Library of Congress Cataloging-in-Publication Data

Boyle, Kevin, 1960–
    The UAW and the heyday of American liberalism, 1945–1968 / Kevin Boyle.
        p.   cm.
    Includes bibliographical references and index.
    ISBN 0-8014-3064-X (alk. paper)
    1. International Union, United Automobile, Aerospace, and Agricultural Implement
Workers of America—Political activity—History. 2. Trade-unions—Automobile industry
workers—United States—Political activity—History. 3. United States—Politics and
government—1945–1989. 4. Liberalism—United States—History—20th century. I. Title.
HD6515.A82I5733   1995
327'.2—dc20   95-9563

Contents

Illustrations

Preface

I have no real memory of a time when liberalism dominated public discourse. I was two years old when African-American marchers braved the fire hoses of Birmingham, three when Lyndon Johnson declared unrelenting war on poverty, seven when Robert Kennedy's funeral cortege wound its way through the cruel June night. I came of age in a period of profound political cynicism, a cynicism that cut through the governed and the governing, a cynicism that maimed and may yet destroy the activist state.

I began this book in response to that cynicism. In particular, I hoped to show the vitality of a political culture that believed government could act in the public good. In the course of my work, that job became more complicated. I became more and more aware that postwar liberals limited their agendas in important ways. I realized that the vision held by the leaders of the United Automobile Workers (UAW) did not match that of their liberal allies. And I began to see how willing the UAW was to compromise its vision to maintain the alliance on which its political power rested. Those complications did not force me to change the original intent of the book, however. Whatever their compromises, the men and women who led the postwar UAW committed their lives to the belief that government action could make American society more equitable and more just. In an age of cynicism, that is a story worth telling.

Every page of this book bears the imprint of Sidney Fine, who for ten years has served as a mentor and model. He read each of the many drafts, sharpening my analysis and my prose every step of the way. He has told me more than once that he considers his students to be members of his family. That is an honor I will always cherish.

I am indebted as well to other scholars who offered suggestions and support, large and small. Gerald Linderman, Terrence McDonald, and Howard Kimmeldorf supplied welcome guidance. Jack Barnard, Elizabeth Faue, Nancy Gabin, Gary Gerstle, Martin Halpern, and Nelson Lichtenstein commented on portions of the project. The critiques of Robert Asher, Bruce Nelson, and an anonymous reviewer improved the book immeasurably. Peter Agree of Cornell University Press shepherded a novice through the publication process with speed, patience, and grace. Barbara Salazar's extraordinary editing of the manuscript made the book more readable and the notes more accessible. At the University of Toledo, Scott McNall and William Hoover helped me to secure several timely grants. And Carol Bresnahan Menning showed tremendous faith in me and my work. She was the ideal colleague. Thanks also to my new colleagues at the University of Massachusetts, who have welcomed me into a friendly and stimulating intellectual environment.

The marvelous staff at the Archives of Labor and Urban Affairs at Wayne State University—Philip Mason, Warner Pflug, Patricia Bartkowski, Raymond Boryzka, Carolyn Davis, Thomas Featherstone, William Gulley, Sandra Kimberly, William LeFevre, Margery Long, Margaret Rauscher, Kathy Schmeling, and Turanda Spencer—were unfailingly helpful and friendly. Going to that library has become the academic equivalent of going home. The staffs of the Library of Congress, the Harry S. Truman Presidential Library, the John F. Kennedy Presidential Library, the Lyndon B. Johnson Presidential Library, the Martin Luther King Jr. Center for Nonviolent Social Change in Atlanta, the Minnesota Historical Society in St. Paul, the Seeley G. Mudd Manuscript Library at Princeton University, and the Michigan Historical Society in Ann Arbor also provided valuable assistance. I benefited from conversations with several UAW officials: Irving Bluestone, William Dodds, Douglas Fraser, Joseph Rauh Jr., Victor Reuther, Paul Schrade, and Leonard Woodcock. Chapter 6 includes material that appears in slightly different form in "There Are No Sorrows the Union Can't Heal: The Struggle for Racial Equality in the United Automobile Workers, 1945–1960," *Labor History,* Winter 1995. I am grateful to the editor, Daniel Leab, for permission to use that material here. The project was funded by the Horace H. Rackham School of Graduate Studies of the University of Michigan, the Henry Kaiser Family Foundation, the Rockefeller Foundation, the National Endowment for the Humanities, and two University of Toledo Summer Fellowships.

I cannot imagine having completed this work without the support of friends and family. Gail Hoffman and Michael Martin, Marty Hershock, Terry and Cindy Hopman, Kevin Hurst, Mike Smith, Joe and Nancy Tolkacz, Brian and Kathy Boyle, and Charlie Trierweiler have done more for me than I can ever repay. Rich Bodek, Jed and Janet Kuhn, Sue Darlington, and Dan Clark made Ann Arbor a special place. Lisa Heinemann, Johanna Schoen, and Glenn and Beth Ames did the same for Toledo. My in-laws, Art and Judy Getis, have shown me how an academic family should work. My parents, Kevin and Anne Boyle, have been constant sources of inspiration. They taught me to love books and ideas, and they taught me simply to love. Abby and Nan spurred me to finish revisions, then have slowed my academic work to a snail's pace. I couldn't be happier. Finally, Vicky has infused my work and my life with more joy than I ever dreamed possible. For that and for so much more, this book is dedicated to her.

KEVIN BOYLE

Amherst, Massachusetts

Abbreviations

ACTU	Association of Catholic Trade Unionists
ADA	Americans for Democratic Action
AFL	American Federation of Labor
ALA	Alliance for Labor Action
AMC	American Motors Corporation
CAP	Community Action Program
CCAP	Citizens' Crusade against Poverty
CEA	Council of Economic Advisers
CIO	Congress of Industrial Organizations
CORE	Congress on Racial Equality
CP	Communist Party
DRUM	Dodge Revolutionary Union Movement
ERAP	Economic Research and Action Project, SDS
FEPC	Fair Employment Practices Committee
GE	General Electric Company
GM	General Motors Corporation
HUAC	House Un-American Activities Committee
HUD	U.S. Department of Housing and Urban Development
ICFTU	International Confederation of Free Trade Unionists
IEB	International Executive Board, UAW
ILGWU	International Ladies Garment Workers Union
IUD	Industrial Union Department, AFL-CIO
JFK	John F. Kennedy
LBJ	Lyndon B. Johnson

Abbreviations

LCCR	Leadership Conference on Civil Rights
MDCDA	Metropolitan Detroit Citizens Development Authority
MFDP	Mississippi Freedom Democratic Party
NAACP	National Association for the Advancement of Colored People
NCC	National Council of Churches
ODM	Office of Defense Management
OEO	Office of Economic Opportunity
PAC	Political Action Committee, CIO
RFK	Robert F. Kennedy
SCLC	Southern Christian Leadership Conference
SDS	Students for a Democratic Society
SLID	Student League for Industrial Democracy
SNCC	Student Nonviolent Coordinating Committee
SP	Socialist Party
SUB	supplemental unemployment benefits
TULC	Trade Union Leadership Council
USWA	United Steelworkers of America
WCLU	Watts Community Labor Union
WFTU	World Federation of Trade Unions

THE UAW AND THE HEYDAY
OF AMERICAN LIBERALISM

Introduction:
Politics and Principle

When Ronald Reagan fired 11,500 striking air traffic controllers in the summer of 1981, he signaled the end of an era in American political life. For thirty-five years, from the end of World War II through the 1970s, the labor movement had occupied a preeminent place in national politics, providing one of the most important voices within the liberal New Deal order that dominated national discourse. Union leaders enjoyed easy access to the White House and Capitol Hill, union activists filled Democratic Party councils, and union dollars financed political campaigns and legislative lobbying efforts. The Republican triumph of the 1980s changed all that. Now, after years of conservative attacks and liberal retreats, the American labor movement is little more than a hollow shell, unable to defend its members from corporate retrenchment, powerless to affect national policy, and devoid of political clout.

The collapse of organized labor has triggered a searching reexamination of labor's role in the postwar United States. How could such a powerful movement have fallen so far so quickly? scholars have asked. The answer they provide is a deeply ironic one. In a series of provocative essays, Nelson Lichtenstein, Ira Katznelson, Alan Dawley, and others have argued that at the height of the postwar liberal ascendancy organized labor sowed the seeds of its own destruction.

In the late 1930s and early 1940s, the emerging interpretation runs, the labor movement's militant wing, under the umbrella of the Congress of Industrial Organizations (CIO), promoted a political agenda that promised to refashion American class relations. That agenda operated on two levels.

The UAW and the Heyday of American Liberalism

On the shop floor, union activists used their newfound power to challenge corporate control of production. Within national politics, CIO spokesmen demanded that they be given a formal role in the management of the economy through some form of democratic economic planning and that national resources be redistributed through a vast expansion of the welfare state. As late as 1945, that is, the industrial unions of the CIO promoted a social democratic program similar to the kind that emerged in sections of Western Europe in the postwar era.[1]

In the immediate postwar years, though, the CIO unions abandoned their hopes for a "social democratic breakthrough" in American politics. The exigencies of wartime allowed CIO leaders to centralize union authority and bureaucratize union practices, actions that undermined the shop-floor activism that had empowered the rank and file in the 1930s. Buffeted by a virulent conservative counter-attack in 1946 and 1947, the industrial unions then forsook class-based politics entirely. First, the CIO aligned itself with the emerging Cold War consensus by purging its Communist members. The remaining CIO unions rejected third-party politics in favor of a permanent place within the Democratic Party. Once safely within the Democratic fold, they abandoned their demands for a say in corporate decision making and a significant expansion of the welfare state. Instead, they accepted the much narrower goal of winning ever larger wage settlements for their members through a collective bargaining process circumscribed by the federal government. By the late 1940s, CIO unions, once the "vanguard in America," had become simply another special-interest group.[2]

The CIO's deradicalization, it is argued, had profound effects both for the labor movement itself and for national politics as a whole. By foreclosing the possibility of forming a third party, the CIO lost much of its leverage within the Democratic Party. Knowing that unions had nowhere else to turn, Democratic leaders offered labor only a token role in setting party policy. The unions' ability to win generous contracts, moreover, caused tremendous resentment among employers and the middle class, who thought the settlements excessive, and among the lower class, who were denied the security unionized workers now enjoyed. For their part, union members grew increasingly complacent under the postwar industrial system, demobilized by a political system that eschewed the language of class and uninterested in supporting reform programs that they themselves no longer needed. Taken together, these factors left the postwar labor movement dangerously weak, dependent on the largess of the corporations and the Democratic Party rather than on its own power within the political economy.[3]

Labor's demobilization likewise constricted the nation's range of political possibilities, Lichtenstein, Katznelson, and others have argued. Without a powerful labor movement pushing them to the left, postwar policy makers of both parties were free to pursue a mild reformism at home and an aggressive anticommunism abroad. The result was a policy mix that left corporate power unchecked, the welfare state underdeveloped in comparison with the polities of Western Europe, and national resources drained by the incessant demands of the military-industrial complex. The labor movement's acquiescence in, indeed support of, this narrow program undermined the Democratic Party's political power. Convinced that it had solved the "labor question" that had bedeviled the nation throughout the first half of the century, the party slowly shifted its focus to the problem of racial inequality. The effort to solve that problem eventually ripped the party apart and opened the door for the conservative triumph of the 1980s.[4]

According to the emerging interpretation, then, the industrial labor movement, by its failure of will in the late 1940s, laid the basis for its and liberalism's collapse in the 1980s. Had organized labor resisted joining the Cold War consensus, the argument runs, had it refused to accept a formal position in the Democratic Party, had it continued to promote a social democratic agenda, perhaps it might have won enough political and economic power to have withstood the conservative onslaught of the Reagan years. The road not taken, it seems, made all the difference.

In this book I hope to contribute to the assessment of organized labor's place in the postwar political order by examining the national political activism of one CIO union—the United Automobile Workers (UAW)—from 1945 to 1968. The UAW offers several advantages as a case study of postwar labor power. Most obviously, the UAW's size and strategic position gave the union tremendous leverage. Throughout the postwar period, the million-member UAW was one of the largest unions in the United States, trailing only the International Brotherhood of Teamsters and the United Steelworkers of America in membership. In economic power it far outstripped even those unions, since it had the ability to shut down an industry that, at its peak, directly or indirectly employed one in every six Americans. The UAW's leadership, among the most sophisticated in the American labor movement, used the union's economic clout to secure much more political power than most union leaders enjoyed. By the 1950s, the UAW sent more delegates to the Democratic national convention, contributed more money and personnel to election campaigns, and maintained a more extensive congressional lobbying apparatus than any other American union.[5]

From the mid-1940s onward, the UAW leadership put its political muscle at the disposal of an array of liberal organizations and causes. Walter Reuther, elected president in 1946, served as a cofounder of Americans for Democratic Action (ADA) and the Leadership Conference on Civil Rights (LCCR). The UAW contributed substantial sums of money to the National Association for the Advancement of Colored People (NAACP), the National Council of Churches, the National Planning Association, the Southern Christian Leadership Conference (SCLC), and other liberal pressure groups. The union maintained warm relations with Hubert Humphrey, Paul Douglas, G. Mennen Williams, Martin Luther King Jr., and other liberal politicians and activists. And the UAW played a pivotal role in the passage of postwar liberalism's most important legislative initiatives, from the Employment Act of 1946 to the Great Society programs of the mid-1960s. A case study of the UAW therefore does more than shed light on one of the most powerful of postwar American unions. It also offers entrée to the inner workings of postwar liberalism.

The UAW, finally, stands at the center of the emerging intepretation of labor's role in postwar politics. More than any other union, Nelson Lichtenstein has argued, the UAW exemplifies the limits of organized labor's vision. During the late 1930s and early 1940s, he contends, the UAW led the struggle to establish social democracy in the United States. When Reuther, a militant anticommunist, won the UAW presidency, he rejected the union's social democratic agenda, routinized collective bargaining, and allied the UAW with the Democratic Party. As a result, Lichtenstein concludes, Reuther "opened the way for the general alignment of his union and the industrial union wing of the labor movement with the . . . conservative, corporate-directed political and economic consensus emerging in the early Cold War years." By examining the UAW, this book directly engages the emerging intepretation of postwar labor's experience.[6]

It also challenges much of that intepretation. Walter Reuther and his supporters, I argue, were not the harbingers of the postwar liberal order but rather the inheritors of the social democratic ideological and political formations Steven Fraser has so effectively traced for the 1930s and early 1940s. The UAW leadership did not abandon this social democratic agenda in the late 1940s. On the contrary, Reuther and the UAW leadership continued to promote democratic economic planning and an expanded welfare state throughout the 1950s and 1960s. They did so, moreover, at the highest levels of government. In the process, however, UAW leaders faced the dilemma that, according to Adam Przeworski and Gösta Esping-Andersen, social democrats invariably confront. Because workers do not make up a majority of the population in advanced industrial countries, these authors demonstrate, social democrats cannot hope to win political power through a strictly class-based party. They therefore must find allies outside the traditional working class. That policy runs the risk of compromising the class-specific nature of the movement's final goals and thus of transforming social democracy into simply another bourgeois political movement.[7]

Such an outcome can be avoided, Esping-Andersen argues, if social democrats promote immediate reforms that offer gains for workers and nonworkers alike rather than reforms that pit one group against another. These positive-sum reforms must have the cumulative effect of marginalizing the role of the free market in determining the citizenry's standard of living. Social democrats thus are able to achieve their ultimate goals without losing the political power that makes reform possible.[8]

The postwar UAW leadership attempted to pursue a strategy similar to the one Esping-Andersen suggests. Throughout the 1950s and 1960s, Reuther and his lieutenants attempted to build a cross-class, biracial reform coalition in the United States. As the UAW activists envisioned it, the coalition would rest on, though it would not be restricted to, three groups: unionists; middle-class liberals in the federal government, in pressure groups such as ADA, in church groups, and in the academy; and African-Americans. The UAW appealed to these middle-class liberals by appropriating two of the issues most dear to them: economic growth and anticommunism. And the union appealed to African-Americans by vigorously supporting civil rights. In each instance, the UAW leaders threw the union's weight behind specific reform measures their coalition partners favored. But the unionists continued to insist that economic growth would not be assured, communism would not be defeated, and civil rights would not be secured until the political economy itself was altered.

The UAW pursued its strategy, however, within political, policy-making, and institutional structures that limited its effectiveness. From 1948 onward, the union had no choice but to work within a Democratic Party sharply divided between northern moderates and liberals on the one hand and southern conservatives on the other. The South's one-party political system and racial caste structure, coupled with the congressional seniority system, ensured southern Democrats disproportionate power on Capitol Hill, power they used to block even the most mild reforms from the late 1930s to the mid-1960s. The southerners' ability to deliver a solid Democratic vote in national elections convinced party leaders that it was better to appease than to confront that power in advancing legislation and in establishing the party's platform. As a result, the postwar UAW promoted its social democratic agenda through a party more concerned with maintaining consensus than with presenting a coherent reform program.[9]

The structures through which the postwar federal government instituted economic and social policy, moreover, hardly lent themselves to social democratic experimentation. By 1946, the federal agencies most amendable to economic planning—the National Resource Planning Board and the War Production Board, for example—had been eliminated. In their place stood agencies, such as the Federal Housing Authority and the Council of Economic Advisers, much less capable of intruding on corporate decision making and the free play of market forces. Similiarly, most of the New Deal–era welfare programs that had survived the war—retirement insurance and unemployment compensation, for instance—remained incomplete in their coverage or decentralized in their administration, a far cry from the cradle-to-grave welfare state the UAW favored.[10]

Such structures dovetailed with the policy preferences of the postwar liberal elite. As Alan Brinkley has shown, by 1945 most liberal policy makers had rejected the notion of a powerful federal state directly involved in the micromanagement of the American economy. Instead, they contended, the federal government should pursue a "commercial" Keynesianism that would promote economic growth and full employment. At the same time, liberals increasingly came to believe that American society was divided not into a handful of large economic blocs but rather into a plethora of relatively small social groupings, precisely the kind of social structure best served by a decentralized and fragmented welfare state. For many postwar liberal elites, the direction of economic and social policy became a technical problem of fiscal manipulation and interest-group management, better solved by experts than by representatives of broad economic interests. Even the UAW's liberal allies in the Democratic Party thus were wary of the social democratic state that the union leadership supported.[11]

Finally, the labor movement's and the UAW's internal structures limited the union leadership's ability to advance its agenda. Throughout the postwar era, the UAW worked within a federated union movement, first as a member of the CIO, then as a member of the AFL-CIO. Consequently, UAW leaders continually had to coordinate their political agenda with those of other union leaders, many of whom did not share the auto workers' commitment to social democracy. Reuther built and sustained his power base in the UAW through a complex political machine, the maintainance of which constrained his freedom of action. The UAW's secondary leaders and rank and file opposed some of the leadership's political initiatives, particularly on racial issues. They therefore undercut Reuther's ability to present his union as the vanguard of reform.[12]

From the late 1940s to the mid-1960s, the UAW leadership attempted to work within these structural constraints. In the process, the UAW made a series of political compromises, accepted some halfhearted reform measures, and supported candidates and programs about which it had serious doubts, all in an attempt to reconcile the realities of postwar politics and the principles of social democratic reform. The effort was in vain; as long as the postwar political and policy-making structures remained in place, the UAW simply could not fashion the reform coalition it sought. In the mid-1960s, however, the political structure suddenly shattered. In a series of dramatic confrontations, civil rights activists, supported by a coalition of forces precisely like the one the UAW had long envisioned, broke the southern Bourbons' stranglehold on the Democratic Party. When the Johnson administration followed that triumph with a wide-ranging attack on poverty, it appeared as if the postwar federal policy-making structures were likewise about to be transformed. Seizing the moment, the UAW threw itself into the antipoverty effort, hoping to push it to the left.

That proved to be a grievous miscalculation. The Johnson administration simply would not be moved; despite its rhetorical commitment to substantive change, the administration believed that the War on Poverty could be pursued within the economic and social constraints of postwar liberalism. The poverty programs thus largely targeted specific social groups, particularly poor blacks, and did not present any challenge to corporate power. The outcome was the opposite of what the UAW had hoped it would be. Many white workers, including many white UAW members, came to see the War on Poverty as a zero-sum game in which they were bound to lose. Conversely, an increasing number of blacks, including many black UAW members, came to see the War on Poverty as an attempt by whites to co-opt the African-American freedom struggle.[13] In order to sustain their influence in the antipoverty effort, moreover, UAW leaders once again compromised their principles, this time by publicly supporting the Vietnam War, the wisdom of which they seriously doubted. That decision alienated the union leadership from the emerging new left, which the UAW had nurtured earlier in the decade, and the growing antiwar segment of the liberal elite. Racked by racial conflict and torn asunder by the war, the reform coalition collapsed, in the process fatally weakening the power base on which the UAW and the labor movement as a whole depended.

In the final analysis, then, *The UAW and the Heyday of American Liberalism* is about labor's failure: its inability to build a cross-class, biracial coalition committed to continued reform; its inability to redefine the nation's policy-making structures; its inability to fashion a more democratic political economy in the postwar United States. The reasons for that failure, though, cannot be traced simply to labor's lack of vision, to its willingness to act as a special-interest group within a pluralist state. The UAW, at least, wanted labor to be much more. Labor's failure, rather, must be seen as grounded in the complex interaction between labor's goals and the context in which they were pursued, between what labor wanted and what it could achieve. The story of labor's place in the postwar political order, in other words, is not just the story of a promise betrayed but also the story of struggles fought and lost.

The first two chapters detail the political culture within the UAW and the nation at large in the mid-1940s, a culture that, in the election of 1948, set the parameters within which the UAW operated for the next twenty years. The following four chapters detail the UAW's struggles to work within those parameters throughout the 1950s and early 1960s. And the final four chapters discuss the triumph and defeat of the reform coalition, starting with the civil rights movement of the early 1960s and ending with the election of 1968, the beginning of the Republican ascendancy in American politics.

During the years from 1945 to 1968, the UAW involved itself in a bewildering array of reform efforts and political campaigns. In order to focus the narrative, I have restricted my attention to national policy and politics, dealing with collective bargaining and state politics only insofar as they had an impact on national issues. Within national political life, I have paid particular attention to four policy areas—full employment policy, federal urban policy, African-American civil rights, and the containment of communism in Asia—and to presidential election campaigns. I could have examined other issues and campaigns, of course: anti-inflation policy, national health care, the rights of migrant laborers, European containment, and senatorial election contests, for example. The five topics selected, however, lay at the center of both the UAW's and the nation's agenda throughout the twenty years under examination, whereas many other issues moved to the center of national concern for much shorter periods of time. By focusing on these issues, then, I am able to examine the UAW's political activity in substantial detail, without fragmenting the narrative.

This book is unabashedly a top-down, institutional history. By choosing that approach, I do not mean to imply that social history is unimportant. The outpouring of extraordinary scholarship since the 1960s has made an invaluable contribution to our understanding of the American experience. But I believe that institutions are also important. In the postwar United States at least, they are important not because they reflect the consciousness of the people they claim to represent. Postwar unions cannot stand as proxies for the American working class; political parties cannot stand as proxies for the American electorate; Congress and the White House cannot stand as proxies for the American people. Rather, unions, political parties, and republican institutions are important because under the liberal New Deal order they had the power to shape national policy, to decide how and for whom the federal government should work, and thus to determine who benefited from the bounty of postwar American society and who did not. The years since 1980 have shown just how important and just how transitory that power was.

[1]

Building the Vanguard

Three months after the Japanese surrender ended World War II, the UAW's Victor Reuther offered his vision of labor's place in the postwar United States. It was hardly an auspicious time for such a pronouncement. The Allied victory had destroyed the tenuous accord that labor, management, and the federal government had built during the war. Conservatives in and outside Congress had turned on the labor movement with a fury unseen since the 1930s; the new president, Harry Truman, had distanced himself from the New Dealers on whom organized labor had so long depended; and corporate officials had boosted prices precipitously while rejecting union demands for expansive wage increases. The onset of peace had also shattered the fragile equilibrium of political forces in the UAW. As early as 1940, the union had divided into two camps, one led by the UAW's Communist cadre, one by Victor's older brother, Walter. During the war, the UAW's factions had barely managed to contain their differences. As soon as the war ended, the internecine battles began again, this time with a ferocity that threatened to engulf the union.[1]

A more cautious unionist might have called for retrenchment. For Victor Reuther, however, labor's troubles simply dramatized the need for union leaders to become more militant than they had been during the war. "Labor today should proclaim a declaration of independence," he wrote in the social democratic journal *Common Sense*. It should

> divorce progressive trade unions from the restrictive concept of "union-
> ism as usual," under which the major function of labor unions has been to

wrestle with business and government for larger shares of scarcity under a
system of "free enterprise." . . . Private ownership of monopolistic industries must be replaced by forms of social ownership. . . . Of course, such
a program is political dynamite; but the task of social engineering that we
face is of such scope that nothing short of political dynamite can blast
away the obstructions to economic abundance and insure the expansion
of political democracy.[2]

Reuther's call to arms was, in part, pure bravado, an attempt to promote
his and his brother's political credentials in national liberal circles and their
radical credentials in the UAW. It was more than that, though. It was also a
statement of principle, a reflection of the Reuther brothers' deepest political
beliefs. In the 1930s and 1940s, the Reuthers developed a simple and
coherent message: If the American people were to enjoy economic growth
and full employment, national economic decision making would have to be
democratized. That goal could be reached, the Reuthers argued, only if the
United Automobile Workers led the way.

At war's end, the UAW seemed to have the power and position necessary
to lead a reformulation of American economic and political life. The UAW
stood at the epicenter of the American political economy in mid-1945. On
the job, the union's million members provided the muscle power that fueled
the nation's most important industry; outside the factory gates, they formed
a broad voting bloc in the swing states of the industrial Midwest, long the
cockpit of national politics, and California, home of the burgeoning aero-
space industry, much of which the UAW had under contract. The UAW's
ability to use its power was severely limited, however, by the union's internal tensions. Scholars have typically described the union's problems in personal terms, tracing the individual conflicts that rent the union's leadership.
To be sure, the UAW did become a personal and political battleground, but
its greatest difficulty was much more fundamental than that. From its
inception, the UAW was torn between two concepts of unionism. Many
rank and filers favored a decentralized union committed to local and shop-
floor activism, whereas UAW leaders operated within institutional and
state structures that demanded centralized, bureaucratic unionism. In the
immediate postwar years, Walter Reuther resolved the tension, winning the
UAW presidency by using the structures the membership feared.

The automobile industry was the twentieth century's quintessential industry, a triumph of innovative technology, integrated manufacturing,
and sophisticated management. Launched in the last years of the nineteenth
century, auto manufacturing became the nation's greatest mass-production
industry in the first three decades of the new century. The Ford Motor

Company led the way in the late 1900s and early 1910s, perfecting complex manufacturing processes that simultaneously sped up production, drove down labor costs, and increased productivity. The General Motors Corporation built on Ford's innovations in the 1920s, constructing management and marketing structures that brought control over the industry's sprawling industrial complex.[3]

Those changes made the auto industry into the United States' economic engine: by 1930, the industry singlehandedly accounted for 13 percent of the value of all manufactured goods in the nation. The industry's changes also concentrated that vast economic power in a handful of massive firms with the resources to exploit the industry's economies of scale; together, General Motors, the nation's largest manufacturing corporation, Ford, and Chrysler made approximately 85 percent of all autos in the 1930s. The Big Three, in turn, concentrated their production in the industrial Midwest. Though the manufacturers maintained plants throughout the United States, 80 percent of their employees worked in Ohio, Indiana, Illinois, Wisconsin, and Michigan.[4]

For the hundreds of thousands of men and women who worked in the plants, auto making was also an insecure and inhumane industry. Auto manufacturers generally paid their workers well, so that a factory hand who worked steadily could enjoy a comfortable, though hardly middle-class, standard of living. Few auto workers worked steadily, however. On the contrary, the industry's marketing strategies and the volatility of consumer demand made auto workers particularly vulnerable to layoffs. Even in the prosperous year of 1925 the typical factory hand lost a month and a half of work as manufacturers cleared inventories or retooled for the annual model change-over. When the economy turned downward, the level of instability increased dramatically: throughout the 1930s, the auto industry had double the layoff rate of manufacturing industries as a whole. Most auto workers thus lived with constant insecurity, knowing that at any time they could face a prolonged period of unemployment that could devastate their family economies.[5]

Inside the factory gates, most auto workers surrendered control over their labor, working to the inexorable demand of the assembly line. The effects of assembly work have been well documented: workers shaking uncontrollably after a day in the plant, workers arriving home too tired to pick up a knife and fork, workers dulled and defeated by years of repetitive labor. Management maintained the work regime with a strict, often arbitrary disciplinary system. A web of foremen, supervisors, and security men enforced petty prohibitions against smoking and talking, kept lunch breaks and rest periods to a minimum, and controlled the right to upgrade, transfer, and fire workers at will. There were "no rules. You were at the mercy of the foreman," a Fisher Body worker explained. "I could go to work at seven o'clock in the morning, and at seven-fifteen the boss'd come around and say: you could come back at three o'clock. If he preferred someone over you, that person would be called back earlier."[6]

In early 1937, auto workers rebelled against the shop-floor disciplinary system, forging the UAW on the factory floors of Flint, Detroit, and other auto centers. The rank and filers were abetted by a phalanx of radical organizers and shop floor activists: Communist Party members, many of whom had been active in auto plants since the 1920s; Socialist and Trotskyist organizers trained in the labor battles of the early 1930s; German- and English-born craftsmen who had learned their radicalism in the coal pits, shipyards, and steel mills of Europe; Catholic unionists committed to their church's vision of a corporatist economy; and others. The factory hands and the radical activists together shattered management's arbitrary power on the shop floor, creating what David Brody has called "workplace contractualism": the detailed classification of jobs and wages, the strict application of seniority in transfers and upgrades, and carefully negotiated procedures for timing jobs, all to be enforced through an elaborate grievance procedure.[7]

The victories of the late 1930s hardly solved all the auto workers' problems. Work rules did not challenge management's control over work pace, and though unionization held out the promise of higher wages, it did not eliminate the specter of unemployment. Whatever the limits of workplace contractualism, though, rank and filers embraced and fiercely defended the rights it provided. They did so in large part by making extensive use of the union's contractual machinery. More spectacularly, workers also took vigorous, often spontaneous action at the point of production. The activist Frank Marquart described the scene at Ford's River Rouge plant when a newly elected UAW committeeman approached his foreman and showed him his committeeman's button. "Do you see this?" the committeeman asked. "Ah, yes," the foreman said. "Congratulations." "Congratulations, hell," the committeeman bellowed. "I'm running this department—you scram the hell out of here!" Such conflicts were not unusual. Between 1937 and 1939, UAW members at GM staged 435 walkouts, despite a contract provision prohibiting strikes.[8]

Auto workers did not simply turn their local and shop-floor power against their employers. Throughout the late 1930s and early 1940s, UAW members also used their locals to draw distinctions among themselves, often in clear violation of the principles to which the industrial union was dedicated. The union's radicals led the way, turning many of the UAW's locals into ideological and political battlegrounds. In 1938, Catholic activists denounced the Communist presence in the UAW. The next year the Communists, Trotskyists, and Socialists, always an unstable coalition, turned against one another with extraordinary ferocity.[9]

The UAW rank and file likewise splintered, though on social rather than political lines. The UAW's social geography remains poorly mapped, but scholar have shown that fault lines cut through the membership. By and large, the auto companies drew their workforces from three sources. For its skilled hands, the industry hired native-born, English, or German tradesmen, long the elite of the American working class. For its production workers, the industry turned to the country's two great pools of unskilled labor, Eastern and Southern European immigrants and rural migrants, white and black. Strikingly diverse, these groups brought an array of often conflicting perspectives and prejudices to their local unions.[10]

Auto workers' varied skill levels created one fissure. By the 1930s, auto makers had dramatically reduced the number of skilled workers required to complete the production process, but a core of tradesmen—approximately 10 percent of the UAW membership—still occupied strategic positions on the shop floor. Steeped in class pride and union consciousness, the skilled hands often feared that their special status would be lost in an industrial union dominated by semi- and unskilled operatives. Almost exclusively white, they also feared that the union might break the strict color line that the crafts traditionally maintained. "A lot of the tool and die makers thought the CIO was a production union," a UAW member recalled, "'and God damn it, [they said,] we don't need a production line.'" As early as 1938, accordingly, skilled workers demanded that the union establish local skilled trades councils empowered to limit the union leadership's control of apprenticeship and the classification of craftwork, a move many production workers deeply resented.[11]

Though more muted, ethnic differences divided auto workers as well. Southern and Eastern European immigrants had dominated the industry's semi- and unskilled jobs in its formative years, but by 1940 the immigrant generation was disappearing from the plants. They were replaced, by and large, by their American-born sons and daughters and by white migrants from rural areas, many of them southern. Together, second-generation ethnic and rural migrants probably accounted for slightly more than half of all UAW members at the start of the decade. These two groups shared at least one key characteristic: they were likely to be militant unionists, favoring aggressive union action whenever they felt their rights to be imperiled. Their militancy was rooted, however, in different cultural traditions and political perceptions. Many young ethnic workers embraced the UAW as a symbol of their Americanization, a primary avenue through which they could exert their rights as citizens. "When we talked to the foreman [after the coming of the union], we talked to the foreman on an equal basis," an Italian-American auto worker recalled. "We did not have to stand up like the Italian boys . . . with their hats in their hands." Historians have paid much less attention to white rural-born auto workers. The extant scholarship suggests that those migrants who came from the rural South took little comfort in Americanism, a rhetoric that ran counter to much of the region's political tradition. Rather, their militancy grew out of a commitment to individual rights and moral justice, values deeply rooted in southern politics and evangelical Christianity. Many migrants from the rural North distrusted federal power and clung doggedly to a nineteenth-century faith in economic independence and individual freedom. Many white rural migrants, northern- and southern-born alike, therefore found less than appealing the UAW's linking of state power and patriotism, which ethnic rank and filers found so attractive. The difference did not have much impact on shop-floor action, but it subtly shaped the two groups' responses to the UAW's political program. Ethnic workers vigorously supported New Deal Democrats, who had incorporated them into the national body politic, whereas rural migrants, though often strongly Democratic, distrusted the party's liberal elites and the reforms they promoted.[12]

The racial fissure cut much more deeply and painfully through the UAW rank and file. Most of the auto industry's African-American workers—about 8 percent of the rank and file in 1945—had come north during or shortly after World War I, hoping to escape the economic dislocation and social brutality of the Jim Crow South. Once in the North, however, they were largely shut out of the auto industry's better-paying jobs. Most auto companies relegated black workers to the least desirable classifications, typically as foundry hands or janitors. The few blacks who were placed in higher paying jobs often faced verbal or even physical attacks from white workers committed to white supremacy. "Coloreds have worked on machines here, years ago," a white worker told an interviewer in 1940. "But there've been 'accidents.' A colored fellow gets pushed into a machine or something else happens." African-American activists, both in and outside the UAW, argued that the union could break down such barriers to black advancement, but many black workers remained wary of an organization dominated by the same white workers who had defended the pre-union color line. "Some of these white fellows come and ask us to join the union," an African-American at a Detroit Dodge plant explained in 1940. "A man doesn't kick you in the ass and then you turn around and kiss him."[13] Black workers had reason for concern. Many early local contracts maintained separate seniority lists or job classifications for black and white workers. A handful of locals went further, barring African-Americans from membership altogether. Some white workers turned to shop-floor action to preserve the color line, walking off the job when an African-American integrated a plant. Such actions did not go unchallenged. By 1945, black rank and filers had begun to fight back, organizing their own caucuses within their locals and, on a few occasions, wildcatting to support integration of the shop floor.[14]

The UAW rank and file also split according to gender. Female auto workers, 7.5 percent of the industry's workforce in 1940, faced many of the same difficulties as black workers. Like African-Americans, women were traditionally relegated to a narrow range of "suitable" jobs: sewing machine operator, small-parts assembler, and trim bench hand, for example. These "girl's jobs" carried a substantial wage differential; on average, women earned half the wage rate of their male co-workers. In the 1930s, Nancy Gabin has shown, most women did not oppose such discrimination. By 1945, however, many UAW women insisted that their union break down shop-floor gender barriers. "Women workers must receive fair and just treatment," a group of rank and filers declared at the 1944 UAW convention. The UAW "must reaffirm the democratic principles that all members should be guaranteed the fullest protection of their union membership."[15]

Such local fragmentation brought the rank and file into direct conflict with the union's organizational structure, which operated according to a much more hierarchical concept of political power. Written by the American Federation of Labor in 1935, the UAW constitution granted ultimate control of the union not to the rank and file but rather to the delegates to the UAW's annual convention. In theory, any rank and filer could serve as a convention delegate. In practice, convention seats usually went to local officials and union activists. This relatively narrow group then elected the UAW's four International officers, the UAW president, secretary-treasurer, and two vice-presidents, who exercised day-to-day control of union affairs. The officers implemented union policy through eighteen regional directors, each of whom was assigned responsibility for those locals within his geographic jurisdiction. Together, the officers and regional directors constituted the UAW's governing body between conventions, the International Executive Board (IEB). Most members therefore had no role, and only a handful of activists enjoyed even an indirect role, in setting union policy. The UAW, in short, was designed as a top-down bureaucracy rather than a grass-roots democracy.[16]

Both government and corporate officials encouraged the union's bureaucracy to take control of the rank and file. The UAW had been able to bring the auto companies to terms only because federal and state authorities were willing to guarantee workers the right to collective bargaining. At first sympathetic to shop-floor ferment, by the end of the 1930s the New Dealers had refashioned labor policy to favor those unions with powerful central leaderships. Similarly, most auto makers insisted that the UAW leadership keep rank and file activism in check as a provision of its contract. Government and corporate officials thus hoped to create an industrial relations system more stable and less confrontational than rank and file activism allowed.[17]

The demands of wartime accentuated the trend toward centralization and bureaucratization. Desperate to maintain continual production of war material and to avoid a ruinous wartime inflation, the Roosevelt administration demanded that unions abrogate their right to strike for the duration and agree to a freeze in wages. The pressure was particularly great on the UAW. The auto industry had linked itself so intimately to the emerging military-industrial complex that it produced 20 percent of the nation's entire military output, and the military's battle plan depended heavily on the booming aircraft industry, many of whose workers the UAW represented. In place of collective bargaining, the administration created a federal grievance procedure governed by a bewildering array of guidelines and directives. The federal government thus attempted to shift the locus of union power from the rank and file to the union bureaucrats, who could maneuver through the byzantine world of federal regulations.[18]

Throughout the war, the UAW rank and file resisted the pressure to centralize union power. Convinced that the cumbersome federal bureaucracy could not or would not protect their shop-floor rights, auto workers staged a massive wave of wildcat strikes. Thousands of white workers likewise walked off the job when the auto companies, under federal pressure, defied the color line by promoting African-Americans to assembly work. By 1945, the rank-and-file revolt had reached crisis proportions; in the course of that year, 50 percent of UAW members participated in at least one walkout. The UAW leadership, a well-informed federal official reported, "has found it impossible to adjust the thinking of its rank and file." Without any control from above, he wrote, American auto plants were being swept by "rebellion and irrationality."[19]

For all its militancy, the wartime wildcat wave accomplished very little. At war's end, the no-strike pledge, the wage freeze, and the federal grievance procedure remained in place; African-Americans and women filled jobs previously closed to them; and union bureaucrats enjoyed more power than ever before. Many auto workers thus faced the return to civilian production in an angry and defiant mood, convinced that both the federal government and the auto makers wanted to roll back the rights they had secured in the 1930s. That fear, in turn, opened the door for Walter Reuther.[20]

W alter Philip Reuther was thirty-eight years old when World War II ended. He was born in Wheeling, West Virginia, in 1907, the second child of German-born working-class parents. Reuther's mother, Anna, was a devout Lutheran, his father, Valentine, a fervent unionist and Socialist: an active member of the Brewery Workers Union, one of the few industrial unions in the AFL, and an ardent supporter of Eugene Debs's Socialist Party of America. Like the German-born Marxists who headed the Brewery Workers, Valentine believed that American society was divided into two antagonistic classes; that in the pursuit of profit capitalists would pauperize workers; and that it therefore was incumbent on workers to organize themselves economically and politically. Like Debs, he believed that workers should use their political power not simply to protect themselves but to transform the social system, replacing capitalism with a democratic "cooperative commonwealth" dedicated to the American tradition of equality and individual freedom.[21]

Valentine ran his family like a socialist *Volksverein*, organizing family debates on social issues, stocking his small library with Socialist tracts, discussing the political applications of his wife's religious commitments, and continually exhorting his children to work for the advancement of the working class. Walter and his siblings—Theodore, the oldest brother; his younger brothers, Roy and Victor; and his sister, Christine—learned their lessons well. By the time they were teenagers, they too had become committed Socialists, high-minded and moralistic in their commitment to social change. ". . . I was very much of a stuffed shirt in high school," Victor recalled years later. "In the class [year]book, one can see a serious face looking out over the caption, 'I think the needs of humanity are more important.' "[22]

Walter combined his politics with a driving ambition. Anxious that his sons avoid the economic insecurity that had plagued him, Valentine encouraged them to learn a trade, a sure path into the upper echelons of the working class. Walter chose tool and die work, one of the newest and most technologically precise of the metal trades. It was a propitious choice, one that placed him at the intersection of nineteenth-century craftsmanship and twentieth-century mass production while instilling in him a precise cast of mind he never lost. Tool and die workers made the elaborate machine tools and fixtures on which mass production depended. Unlike the production workers who used the tools and fixtures, tool and die makers enjoyed a substantial degree of autonomy on the shop floor. They determined proper production methods; they set their own work pace; and even in the largest shops they worked under the direction of a master craftsman, a die leader, rather than a foreman. As a result, tool and die workers combined the skilled worker's traditions of craft pride and self-assertiveness with a modern faith in human ability to master technology. The tool and die maker, the historian Steve Babson has written, "had to be a problem solver. . . . Rationality and logic were prized accordingly. . . . [He] knew how to complete complex and lengthy engineering tasks, and often understood at least as much about the technical intricacies of mass production as his supervisor." Reuther embraced the trade, quitting high school at sixteen to accept an apprenticeship in a Wheeling machine shop. Three years later, in 1927, he left for Detroit, then the world center of mass production.[23]

Nineteen-twenties Detroit was a sprawling amalgam of vast industrial plants, small supply shops, and grimy working-class neighborhoods, all driven by the incessant demands of the automobile industry. As a skilled hand, Reuther escaped the brutal working conditions and financial insecurity that plagued most auto workers. He had no trouble securing work, first at the Briggs Manufacturing Company, then in the toolroom of Ford's River Rouge plant, one of the most sought-after positions in the city. For a time, his entry into the aristocracy of labor undermined his dedication to class solidarity; like many of his fellow tradesmen, he entertained dreams of moving into the middle class. Working nights, he finished high school during the day, hoping to attend college and pursue a career in engineering. The economic collapse of 1929 changed his plans. Though Reuther kept his job, the devastation that hit Detroit led him back to the radical politics his father had taught him.[24]

Staunchly anti-union, Detroit's auto makers maintained the open shop in their plants through a complex of shop-floor informants, blacklists, and physical intimidation. Outside the factory gates, the city was home to a wide variety of working-class radicals, from former members of the Industrial Workers of the World to British union veterans of the 1919 "Red Clydeside." Not surprisingly, Reuther aligned himself with Detroit's Socialist Party, a combination of skilled workers and young activists associated with the City College of Detroit. Victor, fresh from a year at West Virginia University, joined Walter in 1930. The brothers threw themselves into the network of Socialist organizations: Detroit-area discussion groups, the League for Industrial Democracy, Brookwood Labor College, and, in 1932, Norman Thomas's presidential campaign. Valentine was ecstatic. "To me," he wrote Walter and Victor in 1932, "socialism is the star of hope that lights the way, leading the workers from wage slavery to social justice, and to know that you have joined the movement and are doing all in your power to spread the doctrine of equal opportunity for all mankind, only tends to increase my love." The Ford Motor Company apparently thought less of the venture; shortly after the 1932 election, Walter was fired.[25]

Walter's dismissal gave the brothers the opportunity to deepen their radicalism. Eager to "study the economic and social conditions of the world," in Walter's phrase, the pair pooled their savings and in February 1933 left the United States for a two-and-a-half-year world tour, the centerpiece of which was a fifteen-month stint as skilled workers in the Soviet Union's Gorki automobile plant. Both Walter and Victor were impressed by the Soviet effort to build a workers' state; Victor in particular spoke glowingly of "the thrill and satisfaction of participating in genuine working class democracy." They returned to Detroit in mid-1935 convinced, Walter explained, of "the impossibility of acchieving [sic] freedom, peace, and security without a complete change in our social system."[26]

Walter and Victor came back to a city still dominated by the open shop yet dramatically changed by the New Deal's labor policies. The Roosevelt administration's support of union organizing had led auto workers and radicals to launch initiatives throughout 1933 and 1934. None had been particularly effective, but the shop-floor ferment had forced a reluctant AFL to undertake its own industry-wide organizing campaign, to be conducted under the auspices of the newly created United Automobile Workers Union. In 1935, the city's radicals and union activists, including Roy Reuther, by then an organizer for Brookwood Labor College, were pouring into the new organization, hoping to make it into a genuine representative of the auto workers. Walter followed suit, joining the union as a member of a local on Detroit's West Side. Victor joined him as a local staff member shortly thereafter.[27]

The UAW proved to be the ideal platform for Walter's particular talents. His devotion to social change made him a tireless organizer; his childhood training in debate made him an effective public speaker and parliamentarian, unlike most UAW members; and his ideological sophistication and commitment to precision made him a powerful political and bureaucratic infighter. Perhaps most important, the young union's fluidity afforded Reuther the opportunity to promote both his political agenda and his career. Reuther pursued both with single-minded determination. Typically dressed in a three-piece suit, fit, trim, and almost ascetic in his personal habits—he neither drank nor smoked—he looked more like a junior executive than a labor activist. Once on the stump, however, he could turn a speech on even the most mundane topic into a ringing call for social change, a talent that won him ardent admirers. ". . . I was very taken with him," a long-time

1. Roy, Victor, and Walter Reuther (from left to right), 1937. (Archives of Labor and Urban Affairs, Wayne State University)

associate explained. ". . . Reuther was a person who understood the social forces in America, how you work with them to make a better America. . . ." Others found Reuther's soaring rhetoric somewhat less appealing. "I think he's a very chilly fellow," a critic told an interviewer. "Behind that pleasant smile, there's not much interest in his fellow human beings as individuals. He's one of those people who is deeply concerned with mankind in the abstract. The personal relationship means less to him." John L. Lewis was even more brutal in his evaluation. Reuther, he said in his inimitable style, "is an earnest Marxist chronically inebriated by the exuberance of his own verbosity."[28]

Walter rose rapidly through the union ranks. At the UAW's 1936 convention, he was elected to the International Executive Board as a member of the progressive bloc, a coalition of Socialists, Communists, and independent radicals intent on aligning the new union with John L. Lewis's Committee for Industrial Organization (CIO). When the progressives succeeded in bringing the UAW into the CIO fold, Reuther was also named president of the newly formed West Side UAW Local 174. His power was more apparent than real; in mid-1936 the Auto Workers had virtually no members. By the end of 1937, however, the UAW had become one of the largest and most influential unions in the United States. Within a year, Reuther had become the president of one of the UAW's largest locals and a powerful voice in the setting of union policy.[29]

Over the next few years Reuther expanded his power base. In 1938 he was named director of the UAW's General Motors Department, which coordinated union relations with the giant auto maker. Two years later he was elected vice-president, the third highest post in the UAW. At the same time, he worked to build a national reputation, appearing before congressional committees, meeting with White House officials, and writing articles for and granting interviews to major newspapers and magazines. Reuther, the radical Len DeCaux later noted, "worked hard . . . fought well . . . deserved much credit . . . [and] saw that he got it."[30] As Reuther's political stock rose, his political allegiances shifted. Along with many other Socialists, he turned sharply against the UAW's Communist faction in the late 1930s, charging that his former allies were more interested in advancing the Soviet cause than in working for the good of American auto workers. By 1940 the rift had become irreparable; at the UAW convention that year, Reuther sponsored a resolution barring from union office any "member of an organization whose loyalty [is] to a foreign government." Reuther also resigned from the Socialist Party in 1938 when it refused to endorse Michigan's New Deal governor, Frank Murphy, for reelection, and in 1940 he vigorously supported Franklin Roosevelt for president. Reuther did not simply join the Democratic Party parade, however; he remained committed to an ideology rooted in the sociopolitical milieu of his youth: the democratization of industry.[31]

Industrial democracy had been a pivot point of American political thought in the first two decades of the twentieth century. Labor radicals, eager to replace the increasingly shopworn language of artisan republicanism, had introduced the term to the United States in the 1890s. They generally considered industrial democracy to be synonymous with the nationalization of industry, but the term quickly proved to be malleable. Progressive reformers picked it up in the first decade of the new century, in the process stretching its meaning to encompass a range of possibilities, from collective bargaining to shop-floor workers' councils. The United States' entry into World War I transformed industrial democracy from a vague slogan to public policy, as the Wilson administration struggled to direct the wartime economy and reduce the nation's endemic labor conflict by giving reformers, technocrats, union officials, and even workers themselves a say in corporate decisions through a variety of government agencies. The bitter conservative counterattack of 1919 and 1920 ended the administration's experiment in industrial democracy and drove its advocates into the political underground of the 1920s and early 1930s: academia, the tattered remains of the left-wing union movement, and the various organs of the Socialist Party, such as the League for Industrial Democracy and Brookwood Labor College. There they remained until the economic dislocation of the Great Depression once again gave them the opportunity to join the political debate.[32]

Reuther's concept of industrial democracy was not the mild version of early Progressivism. His first encounter with the concept undoubtedly came from his father, whose union had championed the term, and his understanding of it had been strengthened by his connections with Brookwood in the mid-1930s. Neither was Reuther committed to the radical vision of industrial democracy championed by the 1890s laborites. To be sure, Reuther believed that American society was divided into two competing classes, but he was too steeped in his father's Debsian socialism to reject fully the premises and language of artisan republicanism. He remained convinced that, under the rule of law, competing classes could work for the common good, and he generally rejected the traditional Socialist dichotomy of "bourgeois" and "proletariat" for the more vague and more politically charged claim that the nation was divided between "private privilege" and "the people."[33]

That approach had several obvious advantages. By substituting the people for the proletariat, Reuther seemingly rejected European class analysis for the mainstream of American political tradition. He had no interest in fostering class conflict, he implied; he simply wanted to defend the nation's virtue from the corroding effect of avarice. Reuther's defense of "the people," moreover, allowed him to place industrial workers at the center of a multi-class coalition, a pivotal move for a labor movement that represented a minority of American workers. In particular, Reuther envisioned workers as allying themselves with two large social groupings. Like factory workers, middle-class Americans—small business people, farmers, intellectuals, and college students—risked losing their political rights and their economic freedom unless they opposed the nation's economic elite. Likewise, Reuther insisted that factory workers and the poor—especially African-Americans, ghetto dwellers, and the unemployed—faced increased economic insecurity and political marginalization unless they worked together. Despite his attack on the corporate elite, finally, Reuther did not argue that capitalism itself had to be abandoned if national traditions were to be preserved, a position that would immediately have placed him outside the mainstream of American politics. "I have nothing against free enterprise," he insisted. "[But] my concept of free enterprise does not mean license for private institutions to exploit a privilege. It does mean the obligation of an institution, no matter who owns it, to so conduct itself as to serve the public interest."[34]

When he defined the public-interest, Reuther shifted from the traditional rhetoric of republicanism to that of technocracy. Many of the early twentieth century advocates of industrial democracy, particularly on the engineering and academic wings of Progressivism, had been enamored of the possibility of a technological transformation of American society. Reuther took his view of technocracy from the most contentious member of that group, Thorstein Veblen. Following Veblen's lead, Reuther argued that the "inordinate productivity" of modern technology gave Americans the power to create a full-employment economy of unparalleled abundance and "permanent prosperity." The corporate elite who controlled American technology, however, refused to use that power, preferring instead to maximize profit by pursuing a program of "planned scarcity." They did so in two ways. Some industries—Reuther cited steel as the foremost example—intentionally operated their plants far below their productive capacity, thus driving up per unit price while insulating the industry against economic downturns. Other corporations—here he cited the auto companies—used new technology not to increase output but to slash jobs. The auto makers, though, did not pass the resultant savings on to their customers. Rather, the largest firms used their dominant place in the industry to set prices far above what the market would command under open competition.[35]

Such practices wreaked havoc on the American economy, Reuther charged. By limiting output, basic industry ensured that social needs went unmet: forced to compete for high-priced materials, municipalities could not afford to build new schools and hospitals, states could not afford to build roads and bridges, and workers could not afford to build homes. Indeed, the corporate elite robbed Americans of the purchasing power they needed to buy even the reduced number of goods they produced. As inventories mounted, corporations cut their workforces further. Protected from bankruptcy by a low break-even point, the elite then waited until inventories cleared before they rehired. The corporations, Reuther contended, thus locked the nation into a "fitful succession of boom and bust, feast and famine." The cycle could be broken only if production decisions were socialized. "It is my determined belief that there can be no permanent prosperity," he wrote in 1944, "so long as the controls of production remain in the hands of a privileged minority. . . . To win our social war against unemployment and scarcity . . . we must . . . utilize our economic system in the interests of all the people."[36]

Having identified the root cause of national instability, Reuther offered his view of how industrial democracy could be achieved. It was a profoundly social democratic vision, rejecting both the voluntarism of industrial democracy's liberals and the shop-floor empowerment of the radicals in favor of a corporatism informed by the experiments of World War I and the New Deal. National policy, he argued, should follow a "middle way" between the "ideological nonsense which holds that the profit motive is the exclusive incentive for progress" and "the danger of regimentation and dictatorship that characterizes total state ownership of economic resources." The middle way, he contended, should preserve private property whenever possible but bend its use to the public will.[37]

Reuther offered two models for doing so. The federal government could expand the concept behind the Tennessee Valley Authority, he argued, building and running plants in key industries such as steel to provide privately owned corporations with a performance "yardstick." By creating competition, the public corporation would force private firms to expand their productivity. In most instances, though, the state did not need to become a producer itself; it simply needed to direct basic production decisions in the same way the Wilson and Roosevelt administrations had done during the wars and to coordinate those decisions with the manipulation of federal fiscal and monetary policy, as the New Deal's Keynesians proposed.[38]

At war's end, Reuther suggested in early 1945, the federal government should establish a series of regulatory boards to direct peacetime production and federal spending policies. A "Peace Production Board," empowered to set national goals and coordinate the allocation of resources, would head the system that he proposed. Smaller planning councils would make production and pricing decisions for each major industry. And a central government "research agency" would supervise the introduction of new technology to ensure that it was "universally applied in the public interest." Reuther was not willing to entrust the public interest simply to federal officials, however. He insisted that the membership of each planning board be evenly divided among representatives of business, labor, government, agriculture, and consumer groups. Reuther's proposal thus rested on the New Deal's faith in interest-group politics. He insisted, though, that once interest groups were included in the planning process, they would abandon their narrow agendas and work for the common good. A planned economy, he claimed, "would begin the breaking down of narrow fixed economic pressure groups . . . [and] begin to draw into active participation all of the elements whose welfare is affected by the over-all economic pattern established." The result would be an "economic democracy" that would ensure the survival of political democracy.[39]

Here was the culminating vision of the CIO leadership's social democratic wing, a practical plan to move organized labor beyond the shop-floor mass movement of the late 1930s, beyond the workplace contractualism that the mass movement had created, and into the heart of the state apparatus itself. Such a move would transform the American political economy, taking a substantial degree of power away from the corporate sector and placing it in the newly broadened public sector, which would then have the leverage necessary to shift the nation's economic priorities away from individual goals and toward more collectivist ones. For all its promise of sweeping social reform, however, Reuther's program was not inherently democratic. It would not have empowered workers, farmers, and consumers directly: planning agencies would not have altered employer-employee relations at the point of production, and farmers and consumers would still have been subject to pricing decisions beyond their control. It assumed, rather, that a select group of institutional elites, albeit elites who represented a broad range of economic interests, could and should speak for "the people."

It is not particularly surprising that Reuther, a man driven by both personal ambition and the wish to help society, a craftsman trained in the most technologically sophisticated of American industries, should find such a possibility appealing. Promoting a state-centered reconstruction of the American political economy opened Reuther to attack, however. The conservatives who had directed the backlash of 1919 had discredited industrial democracy in large part by raising the specter of government subversion of personal liberty, a specter made all the more alarming by the Bolshevik revolution. A quarter century later Reuther's conservative opponents were quick to revive such fears. As an auto industry official told Congress in early 1945, Reuther's political program was designed to give the labor leader "more, more, and more . . . political, social, and economic power," which he would use to create a "CIO superstate."[40]

Reuther attempted to protect himself from such charges by falling back on his anti-communism. He also opposed statism, he counterattacked, and he had no interest in collectivism. The USSR's centralized state power, he said over and over again, certainly put bread on the table, but it also "put the human soul in chains." Such a system was unacceptable, and he strongly opposed attempts by the Soviets, and by extension American Communists, to expand it. Reuther thus attempted to deflect the conservative attack from his brand of social democratic corporatism to those on his left. That was a dangerous tactic to pursue, since it assumed that the voting public could distinguish between anticommunism and a more general antistatism that had long been a mainstay of American political discourse, a distinction that conservatives were determined to blur.[41]

Reuther's program had other shortcomings as well. For planning agencies to serve the public interest, the federal government had to remain the relatively impartial umpire it had been during the New Deal; it could not become an ally of—or worse, a spokesman for—corporate interests. The program's exclusive focus on class divisions, moreover, underestimated the extent to which noneconomic rifts, particularly racial divisions, rent the nation. This is not to say that Reuther ignored racism. Like many Socialists of his generation, he fervently believed in racial equality. He insisted, however, that racism was rooted in economics and that it could therefore be eliminated by economic change. "There are numerous groups in America who have their special problems, yet the basic problems are common to all groups, and they are economic," he told the National Association for the Advancement of Colored People. "We must work to meet the immediate needs of the various groups, but we must apply ourselves at the same time to solving the basic economic problems. If we go forward to abundance and security and freedom, the Negro will come into his full heritage of justice and equality." That view of American society would prove to be far too sanguine.[42]

The limitations of Reuther's program were more than offset by its political strengths. Reuther's blending of state-centered industrial democracy and anticommunism placed him within the orbit of a powerful group of New Dealers, who promoted him to the national stage. His ideology also allowed him to transcend many of the political divisions within the union and thus to build an electoral coalition that included elements as disparate as Trotskyists and traditional business unionists. Reuther's promise of a full-employment economy free of cyclical downturns, moreover, undoubtedly resonated with rank and filers victimized by repeated layoffs. And his program offered the UAW a way to reconcile the rank and file's tradition of militancy, the union's hierarchical structure, and the federal government's desire for a stable, bureaucratic labor movement. If Reuther were directing the union, the program suggested, UAW rank and filers would not need to defend their rights by militant action on the shop floor; Reuther would defend and even extend their rights for them through the union and federal bureaucracies that the workers now feared. In 1945 and 1946, Reuther traded on those advantages to make himself the UAW's president.

By the war's end, Reuther had already constructed a solid base of support in the UAW, organized as the union's "right-wing caucus." The union's socialist faction was at the coalition's core. It was not a particularly large group—one estimate places the number of socialists below that of the union's small Communist faction—but they were politically sophisticated, well versed in union procedure, and well placed in the UAW hierarchy. Like Reuther, many of the union's socialists had left the party by the early 1940s, but they remained committed to the social democratic principles it had taught them. "Almost none of the people I know in the UAW decided to leave the Socialist party. They sort of drifted out," a former Socialist recalled. "[But] the people I know . . . continued to feel that they had a special approach to trade unionism, a special mission."[43]

In the late 1930s, Reuther also won the backing of the union's Catholic activists, most of whom were affiliated with the Association of Catholic Trade Unionists (ACTU), a small but influential cadre in the UAW. Created in 1937 to promote the church's teachings in the nascent labor movement, the ACTU shared Reuther's opposition to the Communist Party, but it was not simply an anticommunist organization. Drawing on the papal encyclicals *Rerum Novarum* and *Quadragesimo Anno*, ACTU members also favored the creation of corporatist "industrial councils" as an alternative to the "economic despotism" of capitalism. In form strikingly similar to Reuther's planning boards, the ACTU's councils were to serve a much more conservative end. Whereas Reuther believed planning agencies would act as tools for workers locked in a struggle for control of the economic system, ACTU members believed industrial councils would reconcile the classes within a harmonious social structure. In the early 1940s, though, most ACTU members were more than willing to accept the form, if not the substance, of Reuther's program. "We were forced, intellectually and conscientiously," an ACTU spokesmen later said, "to agree with most of his basic policies."[44]

During the closing year of World War II, Reuther added the union's militant "rank and file caucus" to his coalition. A loose confederation of socialists, Trotskyists, and nonaligned shop-floor activists, the caucus had led the union's opposition to the wartime no-strike pledge and had played a central role in the wildcat strikes that had racked the industry. In late 1944, Reuther inched toward the caucus's position, publicly questioning the fairness of the no-strike pledge and supporting wildcatters. Many caucus members, moreover, shared Reuther's antipathy to the Communist Party. Already vigorous opponents of the party before the war, the caucus' socialists and Trotskyists in particular found the Communists' support of incentive pay, the no-strike pledge, and other wartime measures an appalling repudiation of trade union principles.[45]

At the other end of the political spectrum, some of the UAW's traditional business unionists tied their fortunes to Reuther's caucus. Most of these men had little interest in Reuther's social vision; they saw the union as a service organization, processing grievances and negotiating contracts, but certainly not transforming the American political economy. Attracted perhaps by Reuther's top-down approach to union governance, perhaps by his political potential, the business unionists provided the caucus with a bloc of solid, if not always reputable, votes.[46]

While Reuther fashioned his caucus, his opponents built their own bloc, the "left-wing caucus." At its heart lay the UAW's Communist faction, Reuther's most vociferous critics. Never large—the party counted 1,200 members in the auto industry in 1943—the Communist faction neverthe-less controlled some of the most important posts in the UAW, including the directorship of the union's Washington office, its research department, and its legal office. In these and other positions the UAW's Communists worked to maintain the wartime Popular Front, to construct a multiracial, working-class movement, and to institutionalize the party's place in American politi-cal life. Reuther posed the greatest threat to those goals, the Communists believed. Despite his rhetoric, they charged, he was neither militant nor democratic; he was simply an opportunist, willing to do anything necessary, even red-baiting dedicated trade unionists, to promote his career.[47]

As Reuther's reputation grew during the war, some of the UAW's most powerful International officers, including President R. J. Thomas and Secretary-Treasurer George Addes, joined the left-wing caucus. They did so for tactical rather than ideological reasons. Though they considered them-selves to be New Deal liberals, both Thomas and Addes believed that an alliance with the Communists offered the best chance to prevent Reuther from controlling the union. By so doing, they dramatically increased the caucus's ability to expand its base of support, since it now could employ the patronage power of high union office to win adherents on the local level.[48]

The union's African-American activists, finally, provided the left-wing caucus with a critical core of support. Marginal to the organizing cam-paigns of 1937, by the early 1940s African-American unionists had become a powerful force in some of the UAW's largest locals, particularly Local 600, the bargaining unit for Ford's massive River Rouge plant. Using their locals as a base, the activists vigorously attacked racial discrimination on the shop floor, in union offices, and in public policy. In these efforts, African-Americans won the support of the Communist Party, long dedicated to the advancement of civil rights. Reuther, for his part, stayed somewhat aloof from the blacks' wartime agitation. Though he supported the promotion of African-Americans into previously all-white jobs, he opposed a 1943 con-vention proposal that a seat on the UAW Executive Board be reserved for an African-American, a move he claimed would result in "reverse discrimina-tion." African-Americans responded by throwing their support to the Communists; by the mid-1940s, blacks accounted for half of all party members in Local 600.[49]

Despite their relatively broad bases, neither the right-wing caucus nor the left-wing caucus had sufficient strength to win control of the union out-right. The swing vote in any union election thus fell to the large number of uncommitted local officials who attended UAW conventions. Neither polit-ically committed nor eager to rise in the union hierarchy, these unionists—local presidents, recording secretaries, shop stewards, and the like—had no ideological reason to support either group. Local officials did have one pressing practical need in 1945, however. Throughout the war, they had borne the brunt of the rank-and-file revolt: they had to deal with un-answered grievances and slowdowns, hate strikes and wildcats, without undermining the International's no-strike policy. Now they desperately needed to get in front of the rank and file. In November 1945, Reuther gave them a way.[50]

He did so, ironically, by suffering one of the most dramatic defeats of his career. On November 21 Reuther brought General Motors' 320,000 hourly workers out on strike. His demands were extraordinary: GM, he insisted, should increase the wages of its hourly workers by 30 percent, and it should promise to freeze auto prices at their current levels. It seemed to be a brilliant coupling of militant unionism and social democratic principles. If the UAW won the walkout, the rank and file would receive the largest single pay raise in CIO history, while the union would gain the right to participate in the most basic of management decisions, a critical first step in establishing public control of the nation's economy. "All that we have done . . . is say that we are not going to operate as a narrow economic pressure group," Reuther declared in a phrase that would become a standard part of his rhetoric; ". . . we want to make progress with the community and not at the expense of the community."[51]

GM immediately rejected Reuther's demands. The corporation simply could not afford such a large wage increase, its spokesmen insisted, and it would not surrender its exclusive right to determine product pricing, "the very heart of management judgement and discretion in private industry." Reuther then raised the stakes, announcing that the workers would settle for a smaller wage increase if the corporation would prove its inability to pay by "opening its books" to public scrutiny. GM was horrified by the proposal. Reuther did not simply want to look at the books, an executive claimed; he wanted to create "a socialistic nation." "If fighting for equal and equitable distribution of the wealth of this country is socialistic," the labor leader responded, "I stand guilty of being a socialist."[52]

Convinced that it was defending the free enterprise system, the giant auto maker steadfastly refused to discuss any issue that it considered "the sole responsibility of the corporation." In making its case, GM received a critical boost from the Truman administration, which in early 1946 scuttled wartime price controls. Reuther's wage demands also suffered a serious blow early in the year, when both the United Steelworkers and the United Electrical Workers accepted wage increases of 17.5 percent from their employers. Increasingly embattled, Reuther finally ended the strike on March 13, 1946, 113 days after it began, defeated on virtually every point. GM workers received the same wage raise as workers in the steel and electrical industries, and the UAW won no concession on product pricing.[53]

Reuther nevertheless emerged from the strike as the UAW's dominant political figure, having proved to many of the UAW's nonaligned local officials that he was committed to militant unionism pursued through a centralized union management, precisely the combination they wanted to see. He had enhanced his standing at a significant cost: as Nelson Lichtenstein has argued, GM's triumph demonstrated to Reuther the limits of collective bargaining as a tool for sociopolitical change. He did not abandon the idea of pursuing political goals at the bargaining table—throughout his career he continued to believe that the wage increases and fringe benefits the UAW won for its members could serve as yardsticks not only for other unions but for nonunionized workers as well—but he would never again try to use the UAW's bargaining power to redefine the position of the corporations in the political economy. Reuther still believed, though, that he could advance social democracy through political means, and he knew that the GM strike had won him the platform he needed to do just that.[54]

On March 24, 1946, eleven days after the GM strike ended, the delegates to the UAW's annual convention elected Reuther to the union's presidency. As he had anticipated, the vote was largely a referendum on his handling of the strike. Reuther kept his basic constituency in line, then added those delegates who most directly benefited from the walkout: representatives of previously nonaligned GM locals in Flint, Lansing, and Detroit. These forces gave him a razor thin victory: Reuther defeated the incumbent, R. J. Thomas, by 114 of 8,761 votes cast. The victory only accentuated the tensions within the union. The problem was partly racial. Many members of the pivotal GM locals, particularly in Flint and Lansing, were white southern transplants, a fact that deeply concerned many African-American rank and filers, who feared that Reuther now owed his victory to the most socially conservative segment of the UAW population. "Why is it [that] the great majority of the prejudiced element in [the] UAW are Reuther's most vociferous supporters?" the UAW's leading African-American pointedly asked. More fundamentally, Reuther's core constituency was not strong enough to carry the rest of the right-wing caucus's candidates into office. The left-wing caucus consequently retained control of the secretary-treasurer's office, both vice-presidencies, and ten of the eighteen regional directorships. Reuther had won the presidency, but he still did not control the union.[55]

As soon as the convention ended, Reuther launched a two-pronged campaign to sweep the next year's convention. First, he undertook a massive effort to discredit the left-wing caucus by trading on the anticommunist tide then sweeping the nation. By early 1946, Soviet-American relations had collapsed into a maelstrom of distrust. Seizing the moment, the Republican Party raised the politically potent specter of Communist subversion at home. Desperate to defend his administration against such charges and eager to rally public support for his get-tough foreign policies, Truman adopted a similarly strident tone, insisting that communism posed a direct threat to American liberty. In newspapers and magazines, local union meetings and national radio hookups, Reuther joined the attack, repeating the anticommunist themes he had been presenting since the late 1930s. "Communism is in perpetual war with what democracy preaches," he charged in a typical broadside, "for it cannot abide the sanctity of the individual or the interplay of honest differences." It followed, therefore, that the UAW's Communists and their allies threatened both the union and the nation. "The American Communist party is not a political party in the legitimate sense," he said. "Communist party members in America and in our union are governed by the foreign policy needs of the Soviet Union, and not by the needs of our union, our membership, or our country."[56]

Many rank and filers undoubtedly embraced Reuther's anticommunism as a patriotic gesture, just as they had embraced unionism as a sign of their Americanization in the late 1930s. Many others supported Reuther's position as the only practical one for the labor movement to adopt amid the mounting red scare. That scare threatened to engulf the UAW in April 1947, when the Republican-controlled Congress traded on the rising fear to pass the anti-union Taft-Hartley Act. For the most part, the act simply circumscribed organized labor's political and bargaining power, outlawing the closed shop, the use of union funds in political campaigns, and strikes by government employees. But the Republicans also tried to use Taft-Hartley to their political advantage by requiring all union officials to sign affidavits declaring that they were not members of the Communist Party, a provision sure to highlight the extent of left-wing influence in the CIO. The penalty for noncompliance was prohibitive: unions that did not cooperate would be denied access to the National Labor Relations Board, the cornerstone of federal labor policy. Congress therefore presented the UAW with the starkest of choices. It could publicly declare that none of its officials was a Communist, which was not true; it could refuse to comply and thus lose the right to participate in the national collective bargaining system; or, as Reuther insisted it do, it could purge itself of its Communist members. For many local officials, the choice was clear. The UAW simply could not afford to leave the left wing in office any longer.[57]

As he was isolating his opponents on the left, Reuther also was constructing an electoral slate with the widest possible appeal. The result was a carefully balanced, if not coherent, ticket. Reuther divided the unionwide positions between his supporters on the left and on the right, nominating the militant Emil Mazey for secretary-treasurer and the business unionists Richard Gosser and John Livingston for the two vice-presidencies. A committed Socialist, Mazey had been in the front lines of labor conflict since the union's founding, as president of Detroit Briggs Local 212, one of the UAW's most militant locals, as a spokesman for the wartime rank-and-file caucus, and as a Detroit regional director. He was, in Murray Kempton's phrase, the "perennial picket captain," so committed to working-class action that while serving in the South Pacific he organized his fellow servicemen. Richard Gosser, the Toledo regional director, was precisely the opposite. A product of Toledo's working-class street culture—he had spent his teen years as a member of the city's toughest gang and his early twenties running slot machines for a local mobster—he had no ideological commitment beyond serving the immediate needs, desires, and prejudices of his shopmates and friends. His intense localism and rough-hewn manner won him widespread support in the shops, which he then used to consolidate his grip on the Toledo UAW. Gosser ran his region "like a dictator," according to an observer, controlling the hiring gate, manipulating local union politics, engaging in some questionable financial dealings, and strictly segregating the shop floor. John Livingston, the Lower Midwest regional director, did not share Gosser's shady reputation, but neither did he have Mazey's fire. He had begun his union career in 1934 as president of the AFL's auto union local in the St. Louis General Motors plant. He moved steadily up the UAW hierarchy over the next decade and a half, a faithful if unspectacular union bureaucrat. Whatever their limits, though, Gosser and Livingston could deliver their regions' votes, and that made them invaluable to Reuther.[58]

Reuther likewise divided the nominations for regional directorships among a wide array of supporters. ACTU members were given two nominations: the Scottish-born tradesman Joseph McCusker, the hard-drinking former president of Ford Local 600, was named the caucus's choice for directorship of Region 1A, covering Detroit's West Side, and the UAW staffer Patrick Greathouse was named the caucus candidate for Region 4, covering Illinois, Iowa, and Nebraska. Socialists also received several nominations. Reuther chose Leonard Woodcock, who had served on the Socialist Party's national board in 1940, as his candidate for the directorship of the western Michigan region, and Martin Gerber, president of General Motors Local 595 in Linden, New Jersey, as his choice for the East Coast region. Other activists were added to the slate for purely strategic reasons. Russ

Letner and Tom Starling received the caucus's nomination for the directorships of the southern regions, for instance, simply because they could
deliver the regions' votes, though both supported the maintenance of Jim
Crow in southern plants.[59]

Reuther's carefully orchestrated campaign worked precisely as he had
planned. He received two-thirds of the presidential vote at the November
1947 UAW convention; Mazey, Gosser, and Livingston easily outpaced
their left-wing opponents; and the right-wing slate took fourteen of the
eighteen regional directorships. Thoroughly repudiated, the left-wing
caucus quickly collapsed. As soon as the convention ended, Reuther began
purging the UAW's Communists from office; Addes and Thomas left the
union; and many of the UAW's black activists, now isolated, began a slow
and painful shift into the right-wing camp.[60]

Reuther thus resolved the tensions that had torn the union since its
founding, building a bureaucratic, centralized union committed to militant
trade unionism. But he had done so at a cost. By shifting the locus of union
activism from the shop floor to the International, Reuther sapped much of
the locals' vitality. As the locals atrophied, the rank and file grew increasingly disinterested in their union and in the political program it promoted.
Reuther's decision to bring disparate elements into his electoral coalition
imposed order on the union's heretofore chaotic internal politics and gave
him the leverage he needed to solidify his control over union affairs, but it
forced him to turn some of the union's most important positions over to
officials who did not share his commitment to social unionism. Having
aligned himself with the mounting red scare, finally, Reuther reinforced his
loyalty to the national state and thus secured the support of those rank and
filers for whom patriotism had become a badge of honor, but his red-baiting
also helped lay the groundwork for the constriction of American political
debate, which a few years later, would weaken his ability to promote his
cherished agenda. In his moment of exaltation, though, Reuther was not
thinking of limits. He had struggled for years to win a platform from which
he could promote his vision of a more just social system. Now he had done
so. Taking the podium to accept his office, Reuther pledged himself and his
union to the fight. "We are the vanguard in America," he told the delegates
who had just made him the undisputed head of the nation's largest union.
"We are the architects of the future, and we are going to fashion the
weapons with which we will work and fight and build."[61]

[2]

Craven Politics

S hortly before Walter Reuther won the UAW presidency in 1946, the former New Dealer Gardner Jackson privately expressed his hope that the labor leader could redefine liberalism in his image. "Somehow or other, we've got to capitalize the Reuther performance into a political movement," he wrote to his long-time associate Paul Sifton. "It's the only one I see anywhere that has integrity in it, and I still have enough faith in the commonality of folk to feel that they respond to integrity when they know about it." Two years later, such grand hopes had faded, and the UAW faced the unpleasant prospect of endorsing a Democratic presidential candidate who stood to the union's right. ". . . I have stood myself up face to face with the Truman catastrophe and come out with this," the UAW's Washington Office director, Donald Montgomery, wrote Walter Reuther in February 1948. "We shall have to plug for the Democrats on the presidency solely because they are the only instrument at hand for keeping the Republicans out. The Missouri crowd smells bad; but it is less bad than the sewage which will seep into every cranny of government if the Republicans win. This would be a craven program if it stopped with 1948. But our program now must include 1952. Unless it does, we shall not have anything to offer the progressive voters who simply will not truck with Truman."[1]

That the sentiment in UAW circles could shift so profoundly in so short a time reflects the extent to which the political landscape changed in the first few years of the postwar era. In the late 1930s and early 1940s, Walter Reuther had allied himself and the UAW with the Democratic Party's left wing, then dominated by some of the most powerful figures in the Roosevelt administration, who were themselves dedicated to the democratization of the American political economy. The immediate postwar years transformed the Democratic Party, as the party's precarious balance of interests shattered and a new generation of liberals, favoring a less intrusive federal government, eclipsed the UAW's allies. Reuther and his staff tried to reverse the party's direction in 1946, 1947, and 1948, but the vagaries of the 1948 presidential campaign defeated that effort. By the end of the campaign, the UAW was locked into a political structure that did not share the union's vision of a dramatically altered political economy.

The nineteenth-century Democratic Party built its base of support on ethnocultural appeals and the pull of patronage rather than on ideology. For much of the twentieth century, consequently, the party has been rent by serious internal tensions, its spectrum of subgroups struggling to define the Democrats' purpose. The party's liberal wing, largely northern and urban, wanted a federal government actively engaged in the management of national economic and social affairs. The Democrats' southern, white, conservative wing—the "Dixiecrats"—feared that an activist government would destroy the economic and racial hegemony upon which its power rested. Between these poles lay a wide range of moderates: southerners like the young Lyndon Johnson, who favored federal social spending but opposed federal intervention in their region's racial politics; the products of eastern and midwestern machines, whose local power bases were simultaneously enhanced and undermined by a more powerful central state; and others who vacillated between the promise of liberalism and the concerns of conservatism.[2]

Franklin Roosevelt managed for a time to heal the party's rift by accommodating his administration to the party's various factions. FDR offered the Democratic southerners federal funds for a host of economic development projects while avoiding any federal challenge to Jim Crow. He traded federal patronage for the support of urban politicos. And he offered the party's liberals, themselves divided into various camps, the chance to set administration policy. Under FDR's benign direction, in Alan Brinkley's words, the White House became "awash in ideologies" as liberals competed for power and attention. FDR even found a place for both socialists and communists, first in his administration's support for organized labor, then in its attack on fascism.[3]

Reuther was one of those radicals pulled into the New Deal's orbit. As late as 1936, he had condemned the New Deal as "lukewarm" and "inadequate," preferring instead to work for the creation of a Farm-Labor party that could serve "as a resovour [sic] from which we can draw the most advanced workers into our revolutionary party." As he rose in the UAW hierarchy during the next few years, however, Reuther moved toward the Democratic Party. He did so, in part, for practical political reasons. The 1936 election had made clear that the New Deal had won the allegiance of working people and that it was therefore impossible to build an alternative working-class party. "[T]here was enormous feeling for Roosevelt," Reuther's confidant Brendan Sexton recalled. "A great many workers in this country at that time [the late 1930s] had a real class feeling about the Democratic Party. You know, people say we have never had a class party in this country but for an awful lot of workers, the Democratic Party was the class party. They really thought of that as their party."[4]

Reuther also had ideological reasons for supporting the New Deal. By 1937, the year Reuther began his climb to national prominence, the administration's liberal policy makers had essentially divided into two camps. One group, centered on Marriner Eccles, chairman of the Federal Reserve Board, held that the federal government could spur economic growth and address social inequities by making aggressive use of its ability to tax and spend, a policy program that the sociologists Margaret Weir and Theda Skocpol have termed "social Keynesianism." The other group moved beyond Keynesianism to advocate more direct control of the political economy. It was a disparate group, stretching from Harvard Yard to the fledgling CIO's leadership bloc. It encompassed veterans of the Wilson administration's World War I experiments in industrial democracy, such as the Harvard law professor Felix Frankfurter; Frankfurter's Harvard protégés Thomas Corcoran and Benjamin Cohen; activists who spent the early 1930s in the innovative precincts of Progressive Chicago, such as Jerome Frank, and in the private sectors of reformism, such as the Russell Sage Foundation's Leon Henderson and the Yale law professors Thurman Arnold and William O. Douglas; and a handful of strategically placed union officials, most notably John L. Lewis's right-hand man, Philip Murray, and the ubiquitous socialist Sidney Hillman of the Amalgamated Clothing Workers.[5]

This second cadre, spread throughout the administration's agencies, has been variously labeled. The press often referred to the group as antitrusters, but most of its members believed that the concentration of corporate power could not and should not be reversed by federal fiat. Some scholars have called them corporatists, but the term implies a basic faith in business's commitment to the national good, which most of the group did not have. It seems most reasonable to call the cadre members "liberal statists." They argued that the American economy was controlled, by and large, by monopolistic corporations that had used their size and power to set aside the laws of supply and demand. As long as such corporations maintained exclusive control of economic decision making, they argued, the economy would continue to stagnate. If the nation's economic health were to be restored, therefore, the federal government would have to assume a direct role in corporate decision making through the creation of new, more powerful regulatory agencies.[6]

This second group of policy makers, committed to federal control of the economy, embraced the bright young Reuther as one of their own, offering him his first entré into the corridors of power. The relationship began in late 1940, when Reuther advanced his "500 planes a day" proposal, the first embodiment of his social democratic agenda. The administration's liberal statists were then engaged in a vigorous effort to shape the nation's military preparedness program in a way that would expand the government's regulatory power. Reuther's proposal offered them one way of doing so. Since private industry would not meet the nation's pressing need for military aircraft, he argued, production should be taken out of private hands and placed under the direction of a federal Aviation Production Board, whose membership would be evenly divided among labor, management, and government.[7] The New Deal's statist cadre immediately promoted the plan. Hillman, then codirector of the Office of Production Management, and Murray presented the proposal to FDR; Frank arranged for Reuther to discuss it with Roosevelt directly; and Henderson, Corcoran, and Frankfurter publicly promoted it. Despite such high-level support, the plan never moved beyond the talking stage. The auto companies, which controlled aircraft production, vociferously opposed it, and businessmen within the administration's mobilization agencies pigeonholed it. The proposal nevertheless served an important purpose for Reuther, bringing him into alliance with some of the most powerful political figures in the administration.[8]

Perhaps the plan's demise should have told Reuther that the statists' power was already in decline. Throughout the war years, however, it was possible to come to the opposite conclusion, to believe that the regulators were consolidating their hold on administration policy making. FDR responded to the mounting military crisis by creating a web of federal agencies with power to control the economy. The agencies were far from perfect embodiments of the statist ideal—many were dominated by the corporate officials whose power the regulators had hoped to check—but they certainly set a precedent for federal control of heretofore private economic decisions. By 1943, postwar economic planning also seemed to be taking a decidedly statist turn. Even as devout a social Keynesian as the economist Alvin Hansen, the National Resource Planning Board's leading adviser, believed the postwar economy would have to be directed by a central planning agency. Within that context, Reuther's most sweeping proposals—his 1945 call for a Peace Production Board, for instance— seemed both reasonable and, more important, feasible.[9]

As the administration's liberal statists integrated Reuther into their circle, he built his own version of that circle within the UAW. In theory, the UAW's officers were to rely on the International Executive Board (IEB) for advice on setting the union's political policy. Reuther, however, was determined that the board would exercise no real power over union politics: in his view, the board's main responsibility was to validate and administer political policies set by the president's office. That narrow concept of the IEB's authority reflected Reuther's desire to maximize his power over union affairs, but it also reflected the inner tensions of the Reuther caucus. Only Secretary-Treasurer Emil Mazey and a handful of regional directors— Leonard Woodcock, Martin Gerber, Ray Ross, and Ray Berndt—shared Reuther's commitment to social democracy. Both of the union's vice-presidents, Richard Gosser and John Livingston, and a majority of regional directors were mainstream Democrats, committed to the New Deal welfare state but not to the reconstruction of the political economy. Had Reuther given the board control of the union's political program, the UAW undoubtedly would have abandoned the vanguard role in which Reuther so fervently believed.[10]

At the same time, the UAW's bureaucracy offered Reuther the ideal structure for fashioning the union's political program. Like most major unions, the UAW had an extensive staff structure. Most of the men and women who held staff positions performed routine office jobs. But a handful of top staff members served as the officers' principle advisers, helping develop and implement policy from collective bargaining to political action. The union maintained two groups of political advisers. The smaller group, based in Washington, D.C., represented the UAW on Capitol Hill and in executive branch offices, lobbying for legislation and maintaining contact with members of Congress and bureaucrats. The larger staff remained in Detroit, where they gathered and analyzed political and economic data, developed and drafted the union's numerous position statements, and wrote speeches. The two staffs were permeable. The Washington staff returned to Detroit regularly for political strategy sessions, and the Detroit staff shuttled to the capital for Oval Office meetings, congressional appearances, and other political events. As president, Reuther had the constitutional right to appoint both staffs, albeit with the IEB's approval. That power gave him the ability to construct a staff that had the ideological coherence and political commitment that the IEB lacked.[11]

Reuther began building his political staffs even before he won the UAW presidency. He did so by drawing on the broad social groupings that the administration's statists encompassed. Reuther hired New Deal veterans for his Washington staff, men trained in the statists' offices and steeped in their politics. For his Detroit staff, he turned to people much like himself, working-class intellectuals who had spent the 1930s in the cockpits of Socialist and CIO politics and by the early 1940s had come to see the Democratic Party as the best road to social reconstruction.

Reuther started constructing his Washington staff in 1943, when he brought the Department of Agriculture's Donald Montgomery on staff as his consumer counsel. The son of "some very left wing people," according to a close associate, Montgomery had done graduate work at the University of Wisconsin, studying under John R. Commons, himself an advocate of the World War I experiments in industrial democracy. Montgomery joined the New Deal in 1935 as the Department of Agriculture's consumer counsel, a post he held for seven years. Throughout that time, he vigorously advocated greater public control of the corporations' "monopoly power," a theme Thurman Arnold had made central to the late New Deal.[12] In 1945 Reuther added Paul Sifton to his staff as a speech writer and political consultant. Sifton was a gifted polemicist and part-time playwright who, a friend remarked, had "a limitless capacity for indignation." Like Reuther, he had been a socialist in his youth, studying under Harold Laski at the London School of Economics, writing for radical publications, and working for the 1932 Norman Thomas campaign. He left the Socialist Party shortly thereafter, though he remained convinced that capitalism was "fatally flawed." Sifton joined Frances Perkins's Labor Department in 1938 and in 1939 became consumer counsel for the Bituminous Coal Administration, one of the New Deal's most statist agencies.[13] Montgomery and Sifton immediately became central figures in Reuther's emerging brains trust. Montgomery prepared the brief linking wages and prices that Reuther presented to General Motors during the 1945–46 strike, and Sifton gave Reuther the idea of demanding that GM "open its books." As soon as Reuther won control of the UAW, he promoted the pair, making Montgomery director of the UAW's Washington office and Sifton the union's primary lobbyist.[14]

Reuther completed his staff of Washington advisers in January 1948, when he placed Joseph L. Rauh Jr. on retainer as the UAW's Washington counsel. More than any other UAW staffer, Rauh had impeccable New Deal credentials. A Frankfurter student at Harvard Law, he joined the Roosevelt administration upon graduation in 1935, serving as an aide to Cohen and Corcoran and as Benjamin Cardozo's law clerk. Rauh met Reuther when the labor leader brought his "500 planes a day" plan to Washington; he renewed the acquaintance five years later, when, fresh from military service, he headed a public committee supporting the GM strikers. "Joe's back here to complete the revolution, not to practice law," Corcoran told Cohen at the time.[15]

Reuther did not have the power to name the UAW's Detroit staff, most of whom served as heads of the union's departments, until he won control of the Executive Board in 1947. By 1945, though, Reuther had already gathered around him most of the advisers whom he would place in these positions: his brothers, Roy and Victor, and his long-time associate Frank Winn, all already on the UAW staff; Mildred Jeffrey, the head of the UAW's wartime Women's Bureau; Jack Conway, an activist in Chicago UAW Local 6 and a member of the rank-and-file caucus; and Brendan Sexton, president of UAW Local 50, the bargaining unit for Ford's massive Willow Run plant.[16] The group shared many social characteristics. All of them came from working-class or petit bourgeois backgrounds. Roy and Victor came from the German working-class community of Wheeling, of course; Jeffrey was the daughter of Irish Catholic pharmacists in Iowa; Conway was the son of an Irish Catholic Detroit plumber; Sexton was the son of an Irish Catholic worker in western Pennsylvania. Though the extent of their a formal education varied greatly—Conway held a master's degree, Sexton had not gone beyond grade school—all had received training at educational institutions dedicated to reform or socialist activism: Roy, Victor, Winn, and Sexton attended Brookwood in the mid-1930s; Jeffrey received her B.A. at the University of Minnesota and did graduate work at the Bryn Mawr School of Social Economy; Conway did his undergraduate and graduate work in the Sociology Department at the University of Chicago, which he attended on a football scholarship.[17]

Each member of Reuther's inner circle was active in the Socialist Party at least until the late 1930s, and Conway remained a party member until the middle of World War II. All but Conway joined the CIO in its early stages. Roy was one of the first UAW organizers sent to Flint in 1936. Victor and Winn joined Walter in organizing UAW Local 174 the same year. Sexton worked as an organizer for the Steel Workers Organizing Committee in the latter half of the 1930s. Jeffrey did the same job for Sidney Hillman's Amalgamated Clothing Workers and Textile Workers Organizing Committee. Only Conway was a relative latecomer to the labor movement. He joined the UAW in 1942, after he took a part-time job at General Motors' Melrose Park plant in Chicago.[18]

The group's common political experiences and commitments created a web of social and professional relationships that made them natural allies.

2. The making of a UAW cadre: the 1935–36 class at Brookwood Labor College. In the back row, Frank Winn is fifth from the left, Nat Weinberg at the far right. In the front row, Sophie Good, Victor Reuther's future wife, is at the far left; Fania Sonkin, Roy Reuther's future wife, is fourth from the left. Ruth Oxman, Weinberg's future wife, is at the far right of the middle row. Roy Reuther was an instructor for the class. (Archives of Labor and Urban Affairs, Wayne State University)

Victor, Roy, and Frank Winn traced their relationship to Brookwood. Jeffrey had crossed paths with UAW staffers in the late 1930s and considered Roy a friend. In 1943, after Jeffrey completed a stint as a staffer at the War Production Board, again under Hillman, Roy suggested her for the directorship of the UAW's newly formed Women's Bureau. Sexton met the Reuthers through the Socialist Party in the late 1930s, moving to the UAW in 1941 after Walter promised him the chance to enter the political leadership of the new Local 50. Conway came into Reuther's circle through the rank-and-file Caucus, which threw its support behind Reuther in 1944.[19]

Once Reuther secured control of the union, he gave each member of his informal group a position in the UAW hierarchy. He made Roy, the least dogmatic and most politic of the Reuther brothers, director of the UAW's Political Action Department. Victor, the family's ideologue, became director of the UAW's Education Department, a post he held until 1949, when he became director of the CIO's European Office in Paris. Sexton, who had been serving as Victor's assistant, was then promoted to the department's directorship. Reuther appointed Winn as head of the UAW's Public Relations Department, a continuation of the job he had held in Local 174 in the 1930s. Mildred Jeffrey stepped down as head of the Women's Department in 1947; thereafter, Reuther used her as his primary liaison with community and political organizations, particularly the Michigan Democratic Party. Conway, having proved his organizational skills by directing Reuther's 1947 campaign for the UAW presidency, became Reuther's administrative assistant, the UAW equivalent to chief of staff.[20] Reuther rounded out his staff of advisers in 1947 by naming Nat Weinberg as director of the UAW's Research Department and William Oliver and Fair Practices Department director. Weinberg fitted the Reuther mold perfectly. He was a working-class intellectual: he left school at age twelve, finished high school and college at night, taking his B.A. in economics at New York University. He joined the Socialist Party in the early 1930s, serving as a full-time organizer for the Young Person's Socialist League. In late 1935 he attended Brookwood, where he met Roy Reuther. He served as an economist for the International Ladies Garment Workers Union in the late 1930s and in various federal agencies in the mid-1940s. At Montgomery's suggestion, Reuther hired Weinberg for his staff in 1947. Driven by his commitment to social democratic change, he quickly became Walter Reuther's "conscience." Others found him abrasive. Weinberg, a government official complained, "sees a conspiracy in everything."[21]

Oliver, in contrast, fitted none of the staff's typical characteristics. The UAW Executive Board had created the Fair Practices Department in 1944 to investigate charges of racial discrimination in UAW locals and on the shop floor. Under the dynamic leadership of the department's first director, the Detroit labor lawyer George Crockett, the department had become a platform for the UAW's African-American activists and thus for the union's left-wing caucus. When Reuther won the presidency, he fired the popular Crockett, a move that many black Detroiters deeply resented. Reuther compounded the problem when he named Oliver as Crockett's replacement. Oliver had no training in social democratic thought, had not been a member of the Socialist Party, and had not been active in the labor movement during the CIO's formative years. Born in Tennessee, he came north in the late 1930s as a member of an all-black singing group sponsored by the Ford Motor Company. When the company disbanded the group, he took a job at Ford's Highland Park plant, near Detroit. He became the recording secretary for the plant local in 1942, aligning himself with the right-wing caucus, an unusual move for an African-American. That decision, more than any special ability, won him the Fair Practice Department directorship in 1947. ". . . Oliver [n]ever exhibited the kind of personality that would draw people to him," a UAW activist declared. "If anything, he may have lost influence among [those] Negroes he did know."[22]

Oliver was the only crack in an otherwise coherent political bloc. Step by step, Reuther had committed himself, through both his actions and his staff appointments, to an intimate alliance with the New Deal's liberal statist wing. That was an entirely logical thing for him to do. When he began the process in 1940, after all, the administration's statists held some of the most powerful posts in Washington; they shared Reuther's commitment to regulation of corporate decision making; and they welcomed his advice and promoted his ideas. By the time Reuther completed the process in 1947, though, American political life and American liberalism were no longer what they had been in 1940.

Franklin Roosevelt had begun to lose his grip on the Democratic Party as early as 1938, when southern Democrats began to rebel against the further expansion of federal power. The war emergency and the force of FDR's personality stalled an open rupture in the party, but in the immediate postwar years, the Democrats once again split, as new issues, new ideologies, and new politicians reshaped the national agenda in a way that pitted the party's major constituencies against each other.[23]

The greatest symbol of political change came on April 12, 1945, when FDR died and Harry S. Truman became president of the United States. Like Roosevelt, Truman was a product of the Progressive era, but there the comparison ended. FDR had been a scion of eastern reformism, trained in the citadels of the Democratic Party's liberal elite, whereas Truman was a small businessman attracted to the antimonopoly fervor of midwestern populism, the kind of politician who made a passion of good roads and efficient government. He had entered national politics through Tom Pendergast's machine in Kansas City, which orchestrated his election to the United States Senate in 1934. He proved to be a loyal New Dealer during his two terms on Capitol Hill, but he was no liberal ideologue, no champion of a new industrial and political order. In fact, he was not an ideologue of any kind. True to his Missouri roots, he distrusted the rising power of organized labor as much as he distrusted the power of the corporations. He believed that his primary responsibility was to promote the interests of that most nebulous of political constructs, "the people." And he maintained his closest political ties with the Senate's moderates and conservatives. One of the leading Truman scholars captured him best: Truman, Alonzo Hamby has written, "was, above all, a professional politician, for whom party regularity was a way of life." It was that approach to politics that won him the vice-presidency in 1944, and that approach he brought with him to the Oval Office.[24]

Soon after taking office, Truman launched the second great sea-change in American public life, shattering the antifascist alliance FDR had fashioned with the far left. Alarmed by the Soviet Union's behavior in Eastern Europe, the new president adopted an increasingly hard line toward the Soviets in his first few years in office, portraying the Soviets as the totalitarian heirs of Adolf Hitler, intent on subjugating the democratic states of western Europe and undermining the United States' security. In order to block the perceived Soviet advance, Truman committed the United States to a permanent state of military preparedness and massive economic aid to noncommunist nations. When American Communists and their allies condemned the president's actions, the administration responded with a flurry of red-baiting.[25]

As Truman redefined the nation's international commitments, a new generation of liberals began to redefine the course of domestic reform. Unlike the liberal statists, many of the new generation—Mayor Hubert Humphrey of Minneapolis, the Harvard historian Arthur Schlesinger Jr., and the economist John Kenneth Galbraith, for example—had come of age politically during the war, an experience that indelibly marked their views. The rise of fascism left the new generation suspicious of a broad expansion of state power, while the mounting fear of communism led them away from a class-based analysis of American society. Instead, the new liberals increasingly perceived the United States as a conglomeration of social groupings whose interests the federal government carefully balanced, thus maintaining a broad national consensus. They therefore favored extending the piecemeal welfare state that the New Deal had created, typically by expanding existing programs, but also by moving in new directions, such as national health care. At the same time, the practical experience of World War II led the younger liberals to the linkage of social spending and the restructuring of American economic life, a linkage that had been central to both the liberal statists and the social Keynesians. In practice, they argued, the wartime regulatory agencies had not checked corporate power; they had enhanced it, turning the management of the economy over to corporate "dollar a year" men. At the same time, the war seemed to show that Keynesianism did not have to be tied to social reform. Simply by injecting vast amounts of money into the economy, the federal government had wiped out the unemployment that had bedeviled the nation for a decade. The new generation of liberals thus rejected the liberal statism and the social Keynesianism of the late New Deal to embrace a more truncated "commercial Keynesianism," which sought unparalleled economic growth through indirect stimulation of the economy rather than control of corporate activity. "The function of the state," Schlesinger wrote, "is to define the ground rules of the game; not to pitch, catch, hit homers or (just as likely) pop up or throw to the wrong base."[26]

As the new generation of liberals seemingly settled one of the central policy questions of the New Deal era, they took up two issues that had been at best peripheral to the politics of the 1930s: anticommunism and civil rights. Most New Deal liberals had shown little concern for the presence of Communists in American political life. Some liberals had never forgiven the Soviets their cynical alliance with Nazi Germany in the late 1930s or the American Communist Party its slavish support of that alliance, but most had willingly accepted U.S.-Soviet cooperation during the war. As the pressure of the Cold War mounted, though, the new generation turned vehemently against the USSR and its American supporters, condemning them, as Truman had done, as agents of totalitarianism.[27] The horrors of Auschwitz and Bergen-Belsen, meanwhile, led the new liberals to confront the United States' racial caste system. As they did so, they buttressed the growing civil rights activism of the nation's African-Americans. That movement began in the 1930s, when the National Association for the Advancement of Colored People (NAACP) and other African-American activists, many based in radical political parties and the CIO, launched a broad-gauged challenge to Jim Crow and economic injustice. The activists operated both nationally and locally, chipping away at Jim Crow in the courts and the federal bureaucracy while organizing the rapidly expanding black urban proletariat to demand equal access to factory work, equal wages, and the fair distribution of New Deal welfare benefits. The two paths of African-American activism, one focused on social discrimination, the other on economic discrimination, blended together throughout the war years, most notably in mid-1941, when blacks forced FDR to establish the Fair Employment Practices Committee (FEPC) to combat racial discrimination in defense work. Through such struggles, African-Americans thrust civil rights into the center of national political debate.[28]

The civil rights movement naturally horrified the Democratic Party's southern wing, whose power rested on the maintenance of Jim Crow. The successful disenfranchisement of African-Americans and many poor whites in the late nineteenth century had left the South's working class with little influence in the region's politics. The southern Democratic Party thus came to be dominated by the region's economic elite, who appeased poor whites by continually playing the racial card. The absence of Republican competition in the South, moreover, meant that once elected to Congress, a southern Democrat could remain in office for decades, accruing the seniority that gave him tremendous political leverage. The Dixiecrats were now determined to use that leverage to block the party's liberals from attacking racial inequality.[29]

Truman responded to the mounting tension within the Democratic Party by trying to please all sides. "Truman's political hallmark," the political scientist Samuel Lubell remarked, is "the faculty for turning two bold steps into a halfway measure." Truman sided with the New Dealers by ordering the continuation of wartime price and rent controls in 1945, then staffed the relevant agencies with conservatives who lifted most restrictions. He favored extending the life of the FEPC, yet offered only token opposition when congressional Dixiecrats disbanded it. He supported organized labor's right to collective bargaining, then threatened to draft striking railroad workers. Perhaps most important from the UAW's perspective, Truman acquiesced in the evisceration of the 1945 Full Employment bill. As originally drafted, the bill would have committed the federal government to use national economic planning to ensure a job for every American. Truman endorsed the proposal, but when House conservatives objected, he accepted a Dixiecrat-drafted substitute that replaced the bill's planning mechanism with a meaningless requirement that the president present Congress with an annual economic report, to be prepared by a Council of Economic Advisers.[30]

The reorientation of national politics put Reuther and the new UAW leadership in a difficult position. The UAW leadership obviously disagreed with the new liberals on certain key points. The Reutherites rejected the liberals' belief that commercial Keynesianism alone could create prosperity, insisting instead that Keynesianism had to be embedded within a process of broad economic change. They believed that the liberals' willingness to expand the welfare state in bits and pieces was too cautious. And they believed that by retreating from the New Deal's liberal statism the new generation was abandoning the fundamental goal of economic democratization. Many of the new liberals "don't trust the people," Montgomery wrote to Reuther in 1947, "and therefore interpret democracy in terms of doing good for people rather than having the people do it." The UAW leadership and the new liberals, however, also had a good deal in common. They agreed that the welfare state had to be expanded. They favored the use of Keynesianism to increase the working class's purchasing power, and they often invoked the rhetoric of economic growth. They strongly backed civil rights, particularly the FEPC, which spoke directly to the tie between racial discrimination and economic injustice that the UAW leadership believed lay at the heart of the issue. And they welcomed the hostility of the Democrats' southern wing to the new agenda, hoping that the more sharply the divisions in the party could be drawn, the more likely the Dixiecrats would be to bolt the party for the Republicans, their more natural allies.[31]

The UAW leadership believed that it had much less in common with the Truman administration than with the new liberals. Reuther and his supporters shared the president's hostility to communism, of course, and they had no doubt that the United States had the responsibility to block the perceived Soviet advance. They questioned the administration's willingness to use military power to contain the Soviet threat, however, arguing that the United States could stop the advance of communism only by promoting of democracy both at home and abroad. "The chief weakness of American foreign policy," Reuther wrote in 1947, "is the predilection of our State Department for dealing with anybody who will promise to hate communism. . . . Communism breeds on what democracy too often practices; it exploits the lapses of the democratic conscience and thrives on the shortcomings of democratic action. It is the task of democrats to bridge the gap between preachment and practice. We must wipe out the double standard in America and in the world which divides the masses from the minority that controls the preponderance of economic power."[32] The UAW leadership was appalled, moreover, by Truman's vacillations on the domestic front. "Federal authorities," Victor Reuther charged in late 1945, "have indulged every whim of the monopolists, industrialists, and financiers, while shamefully neglecting the basic needs of the returning veterans and unemployed war workers." Victor clearly overstated his case. The UAW leadership's real problem with Truman was not that he was a tool of Wall Street. The UAW disliked Truman because, as Walter Reuther succinctly explained, the president was "retreat[ing] from economic democracy."[33]

The UAW, however, refused to concede that the battle had been lost. In 1946 and 1947 Reuther and his staff tried to reverse the liberal drift away from a powerful regulatory state, working through the one organization that promised to unite the New Dealers and the new generation of activists, Americans for Democratic Action (ADA). At the same time, the UAW leadership tried to push the Democratic leadership to the left, using the greatest threat the union could muster: the creation of a new party committed to the social democratic reformation of the American political economy and opposed to Truman. "[T]he progressives . . . must have leadership," Montgomery argued. "The basic fight is very clear. Monopoly challenges people; [a] private government of big business and banking challenges the public government which voters elect. These economic and political superpowers must be cut down to size. . . . That's the core issue. That's where our program begins and ends."[34]

Founded in 1941 by an amalgam of former socialists, prominent New Dealers, union officials, and middle-class liberals, Americans for Democratic Action, then called the Union for Democratic Action (UDA), served throughout World War II as an explicitly noncommunist pressure group in support of liberal causes. Though it claimed an impressive membership list, it was not particularly powerful; in 1944 it had one active chapter. In early 1946 the UDA's president, the former Socialist James Loeb, decided that with the liberal swing to anticommunism, UDA could be much more. Accordingly, he issued a blanket invitation to the nation's leading noncommunist activists—old and new—to make UDA, now to be called Americans for Democratic Action, into the center of American liberalism. The results were spectacular. ADA's founding meeting, held on January 4, 1947, attracted a stellar collection of 130 progressives, including the New Deal statists Leon Henderson and Benjamin Cohen; the labor leaders David Dubinsky, Emil Reive, and, of course, Walter Reuther; the NAACP's Walter White; and the young liberals Arthur Schlesinger, John Kenneth Galbraith, Hubert Humphrey, and their great intellectual light, the theologian Rienhold Niebuhr. Here, it seemed, was the vehicle the UAW needed to lead liberalism back to the experimentation of the New Deal.[35]

Reuther and his staff immediately tried to use ADA to revive liberals' interest in economic democratization. At ADA's opening session, Reuther made an impassioned plea for a reinvigoration of the liberal imagination. "We are trying to put out a fire," he told the group. "Let's concentrate our power at the source of the conflagration. . . . We must create and apply new techniques for economic democracy, develop a new institutional framework that will make the large corporations responsible to the community. . . . Our watchword must not be back to the New Deal but forward from the New Deal." The UAW also worked within ADA's inner councils to push the organization to a more aggressive position. Paul Sifton urged the delegates at ADA's organizing meeting to develop a "thorough, integrated, forward-looking program" rather than a "bits and pieces expansion of the New Deal." Montgomery went further, drafting an organizational plan that, had it been adopted, would have transformed ADA from an elite pressure group to a mass-based organization intimately linked to the CIO's Political Action Committees (PACs). The CIO, Montgomery suggested, should disband its PACs and "throw [its] weight into ADA on the same basis that the British trade unions participate in the British Labor Party." Reuther and Joseph Rauh, finally, tried to persuade ADA's executive board to turn day-to-day direction of the organization over to Edward Prichard, a Frankfurter protégé who had worked for the prolabor La Follette Committee, the liberal statist Robert Jackson, and the Office of Economic Stabilization.[36]

As the UAW leaders worked to transform the ADA, they also raised the possibility of breaking the union's almost decade-long alliance with the Democratic Party. Victor Reuther fired the first salvo in an article for *Common Sense* in December 1945. "Figuring out political stratagems for persuading either the Republican or Democratic parties to wage a campaign based upon issues like the social ownership of monopolistic industries seems hopeless at present," he wrote. "It is my opinion that the time is now for labor to divorce itself from the two old parties and resolve to build the base for an independent, indigenous new national party—a party designed to mobilize the American people for democratic abundance at home and enduring peace in the world."[37]

The next year Walter, UAW Secretary-Treasurer Emil Mazey, and East Coast regional director Martin Gerber joined A. Philip Randolph, John Dewey, Norman Thomas, and others in launching the National Educational Committee for a New Party. The committee's "Declaration of Principles," written in part by Sifton and Clayton Fountain, the assistant editor of the UAW newspaper, fully embraced the UAW's domestic and foreign policy agendas. Calling the New Deal "a spent force in the Democratic Party," the declaration called for an explicitly noncommunist "political alignment" that would embrace "all useful functional groups, from workers and farmers to small businessmen." The new party, according to the declaration, would pursue a national economic policy based on "industrial councils" of labor, management, and the public "bound together in a national economic council" empowered to provide the United States with "genuine economic planning." In foreign affairs, the party would support democratic regimes around the globe while opposing all forms of imperialism, be they the "monopoly capitalist imperialism" of the West or the "communist imperialism" of "Soviet expansionism."[38] The UAW staff stumped for the committee's proposals in the months after it issued its declaration of principles. Montgomery praised the committee's attack on corporate power as "the heart and core of a liberal program" that "makes the fight worth fighting." Sifton, the committee's director of publicity, claimed that the ideas presented in the declaration "might make politics a nice, not a horrid, word." Only Victor Reuther offered any criticism, saying that progressives had to stop writing declarations and begin the hard work of "unchaining the political energies in America which in the past have expressed themselves in . . . experimental radicalism."[39]

For all its talk, it is unlikely that the UAW leadership ever intended to launch a third party. It certainly had no intention of doing so in 1948; indeed, Paul Sifton complained in late 1947 that the UAW Executive Board had not yet determined its political plans for the upcoming election year.

The UAW's involvement in the National Committee for a New Party was, rather, the mirror image of the UAW's involvement in ADA, both intended to make economic democratization as central to political debate as it had been ten years before. The UAW was outflanked, however, in the course of 1948. First, Henry Wallace's presidential candidacy eclipsed the UAW's threat of bolting from the party. Then Truman claimed the liberal leadership, in the process making the new liberals' agenda the dominant force in American political discourse.[40]

During his thirteen years in the Roosevelt administration, Henry Wallace had been one of the party's most consistent liberals and internationalists. Like most progressives, Walter Reuther had thought highly of him; Wallace, he wrote his brother Roy in 1944, was "much more courageous" in his political positions than most labor leaders were in theirs. In the immediate postwar years, though, Wallace refused to join the liberals in embracing anticommunism. Convinced that world peace was dependent on Soviet-American cooperation, Wallace sharply criticized Truman's policies toward the USSR. Truman responded by firing Wallace from his cabinet in September 1946. Wallace's dismissal made him the champion of those leftists—Communists and noncommunists alike—who shared his interest in maintaining the wartime popular front. Like Wallace, they had grown increasingly isolated from the Democratic mainstream in 1945 and 1946. By mid-1947, the split was irrevocable, and the Popular Fronters began organizing the Progressive Party to challenge the Democrats in 1948. Citizen Wallace aligned himself with the effort in the course of the year, condemning the Truman Doctrine and the Marshall Plan as imperialistic and the Truman administration as a practitioner of "Hitlerite methods." In December 1947 he formalized the connection, accepting the Progressive Party's offer to run as its presidential candidate in the upcoming campaign. Days after he had done so, the Communist Party endorsed him.[41]

With Wallace's announcement the UAW leadership abandoned even the pretense of breaking with the Democrats. To endorse Wallace was unthinkable. He was, after all, the candidate of those political forces that Reuther had been battling within the UAW since 1940. Indeed, many UAW locals still under the control of the left-wing caucus immediately aligned themselves with the Progressive party. Even talk of launching an anticommunist progressive party, moreover, would simply splinter the liberal vote further and ensure a Republican victory in November. As soon as Wallace announced his candidacy, the Reutherites rushed back into the Democratic fold, turning on the Progressive Party with a furious barrage of red-baiting.[42]

Wallace knew his fortunes rested in large part on his ability to win the support of the CIO, and he realized that Reuther was his "greatest obstacle" in his efforts to secure that support. He probably did not realize just how much of a fight Reuther would wage. When the CIO Executive Board met in January 1948 to discuss its reaction to the Progressive Party campaign, Reuther vigorously urged the board to forbid any affiliate to support the party. The Wallace campaign, he charged, was designed not to capture the White House but rather to plunge the United States into chaos. "The Communist party, in the last days of the Reichstag," Reuther argued, "held to the . . . philosophy that if you can create chaos, out of chaos there will be so much poverty, so much human desperation, that out of that we will make bricks. . . . That is the tragic philosophy which the Wallace thing is helping to advance in America." The CIO's left wing responded by insisting that each affiliate be allowed to support the candidate of its choice. Reuther was uncompromising. Any union leader who supported Wallace, he said at one point, was a "political prostitute." After two days of such bitterness, Reuther and his allies on the board, including the CIO's president, Philip Murray, voted 33–11 to condemn the Wallace campaign.[43]

Assured of CIO support, the UAW then stepped up its public attacks on Wallace. Initially the union leadership portrayed Wallace as a dupe of the Communist Party. "I think Henry is a lost soul," Reuther told the *New York Times* days after Wallace had declared his candidacy. ". . . Communists perform the most complete valet service in the world. They write your speeches, they do your thinking for you . . . they inflate your ego as often as necessary." After the CIO condemned Wallace, the UAW drew no distinction between the candidate and the CP. "The Progressive Party is the Communist Party with another label," the UAW Education Department declared in April. "Wallace has placed himself completely in communist hands."[44] The Reutherites also attacked UAW locals that supported the Progressive Party. In April Reuther informed all UAW locals that they were to be "in complete accord with UAW policy in opposition to Wallace." The International wasted no time in enforcing its edict. When Chicago Amalgamated Local 453 endorsed Wallace, the UAW officers wrote directly to the local's rank and file, telling them not to rely on "some of the officers of your local." Reuther took even more drastic action against the officers of Detroit Chrysler Local 51, who had used the local's newspaper to support the Progressive Party. Charging that Local 51's president had "no right" to "peddle propaganda and to carry out ideologies contrary to the basic policies of national CIO and UAW-CIO," Reuther brought the local officer up on charges before the IEB.[45]

As they slashed away at Wallace, the UAW leadership bloc launched a multifaceted effort to integrate the UAW more fully into the Democratic Party. As a first step, Roy Reuther, as director of the Political Action Department, worked closely with August Scholle, director of CIO-PAC in Michigan, to encourage regional directors, local officials, and staffers to take active roles in their state Democratic parties. Those UAW members who did so generally took up the thankless jobs of party regulars, attending precinct caucuses, serving on regional committees, running for seats to state party conventions. The UAW achieved its most complete integration into the party apparatus, not surprisingly, in Michigan: in the first half of 1948, UAW activists and their liberal allies seized control of the state party apparatus from the Old Guard Democrats who had long dominated it. By so doing, the UAW not only gained a voice in state party politics but also created a UAW power bloc at the national Democratic convention. Though hampered by a late start in precinct races, the UAW nevertheless secured a substantial minority of the seats in the Michigan delegation, enough, Scholle carefully said, "to have a considerable influence" over the delegation. Party leaders assumed the UAW's influence was more than considerable. Though Walter Reuther refused to serve as a delegate—he would never do so—party leaders believed he controlled the Michigan delegation. As the convention approached, therefore, Reuther became something of a power broker, whose demands had to be figured into the intricate coalition building that constitutes the central drama of political conventions.[46]

By gaining such access to the Democrats' inner councils, Reuther and his political advisers ran the risk of subordinating their agenda to that of the party. There is no indication, though, that UAW leaders were concerned about that possibility. Throughout early 1948, Reuther and his advisers remained as critical of Truman as they had been in 1946 and 1947: in both private and public discussions, they continued to insist that the party could retain power only if it rejected the president and embraced social democracy. "[M]ost genuinely progressive people are thoroughly fed up and disgusted with both major parties," Montgomery wrote in February. "Out of desperation, a lot of good people will wallow with Wallace until there is something better for them to vote for." Even as Montgomery wrote, however, the party was moving in the opposite direction from the one the UAW advocated. Instead of liberals seizing control of the party, Truman was seizing control of the liberals.[47]

Truman began his transformation from moderate to fighting liberal on the advice of Clark Clifford, one of the few young liberals in Truman's inner circle. Truman was sure to win the Democratic nomination, Clifford argued in a now-famous 1947 memo, because Wallace's candidacy drained away those Democrats most likely to challenge the president within the party. Once he had the nomination, the president was assured of carrying the South. Truman should therefore build his campaign around the issues and rhetoric that would win him the party's northern constituencies: organized labor, middle-class liberals, ethnic and African-American voters. In particular, Clifford suggested that the president offer each of the northern constituencies some advance on the New Deal agenda: the repeal of Taft-Hartley for labor unions, public housing and national health care for working people, a Keynesian tax program for the new liberals, and civil rights for African-Americans. Truman, in other words, should commit himself to the entire agenda of the new liberals.[48]

Clifford's proposal appealed to Truman on political grounds, and it also appealed to his genuine desire to fight for "the people." The president's transformation nevertheless was a slow and halting process: he repeatedly undercut his own rhetoric by taking conservative steps in the first few months of the campaign, leaving many liberals unsure whether his transformation was genuine. Reuther did his best to encourage those doubts. "Our members are demanding exactly what American public opinion is demanding: leadership," an internal UAW memorandum read. "Franklin D. Roosevelt provided this leadership. Harry S. Truman is not providing it, and cannot provide it." Reuther thus supported the ADA's quixotic campaign of March 1948 to persuade Dwight Eisenhower to accept the Democratic nomination, until Conway, Sifton, and Montgomery convinced him that Eisenhower was more, not less, conservative than Truman. Reuther then argued at the ADA's April Executive Board meeting that the organization should call for an open Democratic convention so that the delegates could decide for themselves whether to nominate Truman. The ADA issued an official position paper along the lines Reuther suggested, though many ADAers continued to support Eisenhower well into the summer. When the Democratic convention opened in July, Reuther endorsed one of the leading New Deal statists, William O. Douglas, for the nomination, proclaiming that he represented "the highest standards . . . of liberalism."[49]

The UAW's efforts were futile; as Clifford had assumed, Truman came to the convention with the nomination assured, though many liberals still kept their distance from the campaign. By the time the convention ended, however, Truman had won them over. Without meaning to do so, the UAW contributed to the president's triumph. With the nomination in hand, Truman decided to make a small gesture to the Dixiecrats, suggesting to the platform committee members that they draft an equivocal civil rights plank calling for civil rights legislation but not for any enforcement mechanism. Led by the UAW counsel Joseph Rauh, the ADA drafted a much stronger plank endorsing a permanent FEPC, antilynching legislation, and an end to the poll tax: the new liberals' full civil rights agenda. When the platform committee rejected the liberals' proposal, Rauh, joined by other ADA and CIO activists, decided to take the liberals' case to the convention floor.[50] Hubert Humphrey, then a candidate for the U.S. Senate, agreed to act as spokesman for the plank, but the night before he was scheduled to speak he had second thoughts. Rauh and a handful of others spent the night insisting that Humphrey could not withdraw at that late hour. At 5 A.M. Humphrey agreed to honor his pledge. Rauh and other UAW and liberal delegates spent the next few hours working the convention floor on behalf of the plank. By the time Humphrey took the podium, the majority of the delegates had begun to swing behind the liberals' position. Humphrey's electrifying speech clinched the issue. The convention adopted the ADA's plank as its official position. Through no effort of his own, Truman was on record in support of the liberals' civil rights program.[51] That fact alone made it easier for many liberals to endorse Truman. The next day he gave them an added reason. Appearing before the convention to accept its nomination, he offered a ringing call for the liberal agenda and a slashing attack on Republican reaction, a bravura performance that combined the stemwinding populist style with the rhetoric of the New Deal. "The battle lines of 1948 are the same as they were in 1932," he declared in one of the speech's most memorable passages. But of course they were not. Truman did not propose new economic responsibilities for the federal government; he was not trying to remake the role of the state. He proposed, rather, to build on the welfare state that FDR had constructed and to commit the federal government to the pursuit of civil rights. That was exactly what many liberals wanted him to do, and they were enthralled by the performance. "Unaccountably," the *New Republic*'s TRB reported, "we found ourselves on top of a pine bench cheering."[52]

Truman did not let up when the convention ended. Throughout the fall, he continually invoked the new liberal agenda. In the Northeast he called for more federal housing; in farm states he promised to protect farm subsidies; and he traveled to Harlem to reiterate his support of civil rights. Here was the new liberals' interest group politics in its pure form, relentlessly reformist but never challenging the premises of the American political economy. As Truman made his case, as the crowds grew and the message caught on, the liberals fell into line.[53]

Truman and his advisers also did their best to bring the UAW leadership into line. When Truman agreed to kick off his campaign with a Labor Day address in downtown Detroit, Clifford urged him to remind union leaders that "the only friend they have is the president." The speech, he said, "should be emotional." Truman did not disappoint. The crowd roared its

3. Harry Truman addresses a Labor Day rally in downtown Detroit, September 1948. (Archives of Labor and Urban Affairs, Wayne State University)

approval as he condemned the Republican Party as the defender of economic royalism and called for the immediate repeal of the Taft-Hartley Act. The Truman campaign likewise wooed the UAW with personal appeals. Time and again the campaign asked Reuther to make personal appearances on Truman's behalf, particularly in areas where Henry Wallace's support was strongest. But the UAW leadership continued to hold back. Reuther and his supporters certainly preferred Truman's fighting spirit to his earlier vacillations, and they approved of much of his program. Truman's proposals, however, still fell short of the social democratic program UAW leaders believed had to undergird liberalism. They remained convinced, moreover, that Truman was not a strong enough candidate to win in November. Less than a week after the convention, Reuther was circulating a confidential CIO memorandum conceding the election to the Republican nominee, Thomas Dewey. The union leadership therefore did its best to distance itself from Truman. The UAW Executive Board did not issue its endorsement of the president until mid-September, two months after the

Democratic convention. The UAW's campaign literature rarely mentioned the president. And on the few occasions when UAW officials stumped for Truman, they were less than effusive in their praise. "We recognize that Harry Truman, like everyone else, is not without his faults," Reuther began his most important speech on Truman's behalf.[54]

That is not to say that UAW leaders distanced themselves from the election as a whole. Determined to elect as many liberal state and congressional candidates as possible, the International launched the second stage of its effort to integrate the union into the Democratic Party during the fall campaign. Again led by Roy Reuther and Gus Scholle, the UAW leadership worked to construct a permanent political apparatus within the union, a structure the union could use to perform the pivotal tasks of campaigning. As Reuther envisioned it, the structure rested on four initiatives. The union began fund-raising in the late summer. Prohibited by the Taft-Hartley Act from contributing union funds to political candidates, the International staged a unionwide drive for voluntary contributions, asking members to donate a dollar each to the CIO's Political Action Committee. The union then funneled the money raised to liberal candidates: G. Mennen Williams, for instance, received $10,000 for his gubernatorial campaign in Michigan. In September, the union staged an extensive voter registration drive among its members. The next month the UAW flooded plants with campaign literature and staged political rallies whereever possible. In the closing days of the campaign, finally, the union did its utmost to get its workers to the polls. These were all labor-intensive activities, requiring a large number of volunteers. The International therefore required each regional director to put his staff to work on the campaign from September onward. Staffers were expected to recruit local union officials to rally the workers at the plant level. The UAW thus would be mobilized from top to bottom.[55]

It was an impressive program, a clear reflection of the Reutherites' faith in structured activism. By relying on regional directors for its implementation, however, the UAW leadership ensured that the results would be uneven. According to Reuther's concept of union hierarchy, the regional directors should have simply implemented the political program that he and his staff had formulated. As the Reutherites put their program into place, though, it became clear that Reuther could not simply impose his will on the regional directors. To be sure, the directors were beholden to Reuther for their positions, but the caucus system made Reuther equally beholden to the directors for the votes he needed to keep his office. If the caucus were to run smoothly, Reuther had to respect the regional directors' power bases and protect their privileges. Should a director not enforce a union directive in his region, Reuther could not force him to comply without disrupting the stability of the political machine he had built. As the fall campaign un-folded, conservative regional directors exercised their implicit veto power for the first, but hardly last, time.[56]

The union's political program flourished in Detroit-area regions, where the International's influence was strongest, and in those regions controlled by the Reuther caucus's social democrats. UAW sound trucks passed through Detroit's working-class neighborhoods, local officials ran door-to-door registration drives, and staffers distributed thousands of leaflets at Detroit's plants and union halls. Leonard Woodcock waged a similarly aggressive campaign in the western Michigan region, normally a Republi-can stronghold, sponsoring torchlight rallies and relentlessly pursuing membership contributions. These regions' culminating get-out-the-vote drives were triumphs of grass-roots mobilization. Local volunteers blanketed their areas the week before the election. Dodge Local 3, for instance, had over one hundred volunteers canvassing the heavily Democratic enclave of Hamtramck. Some activists performed Herculean efforts. The staffer Douglas Fraser spent election day at his distict's polling place, checking off CIO members as they arrived to vote. Thirty-five workers were still not accounted for forty-five minutes before the polls closed. Fraser contacted them all, and the local sent out cars to rush them to the polls. Thirty-four of the thirty-five voted.[57]

The program foundered, meanwhile, in regions controlled by the more conservative members of the Reuther caucus. Staffers of Tom Starling, director of the southern region, restricted their efforts to encouraging mem-bers to pay their poll taxes and distributing leaflets. It is possible to at-tribute such lethargy to the stultifying nature of southern politics. Charles Ballard, director of the Toledo region, had no such excuse. Ballard did not even assign staff members to the campaign until the end of September, too late for them to register new voters. Once on the job, the staffers held no plant-level rallies and performed only the most basic fund-raising. By elec-tion day, the Toledo region had raised a grand total of $466 for CIO-PAC.[58]

When staffers did meet with the rank and file, they reported a uniformly grim picture of the Democratic Party's prospects. Staffers who visited locals in North Carolina and Tennessee found stronger support for the the States' Rights Party than for the Democrats, while UAW representatives in Califor-nia claimed that workers there were more excited about Wallace than about Truman. Los Angeles Local 887, an official reported, could attract only 46 of its 9,000 members to a PAC meeting. Rank and filers at Detroit De Soto "displayed utter demoralization," staffer Irving Bluestone wrote after visit-ing the plant. And William Dodds, on the staff of the Chicago Political

Action Department, complained that progressive workers were "sitting this election out. They are lost."[59]

Such reports reinforced the UAW leaderhip's conviction that Truman could not possibly win the election. They became so sure of Truman's defeat, in fact, that they began laying plans for a third stage of political organizing: yet another attempt to redefine the Democratic Party agenda after Truman left office. Reuther pledged himself to that goal in an August editorial in the UAW newspaper that offered a bitter slap at the Democrats. "We must have a political party that meets the needs of people as people," he wrote. "[T]he government . . . must be for something. For example, for an economy that is both free and enterprising, for government expansion and even operation of necessary productive capacity when private enterprise refuses to expand, for producer and consumer cooperatives. . . . Such a government, so elected, will not fail us. As our government, loyal to our principles and our program, it will serve us in the necessary planning and action for prosperity and peace and against depression and war."[60]

The UAW followed up Reuther's commitment by announcing that the union would sponsor a national conference that would serve as the basis for the party's reformulation. Working in conjunction with the Amalgamated Clothing Workers and the National Farmers Union, both strong supporters of New Deal statism, UAW staff members drafted a convention program that combined the programs of the social democrats and the new liberals. The UAW invited two representatives of successful social democratic parties, the British Labour Party's Aneurin Bevan and the Canadian Commonwealth Federation's Tommy Douglas, to speak to the assembly; they offered the keynote spot to Hubert Humphrey, the leading voice of the new generation; and they suggested that ADA serve as a cosponsor. To make sure that the public did not miss the point of all this activity, the UAW scheduled the conclave for January 20, the day Thomas Dewey would take the oath of office.[61]

As the election campaign came to a close, then, the UAW leadership found itself playing a role very different from what it had intended in 1946 and 1947. Reuther had wanted to shape the Democratic Party agenda in a social democratic direction; instead, Truman had embraced the new liberal agenda, while the UAW concentrated largely on supporting liberal congressional candidates and attacking Wallace for his apostasy. The Reutherites had wanted to institutionalize the New Deal's most experimental programs; instead, they were laying plans for a social democratic resurgence while waiting for the Republicans to take control of the White House. But the Republicans did not take control of the White House. Battered by almost a year of brutal attack, the Wallace campaign collapsed: in the end, Wallace managed to win 2 percent of the national vote. Truman's brilliant campaign, in contrast, worked almost precisely as Clifford had predicted. His support for civil rights cost him four southern states, which went to the States' Rights Party, but he still took the vast majority of the region's votes. And he swept the essential elements of the New Deal coalition's northern wing, including the "demoralized" UAW rank and file, an extraordinary 89 percent of whom voted Democratic. The coalition of supporters gave Truman a margin of 3 million votes over Dewey, and it gave the Democrats control of Congress.[62]

The victory was a stunning personal achievement for Truman, but it was also a testament to the power that the New Deal still exerted over American political life. Truman's victory, however, did not mean that the Democrats would simply continue to follow the New Deal's path. In his campaign Truman had chosen to follow the course charted by the new generation of liberals, a piecing together of New Deal welfare programs, commercial Keynesianism, and civil rights. With his victory, the new liberal agenda becoe the dominant force in American political discourse while the UAW's social democratic agenda, itself a critical part of the New Deal, was placed outside the mainstream. Not that the UAW's agenda was dead. Despite its vacillations during the campaign, the union was a vital part of the Democratic electoral coalition and the party's political machinery, and there was always the hope that the UAW leadership could use that position to inject its program into public debate once again. That would not be an easy task, as the UAW's stillborn January political conclave made perfectly clear. Shortly after the election, ADA leaders wired their regrets, claiming that the pressure of organizing the Democrats' annual Jefferson-Jackson Day dinners prevented them from attending. Hubert Humphrey, the newly elected senator from Minnesota, likewise told the UAW that he could no longer serve as one of the conference's keynoters. He would have loved to participate, he wrote, but he had to be in Washington that day, attending Harry Truman's inauguration.[63]

[3]

The Vital Center Shifts

Throughout the late 1940s Donald Montgomery, director of the UAW's Washington office, educated Nat Weinberg, Walter Reuther's primary speech writer, in the UAW's political rhetoric. UAW officials do not speak of "labor's share" of national wealth, he explained; they speak of the "people's share." They do not call for "redistribution of income"; they call for "building mass buying power (without saying where it comes from)." And they do not demand broad change all at once. "What we must do," he wrote, "is build up our case, and its significance will dawn. Like in the morning—the fact is the sun rises and it dawns upon some people, anyhow, that it's time to wake up. But if we insist on starting with the meaning of daybreak, we are just writing poetry, which is fun for the writer, but the readers are few."[1]

It was realistic advice. Though Harry Truman's victory in the 1948 presidential election did not preclude the possibility of social democratic change, the UAW leadership believed, it had set the terms of public debate for at least the next four years. Having affirmed the continued vitality of the New Deal electoral coalition and that coalition's support for the administration's moderate reform agenda, Truman and the party leadership had no political incentive to push for a fundamental restructuring of the nation's economic relationships. Nor were they likely to respond favorably to political appeals grounded in the technocratic language of the early CIO and the late New Deal.[2]

In the election's wake, therefore, the UAW leadership worked to strengthen its connections with the administration by adopting the rhetoric and the agenda of Fair Deal liberalism. In conjunction with African-American groups, the union vigorously supported the administration's civil rights program. It joined middle-class liberals in promoting the growth strategies of Keynesianism and the advancement of the welfare state. And it deepened its commitment to anticommunism by endorsing global containment and finalizing the purge of communists from the labor movement.

In the UAW's view, though, the Fair Deal was simply a starting point, a foundation on which a social democratic political alliance could be built. Democratic and Republican conservatives, in contrast, saw the Fair Deal as a dangerous extension of federal power, a direct challenge to the racial and economic systems they were dedicated to protecting. As the UAW tried to push the Truman administration to the left, congressional conservatives launched a vigorous attack against the White House's program from the right. The attack turned increasingly bitter in 1950 and 1951 as the most reactionary forces in the GOP poisoned American discourse by trying to link liberalism and subversion. They were largely successful in doing so; by the end of 1951 the Fair Deal was dead, and the UAW's dream of social democracy seemed more distant than ever.

Throughout 1949 and the first half of 1950, Reuther and the UAW leadership acted as loyal foot soldiers for the Fair Deal. Truman had promised a raft of liberal initiatives during the campaign, from reform of federal farm policy to repeal of the Taft-Hartley Act. No issue was more central to the new administration's agenda, however, than the advancement of civil rights. Both Truman and the Democratic Party pledged in 1948 to create a permanent Fair Employment Practices Committee (FEPC) to combat discrimination in hiring, to eliminate poll taxes in federal elections, and to make lynching a federal offense. In January the administration moved to keep its promises, first trying to ease the Senate's cloture rule, which would make it easier to break the inevitable southern filibuster, then introducing the package itself.[3]

The UAW lobbyist Paul Sifton led the union's fight for the administration's proposals. Working closely with the CIO Political Action Committee, Americans for Democratic Action, the National Association for the Advancement of Colored People (NAACP), and other groups, Sifton drafted the UAW's proposal for the easing of cloture rules, helped plan the liberal community's legislative strategy, and coordinated its lobbying efforts. The UAW International, meanwhile, maintained a steady drumbeat of support: Reuther demanded that Truman maintain his support for the full package when the president's will seemed to be weakening in mid-March; Roy

4. Paul Sifton, the UAW's primary lobbyist, sometime in the 1950s. (Archives of Labor and Urban Affairs, Wayne State University)

Reuther organized a rank-and-file letter-writing campaign on behalf of the package; and the UAW underwrote much of the civil rights organizations' lobbying efforts.[4]

The UAW likewise continued its accommodation to the demands of the Cold War, both at home and abroad. Emboldened by Truman's victory, Reuther, Philip Murray, and their anticommunist allies in the CIO launched a two-year purge of the CIO's left-wing unions beginning in 1949. In all, eleven unions, with a total membership of 900,000, were expelled from the organization, including such stalwarts of the 1930s as the United Electrical Workers (UE) and the International Longshoreman's Union. The UAW then staged a series of jurisdictional raids against two of the purged unions, UE and the United Farm Equipment Workers, in a further attempt to vitiate their power.[5] At the same time, Reuther spearheaded the realignment of the CIO's foreign commitments. In January 1949 the CIO disaffiliated from the World Federation of Trade Unions (WFTU), the international labor center founded in 1945 as a forum for the labor movements of the Allied powers. Later that year the CIO joined the American Federation of Labor, Britain's Trade Union Council, and other Western European labor federations to form an explicitly anticommunist, rival organization to the WFTU, the International Confederation of Free Trade Unionists (ICFTU). Walter Reuther helped draft the ICTFU's statement of principles at its founding session in London, and in 1951 Victor Reuther became the CIO's liaison to the organization as director of the CIO's European Office, based in Paris.[6]

No matter how loyally they served the administration, though, Reuther and his staff refused to think of themselves as simply pitchmen for the Fair Deal's piecemeal reforms. As they saw it, their role was rather to serve as a "ginger group" within the Fair Deal coalition, continually prodding its allies within and outside the administration to place their programs within a social democratic framework. "[I]f our union has appraised the issues and assigned priority to its concern among them," Donald Montgomery wrote amid the flurry of activity in mid-1949, "we shall be able to tap almost unlimited resources from among those many persons who not only think as we do but see in . . . the nature of auto workers, the tradition of their union, and the spark and power of Walter Reuther the most powerfully potent force at this half-way point through the twentieth century to hold this drunk-driving world on the road . . . so that once again it can read a road map. . . ."[7]

The UAW constructed its case in 1949 and early 1950 by relating the Fair Deal's specific policy proposals to what the union leadership believed was the broader issue of economic power. Victor Reuther's Education Department laid out the union's basic premise in a September 1949 publication.

"The people who are marooned in the Vital Center sometimes call themselves the independent left, progressives . . . liberals, members of the Third Force, ADA'ers, PAC'ers, New Dealers, Fair Dealers, and the Lord knows what else," the publication declared. "But if the Vital Center is not going to become a cream center, it has got to have an economic policy" based on "the mixed economy."[8]

As they worked for the Fair Deal and liberal agendas, Reuther and his staff built on the premise that economic change and social change were inseparable. They did so largely through rhetorical appeals. In the midst of the congressional civil rights struggle, Paul Sifton reiterated the by-now standard UAW line that while a federal FEPC was important, "freedom in your heart needs to have dollars in your pocket to have lasting meaning." Similarly, when ADA called for a federal stimulus package in mid-1949, Reuther argued that jobs programs and road construction, though certainly desirable, would be nothing more than "stop gap measures" unless they were placed within a program of "publicly planned economic abundance." And Reuther told the founding session of the ICFTU that Soviet totalitarianism could not be defeated as long as the Western powers remained committed to unrestricted capitalism. "I am not particularly interested when people talk about free enterprise," he declared. "I am a believer in a planned economy. We may have a private economy, but if we are to give employment to the people who need employment we are going to have to plan for that employment."[9] The UAW leadership also attempted to piggyback its own, overtly social democratic policy proposals on top of its allies' programs. The union lobbied strenuously for an economic expansion bill that would have placed federal fiscal and monetary policy under the direction of a joint government-management-labor board. The idea immediately ran into a wall of opposition. Using the tactics that had proved so successsful against the Full Employment Bill in 1945, business executives condemned the bill for fostering "class warfare." Truman, concerned about losing the support of congressional conservatives, then ordered White House officials to opposed the bill. By year's end, the proposal was dead.[10]

The UAW likewise attempted, and failed, to push the Fair Deal's social welfare program toward social democracy by promoting a fundamental change in the White House's drive for public housing. Wartime population shifts and the postwar housing crunch had increased the pressure for federal action on public housing for low-income Americans, an issue the Roosevelt administration had barely touched upon. In late 1945 Truman endorsed a senatorial proposal that called for a dramatically accelerated building program. The plan typified the constraints within which postwar liberal reform operated. The bill recognized the decay of the nation's inner cities and therefore empowered the federal government to clear large tracts of slum neighborhoods. A portion of the cleared land was to be reserved for public housing, to be built by private contractors at a rate of 100,000 units a year for five years, far short of the nation's needs. The remaining tracts were to be sold to private investors, who could do with them as they pleased. The bill thus made no attempt to compete with the housing industry or local real estate interests, both of which would actually benefit from its provisions. Congressional conservatives nevertheless condemned it as "socialistic" and blocked its passage in 1946, 1947, and 1948. Convinced that his election had undercut the conservatives' power, Truman made the bill's passage a top priority in 1949.[11]

The UAW immediately backed the proposal. The CIO Housing Committee, underwritten by UAW funds, chaired by Walter Reuther and directed by Leo Goodman, of the UAW staff, led the union's efforts. Reuther publicly pledged the CIO's full support of the measure in a meeting with Truman in mid-December 1948, and early the next year he went before the House Banking Committee, where the bill had been sent for consideration, to make an impassioned plea for its swift passage. Goodman, Sifton, and Donald Montgomery lobbied for the plan, tracking key votes in both houses, preparing statements and press releases for the bill's sponsors, and drafting strengthening amendments.[12]

The union's interest in housing was partly personal. A craftsman at heart, Walter Reuther loved carpentry—he single-handedly rebuilt his family home, a modernist retreat of wood and stone in suburban Detroit—and he was fascinated by the possibilities of urban planning. Many UAW staffers, moreover, had lived in Detroit's public housing projects during World War II. The UAW's concern was also motivated by the crisis they saw around them. Metropolitan Detroit's population had increased by 300,000 during the war years, straining the city's already limited housing stock to the breaking point. By 1948, a quarter-million Detroiters lived in substandard housing, many without toilets or running water.[13] Given these conditions, it is hardly surprising that the UAW leadership hoped the administration's housing program could be extended far beyond the provisions of the pending bill. The administration's program "is sound," Reuther told the Senate Subcommittee on Housing, "but we do not believe that [its] sights are set high enough." The problem with the bill, Reuther argued, was that it did nothing to address the root causes of the housing problem: the unemployment that fostered poverty and thus homelessness; the construction industry's ability to limit materials simply to the luxury home market; and the government's unwillingness to spend the federal funds necessary to meet the nation's pressing needs. To address those problems, Reuther insisted, the federal government needed to revamp the very process of low-income home construction.[14]

Reuther presented the UAW's plan to change the housing market in February 1949, at the height of the congressional debate on the administration's bill. According to the Reuther proposal, the federal government would adapt aircraft production facilities, idled since the end of World War II, to the mass production of prefabricated housing. Housing costs would plummet, Reuther contended, while a million workers would be taken off the unemployment rolls. The plan also would boost military preparedness by returning wartime machine tools to active use, where they could quickly be adapted to aircraft production in the event of an international crisis. The entire project, finally, was to be run by a tripartite board of government, labor, and corporate oficials.[15] Reuther attempted to sell the program as a natural extension of the Fair Deal. His proposal, he told Congress, offered a "practical, down-to-earth way" to meet the housing crisis; it would promote economic growth; and it would provide the United States with a powerful tool in the battle against Soviet expansion. "[H]ousing ties in with the problems on the home front and on the world front," he argued. "We, who profess to be the defenders of democracy, of democratic ideals, have got to begin to practice what we preach, and no place in our whole society is the gap between what we preach and what we practice as sharp as it is in housing."[16]

That was a powerful appeal, nicely attuned to the Fair Deal's rhetorical style and the anticommunist mood, and it utterly failed. The UAW's plan won some support, to be sure: the *New York Times* endorsed the proposal's "imagination," and Hubert Humphrey claimed that it "shows again the creative thinking of Mr. Reuther." That was its problem, however. Like the "500 Planes a Day" proposal on which it was modeled, the UAW saw its housing plan as a way to extend federal power over economic decision making in new directions, to create new state structures, and to foster technology for the public good, the goals that had animated Reuther's politics since the early 1940s. These were not the goals of the Fair Deal, though, and no matter how much Reuther tried, he could not make them compatible. Truman showed no interest in the idea, and it quickly dropped from public discussion. The administration, it seemed, was more than willing to accept the UAW's support for its programs, but it was not willing to give the union a say in the setting of the national agenda.

Even if Truman had embraced the UAW's housing proposal, it undoubtedly would have died on Capitol Hill, where even the most moderate expansion of state power was sure to meet almost insurmountable opposition. Technically, the Democrats enjoyed wide margins in the House and Senate in 1949, but in practical terms the numbers were meaningless. Congress was dominated, as it had been since 1938, by a coalition of conservatives, most of them Republicans from the Midwest and West, the balance of them southern Democrats. As Congress opened, the Dixiecrats were determined to block the administration's civil rights program, while congressional Republicans, humiliated in an election they had been convinced they were going to win, were determined to block the White House's attempts to extend the New Deal.[17]

The Dixiecrats led the conservative coalition in 1949, using the Senate cloture rule, which limited floor debate, as its main weapon. Knowing that the Dixiecrats were planning to mount a filibuster against the administration's civil rights program, Senate liberals in early 1949 proposed broadening the upper house's ability to cut off debate by securing cloture. Senate rules then required a vote of two-thirds of senators present and voting to secure cloture, a margin that would require liberals to win the support of northern Republicans. The liberals wanted the requirement lowered to a simple majority; the Dixiecrats countered with a measure that would stiffen the rules for cloture by requiring the approval of two-thirds of all senators, not simply those present and voting. In the ensuing struggle, Senate Republicans supported the Dixiecrats, whose proposal passed by a 63–23 vote.[18]

The cloture fight was more than a fight over procedure. By strengthening the cloture requirements, the Dixiecrats had strengthened their ability—indeed, the ability of any thirty-two senators—to block any liberal legislation the administration advanced, from civil rights to public works. The UAW leadership fully expected the conservative coalition to use that power. "The present deadlock over the change in Senate rules is NOT different from the fight . . . to enact the Fair Deal program," Paul Sifton wrote Walter Reuther. "The bi-partisan coalition that fronts for special privilege has simply succeeded in shifting the first big battle to civil rights, where racist appeals to prejudice, fear, and hate can be used in an attempt to split the people, split Congress, split the Democratic and Republican parties."[19] Events in the balance of 1949 seemed to prove Sifton correct. The Dixiecrat-Republican coalition held firm throughout the year, repeatedly defeating both liberal social and economic initiatives. The president's civil rights package, introduced shortly after the cloture debacle, died in committee, never even reaching the floor, where in any case it would have faced the inevitable filibuster. In the early spring, the coalition defeated the administration's proposal for national health care; in May it turned back the liberals' attempt to repeal the Taft-Hartley Act; and late in the year it rejected the White House's calls for an economic stimulus package. Of all the administration's domestic proposals, only its housing program won congressional approval, and even that measure, which promised to aid real estate developers as much as it helped the urban poor, barely managed to get by a key procedural vote.[20]

The liberal community, including the UAW leadership, was outraged by the conservative congressional coalition's ability to block the Fair Deal, but the UAW also drew a degree of comfort from the coalition's actions. For years Reuther had insisted to his liberal and African-American allies that racial and economic injustice were inextricably linked; now the conservatives had proved it. He had argued that the heart of American conservatism, north and south, was the defense of economic royalism; now the conservatives had proved it. And he had insisted to his supporters that proper principles were meaningless without political power; now the congressional conservatives had proved it. "Now at last we can begin to fight it out along sure lines," Reuther declared. "The difference between those who hope for the future and those who live in the past and fear the future, those who look to people and those who look to property as the source of power can now become the issue of practical politics."[21]

Reuther's optimism was overdrawn, an attempt to put a positive spin on an increasingly bleak political picture, but it was not entirely incorrect. Though they had blocked virtually the entire liberal agenda, congressional conservatives had allowed the liberals to dictate the terms of debate in 1949. In early 1950, however, leadership of the conservative coalition shifted from the Dixiecrats to the conservative wing of the Republican Party, and suddenly the political dynamic changed. Like the Democrats, the Republicans had divided in the immediate postwar years. The GOP's moderate wing, generally based in the northeast urban corridor and linked to some of the nation's largest financial and corporate interests, accepted the centralization of federal power that had been the hallmark of twentieth-century politics. Its leading figures, Wendell Willkie and Thomas Dewey, for instance, favored government intervention in the nation's economic affairs, albeit in support of big business, supported an aggressive American foreign policy, and accepted much of the New Deal welfare state as a necessary "safety net" for the poorest Americans. The Republicans' conservative wing, by contrast, remained committed to the antistatist conservatism of the late nineteenth and early twentieth centuries. Typically based in the small towns and rural districts of the Midwest and West, the conservatives, led by Ohio's Robert Taft, South Dakota's senator Karl Mundt, Michigan's Homer Ferguson, and others, were hostile to the New Deal, sus-

picious of the nation's new international commitments, and virulently opposed to those groups, particularly organized labor, that they considered to
be the vanguard of social change. The moderates had controlled the GOP in
the 1940s, three times winning the party's presidential nomination for one
of their own. As the congressional coalition asserted itself in 1949, however, the conservative wing seized the initiative in the GOP. In the process,
they changed the congressional battle lines from the Fair Deal to the most
explosive issue of the immediate postwar era, anticommunism. As they did
so, even the mildest form of liberalism seemed suspect.[22]

By any rational measure, the administration and its allies, particularly the
UAW, should have been immune to the taint of radicalism. The Republican
right had red-baited the liberal-labor coalition before, most effectively in
the 1946 midterm elections. The White House's fervent pursuit of the Cold
War, however, and the liberal-labor coalition's increasingly bitter attack on
the radical left in the United States had seemingly put such charges to rest.
Then the issue once again slipped out of the liberals' control. Tensions
mounted throughout 1949 as the Communist triumph in China, the USSR's
testing of an atomic bomb, and the discovery of several Soviet spy rings in
the United States convinced many Americans that the Democrats were not
containing the Communist menace. Capitalizing on these fears, the Republicans' conservative wing launched a bitter attack on the administration
and its supporters in February 1950, using as its spokesman Wisconsin's
obscure junior senator, Joseph McCarthy.[23]

McCarthy began his crusade in Walter Reuther's hometown of Wheeling,
West Virginia, on February 9, 1950, announcing that the State Department
knowingly had on its payroll 205 members of the Communist Party. The
spectacular charge won him headlines nation-wide, in the process transforming the public's anxiety into hysteria. Sensing the shift in mood, some
of the most powerful Republicans in Congress quickly rallied to McCarthy's side. Together, McCarthy and his backers slashed away at the administration and its supporters throughout the first half of 1950, using insinua-
tion, innuendo, and lies to portray the liberal left as an ally of Communist
subversion.[24] The UAW leadership again put on a brave public face in
response to the conservative onslaught. The UAW newspaper denounced
McCarthy's Wheeling speech as "utterly irresponsible," and insisted that
"if it weren't for the danger of making him [McCarthy] a martyr there
probably would be a move in the Senate to unseat him." Reuther insisted
that the United States could not defeat the Soviet Union by "turning our
nation into an armed camp at the sacrifice of the very liberties that
distinguish our civilization from totalitarianism." And Paul Sifton blasted
McCarthy for using "smear and goon tactics."[25] Despite its public bra-

vado, however, the UAW leadership was clearly thrown on the defensive by the rise of McCarthyism. In an off-the-record session with his executive board in the spring of 1950, Reuther admitted that he was "sensitive about the socialist label" being applied to the UAW. He subsequently cracked down on the socialist political activities of some union officers and staff members. He told Emil Mazey, the UAW's secretary-treasurer and still a member of the Socialist Party, that while he respected Mazey's loyalty to the SP, the UAW president thought it showed poor judgment. Reuther also roundly criticized Brendan Sexton for participating in a summer school run by the League for Industrial Democracy, an organization that Reuther had long supported.[26]

Reuther undoubtedly believed that such moves were nothing more than tactical retreats made necessary by the temporary aberration of McCarthyism. Indeed, with the outbreak of the Korean War in June 1950, the UAW president himself once again felt safe enough to offer ringing calls for the social democratic reconstruction of the American political economy and the reformulation of foreign policy. But McCarthyism was much more than a temporary aberration; the Wisconsin senator had changed the alignment of American politics. The congressional conservative coalition, now able to cloak its opposition to social and economic change under the banner of anti-communism, had been immeasurably strengthened. Both the Truman administration and the liberal community, conversely, became reluctant to promote even piecemeal reform, much less the systemic change the UAW leadership had been urging upon them. Far from breaking the trend, the Korean War reinforced it, tying the administration more closely to the status quo while fueling the fear on which McCarthyism fed. The vital center, already committed to moderation, thus shifted to the right, where it would remain for the next fourteen years.

The Truman administration's decision to commit American troops to the defense of South Korea in June 1950 seemed to run counter to the UAW's foreign policy perspective. Since the onset of the Cold War, Reuther and his supporters had insisted that military force alone could not stop Communist expansion, since it did nothing to correct the economic injustice that drove nations into the Soviet orbit. Mao Zedong's accession to power in China in 1949 reinforced the UAW's belief that the Cold War could be won only through a positive program of economic aid and the promotion of democratic rights. "We lost China not because of Communist successes but because of democracy's failure," Reuther said again and again in 1949 and early 1950. "We should have known that freedom's fight in China had to be won in the rice fields, not on the battlefields."[27]

Reuther nevertheless applauded Truman's actions in Korea, wiring the president, "The UAW stands unitedly behind you in the courageous and determined leadership which you are giving the free peoples of the world in resisting communist aggression." He had good reason to do so. The administration's show of force offered Truman and the liberals the chance to dampen the unreasoning passions that McCarthyism had triggered. And the sudden need to put the American economy on a wartime basis reopened the possibility of social democracy if labor could secure a meaningful position in the mobilization process.[28]

The UAW leadership immediately moved to take advantage of the opportunity Truman had seemingly given them. In July, Reuther urged the White House to establish control of the economy, including wage and price controls and the allocation of resources, in a single mobilization agency, membership in which would be evenly divided between representatives of management, labor, and the government. He also called on the presidents of the major auto companies to hold a labor-management summit to plan the industry's response to mobilization. And he called for federal management of the steel industry, which he had long changed was artificially restricting production. "We cannot tolerate private economic decisions which block our efforts," Reuther declared, clearly throwing away the caution that he had adopted earlier in the year. "As a matter of survival a free people must act through their government . . . if the normal channels, through which they expect economic responsibility to be met, have failed them."[29] A week later, Reuther sent the White House a detailed proposal for a "Total Peace Offensive" in the Third World. According to the plan, the United States would contribute to the United Nations $13 billion in development funds annually for the next hundred years, the sum to be placed under the management of a People's World Assembly. Each nation would be assigned eighteen assembly seats, to be filled not only by diplomats but also by "dirt farmers, industrial workers, housewives, youths, and . . . labor leaders." The United States would help staff resulting development projects by sending into the field college-age volunteers willing to offer a year of service.[30]

The UAW's expansive hopes for the war were quickly dashed. Indeed, Truman's initial response to the war highlighted his basic commitment to the decentralized economic management of postwar liberalism. Rather than take direct control of the economy through wartime boards, he worked through existing federal agencies, manipulating credit and government contracts to check inflation and promote private investment. He also undercut his only nod to the social democratic agenda, the creation of an Economic Stabilization Agency, by putting the agency under the direction of a conservative academic. And though he considered Reuther's Peace

Offensive "intriguing," he passed it on to his speech writers, who he hoped could borrow its language for White House addresses, rather than to his foreign policy experts.[31]

The UAW leadership deeply resented the White House's moderate approach to the war economy. Donald Montgomery condemned "the unwillingness of Truman to exercise leadership," seeing the president's mobilization program as "impregnable to influence by labor organizations." Reuther agreed. "[T]he Washington scene is very discouraging," he told the UAW Executive Board in September. "You get the feeling that nobody quite knows what is going on." The UAW economist Harry Chester was not willing to give the administration even that much credit. Truman's mobilization plans, he wrote, "were worked up either by the bankers of the federal reserve board or the big business representatives in the Commerce Department. They are all controls of big business, by big business, and for big business."[32]

Far from checking McCarthyism, moreover, the war deepened the hysteria. Defying all logic, Republican attacks on the administration and its supporters continued unabated through the summer and fall. Thoroughly cowed, some congressional liberals joined the conservative coalition to pass the odious National Security Act, which, among other provisions, empowered the president to intern Americans suspected of subversive activity in times of national emergency. The hysteria also spread to the UAW rank and file, particularly to white ethnic workers, among whom the conflation of anticommunism and patriotism was already deeply rooted. In August and September, UAW members in Milwaukee, Los Angeles, Detroit, and New Jersey attacked fellow workers whom they suspected of being Communists. In the worst incident, a mob of workers at the Milwaukee Seaman Body plant carried fifty-five-year old Ray Webb from the factory and dumped him into the street, fracturing his back. Webb had earned the attack by signing a petition calling for nuclear disarmament.[33]

McCarthyism also took its toll in the 1950 congressional election. Though the Democrats maintained control of both houses, the liberal bloc suffered some serious losses. Voters turned out two of the UAW's most trusted allies, California's senator Helen Gahagan Douglas, who lost to Richard Nixon, and Wisconsin's congressman Andrew Biemiller, who had moved straight from the CIO to the House. Ohio's conservative Republican Robert Taft, meanwhile, easily shrugged off a concerted CIO drive to unseat him in a campaign that, according to the analyst Samuel Lubell, "turned out to be a shattering demonstration of labor's political weakness." "This was a genuine nationwide swing of sentiment," a dejected Paul Sifton wrote to Roy Reuther days after the election. Truman clearly agreed. In his

1951 State of the Union message, he surrendered to the conservatives, announcing that he was shelving the Fair Deal for the duration of the war. When Congress opened he made his peace with the Dixiecrats, going so far as to offer Georgia's Richard Russell, one of the faction's most conservative members, the position of majority leader.[34]

By the end of 1950 the administration's economic mobilization program had also swung to the right. When China's entry into the war threatened to prolong the conflict, Truman abandoned the decentralized controls of the previous year and placed the economy under the direction of the newly created Office of Defense Management (ODM). In principle, the creation of the ODM was a progressive move, the kind of central state action the UAW had been demanding since the outbreak of war. In practice, however, the ODM fell far short of the UAW's expectations. The administration made no attempt to integrate organized labor into the ODM's decision-making apparatus. Truman named Charles E. Wilson, president of General Electric (GE) as director of ODM, and Wilson in turn staffed the agency with businessmen and bankers, while labor leaders were given only advisory positions. Far from redistributing economic power, moreover, the ODM seemed intent on making working Americans bear the brunt of the mobilization effort. It established price guidelines that did little to stop inflation at the same time that it instituted a relatively stringent wage freeze. It also placed a cap on the production of consumer durables and restricted the availability of steel, copper, and aluminum—decisions sure to cause layoffs—while offering corporations generous tax incentives for construction of new plants.[35]

The ODM's orders came as a serious blow to rank and filers already concerned about their economic position. Battered by ten years of labor conflict, in the late 1940s officials at Ford, General Motors, and Chrysler had launched wide-ranging efforts to boost productivity and restore shop-floor stability. As part of those efforts, the Big Three had invested heavily in the development of new labor-saving technologies. They also had begun a gradual shift of production from older plants in Detroit, Cleveland, and other auto centers to newly constructed plants in the suburbs, a move they hoped would undermine union militants' power bases. While they poured millions of dollars into these programs, the auto makers had tried to buy labor peace at the bargaining table. The UAW took full advantage of the Big Three's offer. After the 1945–46 GM strike debacle, Reuther had shifted his bargaining strategy from the pursuit of broad social goals to the construction of an economic safety net for union members. On the most basic level, Reuther and his negotiating team had simply demanded that the auto manufacturers boost wages. The UAW thus raised the typical auto worker's hourly wage from $1.53 to $1.74 between January 1948 and June 1950. At the same time, the UAW traded predictable labor relations for a series of innovative contract provisions designed to ensure auto workers' long-term security. The strategy had culminated just weeks before the Korean War began, when the UAW and GM agreed to a five-year contract, far longer than previous pacts. In exchange, GM provided its workers with a cost-of-living allowance, an annual improvement factor—a percentage raise tied to productivity—and a company-funded pension plan. Ford and Chrysler swiftly accepted similar terms.[36]

At the time, commentators had hailed the "Treaty of Detroit" as a bargaining triumph, likely to defuse labor unrest for years to come. With the onset of war, however, the rank and file grew increasingly restive. Workers participated in a frenzy of panic shopping during the first few weeks of hostilities, convinced that shortages would soon make their newfound purchasing power meaningless. The weekend after the United States committed troops to Korea, customers cleared out a Sears store in a Detroit working-class neighborhood. The concern quickly spread to the shop floor. Talk of a federal wage freeze had triggered small wildcat strikes in Detroit-area plants by August 1950. Now, half a year into the longest contract in the UAW's history, the ODM's orders threatened to abrogate the entire structure of wage increases and automatic escalators. The rank and file's worst fears, it seemed, had been confirmed.[37]

The ODM's production quotas were even more damaging to the rank and file than the price freeze. Ordered to produce only 65 percent of their previous year's output, the nation's auto makers initiated a massive wave of layoffs. Just before the Chinese attack in November 1950, the auto industry employed 750,000 production workers; by the end of 1951 the number had plummeted to 614,000. The unemployment rate stood at 5.6 percent in Flint in December 1951, 8.1 percent in Detroit. Those workers who kept their jobs increasingly complained that their employers were speeding up the pace of production, long the most volatile charge rank and filers could make. The mood in the shops was turning "bitter and ugly," a well-informed source reported in January 1951. Shortly thereafter, another, more serious wave of wildcats spread through Detroit, as at least some workers returned to the shop-floor militancy of World War II. The Detroit De Soto plant experienced the greatest upheaval. Workers there walked out of the plant eighty times in the first half of 1951.[38] Discontent was not restricted to neighborhood stores and the factory floor. "Many" auto workers, reported Norman Matthews, Detroit regional director, also blamed the UAW leadership for not taking sufficient action to deal with unemployment. It is impossible to measure the erosion of the rank and file's support for the leadership, but anecdotal evidence indicates that the problem was relatively serious. When the National Labor Relations Board held elections to determine whether the UAW should have a union shop in Detroit's Chrysler plants, for instance, only 60 percent of the company's workers bothered to vote, in sharp contrast to the 90 percent turnout for similar elections in Ford and GM plants the previous year.[39]

The rank and file's disillusionment could not by itself have posed a challenge to the UAW leadership. The disillusionment had to be shaped into a political movement powerful enough to control a bloc of local votes to the union convention, the real center of UAW political power. The Reuther caucus's crushing defeat of the left wing in 1947 had seemed to foreclose such a possibility. Over the next few years, though, Reuther, convinced that he could contain any challenge from below, had allowed the caucus machinery to atrophy. The result had been a flurry of political infighting among local and regional officials, particularly among the most conservative members of the Reuther coalition. The most embarrassing conflict occured in Toledo, where caucus insurgents accused Vice-President Richard Gosser of a range of serious offenses, from misappropriating union funds to taking a share of the profits generated by numbers runners in area plants. In Detroit, meanwhile, the Association of Catholic Trade Unionists (ACTU) lashed out at the Reuther caucus for maintaining ties with such "socialistic" organizations as Americans for Democratic Action. Reuther managed to defuse both conflicts: though they were clearly troubled by Gosser's questionable business practices, an Executive Board investigating committee, following caucus rules of protecting members' perogatives in their regions, cleared him of all charges, and Reuther personally negotiated a truce between the ACTU and social democratic wings of his caucus. Such skirmishes nevertheless damaged the caucus's image of invincibility. Early in 1951, the president of UAW Local 600, Carl Stellato, decided to use the restiveness among the rank and file to see just how weak the Reuther machine had become.[40]

It is not surprising that the first serious challenge to Reuther's leadership since 1947 came from Local 600, the bargaining unit for the Ford Rouge plant. The local's membership, the largest in the UAW, had always been of an independent cast of mind. The left-wing caucus had won the local's elections throughout the 1940s, even as the Reutherites had swept through much of the rest of the UAW. As Nelson Lichtenstein has shown, moreover, Rouge workers had long been partial to direct action at the point of production. That activism had made them one of the first targets of Ford's postwar modernization campaign: the company had shifted thousands of jobs from the Rouge by the late 1940s and cut many others by installing new technologies that speeded up the assembly lines. Rouge workers had responded in time-tested fashion, shutting down the complex for twenty-four days in May 1949 to protest the work pace on the final assembly line.[41]

Reuther had masterfully managed the speedup strike, authorizing the walkout both to appease the rank and file and to wring significant concessions from Ford's management. Early the next year, Stellato, the Reuther caucus's candidate, had won the local presidency. He seemed the ideal choice. Though he had spent the previous few years on the International staff, Stellato was every inch a factory hand. He had an eighth-grade education, had begun working at the Rouge at age eighteen, and had spent most of his work life as a machine setter, a semiskilled job. A few months into his presidency, Stellato had purged the local's left-wing officials. The membership's independence quickly asserted itself, however, as the purged left wing won the fall elections for Local 600 General Council. Stellato switched his allegiance shortly thereafter, joining forces with the left wing he had just attacked and turning against Reuther's handling of the defense emergency.[42]

By combining his left-wing allies with a rank and file willing to take immediate action on the shop floor, Stellato could have offered a radical, even syndicalist alternative to Reuther's social democratic agenda. Had he done so, it is at least conceivable that Reuther would have shifted to the left, perhaps sanctioning and even directing worker action at the point of production. He had done that, after all, during the speedup strike at the Rogue three years earlier. But Stellato did not create a radical movement. Rather, he channeled the rank and file's anger in an essentially conservative direction. He repeatedly condemned Reuther's calls for a revision of the wartime political economy as "ineffective." At the same time, he offered specific policy proposals—the extension of federal unemployment benefits for the duration of the emergency; increased defense contracts for the auto industry; and a thirty-hour workweek for forty hours' pay as an industry standard—that simply demanded that the UAW leadership seek a bigger share of wartime spoils. Stellato therefore accepted labor's subordinate position within the mobilization effort and pressured Reuther to do the same.[43]

Stellato's actions also reinforced a growing perception at UAW headquarters that the rank and file had itself swung to the right. The perception rested in part on many auto workers' seeming embrace of the anticommunist hysteria. More generally, the Reuther cadre increasingly believed that as the UAW reduced its members' economic insecurity, rank and filers became more interested in protecting their gains than in supporting social change. "[T]he union helps [the workers'] economic interests until they can have a front porch," a UAW official claimed in a staff meeting, "and for that they become capitalists."[44]

As the Korean War entered its second year, then, the UAW leadership found itself constrained by a network of conservative forces in Congress, the administration's mobilization agencies, and the UAW itself. The frustration was palpable in the halls of Solidarity House, the UAW's newly opened, modernist headquarters on the banks of the Detroit River. "Today . . . Wilson of GE is virtually a 'domestic president'; Gen. Eisenhower has more political power in foreign relations than President Truman, Defense Secretary [George] Marshall, or Secretary of State [Dean] Acheson," Sifton wrote to Reuther. "Under the imperatives of the world conflict, we drift into a military-industrial receivership because neither in the White House, the Congress, nor in the divided house of labor have we developed the principles, the programs, and the methods for victory."[45] Reuther had tried to fight for his principles during the first year of the war, and he had made no headway. Now, as national political life continued to narrow, he saw no choice but to retreat.

Reuther never stopped calling for social democratic reform of the administration's mobilization program. He repeatedly urged the White House to place the ODM under the direction of a twelve-member mobilization policy board, yet another version of the power-sharing framework he had been promoting since 1940. In mid-1951 he offered another version of his 1949 housing proposal, this plan designed to break the "machine tool bottleneck" that he claimed was stalling military production. The federal government, he suggested, could reactivate World War II–era plants as final assembly centers for machine tools, the program to be overseen by the familiar structure of a tripartite National Production Authority.[46]

Reuther increasingly presented his social democratic proposals, however, within a framework that subordinated fundamental change to political necessity. First, he shifted his rhetoric to protect his union from right-wing attacks. UAW spokesmen had always been careful to avoid the highly charged language of class politics, but now Reuther sprinkled his speeches with disclaimers of interest in any fundamental change in the political economy. He prefaced an attack on the steel industry's "artificial restrictions" of output by insisting that he opposed nationalizing steel production, though he had repeatedly claimed in the late 1940s that he favored federal control of steel plants if such restrictions continued. And before he criticized the corporations' "program of planned scarcity," he claimed that he "believe[d] strongly in the free enterprise system," though as late as

December 1949 he had said precisely the opposite. At times Reuther went so far as to deny his own past. "Certainly I am not a socialist," he told the Detroit Economic Club. "There was a time that I belonged to the Socialist party for about a year. . . . I joined the Socialist party in 1932 during all the unemployment because I felt that it might be a better way of doing things. I have learned a lot since 1932."[47]

Reuther also changed the main thrust of the UAW's program from systemic change to the defense of the rank and file's economic position. He moved first to protect the union's escalator clauses. As soon as he heard that the ODM was considering a wage freeze, he and Richard Gosser rushed to Washington. In a series of hurried meetings with White House officials, including Truman, they took an uncompromising stand: if the administration did not allow the union's escalator clauses to take effect, the UAW would consider its contracts with the auto companies void, and the White House could expect a strike early the next year.[48] Six months later, the UAW leadership launched a vigorous lobbying campaign to bring more defense work to Detroit-area auto plants. In July 1951 Reuther and Emil Mazey asked the White House's mobilization coordinators to earmark more federal contracts for the auto industry; in October the UAW president presented Truman with the same proposal; and in early December, he announced that the UAW would bring eight hundred local officials to Washington, D.C., in January 1952 for a two-day conference on defense unemployment. Behind the scenes, Reuther pushed and prodded the UAW's allies in the Michigan Democratic Party to intercede with the administration on the union's behalf.[49]

The UAW's rhetorical and programmatic shifts made both practical and political sense. Reuther simply could not afford to talk freely of nationalization or to criticize free enterprise if he wished to avoid a devastating right-wing attack; no labor leader could let federal regulations abrogate one of his union's most important contract provisions; and the rank and file clearly needed relief from the mounting layoffs. Reuther's decision to seek that relief by demanding a larger share of defense dollars, moreover, co-opted one of the key demands of the Stellato insurgency and thus undermined its challenge. Perhaps most important, the UAW's lobbying worked. Impressed by Reuther's strike threat, the administration issued regulations in mid-February 1951 designed to allow auto workers the full benefit of the escalator clauses. The administration initially seemed less open to the union's call for increased defense work. One mobilization official bluntly informed the UAW that his agency was not running a welfare program and could not be concerned with pockets of unemployment. At year's end, though, ODM director Wilson buckled under the pressure and announced that henceforth the administration would make every effort to place defense contracts in areas with high unemployment.[50]

As important as those victories were, they did nothing to stop the rightward shift in American public life or to democratize of the American political economy. Indeed, presidential aides realized that the administration's economic concessions to the union enabled the White House to ignore the UAW's demands for a role in the shaping of mobilization policy. "Since we are very likely to have to fuss with Reuther on really basic issues," a presidential adviser wrote in October 1951, "we at least might do him small favors." By adopting a portion of Stellato's program as his own, similarly, the UAW president deepened the union's subordination to the military-industrial complex that Sifton had complained of in early 1951. Reuther's rhetorical concessions to the right were even more troubling. The point of McCarthyism was to destroy the legitimacy of the liberal and noncommunist left, to make reform suspect and dissent disloyal. Even a rhetorical retreat, no matter how understandable or advisable, therefore conceded to the right much of the victory it sought. Nor did Reuther stop with that critical concession. To shore up his position, he also engaged in his own version of McCarthyism.[51]

Trouble began in early 1952, when the House Un-American Activities Committee (HUAC) announced plans to investigate Communist influence in Michigan's defense industries. The probe was clearly motivated by political considerations. HUAC had long served as the conservative coalition's cudgel. Committee members undoubtedly intended the Detroit probe to serve just that purpose. If the hearings could portray the UAW as being soft on communism, the Dixiecrats and Republicans could seriously weaken the union's influence during the upcoming presidential election campaign. Reuther recognized the danger. HUAC, he told the UAW Executive Board, planned "to try to put the union in a position where we were . . . covering up for the communists."[52]

The first week of hearings, held in Detroit in late February 1952, proved to be less than spectacular. The committee subpoenaed several of the areas left-wing activists, most of whom refused to answer the committee's questions. On the final day of its first week in Detroit, however, HUAC produced its star witness, Bereniece Baldwin, dues secretary for the Michigan Communist Party and an FBI informant. In four hours of testimony, Baldwin detailed the party's activities in the auto plants, particularly the Ford Rouge, which, she claimed, the Communist Party had targeted for "special consideration." Soon thereafter, HUAC's chairman announced that the committee would return in mid-March to investigate the CP's activity in Local 600.[53]

Baldwin's testimony touched off a firestorm of concern. The *Detroit News* warned that a "Moscow-controlled fifth column" in "many of Michigan's huge plants and industrial organizations" threatened to "destroy the United States government." Tensions also mounted within the UAW. The ACTU praised HUAC's "shock treatment" as "the only method sufficiently violent to paint on a giant canvas . . . the deep-rooted, rapidly growing Marxian menace." Many of the auto workers Baldwin had identified as party members, meanwhile, became targets of harassment. Seven auto workers so named were fired, and ten more were physically expelled from plants by their fellow workers. At their ugliest, the incidents took on a racist caste. White workers at Chrysler's Jefferson Avenue plant threatened to run a black former party member out of the factory. When local union officials tried to intervene on the worker's behalf, whites, screaming racial epithets, shouted them down. The situation grew more tense the next day, when black workers, determined to keep the man on the job, confronted white workers determined to expel him. To avoid a riot, the local asked the black worker to leave. Tensions remained high throughout the week. One division in the plant hung a black in effigy, and other white workers brandished ropes.[54]

At least some of Reuther's closest advisers urged him to stand up to the pressure: Leonard Woodcock, for instance, claimed that to do otherwise would "dignify" HUAC's "neo-fascist[s]." Reuther disagreed. If the UAW did not cooperate with the committee, he said, "the union will be in jeopardy. . . . The good name of our International has got to be protected." Reuther subsequently moved in two directions. When HUAC returned to Detroit, he ordered two International staffers, Lee Romano, a former vice-president of Local 600, and Shelton Tappes, an African-American activist and former local recording secretary, to testify about their experiences with the local's CP members. Both men also spent much of their time before the committee praising Reuther's record as an anticommunist. The UAW president "is the number one public enemy . . . for the Communist Party, and that's for sure," Romano said, while Tappes argued that under Reuther's leadership the UAW had become "the most active organization in this country against the efforts of the Communist Party."[55]

At the same time, Reuther tried to turn the hysteria HUAC had created to his own political advantage. The UAW president's ability to attract more defense spending to Detroit had already eased the shop-floor tension that had triggered wildcats and thus largely undercut Carl Stellato's challenge to the Reuther caucus. Now Reuther saw an opportunity to crush the opposition. Days after the committee concluded its hearings, Reuther informed Stellato and the Local 600 leadership that the UAW Executive Board was bringing them up on charges of supporting the Communist Party and failing to follow the union's political policies. If found guilty, Local 600's leadership would be removed from office and the local would be placed under receivership, the highest penalty the International could impose.[56]

The IEB hearing exposed the darkest side of the Reuther caucus: its tendency to be run not by democratic procedures but by the iron hand of party discipline. Reuther gave the Local 600 officers just one day to prepare their defense, and he denied them the right to cross-examine witnesses. The presiding officer at the trial, Vice-President John Livingston, had participated in and supported the decision to bring the local officers up on charges. And Reuther was allowed to harangue Stellato for almost three hours before the Local 600 president could say anything in his own defense. As Reuther presented his case, moreover, he made it clear that the key issue was not the political affiliation of the local officers, none of whom, Reuther admitted, was a Community Party member. Instead, Reuther repeatedly condemned Stellato for criticizing the International's policies. The Local 600 leadership strenuously argued that disagreement on policy was a hallmark of union democracy, but the IEB was unimpressed. After more than eleven hours of hearings, the board voted to remove the officers and place the local under the International's control.[57]

The IEB's seizure of Local 600 was clearly a cynical political maneuver. It was also a symbol of just how profoundly the conservative attack had poisoned American political life. In 1949, Reuther and the UAW leadership had believed that by trading on the rhetoric of the Fair Deal they might redirect the national agenda toward social democratic change. Instead, the Dixiecrats and the Republicans had pushed political discourse to the right. The resulting miasma of anger and fear not only destroyed the UAW's hopes of building on the Fair Deal; it also led Reuther to back away from the moral and political core of his ideology, to retreat from what was best in his personality and his philosophy—his profound commitment to social change and economic justice—and to embrace what was worst.

[4]

The Pull of Consensus

In January 1953 Adlai Stevenson, the nominal head of the Democratic Party, phoned Lyndon Johnson, who had recently been elected Senate minority leader. Rumor had it, Stevenson explained, that party liberals wanted the Democratic Congressional Policy Committee, established in 1947 simply to track members' voting records, to set the party's legislative agenda. What was Johnson's opinion of the proposal? "These ADA and UAW people," LBJ said, were lobbying for the idea in order to win control of the party's program, but he had squashed it. The Democratic Party simply could not pursue a liberal agenda, he continued, if it wanted to preserve its base in the South, a point he had recently been making to Hubert Humphrey, the liberals' spokesman in the Senate. "I tried to explain to him that we could not have a completely labor party, and . . . he [should] stop making about forty speeches to the CIO every week and should start making some to the farmers of Minnesota. . . . He is doing that." "That's healthy," Stevenson agreed.[1]

The UAW's attempt to reshape the Democratic Congressional Policy Committee was a minor affair at best. Stevenson and Johnson, however, obviously considered the fight as part of a much broader struggle to reshape the party's program. Democratic leaders had long been concerned that the UAW's brand of aggressive reform would destroy the party's fragile coalition. The right-wing resurgence early in the decade and the consequent constriction of public debate strongly reinforced that view. Moderates such as Stevenson and Johnson thus took control of the party in 1952 and 1953, backed away from even the piecemeal reformism of the Fair Deal, and instead committed the Democrats to a platform that had as its highest priority the maintenance of party unity. Their political power eroding, many of the Democrats' leading liberals likewise tempered their commitment to reform, accepting the moderates' narrow program as a reasonable response to the nation's political and economic configurations. By mid-decade, Franklin Roosevelt's party of the common man had become the party of consensus.[2]

The Democratic Party's shift to the center placed the UAW's leader in a difficult position. If the union hoped to exercise any political power at all, Walter Reuther and his lieutenants would have to support the Democratic Party leadership, but to do so was simply to strengthen the party's ability to build a moderate consensus. The UAW responded to this situation by trying to maintain a delicate balancing act, prodding the Democratic leadership to be more aggressive while adapting its own program and rhetoric to the party's truncated agenda and trying to expand organized labor's political influence by allying the UAW with the labor movement's more powerful and more conservative bloc. The effort was in vain. The Democratic leadership proved largely impervious to the UAW's appeals while the institutional structure that emerged in the labor movement, the AFL-CIO, further limited the UAW's political power.

The Democratic Party's movement toward the center was already well under way by 1952. Pressured by McCarthyism, the conservatives' success in the 1950 midterm election, and the demands of the Korean War, Harry Truman had shelved the Fair Deal and made his peace with the Dixiecrats, who subsequently assumed control of most of the party's key congressional posts. Reuther's accommodation to the party's shift was also well under way. By 1952 the UAW president was publicly denying that his union wanted to change the political economy. He was engaged in extensive lobbying simply to win the union a larger share of defense dollars. And he was trading on McCarthyism to destroy dissent within the UAW. That year's presidential campaign nevertheless marked a dramatic increase in both the Democrats' and Reuther's shifts to the center.

For their part, the Republicans believed that after two decades of defeat, 1952 would be their year. Joseph McCarthy's two-year pillaging of the political landscape, coupled with the stalemate in Korea, had greatly weakened the Democrats. The GOP leadership was divided, however, on how best to exploit the opening McCarthy had given them. The GOP's conservative wing was determined to build on McCarthy's triumph by winning the party's nomination for one of its own, Ohio's Robert Taft. The Republicans' powerful moderate wing, led by internationalists such as Thomas

Dewey, progressive corporate executives such as IBM's Thomas Watson, General Electric's Philip Reed, and Studebaker's Paul Hoffman, and the publisher Henry Luce and other members of the mainstream media, wanted the nomination to go to a candidate who would continue to promote government support of big business at home and American hegemony abroad but who would not advance the New Deal welfare state. In early 1952 they found their man, Dwight David Eisenhower.[3]

On the most immediate level Eisenhower was a political cipher whose commitments were so unclear that, just the year before, Truman had courted him for the Democrats. By training and inclination, though, Eisenhower was everything the GOP's moderates could hope for. As Robert Griffith has pointed out, Ike had spent his adult life in one of the vanguards of the twentieth-century organizational revolution, the military, where he gained an intimate knowledge of state power and bureaucratic process. He understood that the highly integrated economy of mid-century required government assistance, but he opposed state involvement in the management of corporate affairs. He favored the maintenance, by and large, of the New Deal welfare state as a means of fostering interclass harmony, but he was determined to check its growth. He was fervently committed to the pursuit of the Cold War, but he was determined to stop Soviet aggression in a fiscally responsible manner that corporate executives applauded. And, GOP moderates liked to point out, Ike's war record made him eminently electable. The appeal was overwhelming: Eisenhower won the nomination on the first ballot. In the requisite show of party unity, he then offered major concessions to the Republican right, choosing Richard Nixon as his running mate, condemning containment as little better than appeasement, and condoning McCarthy's red-baiting of the Democrats.[4]

Cowed by the Republican resurgence, the Democrats began their campaign in retreat from Fair Deal liberalism. In March 1952 Truman, battered by seven tumultuous years in office, announced that he would not seek reelection. Of the four candidates who subsequently threw their hats into the ring, only the deadly dull governor of New York, Averell Harriman, was to Truman's left.[5] Desperate to expand the field, prominent Democratic moderates and liberals launched a campaign to draft Governor Adlai Stevenson of Illinois, who was coyly disclaiming interest in the nomination. Stevenson was an attractive choice. Witty and urbane, he appealed to the upper-middle-class sensibilities of many liberals. Unlike Harriman, he was a gifted speaker and effective campaigner. He had built a reasonably progressive record as governor. He had only one drawback, in fact, from a liberal perspective: ideologically and programmatically, he was a centrist. He opposed broadening the welfare state; he believed that the federal government should not "put the South over a barrel" by imposing civil rights legislation on the region; and he opposed deficit spending to stimulate the economy. "What do you want from me?" Stevenson asked a delegation from Americans for Democratic Action in March. "I don't agree with your programs."6

The liberals' swing to Stevenson "presents us with a problem," Donald Montgomery wrote Reuther shortly before the Democratic convention in July. The governor's moderation on such fundamental issues as civil rights and economic expansion "do not make a good case for the man," Montgomery argued, but if the party's liberal wing fell in behind him, "we shall have to track along." In that event, he advised, Reuther should concentrate his full energies on pushing Stevenson and the party to abandon their moderation, as the liberals had forced Truman to do four years earlier. That was easier said than done, however. The liberal-labor bloc no longer held the balance of power in the Democratic Party, as it had done in 1948, and Stevenson knew it.7

Events at the Democratic national convention made the decline in the liberal-labor bloc's influence clear. The UAW had further integrated its members into the Michigan Democratic Party in the years since 1948, and thus held an even larger portion of Michigan's convention seats than it had controlled four years earlier: in 1952, twenty-nine of the Michigan delegation's seventy-two members were CIO members, more than in all other state delegations combined. The UAW leadership therefore believed it had the power to secure from the convention two critical concessions, both of which would strengthen Stevenson's ties to the liberals while dealing a serious blow to the Dixiecrats' prestige. Reuther considered it "fundamental" that the party platform reiterate its 1948 pledge to support a strong civil rights program, and he wanted the party's nominee to select a liberal as his running mate. To maximize the union's bargaining power, Reuther ordered the UAW's delegates to stay off the Stevenson bandwagon until the governor made his position clear, and Reuther threatened to withhold the UAW's endorsement of any nominee, including Stevenson, who played to the South.8

Stevenson's closest campaign advisers dismissed Reuther's threats as nothing more than "maneuvering," and moved in precisely the opposite direction from the one the UAW favored. Knowing that the Dixiecrats enjoyed much more power in the party than they had in 1948, Stevenson was determined to appease them. The governor therefore worked with the Dixiecrats to draft a civil rights platform plank considerably weaker than the 1948 pledge. "The 'pros' wrote the civil rights plank," a key Stevenson aide exulted when the work was completed. "It's excellent, but the liberals want to kill themselves." The urge quickly passed. As Stevenson had expected, most of the party's leading liberals accepted the plank, refusing to support Reuther's call for a floor fight in opposition to the platform. Two days later, Reuther, perhaps trying to avoid the UAW's 1948 mistake of distancing itself from Truman, joined the liberals, throwing the UAW's support to Stevenson on the third and decisive ballot.[9]

Stevenson had not yet completed his courting of the south. The day after the governor won the nomination, rumors circulated that he was considering either Senator J. William Fulbright of Arkansas or Senator John Sparkman of Alabama as his running mate. Reuther informed Stevenson that neither was acceptable; the UAW, he said, wanted Senator Estes Kefauver of Tennessee, a liberal on most matters and a moderate on civil rights, for the second spot. Again Stevenson turned the UAW's demand aside and chose Sparkman. "Walter, who worked all Friday night and Saturday morning to get Kefauver in, was terribly shocked," Paul Sifton wrote his wife from the convention, "as was I."[10]

Sifton was not the only UAW insider appalled at Stevenson's convention performance. "Why—why—do we face [this] situation," complained William Dodds, on the staff of the Political Action Department, to Roy Reuther. "We've been compromised and Sparkmanized .... Eisenhower and Stevenson are in fundamental agreement on matters that transcend partisan politics." Roy Reuther, in turn, reported that African-American voters were extremely upset by Stevenson's choice of Sparkman. Donald Montgomery was even more upset by Walter Reuther's apparent willingness to accept Stevenson's actions. "WPR," he wrote to Sifton, "worries me more than S[tevenson] because he has the capacity and the responsibility to do some heavy channelling, and doesn't seem to be showing a taste for it."[11] Indeed, in the weeks after the convention Reuther seemed to be doing his best to accommodate himself to Stevenson. In an August letter to the rank and file, the UAW president argued that the Democratic platform met most of the union's demands, that despite his actions at the convention Stevenson was a liberal, and that Sparkman was a Fair Dealer on every issue but civil rights. Similarly, in a private conversation Reuther reminded the UAW's officers that no candidate was "perfect" and that in any event "politics [is] the art of the possible." In the final analysis, he said, the UAW had to hold Stevenson to "relative" rather than "absolute values."[12]

Stevenson, for his part, had no intention of conceding any ground to Reuther. In late August, the UAW president met privately with Stevenson at his home in Springfield, Illinois. Reuther presented the governor with a detailed list of UAW policy suggestions—a forthright defense of civil rights, repeal of Taft-Hartley, expanded social spending, opposition to "the eco-

5. Donald Montgomery, director of the UAW's Washington Office, sometime in the 1950s. (Archives of Labor and Urban Affairs, Wayne State University)

nomics of monopoly and scarcity," extensive foreign aid to developing nations—all designed to mobilize "the liberal-labor-minority bloc." Stevenson bristled at Reuther's suggestions. "It irritated him to be pressed," an aide recalled. "One of his greatest fears was that the Democratic Party would turn into the labor party. . . . So if Reuther started shoving him around, he bridled. He was never close to Reuther. Few people are. He's a . . . very domineering guy."[13] Stevenson was so determined to distance himself from Reuther, in fact, that he rebuked him at the most public UAW event of the campaign, the Democratic Party's Labor Day rally in downtown Detroit. For years Reuther and other unionists had been condemning the Taft-Hartley Act as a "slave labor law." Michigan's governor, G. Mennen Williams, told campaign aides that Stevenson had to come out strongly for repeal of the act in his Labor Day address, and if the governor was considering "pussyfooting" on the issue, "he'd be better off not mentioning it at all." Stevenson certainly did not equivocate. "I don't say that everything in that act is wrong; it isn't," he told the 30,000 Detroiters in his audience. "I'll say frankly that I don't think it's a slave labor law, either."[14]

Despite Stevenson's centrism, his courting of the South, and his overt hostility to Reuther and his agenda, the UAW devoted its full resources to Stevenson. Roy Reuther had improved the UAW's campaign machinery in the four years since the last national campaign. Rather than simply ask rank and filers to contribute to the the CIO's Political Action Committee, the International staged PAC raffles in the plants. The results were substantially better than in 1948: the Detroit regions had raised more money by the end of September than they had in all of the 1948 campaign. The UAW then used the funds to produce reams of Stevenson campaign literature; the UAW paid for three half-hour television shows in which Reuther spoke for the governor; and the union contributed heavily to Democratic campaign coffers. "[T]he only big money was coming from labor," a Stevenson campaign aide admitted. "[I]f it was not for labor . . . we'd have to close headquarters in a week."[15]

The International also tried to improve the effectiveness of its campaign apparatus at the regional level. As in 1948, the International ordered all of its regional staffers to work on the campaign. Each local was expected to establish a citizenship committee, which would then receive a share of the money raised by the PAC. The International undoubtedly hoped that such a structure would enable it to bypass more conservative regional directors and deal directly with local officials. But again the campaign apparatus proved far more successful in regions controlled by social democrats than in those controlled by the Executive Board's conservatives. Detroit's regions again reported furious campaign activity, with staffers and volunteers incessantly working the plants and union halls. Toledo's regional director, meanwhile, did not enforce the International's order to establish citizenship committees until a month before election day, and the southern regional director did not do so until eleven months after the election. And neither the Toledo nor the southern regions' staffers bothered to inform the International what, if any, activities they were undertaking.[16]

No matter what the level of activity, Stevenson was not an easy sell. Reuther tried to portray the candidate's hostility to the UAW as a sign of his integrity, while the UAW's campaign literature masked Stevenson's views beneath a wave of class-based attacks on Eisenhower and the Republicans. Union flyers labeled the GOP's campaign "the campaign of the four generals"—General Motors, General Electric, General Foods, and General Eisenhower—and the UAW Education Department urged local leaders to link Ike with McCarthy and Taft. The UAW's newspaper turned to the most potent Democratic weapon of all in the campaign's closing days, running full-page inserts that featured photos of Depression-era bread lines and Hoovervilles. "The Wall Street old guard has not changed since 1929," the inserts read. "If they get back into power they will make the same selfish and stupid mistakes that led us into the Depression."[17]

Such classic Democratic appeals obviously still resonated with the UAW rank and file. According to postelection polls, Stevenson won 75 percent of the UAW rank-and-file vote, a full 30 percent above the Democratic total nationwide. Over half of the UAW rank and filers who voted for Stevenson did so because he was a Democrat or because they believed he was "better for the working man," solid evidence of auto workers' continued commitment to the New Deal tradition. The GOP's strident anticommunist appeals, in contrast, seemed to have accomplished little: 81 percent of the UAW's Catholic voters, whom many commentators considered most susceptible to anticommunism, voted Democratic, 10 percentage points above the Democratic margin among the UAW's Protestant members. Subtle warning signs for the Democrats were embedded within the UAW vote, however. As impressive as Stevenson's percentage of the rank-and-file vote appeared, it was still 14 points below the 89 percent Harry Truman had won four years earlier. It is impossible to say in precisely what sectors of the UAW rank and file the erosion occurred, but Stevenson fared worst among those subgroups most likely to enjoy the highest economic standing. Seventy-two percent of the UAW's skilled workers voted for the Democrat, compared to 81 percent of the lowest-paid unskilled workers—a small crack, at least, in the economic bonds that had tied workers to the party of Roosevelt. The vote also divided along cultural lines, at least to some extent. Perhaps put off by Stevenson's urbane manner, perhaps attracted by

Eisenhower's appeal to individualism, rank and filers whose fathers had been farmers were somewhat less likely to vote Democratic than were second-generation laborers. The racial division in the vote was more significant. Despite his equivocation on civil rights, 9 1 percent of the UAW's black members supported Stevenson, whereas 7 3 percent of white members did so.[18]

The decline in the UAW vote seemed small indeed, though, in comparison with the national swing to Eisenhower and the Republicans. Stevenson managed to preserve the essential elements of the New Deal coalition, winning a majority of the labor, northern ethnic, African-American, and southern white votes, but in each instance he secured much smaller margins than Truman had enjoyed. Eisenhower thus added a significant minority of traditionally Democratic voters to his major bases of support, diehard Republicans and a huge bloc of independent voters, particularly white suburbanites. These blocs gave Ike 5 5 percent of the popular vote and the Republicans control of Congress.[19]

Eisenhower's victory was not a repudiation of liberalism, UAW spokesmen argued in the days after the election, but rather a reflection of the general's immense personal popularity. In private, however, union officers and staffers feared the election had institutionalized the Democrats' drift to the center. With Stevenson's campaign, the staffer Bill Dodds wrote, "the Democratic Party itself called a halt to the militant movement that for twenty years has been known as the New-Fair Deal." Now the White House was under the control of a president who was himself committed to centrism, while the Republicans' congressional victory reinforced the Dixiecrats' influence on Capitol Hill. And the UAW simply did not have the power to reverse the tide.[20]

The effects of Eisenhower's victory rippled through both Capitol Hill and corporate boardrooms in the mid-1950s, in the process changing the primary political and economic structures within which the UAW operated. In the wake of the presidential election, the Democratic leadership confronted the divisions within the party. Stevenson would remain the Democrats' titular head until the next presidential election, but the real power in the party now gravitated to the House and Senate minority leaders. The Dixiecrats had the leverage to name their choices for the positions, but they knew that if they chose candidates from the deep South they would touch off yet another party brawl like those that had rent the party during the Truman years. Accordingly, the Dixiecrats threw their support behind congressmen who, like Eisenhower, represented the middle ground of their party, men who, they believed, could unify the Democrats by avoiding the most divisive issues. For House minority leader, every party faction supported Sam Rayburn, a centrist who had held the post since 1937. The Senate minority leadership remained open, since the previous leader had been defeated in the Republican landslide. Days after the election, the Dixiecrats unveiled their choice: Lyndon Baines Johnson, the junior senator from Texas and Rayburn's protégé.[21]

LBJ was essentially the Democratic Party's version of Dwight Eisenhower. Like Ike, he learned his politics in one of the vanguard forces of state expansion, though in the New Deal rather than the military, and he had a profound respect for the federal government's ability to improve the lives of ordinary Americans. He also enjoyed close ties to businesses that benefited from state support, in Johnson's case the construction firm of Brown & Root, the aircraft industry then expanding in Texas, and radio and television interests. He therefore strongly favored the use of government power to stimulate economic growth. At the same time, as the representative of a southern state, he opposed the liberals' support of civil rights. And as a highly ambitious politician who dreamed of the White House, he was determined to avoid any issue that would divide the party he hoped to lead. In the weeks before the new Congress opened, Johnson made it clear how he would pursue these goals if he were elected minority leader. The Republicans had won the right to set the agenda, he argued, but it was not clear precisely what that agenda would be. Eisenhower was committed to preserving the New Deal and continuing containment, whereas some of the GOP's most powerful congressmen, Taft and McCarthy, for instance, intended to dismantle much of the welfare state and reduce the nation's international role. The Democrats, Johnson argued, should support Ike, and by so doing give him the votes he needed to maintain the domestic and international commitments the Democrats had made. Such an approach had obvious advantages. By following Eisenhower's lead, the Democrats could trade on the new president's popularity, and the party would not have to propose any of its own initiatives. That was precisely what the Dixiecrats hoped to hear. With Georgia's Richard Russell leading the way, Senate Democrats made LBJ their leader.[22]

The UAW leadership was incensed by the turn of events in Washington. "How can we get out the vote and win in northern . . . states on a program sparked by champions of . . . tax loopholes, white supremacy, and union-busting?" Donald Montgomery wrote to the Democratic National Committee as soon as he heard Johnson was the front-runner for minority leader. There was every reason for concern. The UAW's political agenda rested on the possibility of extending the New Deal and furthering more systemic economic and social change. Now the Republican and Democratic parties had forged an informal consensus committed to the maintenance of the status quo, favorable to government aid to big business but hostile to government control of corporate decisions, supportive of the New Deal's fragmented welfare state but not of its extension, and opposed to the initiatives the Truman administration had passed. The new consensus, in other words, reversed the UAW's agenda.[23]

Throughout 1953 and 1954, the Republican White House and the Democratic congressional leadership together chipped away at those Fair Deal programs they believed discouraged economic expansion. With Johnson's support, the president eliminated the wartime wage and price controls Truman had established in 1951; congressional conservatives prohibited the targeting of defense dollars to depressed areas; and LBJ and the administration agreed to a housing program that slashed federal construction to a token 30,000 units a year, thus eviscerating the 1949 housing act. Congress also passed a series of measures that extended corporate power over heretofore public resources, such as offshore oil.[24]

The new consensus in Washington, in turn, gave the major auto manufacturers an opportunity to transform their industry. Ford, General Motors, and Chrysler had been investing heavily in new technologies and plant construction since the late 1940s. The federal government had accelerated those efforts during the Korean War by underwriting much of the Big Three's research and construction costs. Now, as the the threat of government regulation all but disappeared, Ford, GM, and Chrysler put their new tools and plants to work. After 1953, the Big Three automated large sections of the production process while shifting more and more work from aging plants in older industrial centers to new, sleek facilities in the suburban Midwest, South, and West. Ford's Brooks Park plant, for example, opened in suburban Cleveland in 1954, used automatic loaders to produce engine blocks twice as quickly as the company's older, nonautomated plants while employing one-tenth the number of workers.[25]

The competitive advantage of such innovations had a devastating effect on the auto industry's smaller producers and numerous parts suppliers. Unable to match the Big Three's extensive capital improvements, independent auto makers such as Studebaker, Packard, Nash, and Hudson saw their share of the auto market plummet. They responded by consolidating their operations: Hudson and Nash formed American Motors Corporation (AMC); Packard and Studebaker merged. As they did so they shut down many of their older plants. AMC closed its Detroit plants in 1955, for example, and centralized production in Kenosha, Wisconsin. The reshuffling did little good; the independents teetered on the edge of bankruptcy throughout the balance of the decade. Parts suppliers fared even more poorly. Many shut down operations as the Big Three, convinced that it was more cost effective to produce their parts in-house, canceled the contracts on which the suppliers had long depended. By the close of the 1950s, auto manufacturing had become largely a three-firm industry.[26]

The industry's restructuring bifurcated the UAW rank and file. After a brief downturn in late 1953 and early 1954, auto production surged as the Big Three took full advantage of their innovations. Despite the introduction of labor-saving technology, then, the major producers added thousands of workers to their payrolls. By December 1955, the auto industry employed 778,000 production workers, the highest total in its history. Wages likewise rose: the average production worker's weekly earnings topped $100 for the first time in 1955. At the same time, the industry's transformation created substantial pockets of poverty as the Big Three shifted production to the suburbs and slashed workforces in inner-city plants. Ford, for instance, reduced its workforce at the Rouge by half between 1950 to 1960. The collapse of parts suppliers and independent producers, meanwhile, wreaked havoc in older auto centers such as South Bend and Detroit. Those workers who could afford to do so followed the jobs to the suburbs. Those who could not do so, many of them black, watched their once-vibrant working-class neighborhoods begin the painful descent into ghettos. Detroit's population fell by almost 10 percent between 1950 and 1960, its white population by 23 percent, while white working-class suburbs such as Roseville and Warren boomed.[27]

The UAW leadership initially responded to the bipartisan consensus in Washington and the concomitant transformation of the auto industry with the same combination of carefully qualified proposals for social democracy and liberal economics that it had put forth during the last years of the Truman administration. In April 1953, Reuther called on the White House to sponsor a labor-management-agriculture conference to "plan for full employment and full production in peace time." He also returned to the rhetoric of Thorstein Veblen, condemning the "scarcity mentality" of "the little men of big business," who once again were reducing production to drive up prices. And at year end he praised Sweden as a model of economic management and social welfare care. As unemployment crept upward late in 1953, the UAW also proposed a spate of short-term stimulus measures perfectly in keeping with liberal growth economics: an increase in the minimum wage, federal supplements to state unemployment benefits, and implementation of public construction projects.[28] In 1954, however, Reuther began to shift the basis of his economic rhetoric, fashioning new messages that moved away from the economic planning that had been central to his agenda. He traded on the auto industry's new order to argue that the Big

Three's consolidation gave them the resources to free their workers from cyclical unemployment. And he insisted that the federal government had to take responsibility for the specific problems that the new industrial order caused.

UAW negotiators had tried to win rank and filers greater security during the 1950 bargaining round by signing long-term contracts with the Big Three. The Korean War layoffs had discredited those agreements, so in 1953 the UAW had persuaded the major auto makers to reopen negotiations on wage rates. Even as the union squeezed the Big Three for more money, though, Reuther insisted that auto workers would not enjoy real economic security until the manufacturers regularized their production schedules and abolished layoffs. In mid-1953 Reuther unveiled the strategy the union hoped would force the change. When the UAW's contracts expired in 1955, the union would demand that its members receive an annual rather than hourly wage. Auto workers would thus be guaranteed their paychecks whether or not they worked, taking from auto makers the financial advantage that layoffs provided. The UAW negotiating team fully expected the Big Three to take long strikes rather than bow to the UAW's demand. By the time negotiations began, however, auto sales were booming and the major manufacturers were desperate to maintain production. Ford cracked first. Though it would not guarantee its workers an annual wage, company negotiators agreed after months of hard bargaining to establish a "supplemental unemployment benefits" (SUB) fund. The company would place 5 cents an hour per employee into the fund. A worker who was laid off would draw a check from the fund each week for up to twenty-six weeks. The SUB check could then be combined with unemployment compensation to provide the worker with 60 percent of his or her take-home pay during the period. General Motors and Chrysler quickly accepted identical plans. Though a far cry from the guaranteed annual wage, it was the Reuther leadership's greatest bargaining triumph.[29]

Even as they won SUB, the UAW leadership increasingly criticized the auto makers for the structural changes that had made the union's victory possible. In particular, UAW officials condemned the Big Three's application of automation and their monopolization of the industry. The union leadership had begun discussing the problem of automation as early as 1949, but the subject did not become central to the union's rhetoric for another four years. The message the union then delivered did not directly attack technological innovation; Reuther and his staff were far too committed to technocracy to do that. Instead, they criticized the corporate officials who controlled the new technology. Corporate managers were not concerned with the social good that technology could bring, the UAW leadership charged; they simply hoped to use new technology to boost their profit margins. By their selfishness, the corporations threatened to impoverish large sections of the working class and thus to unbalance further an economy already skewed in their own favor.[30] The UAW's condemnation of corporate concentration, meanwhile, revived a primary concern of New Dealers in the late 1930s. Increased productivity should result in lower prices on consumer goods, the UAW argued, but the largest corporations— particularly GM—now enjoyed so much power that they could set aside the laws of supply and demand. Corporate officials thus set "administered prices" for their products, high enough to ensure their companies a profit even as they pushed consumers out of the market and risked plunging the nation into depression.[31]

By building its economic message around SUB, automation, and administered prices, the UAW leadership hoped to confront Republican conservatives on their own ground. The UAW's calls for a guaranteed annual wage challenged auto makers to allow workers to share the fruits of capitalism that conservatives were so vigorously celebrating. The UAW's stress on administered prices capitalized on a widespread fear of inflation, a fear fueled by the Eisenhower administration. It also offered a strong rejoinder to the charge, again leveled by the White House, that union settlements like that of 1955 were the primary cause of price increases.[32] The UAW leadership did not shift its rhetoric simply for political gain, though. The union's new message also allowed the leadership to keep its social democratic agenda alive while avoiding the now suspect rhetoric of 1930s social engineering and economic democratization. Like his demands for a say in GM's pricing policy in 1945, Reuther's call for an annual wage pushed the boundaries of postwar collective bargaining, forcing auto makers to admit labor's right to influence, albeit indirectly, decisions long considered management's perogative. By accepting SUB the UAW created a permanent structure that could be used in successive bargaining rounds to win workers even greater security. The UAW's critique of corporate pricing and technological policies rested on the same analysis of the American political economy as had the union's critique of "planned scarcity" in the 1940s. The UAW's proposed solutions highlighted the continuity in the leadership's thinking. To limit price fixing, the UAW suggested, any corporation that controlled 20 percent of its market should have to justify to Congress any proposed price increases. The UAW also called on the government to establish a tri-partite commission, a "technological clearing house," to oversee automation. The UAW thus continued to insist that private economic decisions should be made public through state structures.[33]

The shift in the UAW's economic message nevertheless marked a retreat from its overtly social democratic agenda of the late 1940s and early 1950s. The UAW leadership was still capable of flights of technocratic fancy. "Sensibly, rationally, scientifically," Jack Conway proclaimed in 1955, "we intend to harness this radical new force [of technological change] in our lives, using its potential to produce an era in which well-being, justice, and peace will be the universal possession of all mankind." But such rhetoric was now being used to address not the broad problem of corporate power but specific manifestations of that problem. The UAW had essentially surrendered its claim that the public and organized labor had a right to participate in the management of the economy as a whole.[34]

The UAW's new economic agenda also reinforced divisions within the union. SUB offered substantial and immediate benefits to those employees of the Big Three who faced brief layoffs, but it did not help the auto industry's skilled workers, who generally could count on year-round employment. Many craftworkers thus resented SUB, convinced that the International had won the innovation by accepting a smaller wage settlement for skilled hands. The resentment edged toward revolt by the end of 1955, as 5,000 skilled workers across the country threatened to bolt the UAW for a new union, the Society of Skilled Trades. For all its talk about the social costs of automation and industrial concentration, moreover, the union leadership offered no immediate aid for auto workers who were left permanently unemployed by the industry's restructuring. To be sure, the UAW urged the federal government to provide retraining and relocation for workers and economic assistance for areas victimized by industrial change, ideas drawn directly from Sweden's web of social services. But calls for technological clearinghouses and targeted personnel programs must have seemed distant at best to workers struggling to adjust to plant shutdowns and decaying neighborhoods. The gap between the UAW leadership and the least secure segment of the rank and file thus widened as the union's agenda narrowed.[35]

Even a truncated version of social democracy, however, stood no chance in mid-1950s Washington. The White House rejected the UAW's proposals out of hand. In 1953 Eisenhower politely informed Reuther that full employment could be achieved through "steady vigilance" rather than a government-labor-management summit; he rebuked the UAW president's call for economic stimulation during the 1953–54 recession, charging that he showed a lack of "proper perspective"; and he insisted that "local citizens," and not the government, should be responsible for community adjustments to economic change. The secretary of commerce denounced "'scaremongers' who are trying to frighten automobile workers with the bogeyman of automation," while the secretary of labor saw "no reason to believe that . . . new technology will result in overwhelming problems of adjustment." Secretary of Defense Charles Wilson, the former president of GM, offered the most stinging rebuke. Speaking in Detroit at the height of the recession, he compared unemployed workers to "kennel dogs." He preferred "bird dogs," he said, "who'll go out and hunt for food rather than sit on their fannies and yell."[36]

The Democratic congressional leadership was not much more accommodating to the UAW. In late 1954 Reuther met with Johnson and Rayburn to secure their support for an increase in the tax exemptions for working-class Americans, a small part of the UAW's antirecessionary package. Johnson refused, explaining that, though he was sympathetic, the White House opposed the idea and therefore it had no chance of being enacted. Reuther was livid. "Even though you can't do everything you want to do, you've got to try," he lectured LBJ. "You got to demonstrate that you tried, and if you try and fail, at least we can say the reason you failed is you didn't elect enough good people. Maybe the next time you can do the job." Johnson was unimpressed; the UAW's tax program did not find its way out of committee.[37]

The new bipartisanship also rejected the UAW's brand of liberal internationalism. The Eisenhower administration brought the Korean War to a quick and indecisive end in July 1953. With the cessation of hostilities, Reuther stepped up his calls for a redefinition of American foreign policy. Arguing that Korea had proved that "major reliance upon military strength" was "desperately short-sighted," he again urged that the United States make economic development the basis of its international commitments in the Third World. That premise placed the UAW within the mainstream of liberal thought in the 1950s, but Reuther went further than many of his liberal allies, insisting as well that much of the aid should be funneled to Third World nationalist movements regardless of their support or rejection of American foreign policy. "We should have begun long ago to do more to help peoples and nations who since World War II have been determined to . . . achieve independence, industrial development, and a higher standard of living," he said. "We have allowed our government to be identified with colonialism in the eyes of millions of people. . . ."[38] The administration had no intention of pursuing such a course. Eisenhower used the Korean armistice as a justification for reducing defense costs while continuing to practice global containment. He did so by fashioning, again with bipartisan support, a "New Look" in American foreign policy, relying on the threat of nuclear weapons, the development of mutual security pacts, and covert operations in the Third World, rather than more expensive conventional military action, to combat communism. This combination of tactics put a premium on the creation and maintenance of pro-American governments in the Third World, particularly in Asia, which liberals and conservatives alike increasingly saw as the Cold War's cockpit.[39]

The White House and the Democratic leadership also did nothing to reduce the fever of anticommunism at home. Neither Eisenhower nor Johnson displayed any willingness to confront McCarthy, whose power and bile increased until late 1954, when he destroyed himself during his investigation of the U.S. Army. In the meantime, the Eisenhower administration began seeing Reuther himself as something of a suspect figure. A month after Ike took office, the FBI's director, J. Edgar Hoover, hand-delivered a twenty-page report on the UAW president to the new secretary of the treasury, who was considering Reuther for a position on a national advisory panel. Unusually long by Bureau standards, the memorandum summarized some 1,300 references to Reuther's radical past that the FBI had gathered in the seven years since he had assumed the UAW presidency. Three months later Hoover sent the same memorandum to the attorney general, and a month after that to the mutual security director, both of whom were also planning to appoint Reuther to administrative committees. All three officials dropped the UAW president from consideration.[40]

Blocked from even the most minor avenues of influence and power, the UAW leadership also found that the pull of consensus undercut its influence with its congressional liberal allies. Johnson carefully cultivated Democratic liberals by arguing that they should abandon the broad reform agenda of "bomb throwers" such as the UAW and instead focus their energies on securing a greater share of federal largess for their constituents. By so arguing, LBJ was promoting his own concept of American politics, but he was also subtly shifting the liberals' faith in interest-group politics. When liberals talked of interest groups in the late 1940s, they had generally meant relatively broad social groupings: workers, African-Americans, farmers. Now LBJ was suggesting that they think of much smaller groups, the wheat farmers of Minnesota, for example. Some liberals, most notably Hubert Humphrey, accepted Johnson's advice. Time and again in the mid-1950s, Humphrey backed away from controversial issues that were sure to divide the Democrats, such as civil rights. The UAW leadership was appalled by Humphrey's apparent surrender to LBJ's brand of consensus politics. Hubert's "a goo-goo," Paul Sifton complained, "willing to compromise before he gets going." Those liberals who rejected Johnson's vision of consensus politics were shunted to the fringes of Congress. Paul Douglas of Illinois, one of the UAW's most consistent allies, is a case in point. Because Douglas refused to embrace Johnson's view of interest-group politics, LBJ prevented him from serving on the Senate Finance Committee, where he would have had some control over spending policy. Johnson instead made him chairman of the powerless Joint Economic Committee, where he could give the UAW a platform for its views but could not transform those views into legislation.[41]

Johnson's skillful promotion of party unity through bipartisan centrism and interest-group politics formalized the Democratic Party's commitment to a consensus that largely excluded the UAW. The union leadership was painfully aware of what had happened. "The Demo[cratic] party is supposed to be [for] labor," Brendan Sexton wrote. "Actually . . . the Dem party is probably somewhere to the right of the British Tories." The problem could not be corrected, Sifton said, as long as "the pressure for party harmony" continued to "eclipse" the Democrats' principles. For the foreseeable future, Donald Montgomery wrote Roy Reuther, LBJ "will continue to run the Democratic party . . . further and further from anything we can persuade our people to fight for." The boundaries of political debate, constricting since 1945, had seemingly closed shut.[42]

The pull of centrist politics was not restricted simply to the Democratic Party. It also cut through the heart of the Congress of Industrial Organizations in the mid-1950s, further undermining the UAW's political power. Already weakened by the expulsion of its left-wing affiliates in 1949 and 1950, the CIO suffered yet another severe blow four days after the 1952 presidential election, when its president, Philip Murray, died. With Murray's death the CIO lost its last direct link to the leadership cadre that had created the organization in 1935. Perhaps more important, his death also threw open the question of the CIO's proper role in the American political economy.[43]

As the historian Robert Zieger has pointed out, the CIO never had a controlling vision. Its left-wing affiliates had believed the organization's primary responsibility was the mobilization of the working class; its social democrats believed the CIO should fight for a formal redistribution of economic power through the state bureaucracy; and many of its right-wing affiliates saw the CIO simply as a vehicle for extending bread-and-butter unionism to industrial workers. Murray had used his diplomatic talents and personal prestige to mask these differences until the late 1940s, when Cold War politics had forced him to purge the left. Now his death triggered a bitter battle between the CIO's social democratic center and its right.[44]

The battle began less than a month after Murray's death, when the CIO met in convention to choose his successor. Reuther coveted the post, both for the prestige it carried and for the power it would provide him to advance his social democratic vision. "We must fight the forces of monopoly and scarcity in their opposition to the expansion of our productive capacity and the full development of our material resources," he told the convention. That was exactly what the CIO's business unionists feared. Led by the new president of the United Steelworkers of America (USWA), David McDonald, they hoped to reduce the CIO's social crusading, to move the federation away from its intimate links with the Democratic Party and toward an AFL-style nonpartisanship, and to concentrate on winning better wages and more fringe benefits for CIO members. Rather than run for the CIO presidency himself, McDonald tried to block Reuther's candidacy by throwing the USWA's votes behind the popular CIO director of organization, sixty-four-year-old Allan Haywood, a lifelong union bureaucrat. With McDonald's backing, Haywood made a strong showing, but Reuther carried the vote, 52 to 48 percent.[45]

Reuther's accession to the CIO presidency simply heightened McDonald's antipathy toward the UAW president and his social agenda. "Don't call him Reuther," he told an aide. "Refer to him as that no good, red-headed socialist bastard Reuther." McDonald did more than complain. Within the year, he circulated rumors that the USWA was planning to pull out of the CIO and form a new federation with John L. Lewis's United Mine Workers and the International Brotherhood of Teamsters. Such a move not only would have crippled and perhaps destroyed the CIO; it also would have created a rival federation perfectly attuned to the contours of consensus politics. Lewis was an outspoken critic of liberal reformism, and both Dave Beck, the Teamsters' president, and McDonald were committed, in Robert Zieger's phrase, to "centrist non-partisanship." It is impossible to know whether McDonald actually planned to forge a new labor center or if he simply intended to use the threat of it to move Reuther to the center. Whatever McDonald's intentions, Reuther did in fact move to the right, forging an alliance with the very embodiment of business unionism, the American Federation of Labor.[46]

The CIO had always viewed the AFL as its antithesis. Dominated by the exclusionary building trades, its executive board controlled by bread-and-butter unionists, some of its largest affiliates profoundly corrupt, hostile to radical political change, the AFL had none of the CIO's élan. What the AFL lacked in verve, though, it made up in membership: 10 million workers belonged to the federation in 1953, double the number of rank and filers in the CIO. That fact alone made the AFL an inviting ally for the increasingly embattled Reuther, whose political base both within and outside the labor movement seemed to be eroding so quickly.[47]

The change in AFL leadership added to Reuther's interest in an alliance. William Green had served as the AFL's president from Samuel Gompers's death in 1924 to his own in late November 1952, a mere two weeks after Philip Murray died. Green had been labor's most implacable conservative. By comparison, his successor, George Meany, the AFL's fifty-eight-year-old secretary-treasurer, appeared to be nothing less than a Young Turk. To be sure, Meany seemed the very caricature of a labor boss. A burly, cigar-smoking Irish Catholic plumber from the Bronx, he was brusque, short-tempered, and tactless. Despite his demeanor, though, he was not completely wedded to the past. His career had taught him that the AFL's traditional distrust of state power and political action was no longer viable. As the federation's spokesman on the National War Labor Board during World War II, he had learned to deal with the New Deal bureaucracy, and in the immediate postwar years he had revamped the AFL's political apparatus, moving the AFL toward a closer alliance with the Democratic Party.[48]

The point should not be pushed too far. Meany never believed that the labor movement should use its political power to transform society. He fervently believed that labor's overriding responsibility was to provide for the economic well-being of its members, and he was committed to doing so through the capitalist system. At the same time, Meany was a militant anticommunist who saw even the mildest détente with the Soviet Union as nothing more than appeasement. Finally, Meany was by both training and inclination a labor bureaucrat. He had never participated in a strike; he had not worked as a plumber since 1922, when he went on the staff of his Bronx local; and he had spent thirty years climbing the AFL ladder. His management style reflected his background. He jealously guarded the prerogatives of his office, interpreting others' actions as assaults on his position in the hierarchy. He was an accomplished bureaucratic infighter, and he excelled in back-room politics.[49]

Reuther was aware of Meany's shortcomings as an ally. Bringing the AFL and CIO together, the UAW president admitted to the CIO Executive Board, would "not [be] perfection," and he considered Meany's foreign policy perspective to be "a hell of a problem." Reuther was nevertheless convinced that an alliance with the AFL was the best way to prevent the disintegration of the CIO. And he genuinely believed that a single national labor center, 15 million members strong, could be used to break the political consensus that stymied reform. "We can see what's going on in America," he told the UAW convention in 1953. "The enemies of labor are united . . . and labor remains divided." A merger of the AFL and CIO, Reuther believed, could solve that problem by giving organized labor "great power to fight [the] political battle."[50]

Reuther understood that Meany and the AFL leadership would not automatically use that power to back substantive reform, but he was sure that the UAW could force them into action. "It is possible to get the old crusading spirit going," he told the UAW Executive Board,

> where we go out and organize the unorganized [and] build our forces stronger in the political field. . . . Now I believe that you can create that kind of climate," but if it is to be created we will have to create it. The UAW-CIO will have to lead that parade. No one else will head it. . . . I think it is possible to take some of the AFL unions who have had no imagination and no vision for many years, but who have tremendously large and impressive treasuries. . . . Maybe you can't get some of these [AFL] fellows to work any harder, but maybe you can open up their bank accounts and get some young fellows who will do the work. I think that's the key to it.[51]

Working from that premise, Reuther initiated a series of negotiations with Meany to bring the AFL and CIO together. The UAW president first raised the possibility of united action in December 1952. Meany was interested, and over the next two years he, Reuther, and their advisers hammered out their affiliates' jurisdictional conflicts, created a new institutional structure that could accommodate both the AFL and CIO staffs, and drafted constitutional language that addressed the AFL's racial practices and its accommodation of corruption.[52] The negotiations reached a pivotal point in early 1955, when Reuther and Meany began to discuss the merged federation's leadership structure. Reuther readily conceded that Meany should be named the AFL-CIO's president, since the AFL was bringing to the new organization twice as many members as the CIO. Meany offered Reuther the federation's second highest position, secretary-treasurer, but Reuther was not interested. As secretary-treasurer, he realized, he would have no power base independent of Meany and therefore would have no leverage to push the new federation toward political activism. Reuther suggested an alternative: an AFL official could be named secretary-treasurer if Reuther were named director of a new Industrial Union Department (IUD) within the AFL-CIO. Every former CIO union would belong to the IUD, and a portion of their federation dues would go to it. The IUD, it was clear, was to serve as the institutional structure through which the UAW would play its vanguard role.[53]

When Meany reluctantly agreed to the proposal, he cleared the final significant hurdle in the way of the merger. In February 1955, the AFL and CIO negotiating teams announced that the two federations would be joined in convention on December 5, 1955. On December 2 Reuther presided over the CIO's final convention, closing with a ringing call for a new labor movement. "I say to you this is not the end," he proclaimed. "This is part of that great historic struggle that goes on as long as hope beats within the human breast . . . that dream that mankind can fashion a world in which . . . the great power of creation which God gave us can be used by man to create a better world." Three days later, beaming with satisfaction, he joined Meany in opening the first convention of the AFL-CIO.[54]

Few of Reuther's closest advisers shared his optimism about the merged federation. Throughout the negotiations, Victor Reuther, Donald Montgomery, Brendan Sexton, and other staffers had repeatedly tried to convince Reuther that he was fooling himself about the federation's potential. Meany and the AFL leadership, they insisted, were too conservative to allow the new federation to serve as a vehicle for social reform, and no matter how much power he managed to carve out, Reuther would be unable to change them. The merger "broke my heart," Sexton recalled. "I was absolutely against it . . . and I argued endlessly about [it]." On the first night of the AFL-CIO's convention, he and other UAW staffers held a party to honor the CIO's passing. The folk singer Joe Glazer played the guitar, Sexton remembered, "and we sat around and wept. I know that I wept. I was just heartbroken." He had reason to be. In his desperation to break the hammerlock of consensus, Reuther had placed the UAW within yet another institutional framework that would constrain its activism.[55]

George Meany signaled his desire to align the AFL-CIO with the political consensus days after the merger. He chose to do so, not surprisingly, on a foreign policy issue. By late 1955, Eisenhower was well on his way to fashioning American foreign policy's "New Look." As part of that effort, the administration had forged a series of military pacts in the Third World, and administration officials were suggesting that the United States would not look kindly on emerging nations that refused to join the U.S. orbit. Meany endorsed the White House's view in a speech on December 14, 1955. "No country, no people, no movement can . . . be neutral" in the face of the Soviet-U.S. struggle, he said. Then, in a blast that won him national headlines, he singled out two nonaligned nations, India and Yugoslavia, for particular criticism. "[Prime Minister Jawaharlal] Nehru and [President Josip Broz] Tito are not neutral," he charged. "They are aides and allies [of the Soviet Union] in fact and in effect, if not in verbiage."[56]

The speech reflected Meany's own views, but it also bore the imprint of his primary foreign policy adviser, Jay Lovestone. Lovestone had long been one of the shadowy figures of American politics. In the 1920s he had served as executive secretary of the Communist Party of the United States (CP). Expelled from the party in 1929, he had led several anti-CP communist splinter groups in the 1930s. Late in the decade he threw himself into the CIO's internal battles, for a period advising the UAW's first president, Homer Martin, in his attempt to purge the UAW's CP and socialist factions. From there Lovestone drifted into the AFL, where he abandoned communism altogether and embraced a virulent anticommunism that placed him to the right of most cold warriors.[57] The Reuther brothers despised Lovestone, both for his role in the UAW's factional fight two decades earlier and for his ability to move the AFL-CIO's foreign policy position in the opposite direction from the UAW's liberal internationalism. They therefore decided to make Meany's speech a test case of the UAW's power to influence the federation's policies. At Victor's suggestion, Walter Reuther announced that he would make a ten-day goodwill tour of India in April 1956, traveling as the guest of the Indian government.[58]

Reuther went out of his way to contrast himself to Meany in the weeks before the trip. Meany took his foreign policy advice from Lovestone; Reuther turned to Norman Thomas for help in preparing his speeches. Meany condemned India's neutralism; Reuther said he was eager to learn more about the subcontinent's "great democratic undertaking." And the day before he left, he openly criticized the AFL-CIO president. "I respect Mr. Meany's point of view," he told reporters, "but I disagree with it. . . . [T]he leaders of India are irrevocably dedicated to finding a democratic solution to India's basic problems."[59] Reuther was no more subtle during his trip. He traveled constantly, visiting with Indian trade union and government officials, including Nehru, touring factories and villages, and delivering 118 speeches. He praised Nehru for following in the tradition of the United States' founders; he praised the government's five-year development program as "a practical demonstration of democratic economic planning at its best"; and he defended India's neutrality, which he claimed was the result of the nation's "religious and community make-up."[60]

Reuther returned to the United States amid a wave of positive publicity: a front-page story in the *New York Times* quoted an Indian newspaper that called him "the true voice of labor." The acclaim simply fueled his desire to mount a frontal assault on the AFL-CIO's foreign policy position. Victor Reuther prepared an extensive brief for his brother to present to the AFL-CIO Executive Council when it next met, on May 1, 1956, calling for a thorough overhaul of the federation's foreign policy. Meany was not willing to give an inch of ground. Before the council meeting he sent a blistering letter to the *Times*, insisting that "Americans and liberty-loving people everywhere have a right, indeed a duty," to oppose nations that sat on the sidelines in the struggle against Soviet expansion.[61] When the council met, he moved from rhetorical counterthrusts to his greatest weapon, his incomparable skill in bureaucratic warfare. Before Reuther could present his brief, Meany accused the UAW president of trying to destroy the merger by questioning his right to speak for the American labor movement. "If I don't speak for the labor movement," Meany reportedly asked, "then who does?" Instantly Meany had transformed a legitimate policy question into a personal challenge to his authority. Thrown on the defensive, Reuther said that he had no conflict with Meany but objected strongly to Lovestone. For the next hour and a half, the two men debated Lovestone's role in the federation, the meeting degenerating at times into a "knock-down, drag-out affair," according to a participant. Finally Meany proposed that Lovestone's office be placed under the supervision of the federation's international affairs committee, then chaired by the CIO's Jacob Potofsky. It was a meaningless gesture, since the committee could not limit Lovestone's access to Meany, which was the real source of his power. Reuther, however, had no choice but to accept the offer; to have done otherwise, Meany had made clear, would be nothing less than an assault on his presidency. A year later Victor Reuther privately conceded that the federation's foreign policy was as conservative as it had ever been.[62]

Reuther's failure to push the AFL-CIO's foreign policy to the left was only the first of many such defeats for him. Meany repeatedly undercut Reuther and the UAW in the course of the next decade, not simply on foreign policy but on domestic issues as well. Time and again the UAW president tried to play his vanguard role, and time and again Meany defeated him. As he did so, Meany pulled the labor movement more and more into the political consensus that Reuther so desperately wanted to break.

By the mid-1950s, the UAW leadership was locked into a series of alliances and structures—the Democratic Party, the Congressional–White House nexus, the AFL-CIO—whose primary commitment was to maintain the national status quo, a status quo that the UAW believed fostered inequality and promoted injustice. The UAW seemed utterly incapable of transforming these structures into vehicles for social change. The problem extended into every portion of the UAW's political agenda, from national economic policy to foreign relations. The politics of consensus exerted itself most strongly, however, on the one issue that had the greatest potential to transform American political life, the issue that cut most deeply through the UAW itself: civil rights.

[5]

The Crucible of Race

The twenty-two local UAW officials gathered in the CIO hall in Jacksonville, Florida, were already in a bad mood by the time Harry Ross, of the Fair Practices Department staff, arrived for their meeting on the evening of April 5, 1956. Ross therefore opened his presentation with a proposal: if the officials would listen to him without interruption for a half hour, he would listen to them for the rest of the evening. For the next thirty minutes he laid out the UAW's civil rights program: its support for the National Association for the Advancement of Colored People (NAACP); its opposition to the White Citizens' Councils then sweeping the South; the union's support for liberal politicians. When he was finished, Lloyd Jackson, the president of UAW Local 20 in Jacksonville, rose in protest. "He charged that the NAACP was communistic," Ross reported, "that Walter Reuther was a communist; that Walter Reuther went to Russia; that all Walter Reuther wanted was the 'nigger' vote so that he could be president some day. . . ." By now Jackson was on his feet, standing inches from Ross, trembling and white. "Shaking his finger in my face he said that when the time comes, and 'nigger' loving Reuther lined up his 'niggers,' Reuther would be the one he was going to draw a 'bead on.'"[1]

The atmosphere was less heated but no less tense three months later, in late July, as the UAW's chief lobbyist, Paul Sifton, worked the marble halls of Congress on behalf of the pending civil rights bill. Backed by a host of civil rights organizations, the bill had passed the House of Representatives days before the end of the session. Determined that it go no further, Senate Majority Leader Lyndon Johnson planned to send the bill on to the

Dixiecrat-controlled Judiciary Committee. The civil rights lobbyists were equally determined to bring the bill up for a vote of the full Senate before the session ended. As the civil rights lobbyists scrambled for support, however, they found themselves blocked not by the Dixiecrats but by two of the UAW's closest allies, Hubert Humphrey and the AFL-CIO.[2]

Humphrey first tipped his hand when he met the civil rights lobbyists in his office the day before the lobbyists planned to mount their challenge. For over two hours the lobbyists pleaded for his help, but to no avail. This was not the time, Humphrey repeatedly insisted, to challenge LBJ. Joining the meeting midway through, two powerful lobbyists for the AFL-CIO, Andrew Biemiller and Robert Oliver, immediately backed Humphrey, saying that any senator who opposed Johnson would "be personally responsible" to the AFL-CIO. The next morning, as Sifton and his allies desperately tried to force a vote, Humphrey, Biemiller, and Oliver stepped up their opposition, lobbying other senators to abandon the bill to committee. The pressure worked. When Johnson called a key procedural vote that evening, the civil rights activists managed to win only six votes. The bill was dead, its advocates humiliated.[3]

Hubert Humphrey's careful calculation of political interest was far removed from Lloyd Jackson's rabid racism, but together they created the political dynamic that most deeply troubled the UAW leadership in the 1950s. Throughout the decade, the union leadership supported the growing assault, both in Congress and in the UAW itself, on racial inequality. They did so in part because they believed civil rights to be the greatest moral issue of the postwar era. But they also believed that the civil rights issue cut to the very center of American political life—that it, more than any other issue, could shatter the iron grip of consensus, that it could reinvigorate reform. The consensus could not be broken, however, nor could a reform coalition easily be built. On the contrary, the UAW leadership proved to be no match for the Democratic Party leadership, which repeatedly blocked even the smallest of initiatives. And the configuration of racial and political forces in the UAW forced the leadership to take a gradualist approach to racial change within its own ranks. That gradualism, in turn, led some black activists, both within and outside the UAW, to question the union's commitment to the cause.

By his support of civil rights in the 1948 presidential campaign, Harry Truman had ensured that the question of racial equality would become a central element of national debate. UAW leaders applauded that fact; they had been pivotal, after all, in drafting the liberal civil rights platform plank on which Truman had run. The Reutherites continued to insist, as they had done since the late 1930s, that racial discrimination had to be understood as a component part of economic injustice. In the late 1940s and early 1950s, the congressional conservative coalition of Dixiecrats and Republicans seemed to prove that linkage, repeatedly combining to defeat the Truman administration's attempts to pass a Fair Employment Practices Committee (FEPC) bill. The coalition's opposition to FEPC brought it into repeated confrontion with the liberal civil rights forces, a conflict the UAW believed reinforced their message that the liberals could defeat both social and economic reaction only by forging a powerful counterforce committed to fundamental political change. By 1955, though, Lyndon Johnson's consensus politics had managed to undercut the liberal forces and threatened to remove civil rights from the national agenda.[4]

The defeat of the Truman administration's FEPC bill in the early days of the Fair Deal did in fact lead to greater organization of the liberal–civil rights bloc. In early 1950, the NAACP called on a range of liberal, labor, and African-American organizations to join with it in creating a permanent umbrella committee, first called the National Council for a Permanent FEPC, later the Leadership Conference on Civil Rights (LCCR), through which the groups involved could coordinate their lobbying efforts on behalf of an FEPC. The invitation was tailor-made for the UAW. The leaderships of the Auto Workers and the NAACP had enjoyed a friendly relationship since the late 1930s, when the NAACP's Detroit branch had offered pivotal support for the union's campaign to organize the Ford Motor Company. Local NAACP chapters maintained their close ties to the African-American working class throughout the 1940s and early 1950s, ties that gave the organization widespread legitimacy in black communities north and south. The national NAACP, meanwhile, forged ever closer political and personal links with the anticommunist liberal-labor nexus. By the early 1950s, the NAACP leadership increasingly pursued integration through legislative and judicial action, rather than through direct action. It had no formal ties to the Communist left, unlike many other African-American organizations, most notably the militant National Negro Labor Council. And it maintained strong ties to the liberal community: the NAACP's president, Walter White, served on ADA's executive board, and several white anticommunists, including Walter Reuther, sat on the NAACP's board.[5]

The UAW leadership threw the union's full weight behind the LCCR, working to make it into a vehicle for the UAW's brand of reform. UAW representatives took control of the group's credentials committee at the inaugural meeting, then used it to exclude any African-American organization with left-wing connections. Roy Reuther, Paul Sifton, and William Oliver, director of the UAW's Fair Practices Department, were named to the organization's steering committee; Sifton was put in charge of its lobbying efforts; and Joseph Rauh signed on as its general counsel. With such strong Reutherite influence, it is hardly surprising that in its final form the LCCR reflected the UAW's approach to political action. It was explicitly noncommunist. It embodied the liberal-labor-black coalition that the UAW saw as central to its political program. And it was clearly a top-down affair through which institutional elites representing a variety of functional groups worked for social change. "The Leadership Conference is less concerned with numbers than with the leadership qualities of those who will attend," an early LCCR statement bluntly explained.[6]

Despite the new level of organization, the civil rights forces could not overcome the roadblock formed by the congressional conservative coalition, as the 1950 struggle for FEPC made painfully clear. The UAW knew that FEPC stood little chance of passing in the 1950 congressional session—Sifton admitted it would take a "political miracle" to get the bill through Congress—but the civil rights forces were at least determined to force a vote on the Senate floor. The UAW and the LCCR launched their lobbying campaigns, both under Sifton's direction, as soon as the session opened. They immediately ran into trouble. First, the House majority leader, Sam Rayburn, tried to pigeonhole the FEPC bill in committee; then, failing that, he orchestrated passage of a substitute bill that rendered the measure meaningless by omitting any enforcement mechanism. The LCCR fared even more poorly in the Senate. When the FEPC bill reached the floor in May 1950, the Dixiecrats launched a filibuster, as they had threatened to do the previous year. Twice Senate liberals tried to cut off debate by voting cloture, and twice Senate Republicans joined with the Dixiecrats to defeat the motion, first by a margin of 12 votes, then by 9.[7]

Shortly after the Senate's defeat of FEPC for the second time in as many years, Roy Reuther suggested that the LCCR consider a change in tactics. No civil rights legislation, he argued, could possibly be enacted under the existing Senate rules, which required a two-thirds vote of the full Senate to break a Dixiecrat filibuster. Rather than expend energy on fights it was sure to lose, therefore, the LCCR should try to change the Senate rule governing cloture, Rule XXII, from two-thirds to a majority of the full Senate. The proposal seemed to signal the willingness of the civil rights forces to retreat from the congressional battle. On the surface, Rule XXII was a technical, even prosaic issue, far removed from the day-to-day brutalities of Jim Crow and the burden of economic injustice, certainly not the sort of issue that mobilized mass protests or inflamed public passions. In the UAW's view, though, it was the linchpin of the conservative coalition's power to define the national agenda. Jim Crow must be understood, Walter Reuther argued, as part of a "deeply entrenched and far-reaching system of economic social and political injustice and exploitation" that rested, in the final analysis, on the denial of economic democracy, north and south. The Dixiecrats and Republicans maintained that system through the filibuster, Paul Sifton contended, the Dixiecrats trading their votes against economic reform in exchange for the Republicans' refusal to vote cloture on civil rights bills. The filibuster thus served, in Sifton's words, "as a cloak for opposition to virtually all labor, economic, and welfare legislation."[8]

Any attack on the filibuster faced one seemingly insuperable problem: the Dixiecrats, anticipating a liberal assault on the cloture rule, had themselves changed the rule in 1949 to disallow a cloture vote on any motion to change Rule XXII. The first time the liberals tried to lower the requirements for cloture, then, the Dixiecrats could launch a filibuster against the effort, and the liberals would be powerless to end it. In effect, the Senate now required unanimous consent to change its requirements for cloture. At the UAW's request, Joseph Rauh took up the problem, working throughout the first half of 1951 to find some formula to overcome the Dixiecrats' manipulation of the Senate rules. In September 1951, the former Supreme Court clerk presented his findings. The Dixiecrats' restriction on cloture did not apply, he argued, at the beginning of a new Congress, when the Senate adopted its rules for the upcoming session. At that point, a simple majority of senators could liberalize the cloture requirements from two-thirds to one half, thus breaking the power of the filibuster.[9]

At the UAW's insistence, the LCCR immediately placed Rauh's proposal at the top of its legislative agenda, where it remained until the late 1950s. The Dixiecrats, meanwhile, denounced the proposal as an effort to institutionalize the tyranny of the majority. Changing the cloture rule, Senator Richard Russell of Georgia proclaimed on the Senate floor, would be nothing less than a "death blow to our institutions of government." Such claims had tremendous resonance in the South, but they bore no resemblance to reality. Democratic liberals did not control the majority of votes in the Senate. They were the minority, outnumbered by the conservative coalition, who proved their numerical superiority at the first opportunity.[10]

The UAW and LCCR, again directed by Paul Sifton, first put Rauh's proposal to the test at the opening of the 82d Congress, in January 1953. After extensive lobbying, Sifton had persuaded a small group of liberal senators, led by New York's Herbert Lehman, Illinois' Paul Douglas, and Hubert Humphrey, to move for the alteration of Rule XXII. The conservative coalition responded in classic form. The Dixiecrats' spokesman, Richard Russell, promised the Republican leader, Ohio's Robert Taft, that he could count on future favors if he delivered the Republican vote against the proposed rule change. Taft then used the threat of poor committee assignments to bring the GOP's senators into line. Together the Dixiecrats and Republicans defeated the liberal motion by a 70–21 vote.[11]

Such a display of raw political power, pitting Democratic Party factions against each other, was typical of the bitter politics of the early 1950s, and it was precisely what the new minority leader, Lyndon Johnson, hoped to avoid. Unlike the Dixiecrats who made him minority leader, LBJ did not want to confront the civil rights forces in the Senate directly, even if he was sure to defeat them. He wanted to keep civil rights off the Senate agenda altogether and thus to avoid even the possibility of a party split. He hoped to do so, moreover, with the aid of his liberal Senate colleagues. In the course of 1953 and 1954, therefore, Johnson carefully wooed those liberals he could and isolated those he could not. When the UAW and LCCR again tried to change Rule XXII in January 1955, he was ready.[12] Sifton and the LCCR's other lobbyists lined up most of the Senate's leading liberals in support of the rule change. Time and again in the days before the session opened, though, Hubert Humphrey, LBJ's closest ally in the liberal camp, refused to meet with the LCCR's representatives. Humphrey was still un- committed when he arrived at a final planning caucus called by the LCCR's supporters the evening before Congress met. He did not remain uncommit- ted for long. Taking the floor, he argued strenuously against a challenge to Rule XXII, insisting that it had no chance of success. "Debate was hot and heavy," Sifton recalled. Paul Douglas, Michigan's Patrick McNamara, and New York's Lehman insisted that the fight had to be made, regardless of the outcome. Other liberals at the Senate caucus were swayed by Humphrey's opposition, however, and in the end the caucus, its ranks divided, decided not to challenge Rule XXII the next day.[13]

The collapse of the Rule XXII challenge was only the beginning. Liberals introduced forty-four separate civil rights bills in the first half of 1955, but Johnson, by then majority leader, made sure that none reached the floor. The Democrats' other leading spokesman, Adlai Stevenson, laying the groundwork for another run at the Democratic nomination, supported LBJ, explaining that the party could not take any legislative action that might alienate the Dixiecrats. Humphrey, who likewise entertained dreams of national office in 1956, announced in midyear that the time had come for the supporters of civil rights to relax their efforts. Even some members of the LCCR called for retrenchment. Shortly after the 1955 Rule XXII deba- cle, Sanford Bolz, LCCR member from the American Jewish Conference, argued that the LCCR should undertake "a complete reappraisal" of its civil rights priorities, reducing its demands to a bare minimum so as not to alienate its liberal supporters in the Senate.[14]

The UAW was furious with the liberals for their sudden retreat. "Nice work," Paul Sifton wrote to Roy Reuther in July 1955. "Liberals smother the civil rights issue, try to split the ranks of the civil rights forces, seek to divert attention to other issues that result in compromise or defeats and then announce that the civil rights issue is dead for the time being. Of course it isn't. It's hot. It will be as long as the unemployment rate among non-whites is twice the unemployment rate among whites." Sifton was right; the issue was hot. It was hot in the factories and the union halls of the North, and it was hot in the schools and churches of the South. In the halls of Congress, though, civil rights had gone cold, frozen out by the power of consensus politics.[15]

As UAW leader struggled to keep civil rights on the national agenda in the late 1940s and early 1950s, they also grappled with racial tensions within the union. In the late 1930s, many white auto workers had used their newfound bargaining power to institutionalize the auto industry's traditional color line, which relegated African-Americans to a narrow range of low-paying and undesirable jobs. The UAW's skilled workers, whose racism was often deeply rooted in artisanal consciousness, adopted the most uncompromising position, typically barring African-Americans from apprenticeship programs or skilled classifications. Some semiskilled workers were equally uncompromising. The Atlanta Chevrolet local excluded African-Americans from the bargaining unit altogether, and the St. Louis General Motors local maintained separate seniority lists for "white" and "colored" members. Many other locals, north and south, used more indirect means to maintain segregated shop floors, establishing one seniority list for all-white semiskilled job categories and another for the unskilled classifications African-Americans typically filled. White workers in locals that did not have discriminatory agreements often used informal channels to limit the rights of blacks. African-American auto workers in the Detroit area repeatedly complained that shop stewards would not process their grievances, and blacks throughout the industry were subject to harassment and intimidation by white workers.[16]

Convinced that the International was not strong enough to combat its locals, the UAW's officers largely ignored shop-floor discrimination in the late 1930s. World War II changed the balance of power within the union, though, and together the International, the federal government, and working-class black activists forced most UAW locals to abandon their most discriminatory practices for the duration. African-American auto workers made significant gains as a result, though they continued to be shut out of skilled classifications. In early 1942, blacks made up 2.7 percent of the semiskilled workers in Detroit auto plants; by mid-1943 they held 9.3 percent of the semiskilled jobs. Change did not come easily: tens of thousands of white auto workers walked off their jobs for days at a time when African-Americans were promoted into previously all-white classifications in 1942 and 1943. Nor did the changes prove permanent. According to UAW estimates, over half of black wartime workers were laid off by the end of 1945, thus reducing the number of African-Americans in the industry to prewar levels. Many UAW locals also returned to their prewar discriminatory practices. In 1942 and 1943, for example, hundreds of black workers in the Dodge Main plant in Hamtramck, Michigan, had been upgraded to semiskilled classifications. By 1946, the Dodge Main local, UAW Local 3, had reinstituted its prewar departmental seniority program, and most of the plant's departments were once again staffed exclusively by whites.[17]

Like his predecessors in the UAW presidency, Walter Reuther was formally committed to the eradication of racist practices within the union. He was constrained in his ability to do so, however, by a series of political and institutional forces, some of his own making. Since most UAW African-American activists had opposed Reuther's caucus in the factional fights of the 1940s, Reuther had no political obligation to meet their demands for an end to racial discrimination within the union, nor did African-Americans hold any elected position in the International. Regional directors, conversely, could use their power in the Reuther caucus to ignore union policies they disliked, as the UAW's 1948 and 1952 political campaigns had made clear. "In the UAW, regional directors are very powerful," Mildred Jeffrey explained. International staffers "don't go into a region without the permission of the regional director." Throughout the late 1940s and early 1950s, the most conservative members of the UAW Executive Board—Vice-President Richard Gosser; Joseph McCusker, Detroit regional director; Toledo's Charles Ballard, Russ Letner, border states director; and Tom Starling, southern director—used that power to defend the UAW's color line.[18]

The lack of real authority on the part of the UAW Fair Practices Department, the International department empowered to enforce the UAW's anti-discrimination policies, increased the regional directors' power to resist racial change. When it created the Fair Practices Department at the peak of the wartime hate strikes, the UAW Executive Board was careful to limit the department's ability to intervene in the affairs of the regions. The department could not launch its own investigations, but could act only on formal complaints brought to it by rank and filers or local officials. Once a complaint was received, it was transferred to the regional director for investigation and adjustment. Only if the regional director did nothing could the department undertake its own investigation and offer its own recommendations, which were to be implemented by the very regional director whose disinterest had triggered the investigation in the first place. Reuther further compounded the department's problems by placing it under the direction of William Oliver, who lacked the imagination and fire necessary to overcome the regional directors' hostility.[19]

Reuther and the International staff were thus caught between their own commitment to racial equality and the political and structural constraints imposed on them by the caucus they headed. That tension, in turn, determined the contours of rank-and-file racial conflict in the late 1940s and early 1950s. African-American auto workers insisted that the International live up to its promises and use its institutional power to break the local color line. Many white workers used the residual power of the locals and the regional directors to defend traditional racial practices. The two sides jockeyed for position throughout the period, with the International caught in the middle.

African-American rank and filers brought their demands to the International in a variety of ways. On occasion, an individual worker sought to capitalize on the national UAW's commitment to racial equality. In December 1955, for example, James Major, a production worker at Dodge Main, was fired for kissing a white female co-worker. When he asked his local officers for help, they said that the dismissal was justified. Major then contacted the Fair Practices Department, making sure to cite Walter Reuther's civil rights record to support his demand for reinstatement. Similarly, Robert Ellis, a rank and filer at the Chevrolet transmission plant in Saginaw, Michigan, claimed that his local was denying blacks the right to be upgraded despite their commitment to the union cause. "The Negro," he wrote Reuther, "continues to pay his union dues, wear his button, give full support to the union . . . and watch a select group into the higher bracket while he remain [sic] in the underprivileged group because of a difference of race."[20]

Appeals of this sort were fairly unusual. It was much more common for African-American auto workers to form factory-level protest groups, an action that their isolation within the plants undoubtedly facilitated. The inner dynamic of these groups remains obscure, but it seems clear that they were led, and at times held together, by a rank-and-filer well placed in the local black community. In the late 1940s, African-American workers in a Kansas City local organized to protest their local's blatantly discriminatory seniority system. They chose as their spokesman fifty-three-year-old Walter Hargreaves, a Mason, a member of the Bethel Methodist Church, and a member of American War Dads Chapter 12. Blacks in the St. Louis Ford

6. UAW staffers: from left to right, Joseph Tuma and Lillian Hatcher, of the Fair Practices Department; Mildred Jeffrey, director of the Community Relations Department; and William Oliver, director of the Fair Practices Department. (Archives of Labor and Urban Affairs, Wayne State University)

plant selected Francis Hicks, a twenty-six-year-old cabinetmaker and World War II veteran, to lead their attack on shop-floor discrimination.[21]

Some African-American rank and filers allied themselves with pressure groups and political organizations outside the UAW. In 1953, twenty black workers at the Allison plant in Indianapolis turned to their local NAACP chapter to break the color line in their local. Two years later, black workers at the Chance-Voight Corporation plant in Dallas, one of the most discriminatory in the UAW, filed formal charges against their local with that city's NAACP chapter. Throughout the 1950s, black workers at the St. Louis GM plant turned to the Urban League for support. Before they approached the NAACP, African-American rank and filers at Chance-Voight appealed for help from the Baptist Ministers Union of Dallas. And many black activists at the Ford Rouge plant allied themselves with the Communist Party.[22]

White auto workers, meanwhile, attempted to maintain the color line by exerting their control of the shop floor, their local, and the regional office. On the most basic level, white rank and filers insisted that they had the right to determine the sort of person they worked beside, a right they protected through the workplace action that had been the hallmark of the early UAW. Local UAW officials in Hurst, Texas, broke the color line in one plant in 1953 by upgrading three African-Americans to a previously all-white department. "They were met," an official reported, "by an organized group of the entire department, and a noose was hanging in the department. The colored guys were told to go back where they came from, or else." Contrary to the conventional view, white workers also continued to stage "hate" strikes well into the postwar era. Three hundred white workers walked out of the Cleveland Fisher Body plant in 1947 when two blacks were moved into production jobs; in 1955, white women at the Toledo Champion Spark Plug plant struck twice after an African-American was upgraded to their department; and in December 1956 white workers in the St. Louis GM plant shut down their facility to protest black upgrades.[23]

Other white rank and filers manipulated local union policy to block blacks' demands. The Dodge Main local gerrymandered steward election districts so that the plant's African-American workers would be less likely to elect black representatives. Local officials in the Toledo Willys-Overland plant refused to assign a steward to the department with the greatest number of black workers. Polish-Americans at the Chrysler Highland Park plant, near Detroit, refused to accept black workers on the local election slate. And one southern plant held its local meetings at 3:30 P.M., half an hour after the all-white production workers ended the day shift but two hours before the janitors, the only black workers in the plant, finished their workday.[24]

White workers and officials used claims of local autonomy and their political leverage in the Reuther machine as their last lines of defense. A St. Louis local official claimed that he approved of the UAW's commitment to integration, but International officials "want to move too quickly and their attitude of forcing things through and letting the attitude come later does not work in our plant." Other St. Louis officials reported that they could not be elected to office if they took a "fair position on the upgrading of Negroes." In Toledo, Ballard similarly informed UAW headquarters that although he supported racial equality, the Fair Practices Department "only tend[ed] to make trouble" because it interfered in local bargaining and injected itself "into the political stream of local unions." And the regional staff in the deep South insisted that white workers would not contribute to the UAW Political Action Department's fund drive if the Fair Practices Department interfered in their affairs.[25]

The International responded to the conflicting pressures from below with piecemeal moves against shop-floor and local discrimination. When the International enjoyed substantial leverage, it broke the color line, though political considerations often dictated just how quickly it did so. When the International did not enjoy such leverage, the color line remained intact. The UAW was most successful in dealing with locals and regions closest to Detroit, the same regions in which the UAW's political program had flourished. The International's political hegemony in the area enabled it to bring tremendous pressure to bear on recalcitrant locals; International staffers had almost immediate access to the shop floor and to local union halls; and the social democratic regional directors—Leonard Woodcock, for instance—shared Reuther's commitment to racial equality. The Fair Practices Department often simply worked through regional directors to rewrite local contracts and to oppose discrimination on the shop floor. Woodcock maintained a vigorous Fair Practices program in his region, as did Ray Berndt in Indiana.[26]

When regional directors or rank-and-filers proved uncooperative, the International could take decisive action. Roy Reuther pressured Ballard into allowing the Fair Practices Department into Toledo, and the International dispatched a staffer to the region to rewrite the locals' discriminatory seniority agreements. When white workers at Detroit's Motor Products plant wildcatted to protest the upgrading of an African-American in September 1947, the Fair Practices Department's staffer Joseph Tuma informed a hastily called local meeting that the International would not defend the strikers against any disciplinary action the company might choose to impose. The workers returned to work the next day. The pace of reform, however, was often dictated much more by politics than by principle. The Fair Practices Department forced an Indianapolis International Harvester local to integrate immediately after the left-wing United Farm Equipment Workers made an issue of the local's racial policies during the bitter organizational battles between the two unions in the late 1940s. On the other hand, the department allowed St. Louis Local 25 to maintain a discriminatory seniority system thirteen years after the first complaint against the local was filed, at least in part because the regional director claimed the local would break with the Reuther caucus if the department moved against it. Similarly, the Fair Practices Department vigorously opposed the Negro Labor Council's attempt to pass a Fair Employment Practices ordinance in Detroit, which would have given the International a powerful tool to combat shop-floor discrimination, simply because the council had been aligned with the left-wing caucus in the late 1940s.[27]

Despite such gamesmanship, the International managed by the mid-

1950s to erase much of the color line in plants in northern and many border states. With equal access, the percentage of African-Americans on the shop floors of the North rose dramatically: by 1957, African-Americans accounted for 20 percent of hourly workers at Ford's Detroit-area plants and 24 percent at Chrysler's Detroit plants. Integration did not create racial harmony, to be sure: day-to-day racial incidents continued throughout the decade. In those sections of the union over which the International had no leverage, moreover, the color line remained firmly in place.[28]

The problem of discrimination was most noticeable in the UAW's skilled trades. The International had no intention of seriously challenging the trades' starkly drawn color line because to do so would have been to question the skilled workers' most basic right, their power to determine entry into the craft. The International had no intention of mounting such a challenge, particularly after the tradesmen's threatened revolt of the mid-1950s. Instead, the Fair Practices Department launched a series of token efforts to integrate the trades. In 1951 the Fair Practices Department sent two black apprentices to the Detroit Fleetwood plant, but withdrew them days later when the white workers struck in protest. Two years later the department persuaded the two largest tool and die locals in Detroit to include nondiscrimination clauses in their contracts, and the International made some effort to place black youngsters in the city's all-white apprenticeship programs. Again the tradesmen resisted and again the International did not push the issue.[29]

The Fair Practices Department did not make even a token effort to confront the racial practices of its southern locals. At its founding, the UAW had few southern members, but in the late 1940s and early 1950s the number grew as auto manufacturers began shifting to plants in the South and West as part of their effort to decentralize production. By 1955 the UAW had fifty-six southern locals, which together accounted for approximately 5 percent of the union membership. The shift of jobs to the South posed some obvious problems for the Fair Practices Department. The region was far removed from the union's center of power; International staffers could not simply drop in on a trouble spot. When International officials complained of discriminatory practices, corporate spokesmen and regional and local UAW officials retorted that they were simply following community standards in segregating their workforces or union halls. And when staffers actually visited southern locals, rank and filers generally rejected them as northerners who had no appreciation for southern traditions. For the most part, though, Fair Practices Department staffers simply did not visit the South, preferring to ignore the locals' blatant disregard of the union's racial policy. When the staffer Harry Ross attended the region's summer school in June 1952, he found a "noticeable lack of knowledge" about the union's racial policies. Oliver did nothing to correct the problem. He admitted in 1954 that the department had no viable program in the South, but he did not appoint a full-time staff member to the region until 1956.[30]

Civil rights activists generally blamed Oliver for the union's caution and equivocation. The Fair Practices Department, a UAW local newspaper charged, "could be an important and powerful one if the director had the fortitude to be forceful enough." Herbert Hill, the NAACP's labor secretary, agreed. "I believe it is obvious to any serious person," he complained in a private letter, "that the Fair Practices Department has no plan, suffers from a complete lack of fundamental thinking on the race question, but merely goes through a routine of hollow rituals while spending a fantastic amount of money which might otherwise be used in a very positive and constructive manner."[31]

Oliver's critics missed the point. His shortcomings, though substantial, were more a reflection than a cause of the UAW's caution. The UAW leadership, from Walter Reuther downward, had come to believe that institutional and political considerations made a frontal assault on racial discrimination in the UAW impossible. The color line thus remained in place, cutting across the UAW just as it cut across the nation.

Despite the forces arrayed against it, the civil rights movement could not be contained. Just as the pull of consensus and compromise seemed most powerful, both in national politics and in the UAW, the movement suddenly surged forward. The NAACP won the first pivotal victory in the landmark Supreme Court decision *Brown* v. *Board of Education of Topeka* in 1954. At the same time, a new grass-roots protest movement, based in the urban South and grounded in the network of church, family, and community, initiated a series of attacks against the segregation of public transportation. That effort peaked in the successful bus boycott in Montgomery, Alabama, in 1955 and 1956, initiated by local NAACP and union activists and led by twenty-six-year-old Martin Luther King Jr., then the pastor of Montgomery's Dexter Avenue Baptist Church.[32]

The new wave of activism triggered a massive backlash among white southerners. Whites across the South correctly saw the *Brown* decision as a fundamental challenge to the racial caste system that had defined the region for generations. In response, segregationists pledged massive resistance to the Court's decision. Southern governors and congressmen provided the backlash with its intellectual underpinnings, such as they were, by reviving the antebellum concept of interposition. Tens of thousands of middle- and working-class southern whites served as the movement's foot soldiers by joining White Citizens' Councils and reviving the long-moribund Ku Klux Klan. The bus boycott simply fueled the fire. Segregationists used the boycott to step up their recruiting drives, while the Citizens' Council of Montgomery turned it into a testing ground for white intransigence. In the course of the 382-day boycott, King and his fellow activists endured repeated threats, bomb scares, and physical attacks.[33]

The mounting racial crisis in the South shifted the focus of the national civil rights movement away from the UAW's agenda in several important respects. The primary venue of civil rights activism moved from Washington, D.C., where the UAW's political apparatus made it an invaluable ally of the movement, to the deep South, where the UAW had largely abdicated whatever influence it had. More important, the new activism focused public concern on the social manifestations of racial injustice, rather than on the linkage of racial and economic inequality. This new agenda thus redefined the UAW's position in the movement. In the late 1940s and early 1950s the union had helped to set the movement's course; with the new ferment in the South it was moved to a supporting role.[34]

The Auto Workers played that role easily in the NAACP's attack on school segregation. The national NAACP's legalistic approach to the issue dovetailed perfectly with the UAW's formalistic, bureaucratic approach to ocial change. The UAW leadership was unstinting in its help: a $75,000 contribution from the UAW helped to underwrite the NAACP's final push to the Supreme Court; the UAW's legal department submitted an *amicus curiae* brief to the Court in support of the NAACP's position; and union officials immediately embraced the decision, Reuther hailing it as "a heart-warming affirmation of . . . American democratic principles."[35]

The UAW leadership was slower to embrace the Montgomery bus boycott. The union offered some financial and moral support: the UAW contributed almost $5,000 to the boycott's organizing committee through direct donations and a series of fund-raising rallies at Detroit-area locals, and the UAW's officers repeatedly praised the boycotters' aims and personal courage. These efforts, however, fell far short of the contributions made by at least two other unions, the United Packinghouse Workers and the Brotherhood of Sleeping Car Porters, both of which offered the boycott much greater financial assistance. The Sleeping Car Porters also provided critical tactical advice. The UAW's hesitancy was largely a reflection of the significant cultural gap between the union leadership and the nascent movement. The bus boycott's grass-roots activism was markedly different from the top-down, carefully calibrated actions the UAW favored; the movement's Christian idiom contrasted with the UAW's thoroughly secular, often technocratic rhetoric; and the boycott's penchant for ad hoc decision making rather than centralized management convinced some of the UAW's staffers, particularly the bureaucratic Oliver, that the movement would not last.[36]

The UAW leadership clearly recognized, nevertheless, that the Montgomery movement, more than any other activity of the civil rights community, had the potential power to break the grip of consensus, to force, by sheer moral example, the question of racial injustice back into the center of American political debate. "[T]hings are moving in the right direction. . . . There is great ferment in the south," Walter Reuther told the Fair Practices Department staff in late 1956. "I think what we have to do is . . . to keep up the struggle . . . . I think we're on the threshold of breaking through." The UAW welcomed King's decision in early 1957 to build a permanent protest organization, the Southern Christian Leadership Conference (SCLC), to engage in nonviolent direct action throughout the South. The UAW cosponsored SCLC's first major event, a highly publicized prayer pilgrimage on the steps of the Lincoln Memorial in May 1957. The union welcomed SCLC into the Leadership Conference on Civil Rights, and the UAW Political Action Department provided SCLC's first sustained program, a voter registration drive, with advice and regular, though not large, financial contributions.[37]

More fundamentally, the UAW tried to build on the upsurge of activism in the South to revive the legislative initiatives that the Democratic Party's consensus politics had smothered. In February 1956 the Leadership Conference on Civil Rights endorsed an eight-point civil rights package that combined its standard demands—FEPC, antilynching and antipoll tax provisions, and the alteration of Rule XXII—with new demands generated by the southern movement: the elimination of federal funds to educational institutions that practiced segregation; an end to segregation in interstate travel; and the establishment of a Civil Rights Division within the Justice Department empowered to seek injunctive relief for African-Americans denied their civil rights. The UAW likewise urged the Democratic National Committee, then preparing for the upcoming presidential campaign, to present to the party's August convention a civil rights platform that unequivocally endorsed the southern freedom movement, particularly the *Brown* decision, and supported the LCCR's legislative agenda. "Once and for all," Joseph Rauh told the committee, "the Democratic Party must set to rest the notion that the geographical division of the party requires compromise. Once and for all the party must surmount this geographical division and put itself wholeheartedly on the side of civil rights."[38]

Party leaders had no intention of following Rauh's advice. Just as he had been the year before, Lyndon Johnson was determined to keep civil rights from coming before the Senate, and Adlai Stevenson, sure to be the Democratic nominee for president, was convinced that he could win the election only if he did not, in the words of a key adviser, "inflame southern passions." Throughout the early months of 1956 it seemed as if LBJ and Stevenson would once again have their way. The LCCR's civil rights package made no headway in Congress, and party spokesmen politely but firmly rebuffed the UAW's repeated demands. In April, however, the civil rights forces received help from a most unlikely quarter. Dwight Eisenhower submitted to Congress a relatively broad civil rights package endorsing the LCCR's call for a civil rights division with injunctive powers.[39] A segregationist at heart, Eisenhower had done virtually nothing to promote civil rights during his first term in office. As southern opposition to the *Brown* decision stiffened in 1955, though, Attorney General Herbert Brownell convinced the president that the administration needed to take some action to protect the integrity of the federal government. Ike also realized the political advantage of introducing a civil rights bill in an election year. If LBJ allowed the administration's bill to come up for consideration, the resulting conflict between liberals and Dixiecrats would undermine Democratic unity. If, on the other hand, LBJ bottled up the bill, the Republicans could claim that they, rather than the Democratics, championed equal rights.[40]

The UAW immediately endorsed the bill Eisenhower had proposed, convinced that it was at least a first step toward breaking the Johnson consensus. While the UAW and their civil rights allies organized on behalf of the proposal, however, LBJ organized against it. Johnson's mentor and closest political ally, Sam Rayburn, won him valuable time by slowing the bill's movement through the House to a crawl. While the House deliberated, LBJ carefully built a consensus against the bill. He convinced the Dixiecrats that quietly killing the proposal was preferable to a highly public filibuster; he convinced Democratic moderates that bringing the administration's package to the Senate floor would simply hurt Stevenson and the party in November; and he convinced Hubert Humphrey that by opposing consideration of the bill he would boost his chances of winning the vice-presidential nomination at the upcoming Democratic convention. Johnson even won AFL-CIO support for tabling the proposal by arguing that a bloody fight on civil rights would threaten legislation of more immediate concern to working people, particularly a pending increase in social security benefits. It was another masterful performance. By the time the House finally passed the bill and sent it to the Senate just days before the end of the session, only a handful of liberal diehards still wanted to bring it up for a vote.[41]

Paul Sifton, Roy Reuther, and the UAW's other lobbyists made a desperate bid in the session's closing days to save the administration's package, but the Johnson consensus held firm. LBJ shunted the bill to the Senate Judiciary Committee, whose chairman, Senator James Eastland of Mississippi, was sure to pigeonhole it. Humphrey and the AFL-CIO then joined forces to defeat the liberals' attempt to discharge the bill. Finally, on the last day of the session, July 27, the civil rights forces conceded defeat. Sitting in the Senate gallery, Sifton watched in silent rage as Humphrey made an impassioned plea for his colleagues to pass a comprehensive civil rights bill in the next session. "Anyone," Sifton commented shortly thereafter, "can come to a funeral."[42]

Defeated in Congress, the UAW was humiliated at the Democratic convention a few weeks later. Party leaders hoped that the convention would be a celebration of the Democrats' hard-won consensus. This time, unlike 1952, there was to be no struggle for the presidential nomination. The party's power brokers had coalesced around Stevenson early in the year, and he was assured of a first-ballot victory. The platform committee was firmly under the control of party moderates, who were determined to produce a civil rights plank so innocuous that none of the party's factions would be offended. And the convention was to be chaired by one of the architects of the congressional consensus, Sam Rayburn. The UAW leadership was willing to accept part of the party's consensus—the Reuthers had pledged their support to Stevenson early in the year, despite some grumbling from staffers that the governor had been a less than inspiring candidate in 1952—but they were determined to insert a forthright endorsement of civil rights in the party platform. "Since 1944 many pledges on civil rights have been made. They have not been fulfilled," Walter Reuther told the platform committee. "The political parties seeking [our] support in 1956 will, we insist, have to adopt language [that is] clear, simple, and unequivocal. . . ."[43]

The platform committee initially reacted to the UAW by shrouding its deliberations in a veil of secrecy during the convention's first few days. The UAW repeatedly demanded to see a draft of the committee's civil rights plank, but the committee refused. Reuther then organized a high-powered delegation of party liberals to secure a copy, but the committee again refused. Even Mildred Jeffrey, who at the UAW's insistence had been given a seat on the platform committee, was not permitted to see the plank. The committee finally unveiled its handiwork a few hours before it was to go before the full convention—too late, party leaders hoped, for the civil rights forces to organize any opposition. The plank was exactly what the UAW had feared. It made no mention of *Brown* except to say that it had "brought consequences of great importance." It made no pledge to enforce the Court's order, and it promised no federal legislation.[44]

As soon as the platform plank became public, Reuther called an emergency meeting of the civil rights forces in his hotel room. There, Reuther, Rauh (then the executive director of ADA), the NAACP's Clarence Mitchell and Roy Wilkins, Senator Herbert Lehman of New York, Governor G. Mennen Williams of Michigan, and other party liberals decided to oppose the civil rights plank on the floor of the convention that evening. "[The] question [is] whether or not [the] Democratic Party will symbolize political morality . . . ," Reuther told the group. "We have tried to work reasonably. Now we fight." The rest of that afternoon and evening, Rauh worked the convention floor, lining up support for the challenge, while Reuther worked the phones, trying to convince the Stevenson camp that the plank had to be strengthened. The UAW, however, proved no match for Sam Rayburn, who moved decisively to preserve the plank as written. Rayburn first prevented the floor debate from beginning until 1 A.M., long after the national television audience had gone to bed. He then allotted the spokesmen for civil rights, Lehman, Williams, and Paul Douglas, a total of ten minutes to make their case to the convention. When the liberals had finished, Rayburn turned the microphone over to Harry Truman, who delivered an impassioned speech in support of the platform committee's plank. As soon as Truman left the rostrum, Rayburn called for a voice vote on the plank. In the bedlam of the convention floor it was all but impossible to judge the response, but Rayburn immediately announced that the delegates had voted in favor of the platform committee's work. Ignoring Lehman's pleas for a roll-call vote, he adjourned the convention for the evening. The entire proceedings were "a disgrace," Jack Conway complained. "Old Sam Rayburn chaired the convention like Mussolini."[45]

The UAW exacted a measure of revenge two days later. Having won the presidential nomination, Stevenson tried to enliven the convention by placing his choice of a running mate in the hands of the delegates. The convention immediately turned into a mad scramble as a host of up-and-coming Democrats—including John Kennedy, Senator Estes Kefauver of Tennessee, and Hubert Humphrey—declared their candidacies. Convinced that his support of LBJ had made him acceptable to the south, Humphrey now turned back to the UAW for its support. Early in the morning before the vote, Conway and Reuther's staffer Douglas Fraser arrived in the senator's hotel suite with the union's response. Humphrey, they said, had been "too weak" on civil rights to deserve the UAW's support. They would back Kefauver, who had championed civil rights throughout that year's primaries. Without the auto workers' support, Humphrey's candidacy collapsed. Kefauver took the vice-presidential nomination on the second ballot, Humphrey finishing a humiliating sixth.[46]

Punishing one's friends was hardly the same as advancing civil rights, however. The UAW had failed to capitalize on the nascent civil rights movement in the South to break the Democratic Party's commitment to the status quo. Johnson, Stevenson, and the Democratic leadership had made it clear that the demands of party unity outweighed the moral demands of the civil rights cause. The South might slip deeper and deeper into racial crisis, but for the moment, at least, Washington remained wrapped in the comfortable protection of consensus.

Although the upsurge in civil rights activism in the South had apparently not had a great impact on national politics in the mid-1950s, it had a profound effect on the racial dynamic within the UAW. As the battle over the industry's color line grew in intensity in southern auto plants, black UAW staffers attacked the racial configuration of the union hierarchy. Caught between the conflicting pressures of union politics and the racial principles it professed to espouse, the International responded by falling back on the same sort of gradualism it had pursued in the early 1950s. For more and more African-Americans, though, gradualism appeared to be dangerously close to appeasement.

The white backlash that tore through the South in the wake of *Brown* also struck the UAW's largest southern locals. According to the International's estimates, over 80 percent of the white members and half of the officers of the Memphis International Harvester Local 988 joined that city's White Citizens' Council within forty days of its formation. In Atlanta 1,500 members of amalgamated Local 882, 2,500 members of Buick Local 874, and 1,400 members of GM Local 34 joined the Georgia Klan shortly after its revival, and one member of Local 34, Eldon Edwards, was named the Klan's imperial wizard. Union organizers in the south, a confidential 1956 report stated, "have never seen the membership of local unions so stirred up over any issue as they have been by the racial crisis in the south. The union members eagerly follow the Dixiecrat demagogues . . . and have joined the White Citizens Councils by the thousands."[47]

At times the backlash among the rank and file seemed about to erupt in open revolt. To gauge the depth of white discontent, William Oliver sent a white staffer, Harry Ross, on a two-week tour of southern locals in April 1956. Everywhere he went, Ross reported, the reaction was the same: rank and filers were incensed that the UAW supported the NAACP, that Reuther was "cramming [civil rights] down our throats," that UAW newspapers continually published photos of blacks and whites together, and that the

UAW favored racial mixing. Shortly after Ross completed his tour, rank and filers in Atlanta sent Reuther a thirty-page petition demanding that the International stop funding the NAACP. Several UAW locals made substantial donations to their areas' White Citizens' Councils, and some locals threatened to disaffiliate from the UAW altogether if the union continued its efforts to end Jim Crow. "The time is soon coming," a local official warned Ross during a heated membership meeting in early 1956, "when the workers of the South will decide whether we want your union with desegregation or we want our own union with segregation. When the showdown comes we'll take segregation and leave you guys up in Detroit. We won't stand for it."[48]

As massive resistance swept through the white rank and file, the spirit of Montgomery spread through African-American auto workers in the South. Never particularly numerous, in the late 1950s blacks accounted for less than 5 percent of the region's membership. African-American auto workers were generally relegated to only a handful of classifications and were subjected to repeated physical and psychological intimidation, and as a consequence had not been as forceful in demanding integration as their union brothers and sisters in the northern and border states had been in the early 1940s. As the southern freedom struggle developed, however, southern auto workers began to organize. The pattern was familiar. Some southern black rank and filers aligned themselves directly with the International, invoking the union's principles. ". . . [W]e only wish there was some way a local union could forbid members of a local union from electing . . . officers that don't believe or abide by the Constitution and Policy of UAW-CIO," a black worker wrote Oliver. "The Negroes in our Local believe in the UAW-CIO[,] the greatest union in the world." Others—black workers in Atlanta Local 34, for instance—turned to the NAACP for support. Many built shop-level protest groups directed by community elites. Two fifty-year shop-floor veterans, both of them sweepers, led African-Americans in Atlanta Local 10, while the black members of Memphis Local 988 organized under the direction of George Holloway, the son of a Pullman porter, a former Tuskegee Institute student, and a long-time union activist whom local blacks referred to as "Mr. UAW."[49]

For the most part, the clash between white and black rank and filers played itself out in small confrontations. When Leon Bradford, a member of Atlanta Ford Local 882, demanded that he be upgraded from sweeper to a production job, his local committeeman and area director pulled him off the shop floor and spent twenty-five minutes berating him for wanting to mix the races. Some UAW locals, such as Memphis Local 988, teetered on the edge of violence. The local had enjoyed relatively amicable race relations in the late 1940s. It was one of the few large UAW locals in the South to have a plantwide seniority system and the only UAW local in the region to have an African-American on its bargaining committee. The white back-lash swept through the local in 1954 and 1955, however, and conditions quickly deteriorated. Led by several of the union's officers, white workers joined the Memphis White Citizens' Council en masse; hate literature circulated throughout the plant; union meetings degenerated into diatribes against the UAW leadership and its ties to the NAACP; and, in an obvious test of the International's resolve, the union leadership decided to segregate the union hall's toilets and drinking fountains. The local's African-Americans fought back. In the midst of a particularly bitter meeting in late 1955, George Holloway seized the microphone and defended both the UAW and the NAACP. White workers responded with cries of "Nigger," and the meeting almost turned into a brawl. By year's end, a regional official reported, Local 988 was descending into "open war."[50]

The International was completely unprepared to deal with the mounting racial tension in its southern locals. Because of its benign neglect of the region in the early 1950s, the Fair Practices Department had no program and no staff in place in the South, nor was Oliver temperamentally equipped to deal with the extraordinary level of hostility there. The International's problem was compounded by the breakdown of the much-vaunted Reuther machine in the region. The southern delegates to the 1953 UAW convention had rejected Reuther's choice for regional director, Tom Starling, in favor of one of his staffers. For the next two years, the International had refused to support the new director. By the time the caucus candidate regained the regional directorship at the 1955 convention, the International's connection to the southern locals had weakened dramatically.[51]

The UAW tried, unsuccessfully, to finesse the mounting crisis in its southern locals, gently prodding the white members to abandon their protest but not demanding that the locals comply with the union's racial policy. The Fair Practices Department repeatedly tried to persuade the Atlanta GM locals to rewrite their contracts to eliminate the discriminatory seniority systems, but the local leadership refused. A department staff member tried seven times to convince the leadership of Local 882 that they had to up-grade African-Americans; they refused seven times. Even in the face of the most extreme intransigence, as in Memphis, the International offered a careful, measured response. The International first intervened in Local 988 in March 1956, when Vice-President Pat Greathouse sent a staffer to meet with the member and hear their grievances. The session went badly. When the staffer called for the member to pull together, the 450 unionists crowded into the hall yelled "Go on back north!" and "We'll settle our own problems our own way!" The International sent another staffer to the local several months later, but the white membership rebuffed him, too. Still the International equivocated. When the regional director suggested that the UAW revoke Local 988's charter, Oliver vetoed the idea as too provocative. Instead, the International tried to seize control of the local by backing a liberal candidate for the local presidency in 1957. He finished fourth, far behind the incumbent, a member of the Memphis White Citizens' Council. The new president then purged all African-Americans who had managed to retain elective positions in the local—including Holloway—and local whites physically threatened any black who attended a meeting. Again the local's African-Americans pleaded with the International for help, and again the Fair Practices Department equivocated, this time simply dispatching a series of warning telegrams to the local president. By the late 1950s, the local's blacks had begun to doubt that the International would ever take action. "We don't know what to do," twelve members of the local wrote Oliver, "so we are calling upon you and others to tell us . . . how to get out of this darkness. [We] hope you understand what we are asking for: some type of . . . leadership from the Fair Practices Department."[52]

The upsurge of black activism within the Reuther caucus followed a very different dynamic from the one generated by the racial conflict in the South. Like southern African-American rank and filers, northern UAW activists took their inspiration from the southern attack on Jim Crow. The northern activists were not rank-and-filers, though; they were some of the most highly placed African-Americans in the UAW hierarchy, all long-time Reuther caucus loyalists who held secondary International staff positions. The principal activists were Horace Sheffield and Shelton Tappes, both of whom had served the caucus faithfully and effectively since the Ford organizing drive of 1941, and Willoughby Abner, who helped direct the UAW's political action program in Chicago in the 1950s. This high-powered group was not seeking equal access to jobs or equal treatment in local union affairs. They were trying to give themselves, and through them other black politicians in the UAW, a greater share of the union's institutional power. In particular, they hoped to build a black caucus—they named their group the Trade Union Leadership Council (TULC)—within the Reuther machine, and to use that caucus to gain entry into the UAW's most powerful all-white bastion, the International Executive Board (IEB).[53]

The UAW's left-wing caucus had made black representation on the IEB a major concern in the early 1940s, but Reuther had buried the issue after his victory in 1946. It remained off the UAW's agenda, though not off the agenda of the UAW's black members, until the 1955 union convention, when Local 600 called on Reuther to nominate an African-American for one of the union's two vice-presidencies. Since Local 600's delegates were not members of the Reuther caucus, the resolution carried no weight, and Reuther simply brushed it aside. Once raised, however, the issue could not again be suppressed. Indeed, Reuther's rejection of the request simply intensified the African-Americans' desire to try again. "[K]nowing the strong feelings of our Negro members on this question," Horace Sheffield wrote Emil Mazey shortly after the convention, "I have no doubt that [it] will rage with even greater intensity immediately before and during 1957."[54]

The TULC waited until the 1959 convention to demand black representation on the board once again. As was traditional, the Reuther caucus met during the first day of the 1959 convention to decide who should be nominated for IEB seats. Without first notifying Reuther of his intentions, Sheffield took the floor to ask why no black was to be nominated. George Burt, Canadian regional director, responded that the caucus would be pleased to support an African-American when it found one who was qualified to sit on the board. Infuriated, the TULC leadership decided to take the issue to the convention floor the next day. The TULC's organizers realized that by staging a floor fight they would be defying the caucus's decision, the gravest sin in the Reuther caucus, and thus would be risking their careers in the union. They nevertheless were determined to proceed. "If Jesus himself had said, 'Don't do it, Shef', I would have ignored Jesus," Sheffield recalled. "I figured I had had enough. You know all these years we had waited, that this was the time to unplug the thing." When the convention chairs called for nominations the next afternoon, Sheffield demanded to be recognized. First he attacked the notion that blacks were not qualified for a seat on the IEB. "Negroes," he said, "are sick and tired of the matter of qualifications being raised only when a Negro is being considered for some particular office. . . . I think it is fairly evident to everyone here that it is not necessary to be a Rhodes scholar to sit on the International Executive Board." He then nominated Willoughby Abner for a vice-presidency. Abner, following the TULC's plan, immediately declined the nomination, but the TULC had made its point.[55]

In absolute terms, the TULC's 1959 convention challenge was a minor act, particularly in comparison with the raw courage of the rank and filers' attack on the southern color line. The TULC had not meant its challenge to be a genuine rebellion against the UAW leadership, however. It was a symbolic rebellion, intended to highlight the contradiction in the UAW's civil rights position. Throughout the 1950s, Reuther and the UAW leadership had strenuously advanced the national civil rights cause, hoping that by so doing they could shatter the political status quo. At the same time, they had adopted a gradualist approach to racial discrimination on the shop floor and in the International because they did not want to upset the balance of political and structural forces within the union. The TULC had forced that contradiction into the open in the Reuther machine's most public forum. The UAW's African-Americans had sent a clear and unequivocal message to the UAW leadership. In the new decade, they declared, gradualism would not be enough.

[6]

Something Less than Perfect

By June 1961 Victor Reuther had seen enough of the Kennedy administration's vacillations. "To some of us," he wrote, "it seems that something tragic happened between the 1960 campaign and the taking office of the new administration in 1961. . . . Instead of the fresh beginnings for which we worked and voted, instead of changing from old policies that had failed and were described as a failure in the 1960 campaign, the word and practice in recent months too often has been, because of the "narrow margin," because of the realities of practical politics, because of the bipartisan coalition of reaction in the Congress . . . not to *begin* but to *continue*."[1]

Reuther really should not have been surprised by Kennedy's caution. In the late 1950s Democratic Party leaders had gradually moved away from the bipartisanship that Lyndon Johnson and the Eisenhower administration had forged in 1953, but they remained convinced that substantive change was neither feasible nor desirable. Democratic leader consequently committed themselves to essentially symbolic gestures late in the decade, designed more to appease the party's constituencies than to revive its long-moribund reform agenda. JFK followed that policy to the letter. For all his liberal campaign rhetoric, his ringing call to arms, he was more interested in maintaining the status quo than in moving the nation in a new direction. He therefore ignored the UAW's demands for sweeping reform, convinced, like the party leaders who had preceded him, that the union had no choice but to support him. At first that assessment seemed correct. Throughout 1961 and 1962, UAW leaders pleaded with Kennedy to do more, sputtered with anger when he refused, but seemed powerless to change the administration's direction. In the last year of the Kennedy administration, however, the UAW leadership began to search for a new way, outside the bounds of party politics, to shatter the consensus that continued to grip American public life.

B y virtually any measure, the 1956 presidential campaign was a disaster for the Democratic Party. Adlai Stevenson, having run a lackluster campaign, was swamped by Dwight Eisenhower, who won by 5 million more votes than he had garnered four years earlier. Eisenhower made significant inroads among those groups that were the heart of the New Deal coalition's northern wing—workers, Catholics, and African-Americans— while carrying six southern states, the largest number the GOP had ever won in the region. In the election's wake, the bipartisan consensus began to weaken as the Democrats tried to stop the dangerous erosion of their political base. When they abandoned bipartisanship, however, party leaders had no intention of reinvigorating reform. They were willing simply to take on the appearance of action. They made that clear on the two issues of greatest concern to the UAW in the last years of the 1950s, civil rights and unemployment.[2]

Party leaders moved first to stop the movement of African-Americans to the Republicans. Eisenhower had helped trigger the defections by submitting a broad civil rights bill to Congress in 1956, a bill that Lyndon Johnson then helped to defeat. GOP spokesmen had hammered away at LBJ's actions in the campaign, and Eisenhower had pledged to resubmit his proposal in early 1957. Shortly after the election, Johnson decided that this time the bill would pass, but it would do so on his terms.[3]

As the bill wound its way through the House in the spring of 1957, the UAW and its allies in the Leadership Conference on Civil Rights (LCCR) girded for the inevitable southern filibuster in the Senate. The House finally passed the bill on June 18, 1957. It came before the full Senate two days later. But the Dixiecrats mounted no filibuster. Instead, they simply amended the bill, removing the section that empowered the federal government to protect civil rights and replacing it with a provision granting blacks whose civil rights had been violated the right to jury trials. The change essentially emasculated the bill—blacks could not expect a fair hearing in most southern courtrooms—transforming it from a substantive step toward racial equality to a symbolic gesture. The LCCR immediately switched tactics, desperately lobbying senators to restore the enforcement provisions, but LBJ held the Democrats in line. The Senate approved the crippling amendments on August 6. Johnson scheduled a final vote on the measure for the next day.[4]

The UAW and the LCCR were unsure how to respond to Johnson's actions. If they endorsed the bill, they feared, they would be giving LBJ the imprimatur of the civil rights movement, precisely what the majority leader wanted. Yet, if they asked their liberal allies in the Senate to vote against the bill, the LCCR would almost surely kill the first civil rights package since the end of Reconstruction to have a chance of winning Senate approval. Most LCCR representatives, including the UAW leadership, were initially inclined toward the latter position. As the senators filed out of the chamber after approving LBJ's amendments, however, the UAW's lobbyists, Paul Sifton and Joseph Rauh, ran into Vice-President Richard Nixon, and suddenly they changed their minds. "Boys," Nixon told them, "I think we ought to let the civil rights bill die and we'll get you a better one next year." Sifton and Rauh immediately realized that the Eisenhower administration wanted the LCCR to oppose the bill so that the Republicans could again blame the Democrats for blocking civil rights. When the LCCR met the next morning to finalize its strategy, Rauh and Sifton vigorously argued that the group should endorse the bill as better than nothing. "It was a difficult session," the NAACP's Roy Wilkins recalled. LCCR affiliates opposed to saving the bill almost stormed out of the meeting at one point, but after hours of debate the UAW spokesmen won out. The LCCR endorsed the bill and gave LBJ and the Democratic congressional leadership the consensus they were seeking. That evening, with the LCCR's blessing, Senate liberals joined with the Dixiecrats to pass the 1957 Civil Rights Act.[5]

LBJ responded to the UAW's repeated attempts to weaken Rule XXII, the Senate cloture rule, with the same combination of symbolism and obstruction. With Hubert Humphrey's help, Johnson had defeated the LCCR's attempt to alter the rule at the beginning of Congress in 1955. LBJ again tried to line up support to block the LCCR's efforts in early 1957, but this time most liberals refused to cooperate. The motion to change the rule still went down to defeat, but by a much narrower margin than before, 55–38. The UAW therefore concluded that the civil rights forces had a chance of success at the 1959 opening of Congress. The number of liberal Democrats had been substantially increased as a result of the party's victory in the 1958 congressional election. Humphrey, hoping to restore his liberal credentials in advance of his run for the presidency in 1960, was vigorously lobbying the newcomers to support the change. Sensing the liberal tide, Johnson proposed a compromise: rather than reduce the cloture requirement from two-thirds of all senators to a simple majority, he would support a motion to change the requirement to two-thirds of all senators present and voting. The UAW and LCCR rejected the proposal, since every senator was likely to be present on a civil rights vote, but LBJ was not to be denied. Threatening new senators with poor committee assignments, he easily defeated the LCCR's proposal, 60–36.[6]

Party leaders responded to the UAW's other primary concern—unemployment—in similar fashion. As they had restructured the auto industry earlier in the decade, the managements of General Motors, Ford, and Chrysler had created pockets of structural unemployment, but they had also boosted their own hiring to record levels. The auto factories had hummed throughout 1955 and 1956, producing more cars than ever before. In late 1957, however, the national economy slid into recession. The downturn was severe; at its worst point in June 1958, the national unemployment rate stood at 7.8 percent. Saddled with massive inventories, the Big Three reduced by half the number of production workers they employed. Even SUB could not protect many UAW members: by December 1958, 13,400 Detroit-area workers had exhausted both their unemployment benefits and their SUB payments. Within a year and a half, the specter of cyclical unemployment, seemingly exorcised from the auto industry by the mid-1950s boom, had returned.[7]

The recession also accelerated the process of consolidation, threatening to plunge heretofore secure workers into permanent unemployment. Protected by its massive competitive advantages, GM increased its share of the car market to over 50 percent during the downturn, in the process turning a tidy after-tax profit of $12.6 million. Chrysler, long the weakest of the Big Three, lurched toward bankruptcy as its market share fell from 19 percent in 1957 to 11 percent in 1959. Chrylser's management subsequently cut its blue-collar workforce by 43,000; workers at the company's Dodge Main plant needed twelve years of seniority to avoid being laid off. Workers at smaller companies had even more to fear. Studebaker-Packard officials, for example, managed to keep their company solvent only by abandoning multiline production.[8]

The recession also helped the auto makers deal the UAW its first defeat at the bargaining table since 1946, in the process triggering the first sustained shop-floor upheaval since the onset of the Korean War. The union's contracts with the Big Three expired in June 1958, just as the recession reached its deepest point. Realizing that a strike would simply allow the major manufacturers to clear their inventories, Reuther announced that union members would work without contracts while negotiations proceeded. But of course that strategy gave the UAW no leverage whatsoever with management. When Ford finally signed the first major contract of the year in September, consequently, the company agreed only to minor increases in wage rates, pensions, and SUB benefits. That was not the most brutal blow of the summer for rank and filers, however. No longer constrained by contractual limits on work pace, Big Three officials sped up production dramatically during the summer months. Factory hands responded by staging a series of wildcat strikes: 78 in all in 1958, six times the number of the previous year. Conflict swept through Chrysler's plants in particular, as the financially pressed corporation pushed its workers harder and harder. In the worst case, workers at the Briggs Body plant in Detroit wildcatted four times between early June and late July.[9]

The multiple crises in the union ranks led at least some UAW officials to look beyond the circumscribed economic program that the union had presented in the mid–1950s. Unless the union reacted vigorously to the recession, Roy Reuther and Nat Weinberg predicted, rank and filers would begin "drifting from us and getting other loyalties." To avoid such a possibility, they contended, the union had to "carry its program" into working-class neighborhoods, establishing counseling centers and leagues of the unemployed. Walter Reuther, similarly, argued that the AFL-CIO should stage a massive march of the unemployed in Washington, D.C. These were compelling proposals, hints that Solidarity House was beginning to seek new departures, but they did not move beyond the talking stage. In the end, Reuther confronted the recession by placing it on the truncated social democratic agenda he and his advisers had formulated earlier in the decade. The results were predictable.[10]

The nation was mired in recession, Reuther argued over and over in the late 1950s, for two interlocking reasons. Throughout his term in office, Eisenhower had refused to use government spending to expand the purchasing power of the working class. Massive corporations such as GM, meanwhile, had used their monopoly power to set prices so high that large numbers of consumers were shut out of the marketplace. "The law of supply and demand has been repealed in America," Reuther said on *Face the Nation*. "And what we have in the place of the law of supply and demand is . . . administered pricing." The only way to end the recession, therefore, was for government to reverse its spending policies and to use its power to challenge corporate pricing policies.[11]

To those ends, the UAW strenuously backed two congressional initiatives: a package of short-term stimulus measures advocated by Senate liberals and an in-depth investigation of GM's pricing policy under the direction of Senator Estes Kefauver of Tennessee. The liberals' program reflected their faith in commercial Keynesianism. Led by Paul Douglas, they called on Congress to reduce the tax rate for and temporarily suspend withholding taxes from working-class Americans, to increase the minimum wage and social security payments, to establish minimum standards for unemployment compensation, and to undertake an extensive public works program, with particularly hard-hit areas such as Detroit targeted for special relief through a newly created Area Redevelopment Agency.[12] Kefauver's probe, meanwhile, reflected his populist roots. In early 1957 the Tennessee senator, long a UAW favorite, proposed that he direct a special subcommittee to investigate corporate pricing policy. His initial investigation of the steel industry garnered little attention, but when he announced that in early 1958 the committee would begin an examination of the auto industry, the auto makers tried to have the committee's funding cut off. The UAW countered with a concerted effort to save the hearings, which union leaders realized would give them the most public forum in years to attack corporate power.[13]

Johnson and the congressional leadership again tried to give the appearance of action on the programs that the UAW supported, but again they refused to move beyond appearance to substance. Johnson repeatedly excoriated the administration for its complacency in the face of recession, and he backed several public works projects, including Area Redevelopment. In a series of private meetings with administration officials, though, LBJ agreed to block the liberals' attempts to reduce taxes. When Eisenhower criticized the Democrats' call for increased spending as likely to trigger inflation, LBJ scaled back even his own public works proposals, and he mounted no serious effort to override the president's veto of the Area Redevelopment Bill, though it had passed Congress easily. Again the UAW tried to build pressure for something more, most notably by staging a widely publicized "Get America Back to Work" conference in Washington in April 1959. Johnson responded with another empty gesture, announcing two weeks before the conference that he was asking Paul Douglas to head a special Senate committee, comparable to the 1938 Temporary National Economic Committee, to undertake a broad investigation of the causes of unemployment.[14]

After weeks of intensive lobbying, the UAW likewise won the party leadership's backing for the Kefauver investigation. The resultant hearings turned out to be every bit the showcase the UAW had hoped they would be. Reuther, the committee's lead-off witness, delivered a condemnation of GM's pricing policy that drew on the economic analysis he had been offering since 1940. He then proposed the public control mechanisms that he had developed in the mid-1950s. Any corporation that had at least 20 percent of the market share in its industry, he suggested, should be required to explain a proposed price increase to a federal review agency. Thrown on the defensive by Reuther's performance, auto industry representatives sounded like economic troglodytes when they appeared before the committee. GM's president, Harlow Curtice, for example, called Reuther's proposal dangerous—it would mark "the beginning of the end of the free enterprise system," he declared—and unnecessary. The auto industry was just as competitive as it had always been, Curtice insisted. The only difference was that now the competition was between GM's divisions rather than among different companies.[15]

For all its sound and fury, the Kefauver hearing produced no tangible results. Democratic Party spokesmen incorporated mention of the administered price problem in their speeches and platforms in the hearing's wake, and Senator Joseph O'Mahony of Wyoming went so far as to introduce a bill embodying the UAW's price hearings proposal. The congressional leadership, though, made no substantive attempt to confront the auto industry's power, and O'Mahony's bill never reached the Senate floor. Like the Civil Rights Act and the Democrats' antirecession program, the Kefauver hearing was nothing more than window dressing, a way of reinforcing the New Deal coalition's loyalty to the Democratic Party without risking any action that might threaten the congressional consensus that Johnson had so carefully built.[16]

The UAW leadership's frustration finally boiled over in early 1959. Shortly after that year's cloture fight, the normally mild-mannered Roy Reuther confronted Bobby Baker, Johnson's young chief of staff, in the Senate hallway. LBJ's gamesmanship, Reuther told Baker, had seriously hurt the Democratic Party's chances in the 1960 election. Baker testily responded that "the real strength of the Democratic Party" was in its diversity of opinion. "[I]f diversity was the key to the Democratic Party's strength," Roy shot back, "why [are] they working so hard to get conformity?" It was a telling exchange. As late as 1959, even the most politically sophisticated UAW official saw the defeat of the union's agenda in personal terms. In the UAW leadership's view, the nation's political system was not deadlocked because the Democratic Party's configuration made it incapable of action, or because of the party's pervasive commitment to consensus. It was deadlocked because of Lyndon Johnson, whose machinations had prevented the Democratic Party from fulfilling its genuine commitment to social change.[17]

It was reassuring to personalize the nation's political deadlock. If the Democratic Party could be led astray by the wrong leadership, after all, it could also be put right by the correct leadership. And with the presidential election only a year and a half away, the Democrats had the chance to find that leadership. Battered by the recession and weakened by Eisenhower's impending retirement, the Republicans appeared beatable. The key to the campaign, then, was to secure the nomination for a representative of the party's liberal wing. If the Democrats then carried the election, Johnson would surrender control of the party to a president who would restore to the Democrats the better angels of their nature. Jack Conway recalled the common opinion in Solidarity House in 1959. "[W]e felt . . . that Lyndon Johnson represented the worst of the Democratic Party, the southern bloc dominating the Congress. . . . We'd been fighting that for a decade. We just assumed that time would work in our favor if we could elect a president and gradually bring about . . . changes."[18]

The UAW's political operatives began to lay the groundwork for the union's participation in the 1960 campaign in early 1959. "[T]he great task is to keep the liberals together," Mildred Jeffrey wrote Walter Reuther in April. "Unless we do so we will not nominate [a] candidate whom the American people will elect." At first the UAW was unsure who that candidate should be.[19] Three representatives of the postwar Democratic generation, John Kennedy, Hubert Humphrey, and Senator Stuart Symington of Missouri, had announced their intention to seek the nomination. Adlai Stevenson was once again considering a run, and it was widely and correctly rumored that Lyndon Johnson wanted the nomination, though he denied having any such interest. The UAW leadership was cool to the idea of another Stevenson candidacy—as they saw it, he had had two chances and he did not need another—and they were positively hostile to the possibility of Johnson's representing the party in 1960. Humphrey and Symington were acceptable, since despite lapses, they had established liberal records during their Senate careers. Kennedy's case was somewhat less clear. He had been something of a nonentity during his first ten years in Congress. LBJ remembered him as "a whippersnapper, malaria-ridden and yellow, sickly, sickly. He never said a word of importance in the Senate and he never did a thing." When JFK took a position, it was generally a moderate one, and for the most part he was considered an attractive though not particularly effective legislator, committed more to advancing his career than to any particular ideology. In the course of the 1960 primary campaign, however, the union leadership became more and more convinced that Kennedy offered them the best chance to end a decade of Democratic Party gridlock. They were wrong.[20]

Kennedy first burst onto the national scene when he made a bid for the vice-presidential nomination at the 1956 Democratic convention. The UAW had opposed him then in favor of Kefauver, whom they considered more reliably liberal. At one point during the convention JFK and Reuther found themselves in the same elevator. Kennedy took the opportunity to ask the UAW president what it would take for him to win the union's support. "Improve your voting record," Reuther had replied. After the

1956 election, as Kennedy positioned himself for a run in 1960, he did just that, moving closer to the UAW in the process. Searching for an issue that would give him national stature as a legislator, he had championed a labor reform bill designed to protect rank and filers' rights. At the same time he and his brother Robert took leading roles in a highly publicized Senate investigation of labor racketeering, directed by Senator John McClellan of Arkansas.[21]

For the most part, the McClellan Committee concentrated on the profoundly corrupt Teamsters' Union, an investigation Reuther fully endorsed. At the Republicans' insistence, however, the committee also held hearings on the UAW's bitter four-year strike against the Wisconsin-based Kohler Company, a manufacturer of bathroom fixtures, and on long-standing charges of corruption against UAW Vice-President Richard Gosser. The UAW realized that the hearings could be embarrassing. "Our hands weren't completely clean" in the strike, Jack Conway admitted: the UAW local had intimidated nonstrikers and had been guilty of some violence. And the Reutherites had long been aware of Gosser's questionable financial practices. Once the hearings began, the Kennedys did all they could to help the UAW avoid trouble. Robert Kennedy, the McClellan Committee's chief counsel, met daily with Joseph Rauh to keep him updated on topics of future discussion; Kennedy's aide Kenneth O'Donnell made sure that Conway was informed of all decisions the committee made in executive session; and, perhaps of greatest importance, John Kennedy was sure to be on hand any time UAW witnesses were having trouble in the public hearing. "Every time we were getting into trouble," Rauh recounted, "Jack would enter the hearings room, take his seat on the committee dais and help us out. It got to be a joke inside our crowd."[22]

The extra effort paid off. By the time Kennedy declared his candidacy for the presidency, the UAW high command had come to see him as a friend and ally. The union was not yet ready to back him for the Democratic nomination, however. Stung by the party's willingness to ignore the union's demands in the 1952 and 1956 elections, Reuther announced in early 1959 that the auto workers would endorse no candidate until after the 1960 convention. Behind the scenes, the UAW worked to bolster the liberals' strength in the upcoming campaign.[23] The union first attacked the party's convention procedures, which Democratic leaders had used in the previous two campaigns to block liberal initiatives. Knowing that a repeat of the 1952 and 1956 conventions would play into LBJ's hands, the UAW quietly urged the Humphrey and Kennedy camps to take control of the 1960 convention. "[W]e formed a kind of informal crap game," Conway, the UAW's liaison with convention planners, recalls, "and got each of the potential candidates to designate someone that could, in effect, represent their interests . . . This group met from time to time and talked about convention arrangements. . . ." The results were very much to the UAW's liking: the liberal Chester Bowles was appointed chairman of the platform committee; Senator Frank Church of Idaho was asked to deliver the keynote address; and, in a weak nod to the South, Governor LeRoy Collins of Florida, a moderate on civil rights, was named convention chairman.[24]

Reuther tried to strengthen the UAW's influence with the Humphrey and Kennedy campaigns by freeing both his staff and the union's regional directors to support whomever they pleased. It was an unusual step, a break from Reuther's past practice of personally setting the union's political policy, then expecting regional directors to follow the party line. Reuther did not surrender complete control of the UAW's agenda in the upcoming campaign, however: he insisted, according to Conway, that "when it became clear where things were going to fall, we would go as a unit." Some staffers and officers quickly joined the Kennedy and Humphrey campaigns. Rauh became Humphrey's speech coordinator, and the Executive Board members Harvey Kitzman and Patrick Greathouse worked to strengthen the senator's campaign in the Midwest. Conway, who had grown fond of Kennedy during the Rackets Committee hearings, joined the Kennedy camp, while Leonard Woodcock and Mildred Jeffrey lobbied for JFK among the Michigan Democrats.[25]

For his part, Reuther refused to choose between the two men until one proved himself the stronger candidate. At first Humphrey seemed to have the upper hand. When the two candidates addressed the UAW's 1959 convention, Kennedy received a polite reception, whereas Humphrey, whose stemwinding speaking style had always played well with labor audiences, received a twelve-minute standing ovation. JFK also did not particularly distinguish himself in private conversations with Reuther. When Reuther pressed Kennedy to explain his position on civil rights, the candidate responded that he simply followed Humphrey's lead, hardly an impressive way to distinguish oneself from a rival.[26]

JFK did have one striking, and in the end decisive, advantage over Humphrey. He ran a better campaign. The candidates first met head to head in the Wisconsin primary in April 1960. The Wisconsin UAW, led by Harvey Kitzman, put its political apparatus at Humphrey's disposal, and the senator spent weeks stumping throughout the state, all to no avail. Making effective use of television, spending money liberally, and trading on his Catholicism in the ethnic neighborhoods of Milwaukee, Kennedy carried blue-collar areas by wide margins and won the primary with 56 percent of the vote. "Once the Wisconsin primary was over," Conway recalls,

"Walter's attitude toward Jack Kennedy changed in the sense that he saw for the first time a guy who did have the potential to be nominated. . . . Hubert ran like he was running for sheriff and . . . Kennedy ran like he was running for president." Rauh saw Reuther's shift to JFK in somewhat more cynical terms. The UAW president "didn't go for Hubert," he said, "because he felt that was kind of a useless gesture and that's the kind of thing you let idealists do."27

Whatever his motivation, Reuther decided that the time had come for the union to fall in behind Kennedy. Acting with Kennedy's approval, Reuther and Conway met with Humphrey and tried to persuade him to quit the race, offering to pay his mounting campaign debts if he did so. Convinced that he could win the upcoming West Virginia primary, Humphrey refused. Reuther did not let the matter drop; during the next few weeks he repeatedly asked Rauh to persuade Humphrey to withdraw. After JFK won in West Virginia, Rauh accepted the assignment. Sitting in the senator's bedroom, he impressed on Humphrey the futility of continuing the race. With Humphrey's reluctant consent, Rauh spent the night typing up his withdrawal speech. UAW lobbyists began to recruit Humphrey delegates for the Kennedy camp immediately thereafter.28

With Humphrey out of the race, the UAW turned its full attention to unifying liberals behind Kennedy. The union followed two paths. Reuther pressed JFK to choose Humphrey as his running mate, while Nat Weinberg, Paul Sifton, and Victor Reuther prepared a laundry list of platform positions: a promise of meaningful civil rights legislation; an aggressive program to end the lingering recession; the creation of a national clearinghouse for technological change; a dramatic increase in foreign aid; and the creation of a "youth peace corps" to be sent to developing nations.29 The UAW could not have been happier with Kennedy's response. In early summer he all but agreed to add Humphrey to the ticket, telling Rauh that he would tap the Minnesotan "or some other midwestern liberal." During the opening days of the convention, moreover, the Kennedy forces drafted the most liberal platform in the party's history. "We knocked a home run on the platform," Reuther gloated in a meeting with UAW staffers. Two days later, JFK won the nomination on the first ballot.30

Kennedy's nomination was not, however, a clear-cut victory for the party's liberal wing. JFK was, as Walter Lippman put it, an "enlightened conservative," eager to maintain existing power relationships in both his party and the nation at large. He considered himself to be a moderate, more than willing to woo liberals and labor, as he had wooed the UAW, or to compromise with conservatives, as the situation demanded, but not willing to dedicate himself to any substantive change in the nation's political order.

He distrusted class-based politics, assuming that the nation was divided into a plethora of small interest groups; and he believed that domestic problems were, by and large, technical, to be solved by the carefully circumscribed application of government power. The torch was being passed to a conventional Democrat as committed to consensus as Lyndon Johnson had been. As such, Kennedy was not the person to fulfill the hopes that the UAW was beginning to invest in him.[31]

K ennedy shifted away from the liberal agenda in his first major decision as the Democratic nominee, moving decisively to shore up his conservative support. The morning after JFK won the nomination, Reuther met with Robert Kennedy to stress that the UAW expected the candidate to choose a liberal running mate. RFK said nothing to indicate that his brother had other intentions, but shortly thereafter Reuther, back in his hotel suite, heard on television that Kennedy had asked Lyndon Johnson to join him on the ticket.[32] The UAW contingent was incensed by Kennedy's announcement. Not only had he appeased the Dixiecrats, but he had done so by placing the architect of congressional consensus on the ticket. "If you do this you're going to fuck up everything," Conway told Robert Kennedy when he arrived at the UAW suite to explain his brother's decision. Reuther was even more furious. Believing himself double-crossed, he told RFK in no uncertain terms that the UAW would not support Johnson. On the convention floor, Rauh and Governor G. Mennen Williams of Michigan were calling on liberals to oppose the nomination. If Reuther gave his approval, the Michigan delegation and the ADA were sure to lead an embarrassing floor fight. Faced with such a possibility, LBJ's supporters moved quickly to appease Reuther. David Dubinsky of the International Ladies Garment Workers Union, a long-time Johnson ally, phoned Reuther to tell him that in his opinion, Johnson's selection was a stroke of genius, and the AFL-CIO lobbyist Robert Oliver arrived at the suite with a statement from LBJ endorsing the strong civil rights plank in the party platform.[33]

Reuther finally relented, conceding that a floor fight would be a "useless gesture" that would simply hurt the Democrats' chances in November. His mind made up, he then moved to squelch the discontent on the convention floor. He sent Paul Schrade, an up-and-coming staffer, to the Michigan delegation to call off any challenge to Johnson. Finding the delegates already in caucus on the question, Schrade passed on Reuther's instructions to Leonard Woodcock, the UAW's spokesman in the group, who then made an impassioned speech in support of Kennedy's decision. "He ticked off the reasons," Williams recalled, "and we all exorcised whatever devils we had." LBJ was nominated by acclamation that evening. Reuther still was not pleased by the turn of events, but, he admitted days later, the union had no choice but to back JFK. "In politics," he told the UAW staff, "you arrive at that point you arrive at in collective bargaining. You exert all your influence, fight as hard as you can, and then you have to make a decision. . . . You wind up with something less than perfect. . . ."[34]

That was undoubtedly the response Kennedy had hoped for, but he was too sophisticated a politician to allow the UAW's anger to simmer. In the weeks after the convention, Kennedy again carefully cultivated the UAW leaders, integrating them into his campaign apparatus, listening to the Reuthers' advice, and incorporating UAW themes and proposals in his speeches. Kennedy asked Roy Reuther to direct a blue-collar voter registration drive that the campaign's strategists touted as the "key to victory." Funded by a $300,000 grant from the AFL-CIO and $200,000 from the UAW, the effort proved to be of limited practical value. According to a postelection Harris survey, union turnout rates were 5 to 6 percentage points lower than that of nonunion members. The drive was important to the UAW's spirits, though. "[I]t was a good interim activity," Jack Conway contends. "It was the thing that got everybody kind of lined up and functioning, and they forgot about the Lyndon Johnson thing."[35] Kennedy likewise courted Walter Reuther's favor. In August JFK invited the UAW president to Hyannisport to discuss economic policy. Reuther arrived on the same day that Kennedy was meeting with Paul Samuelson, Gardner Ackley, and other economic advisers. Asked to join the discussion, Reuther soon dominated it, lecturing the economists on the dire need for more public spending, a tax cut, and other mainstays of the UAW's antirecession program. Kennedy listened intently, and Reuther left the meeting pleased with his performance, but the economists were upset that Reuther was telling them how to do their jobs. JFK immediately reassured them. "Forget it," he told the group as soon as Reuther had gone. "You don't have to report to anybody. Just do the best job you can and don't clear it with them."[36]

Kennedy, however, did avail himself of Reuther's ideas, making them the centerpiece of his Labor Day speech in downtown Detroit. Adlai Stevenson had publicly rebuked Reuther during his Labor Day address in 1952. Kennedy praised the UAW as a champion of "the public interest," then spent the bulk of his speech stressing the need for economic growth and chastising the steel and auto industries, Reuther's favorite targets, for limiting production. It was a masterful performance, perfectly attuned to the UAW's agenda. When the candidate returned to Michigan in mid-autumn, he again followed the UAW line, this time on foreign policy. At the University of Michigan, he pledged to create a Peace Corps, an idea that Reuther had first proposed in 1950.[37]

7. A UAW member seeks to register voters in Detroit, c. 1960. (Archives of Labor and Urban Affairs, Wayne State University)

Kennedy's careful cultivation of the UAW paid off handsomely for the Democrats. The union threw itself into the campaign with unparalleled vigor. It flooded Kennedy with suggestions for speeches and tactics; it paid to reproduce two hundred film prints of JFK's pivotal address on religious freedom; it provided emergency funds for television broadcasts late in the campaign; and Reuther campaigned for the Democrats at a host of labor gatherings. Most important, UAW rank and filers gave JFK their overwhelming support. According to a postelection Harris poll, 73 percent of UAW voters cast their ballots for JFK, as compared to 59 percent of the rank and filers' neighbors who were not UAW members and 49.6 percent of the American public as a whole. Such a wide margin, the pollsters argued in a report prepared for the UAW, made the UAW "the anchor point" for the American labor vote, "the most heavily Democratic sector of the electorate."[38]

The UAW rank and file's support for Kennedy was rooted in a complex of factors. JFK's religion helped him with the large number of Catholics in the UAW's ranks: according to the Harris survey, Kennedy won 96 percent of their votes. More fundamentally, JFK benefited from the unemployment that continued to cut through the rank and file. Though the economy had taken a slight upturn in 1959 and early 1960, auto makers employed, on average, 150,000 fewer production workers in 1959 and 1960 than in the peak year of 1955. Sixty-five percent of auto workers thus cited "bread and butter problems" as their major concern in the 1960 campaign, a response rate almost three times higher than that of any other issue. "[It] is perfectly apparent," the pollsters concluded, "that the economic pinch dominates all else. . . . Their concern over jobs is deep and abiding." That concern, in turn, played into many auto workers' long-standing faith that the Democratic Party protected their economic interests. A third of the UAW members who voted for Kennedy did so, the Harris survey showed, because he was a Democrat or because he was "for working people."[39]

The Harris poll also revealed, however, that the rank and file's social and economic fissures had further splintered the UAW vote in the eight years since similar election statistics had been compiled. Skilled workers' allegiance to the Democrats fell substantially: in 1952, 72 percent of the UAW's skilled workers voted for Stevenson; in 1960, 64 percent supported JFK. White rank and filers were somewhat less likely to vote for Kennedy than they had been to vote for Stevenson in 1952, whereas African-American rank and filers kept their vote totals constant. There were also marked differences within the white vote. Kennedy won 96 percent of the UAW's Polish-American vote, for example, 77 percent of auto workers born in the South, and only 46 percent of the Anglo-Scot membership. Female auto workers, finally, were much more likely to vote for JFK than were male auto workers. It is impossible to unravel the various social strands that caused these differences. Many white auto workers undoubtedly opposed JFK's support for civil rights; many Polish-Americans probably embraced Kennedy because of his Catholicism; and many Anglo-Scots probably opposed him because of his religion. The economic differences between rank-and-file voters were clearer. As the Reutherites struggled to build a cross-class coalition committed to social change, they was beginning to lose the political allegiance of auto workers most likely to have the highest paying, most secure jobs. The foundation on which the union hoped to rebuild the American political structure was continuing to weaken.[40]

There is no indication that the UAW leadership recognized the problem. On the contrary, Reuther exulted in the overwhelming UAW vote, claiming in his postelection analysis that the UAW had given JFK his margin of victory. The Kennedys did nothing to discourage that perception. "Bob [Kennedy] used to say flatly that the UAW was the spine" of the whole election, Conway recalls. Given JFK's debt to the union, the UAW leadership had great hopes that he might at last break the political deadlock that had frustrated reform for the previous decade. "I am confident," Reuther told the union's Executive Board shortly after the election, "that Senator Jack Kennedy, when he takes the presidency on the twentieth of January, will implement the program upon which he was elected. There is no question whatsoever in my mind about that."[41]

Even in the flush of victory, though, the UAW picked up indications that JFK was more committed to consensus than to confrontation. Years later Conway remembered one revealing moment. He was watching television news reports the morning after the election when Kennedy called to thank him for his support. Ecstatic, Conway went back to the television to watch the president-elect make his first public appearance. "That's when he, in effect, accepted the fact that he had won," Conway said. "And then he proceeds to announce that the first thing he wanted the American public to know was that he was reappointing J. Edgar Hoover and [CIA Director of Central Intelligence] Allen Dulles. And I said, 'shit.'"[42]

During the Kennedy years, Reuther enjoyed easier access to the White House than he had ever had before. Though he was only ten years older that JFK, the labor leader believed himself to be the administration's éminence grise. Conway, who usually arranged Reuther's meetings with Kennedy, recalls that the labor leader "was, in effect, giving the benefit of his experience and wisdom to this young man who happened to be president." Reuther typically would arrive at the White House armed with a briefcase full of documents and proposals for Kennedy to consider and the two would spend several evening hours in conversation. JFK, however, was not particularly interested in putting Reuther's advice into practice. "[T]here were many, many times when I had the feeling that the president was indulging Walter," Conway contends, "that this was a way of, you know, being decent and also keeping good relations, and so on."[43]

Kennedy displayed his indifference to the UAW's agenda in a variety of ways. Despite the union's herculean efforts during the campaign, the UAW fared poorly in presidential appointments. Two Reutherites were offered relatively minor positions: Leonard Woodcock declined Kennedy's offer to serve as ambassador to Pakistan, and Conway, who had grown increasingly restless in Reuther's shadow, accepted an appointment as deputy administrator of the Housing and Home Finance Administration. Reuther received even less. At George Meany's insistence, JFK reneged on a promise to name Reuther to the American delegation to the United Nations, an honorary post he had long coveted. "If anyone except a trade-union president . . .

had ordered as much cash and manpower into an election campaign as Walter Reuther mobilized for Jack Kennedy," an observer wrote, "he would have gotten a ticket entitling him to this many places in the Cabinet. . . . But when you tote up what Walter Reuther got . . . the sum is less than nothing."[44]

Kennedy's domestic policies, moreover, showed none of the courage and energy that the UAW had hoped to see. The UAW called on the administration to launch a massive urban renewal program, the centerpiece of which was to be the construction of 400,000 new units of low-cost housing a year, but in 1962 the administration built 30,000 units, the lowest total since 1956. With vigorous UAW support, JFK shepherded the Area Redevelopment Act through Congress, then left the program woefully underfunded. The UAW pleaded with Kennedy to support the union's 1961 attempt to weaken the Senate cloture rule, but JFK maintained a studious silence. "No one can argue that we didn't have the votes," the UAW's new lobbyist, Ralph Showalter, reported after the rule change was defeated by a 50–46 vote. "Just a word from Kennedy . . . would have made the critical difference."[45]

The administration's housing and civil rights programs were secondary concerns for the UAW in 1961 and 1962, far less important than the White House's economic policy. The economy had never fully recovered from the 1958 recession. To be sure, the unemployment rate had dropped to 5.7 percent in 1959 and 1960, but the economy had not regained the robustness of the mid-1950s. In late 1960 the economy slipped back into a recession: by February 1961 the unemployment rate had skyrocketed to 8.7 percent, its highest level since 1950. Employment levels in the auto industry immediately plunged downward as the Big Three launched another round of layoffs. Studebaker-Packard, one of two remaining independents, shut down permanently, as did several suppliers, including such UAW bastions as Toledo Auto-Lite. "Everybody was bawling and crying," a Studebaker worker recalled of the day he lost his job, "especially oldtimers because they couldn't get jobs anywhere else."[46]

The UAW responded to the latest downturn by pressing on Kennedy the same Keynesian program of spending proposals and working-class tax cuts that it had advocated in the late 1950s. Convinced that the new leadership had shattered the conservative pall of the 1950s, though, the UAW no longer saw the need to limit its economic agenda to such measures. "The National Association of Manufacturers has characterized every effort to make our free enterprise system socially responsible as socialism," Reuther told a labor group in March 1961. "Everything that Franklin Roosevelt proposed was socialism, everything that Harry Truman proposed was so-

cialism. . . . We've got to recognize the basic deficiencies in the structure of
our free economy. And we've got to deal with those deficiencies with
courage and honesty. . . . I have unlimited faith in President Kennedy because I think he will provide the kind of leadership we need." UAW spokesmen therefore embedded the union's Keynesian proposals within a framework as overtly social democratic as anything they had advocated in the
1940s.[47]

Having made their case for immediate federal action, UAW officials argued that taxing and spending programs could not in themselves solve the
nation's economic ills, since their effectiveness could easily be offset by the
investment and production decisions of corporate managers. "Government
decisions as to monetary and fiscal policy . . . may have as their goal the
achievement of a desired state of economic affairs," Nat Weinberg wrote,
"but they . . . have to be made with more hopefulness than assurance . . . as
to their impact on private economic decisions." The federal government
could manage the nation's economy, according to the UAW, only if it found
a way to coordinate public and private economic activity. Reuther had tried
to make that argument in the 1950s largely by indirection, advocating a
variety of mechanisms, such as production boards during the Korean War
and a technological clearinghouse in the mid-1950s, that would broaden
state power. Now the UAW leadership once again embraced the social
democratic rhetoric and policy proposals it had championed before the
decade's restriction of political debate. To create an economy of abundance,
they insisted, the federal government must undertake democratic economic
planning.[48]

Ostensibly the UAW based its planning proposal on the Western European, particularly the French, model, which was then enjoying widespread
play in the American press. In fact, the mechanism that the UAW proposed
in the early 1960s was remarkably like the production boards it had advocated at the close of World War II. Working through a National Planning
Agency, labor, management, and government representatives would determine national priorities and set appropriate economic goals. For the most
part, corporations would not be bound by the agency's decisions. An auto
maker could decide to cut production, for instance, although the agency
had called for an increase in output. The agency, however, would have a
wide variety of tools at its disposal—tax policy, federal spending, and
regulation—to bring the recalcitrant company back in line. The agency also
would be given a say in corporate decisions that had the greatest impact on
the community, such as pricing and plant location. "[T]he best response to
the concentrations of private power in this country," Reuther argued in
1963, echoing his rhetoric of 1945, "is . . . to set them [at] a task which will

fulfill and transcend their private goals and absorb their best energies not in the defense of acquired positions but in reaching out . . . toward new achievement in behalf of man and free society."[49]

The Reutherites were not naive. However much they praised JFK's vision, they realized that, left to his own devices, the president would not lead a crusade for social democratic change. Throughout the Kennedy years, therefore, the UAW continually pressed its program on the administration. Reuther first raised the need for planning at the March 1961 meeting of the new president's Labor-Management Advisory Committee, a largely symbolic committee that brought together union and corporate presidents for discussion of a range of economic concerns. He took the union's proposals to the congressional Joint Economic Committee early the next year. A few months later he made an impassioned plea for planning at a White House Conference on Economic Issues. And in mid-1962 he presented JFK with a detailed explanation of the UAW's program during a private meeting. UAW spokesmen also pushed planning in a range of nongovernmental forums, from local union meetings to national political conferences, and in early 1963 the union placed the idea at the top of its legislative agenda. By then, however, it had become painfully clear that the pressure was not working, that in fact the administration's economic policy was moving in a very different direction from the one the UAW advocated.[50]

During the 1960 campaign, the UAW leadership had feared that Kennedy was moving beyond the commercial Keynesianism of postwar liberalism to the qualitative liberalism of John Kenneth Galbraith. Kennedy had invited Galbraith into his inner circle of economic advisers, and had built his campaign on the theme of individual sacrifice for the public good, the same theme on which Galbraith had premised his 1958 book, *The Affluent Society*. The union had nothing to fear. JFK "had no taste for economic theory," according to Theodore Sorensen, and had no intention of committing himself to any school of thought. JFK narrowed his range of choices, though, balancing his economic programs between the fiscal conservatism of the Eisenhower years and the limited activism of the commercial Keynesians.[51]

Hoping to appease Wall Street, Kennedy followed the conservative path in 1961. In early February he called for structural measures to combat the recession, including the swift passage of the area redevelopment bill that Congress had twice passed in the late 1950s. But he eschewed a more overtly Keynesian approach, such as a lower-income tax cut, preferring to maintain "sound fiscal policies," a phrase that, a critic noted, "could have been said . . . by Eisenhower." At the same time, the president proposed an 8 percent investment credit to encourage businesses to modernize their plants.[52] The UAW publicly applauded Kennedy's limited initiatives, Reuther praising JFK's "compassion." In private, however, the UAW leadership was upset by Kennedy's caution. The administration's proposed tax incentive, Weinberg charged, "is essentially a warmed-over and somewhat more sophisticated version of the 'trickle-down' theory so dear to the hearts of Andrew Mellon and George Humphrey." And in an August meeting Reuther pointedly presented Kennedy with a copy of the Democrats' 1960 platform, which pledged the administration to fight for a 5 percent annual growth rate. Only Emil Mazey made the union's complaints public. "Write to the president and tell him we are sympathetic to the problems of Berlin, but we have some serious problems here at home," he told a rally at a Detroit local. "If he can use his full powers to protect . . . the people of Berlin, why doesn't he use them to protect the rights of the five million unemployed Americans right here at home?"[53]

Kennedy shifted toward the liberal position in 1962. Throughout 1961, the chairman of the Council of Economic Advisers (CEA), the liberal academic Walter Heller, had educated the president on the logic of commercial Keynesianism, insisting that a quick tax cut could spur economic growth. At first Kennedy resisted, convinced that any sign of fiscal irresponsibility would frighten business. After the stock market plunged in May 1962, however, "Kennedy was clearly a changed man," in the historian Alan Matusow's estimation. "Now he was practically a Keynesian, willing to contemplate policies that would be good for business whether business knew it or not." The president began at last to consider a massive tax cut. To preserve the national consensus, though, Kennedy sought to win business's support for the cut by aiming it at corporations and upper-income families rather than at the middle and lower classes.[54] JFK announced the administration's plan before the sterling New York Economic Club in December 1962, sounding as pro-business as any Republican. By reducing taxes on the wealthy, the president contended, the administration would induce business activity and boost economic growth. The cuts were not to be made in haste; they were to be spread over three years, so as not to frighten businesspeople with massive deficits. As a sop to labor, Kennedy tied the cuts to the closing of corporate tax loopholes.[55]

It would take more than that to win the UAW's support. The union had been advocating a tax cut for years, but not one for the rich. "This, of course, is exactly the reverse of the kind of tax reduction needed," Weinberg complained to Reuther. UAW economists calculated that under Kennedy's proposal a family with a $5,000 annual income, approximately that of the average auto worker, would receive a tax break of $7, hardly the kind of income redistribution the UAW hoped to see. Troubled by such dismal projections, Reuther made public his dissatisfaction with the administration's proposal, telling the Joint Economic Committee that the White House "has been far too conservative in its appreciation of the urgency of the situation we face . . . The goals it has set," Reuther said, "have been far too low, and the programs it has proposed have been too limited even to achieve those inadequate goals." Congressional leaders, for their part, considered Kennedy's proposal too liberal. They therefore exacted a heavy price for their support, demanding that the administration reduce federal expenditures and eliminate most of the bill's tax reform provisions. By the time the measure emerged from the House Ways and Means Committee in August 1963, it was so weak, in Weinberg's view, that it threatened to discredit tax cuts for years to come.[56]

Administration officials duly noted the UAW's anger. "Their main gripe this year centers around . . . federal tax policy," Heller wrote Kennedy in late 1962. "They think they will wind up next year, like this year, with the dirty end of the stick—big cuts for the fat cats, some crumbs for the little folk, and no reform. They wonder if they wouldn't do better if this so-called 'anti-business' administration reversed itself and became violently anti-labor." Heller was sympathetic to the union's position, but even he recognized the politics of the matter. No matter how great their frustration, he concluded, UAW leaders, like the labor movement in general, had "nowhere else to go." In private, Reuther admitted as much. "[I]t is a very tragic thing in America when the only militancy is the John Birch Society, when . . . there is no counter thrust [to the left]," he complained to the Executive Board. "It is more difficult during the Kennedy administration than it was during the Eisenhower administration because when you get an administration that is reasonably friendly it tends to immobilize the left."[57]

Kennedy's economic policies had precisely the effect Reuther described. JFK's tax cut was in principle impeccably liberal. Since the late 1940s, liberals had been urging the Democrats to offset the business cycle through the careful application of fiscal policy—the basic premise of commercial Keynesianism—and now Kennedy was willing to do so. Most liberals thus supported Kennedy's tax initiative, hailing it as a victory for the "new economics" that they had been championing for years. Most of the liberals and union officials who objected to the specific form of the cut, moreover, were unwilling to challenge the president's plan for fear of undermining public support for Keynesianism in general. In mid-1962, Chairman Heller of the CEA had tried to persuade JFK to direct the tax cut at middle- and lower-income families, but Kennedy had dismissed the suggestion as impractical. Hoping to bring greater pressure to bear, Heller asked Reuther and the AFL-CIO economist Stanley Ruttenberg, both of whom favored

Heller's approach, to discuss the planned cuts with Kennedy. JFK agreed to see the pair on June 15, and the UAW president and Ruttenberg began to plan their presentation. When George Meany heard of the meeting, however, he immediately ordered Ruttenberg to withdraw. Reuther plunged ahead, presenting the president with the UAW's plan for an immediate $10 billion tax cut. Reuther could not make a very strong case without the federation's endorsement, however, and Kennedy politely rejected Reuther's proposal as unacceptable to Congress. Kennedy's willingness to endorse a tax cut, then, actually constricted the liberals' agenda by forcing them to support the mildest form of commercial Keynesianism, a form that bolstered corporate power.[58]

Kennedy thus undercut whatever appeal the UAW's calls for economic planning might have had in the early 1960s. *Newsweek*'s influential commentator Hobart Rowen, for example, dismissed the UAW's call for a National Planning Board as "wishful thinking," and even the UAW's allies on the president's Labor-Management Advisory Committee firmly rejected the UAW's attempts even to mention the concept in the committee's report. For its part, the White House dismissed the UAW's agenda as grandstanding. "Reuther has no fear of broad public policies," a White House staffer reported, "partly because they afford him a wider personal public platform and partly because he is confident that he can insulate his own union and industry from any serious application."[59]

Kennedy's cautious economic policies had precisely the opposite effect on the UAW than they had on the liberals in general. Frustrated and angered by the administration's moderation, the UAW leadership finally admitted that the union could not influence the course of national policy by working within the traditional political structure. No matter how strenuously the UAW pleaded for action, Reuther concluded, the pull of consensus was simply too strong. Reuther lashed out at Kennedy in an Executive Board session in March 1963. "In 1964 the New Frontier is still not going to be off the ground," he complained. "I think at that point [JFK]'s going to be in trouble." A few months later, Reuther extended his criticism to the liberal community as a whole. "There is a need for a force to be ahead of the administration," he declared, "to be pointing out that more has to be done toward creating pressure in the right direction to counteract pressure that is in the wrong direction. In American politics there is not that force."[60]

Here, at last, was a moment of revelation. For almost two decades the UAW, his UAW, had worked within the bounds of conventional politics, hoping all the while to change those politics. The UAW's efforts had culminated in the Kennedy campaign; never before had the union brought so many resources to bear on behalf of a presidential candidate. And still, two years after JFK's inauguration, American politics remained at dead center. The lesson was clear. The UAW had failed, and until the national political structure was transformed, it would continue to fail. During the last year of the Kennedy administration, therefore, Reuther began to look for allies outside traditional political boundaries, beyond the White House, beyond the halls of Congress, beyond Americans for Democratic Action and the Democratic Party. At midyear he found what he was looking for in the streets of Birmingham, Alabama.

R euther was unwilling to admit that the political deadlock could be broken without organized labor. "The labor movement . . . by its very nature, by its philosophy and its commitment," he argued in 1963, "has to be the core of any progressive political force." In the eyes of some critics, however, the UAW itself had lost its commitment to progressive unionism. Years of one-party rule, bureaucracy, and repeated political compromise, they charged, had robbed the union of the vitality, militancy, and democracy it had once enjoyed. By embedding itself in the AFL-CIO, more-over, they claimed, the UAW had subordinated its social vision to business unionists who condoned corruption and discrimination. Despite his ringing denunciations of the status quo, Reuther, Murray Kempton wrote, "seems a little obsolete," his union little more than "a nursing home" for tired activists no longer able to carry the standard of social change.[61]

The critics had a point. Without a meaningful opposition party within the union, UAW politics had become stultifying, union conventions often exercises in showmanship rather than democracy. "There was the usual hippodrome stuff," a UAW insider wrote in her diary after one convention. "But the noise was nothing like what I went through the year when Walter was first elected president. Partisanship then was so wild." For the most part, rank and filers were less concerned with union politics than with the UAW's seeming inability to combat the threat of unemployment. That concern, according to a 1961 survey, was gradually eroding the rank and file's faith in the union. Only 11 percent of UAW members thought the International was doing an "excellent" job, whereas a quarter rated the International's performance "only fair" or "poor." Another quarter had no idea what the UAW was doing for them.[62]

The centralization of union authority also left many rank and filers convinced that the UAW was just another distant bureaucracy. UAW locals paid a particularly heavy price for the rank and file's distance from union affairs. Emil Mazey's Local 212 had been unable to muster so much as a quorum for several years in the early 1960s. Local 212 was hardly unique; half of the UAW's rank and filers, a 1961 survey indicated, had not attended a local meeting in over a year. Most of those who did not go to meetings explained that it was either too much trouble to attend or that everything had been decided before they even arrived. "If fifteen thousand of us went to a union hall and voted unanimously to remove an international representative," a disgruntled rank and filer believed, "this would carry no weight if Reuther didn't want to do it. . . . Sometimes six or seven out of ninety go to [local] meetings. . . . They have discouraged men by ignoring them for so long that the men don't want to go there." Without membership involvement, it became increasingly difficult for local leaders to keep the International apprised of rank-and-file sentiment. "I think we are kidding ourselves when we say we know what the membership's attitude is," Regional Director Ray Ross admitted at an Executive Board meeting in March 1963. "I think we'd be very surprised if we conduct[ed] a poll."[63]

The sense of anomie reached even into Reuther's inner circle. The union's original brains trust had begun to disintegrate by the early 1960s. Donald Montgomery, despondent over the death of his wife, committed suicide in 1957; Conway left the union to join the Kennedy administration in 1961; and Paul Sifton retired in 1962. Reuther tried to replace the three with men who shared their backgrounds and commitments. He named Victor Reuther head of the UAW's Washington Office; Irving Bluestone became Reuther's administrative assistant; and Ralph Showalter took over the union's lobbying duties. Like Conway and Sifton, Bluestone and Showalter had both been active in the Socialist Party in the 1930s, Bluestone in New York City, Showalter in Chicago. Both had joined the UAW during World War II, had been early adherents of the Reuther caucus, and had worked their way up the UAW hierarchy.[64]

As dedicated as Reuther seemed to maintaining the spirit of the 1940s, at least some staffers believed that two decades of political compromise had robbed him of the will to fight. The UAW "is rapidly becoming an organization of mediocrity," a high-level staff member wrote in 1963. "There [sic] becoming so bloody conformist. . . . Everything must be screened, rewritten, censored, cleared for historical purposes and in almost every case, robbed of its vitality and forthrightness." Brendan Sexton and Nat Weinberg, friends reported, had grown so frustrated by the union's compromises over the past decade that they had considered resigning. The UAW's public relations director, Frank Winn, "drowns himself in reading, music, hobbies . . . ," another friend explained, "and does his job without letting his heart be touched, or hurt."[65]

Walter Reuther recognized the growing frustration. The weakness of the labor movement, he admitted in a rare moment of self-deprecation, "has never been with the workers. It has always been in the leadership of the labor movement. I include myself in that." In 1962 and 1963, accordingly, he took a series of steps he hoped would revitalize the union. First, he made his first significant move to weaken the conservative faction on the UAW Executive Board. He removed Vice-President Richard Gosser, who had long been dogged by charges of corruption, from the IEB and added four new board members. Nelson Jack Edwards became the UAW's first African-American board member; Douglas Fraser and Kenneth Bannon became board members at large; and Paul Schrade was elected West Coast regional director.[66]

Fraser and Schrade in particular seemed to demonstrate Reuther's commitment to revitalizing the board. The two came from strikingly different backgrounds. Born in Scotland, the son of an electrician, Fraser grew up in Detroit. He quit high school to take a job on the assembly line, helped to organize his local, and battled his way up through the union. Schrade, by contrast, grew up in a middle-class New York family and attended Yale University. In his senior year he dropped out of school and headed west, intent on securing factory work and pursuing working-class politics. He took a job at the North American Aviation plant in Los Angeles, already organized by the UAW. His academic credentials quickly won him the attention of his local officers, then of the UAW International. Within a few years of joining the union, he was working as Leonard Woodcock's administrative assistant in Detroit. Despite their differences, Fraser and Schrade had quite a bit in common. Both were considerably younger than Reuther and most of their fellow board members: Fraser was forty-six years old in 1962, Schrade thirty-seven. Both had been Socialists in the 1940s. And both believed that the UAW should serve as an agent of social change.[67]

In addition to membership changes, Reuther also instituted structural changes designed to reinvigorate the union. At Reuther's insistence, the Executive Board undertook an intensive self-examination during several week-long retreats in the Poconos. At the 1962 UAW convention Reuther championed the creation of a $1.5 million Free World Labor Fund, financed by the interest on the union's strike fund, to promote trade unionism and liberal internationalist organizations abroad. And in May 1963 he established a leadership study center, under Brendan Sexton's direction, to instruct union staffers and organizers in new methods of reaching the rank and file. "If you go back home and do everything the way you did before," he told the first class, "this school will be a failure."[68]

Finally, Reuther actively considered taking the one action that his most militant staff members had hoped he would take: he considered pulling the UAW out of the AFL-CIO. Throughout the Kennedy years, Reuther and George Meany continued the sniping and mean-spirited maneuvering that had marred their relationship since the merger. For his part, Reuther became increasingly vocal in his criticism of Meany's conservatism, which he blamed for the malaise that seemed to grip organized labor. "[T]he situation in the AFL-CIO becomes more difficult, if not impossible, each day," he wrote Eleanor Roosevelt in 1961, "because of Mr. Meany's . . . seeming willingness to submit to the pressure of the most backward forces in the labor movement instead of joining with those who want to make the labor movement more than a narrow economic pressure group." Meany publicly dismissed Reuther's charges as little more than misplaced nostalgia. "Those who miss labor's crusading spirit," he told reporters, "[should] go back to the days when their daily bread and beer came from the WPA or from anemic union payrolls." The AFL-CIO president also lashed out at Reuther in a series of petty bureaucratic thrusts undoubtedly intended to demonstrate that he, not Reuther, controlled the levers of power in the labor movement. Meany blocked Jack Conway's 1962 appointment as under secretary of labor, for instance, and he omitted Reuther's name from a list of officials to serve on an international affairs committee in the Labor Department.[69]

The break finally came in August 1962, when the United Rubber Workers' president retired from the AFL-CIO Executive Council. Reuther considered it his prerogative to name a successor, since the seat had belonged to a former CIO union. Reuther nominated Ralph Helstein of the Packinghouse Workers, one of the nation's most liberal union presidents. Meany, who distrusted Helstein, rejected the nomination, accusing Reuther of making the selection just to anger him. In an exchange during an Executive Board session that highlighted the chasm that separated the two men, Reuther said to Meany, "As far as you are concerned I have no honesty or integrity," to which Meany simply replied, "Yes." Livid, Reuther decided to withdraw the UAW from the AFL-CIO. At the last moment, though, politics again intervened. At JFK's request, Reuther agreed to remain in the federation until after the 1964 election.[70]

After the Helstein affair, Reuther increasingly turned his attention away from the AFL-CIO and sought instead to reinvigorate its Industrial Union Department. The IUD had never lived up to its mandate of 1955. Instead of organizing the unorganized, it had become something of a sinecure for former CIO officials. "The phones never ring," an IUD staffer told a reporter in early 1963. "No one has any sense of purpose." Reuther tried to correct the problem in March 1963 by appointing Jack Conway, who had left his government post in frustration with the Kennedy administration, to the IUD directorship, a move warmly applauded by labor activists.[71]

By itself, Reuther's maneuvering could not make the labor movement into the "counter force" that he believed American politics needed. As long as organized labor operated within a context of consensus and complacency, the UAW president's attempts to revitalize the IUD and UAW seemed to be little more than house cleaning. The IUD, institutionally subordinate to the AFL-CIO, could not act as the shadow labor movement that Reuther envisioned. The best Conway could do with his new post was to funnel AFL-CIO funds into progressive causes that otherwise would not have received federation support. And for all its internal activity, the nation's leading labor journalist wrote in 1963, the UAW seemed to be "a union in search of a mission." Reuther's tirades against Meany, meanwhile, struck many observers as childish and churlish. David Dubinsky dismissed Reuther's criticism as the consequence of his "enormous ambition," and a White House official said that in the administration's view, the UAW president's performance in the AFL-CIO was "pitiful." The best solution to the bickering between the labor leaders, another official suggested, was to make Reuther ambassador to India.[72]

Had Reuther focused exclusively on reviving the labor movement as a vehicle for social change, he undoubtedly would have failed. As he struggled to revitalize the UAW and the AFL-CIO in 1962 and 1963, though, he was also working to strengthen the labor movement's ties to groups that had served as the backbone of social change in the past. The UAW targeted two groups in particular for support: student activists and African-Americans. By so doing, the union helped to lay the foundation for the movements that with stunning speed would shatter the deadlock that had gripped American politics for fifteen years.

By the early 1960s, many UAW leaders feared that, having reached middle age, they were losing touch with the younger generation of activists who would someday replace them. "We're all getting older," an Executive Board member explained. "You can't keep talking to a guy about what happened in the Depression when he wasn't even born then." It was an article of faith in UAW circles that the younger generation lacked the political zeal that had so animated the Reutherites in the 1930s. Young workers showed little interest in their union, UAW leaders believed, and college students were more attracted to the conservatism of William Buckley than to crusades for social change.[73]

The UAW had two solid connections to the few college students who were active in liberal politics in the early 1960s. UAW funds had long helped to underwrite the Student League for Industrial Democracy (SLID), the socialist group that in the 1930s had been a mainstay of radical student politics. And in the early 1960s the children of UAW activists and friends began to enter college, most typically at the University of Michigan. Highly politicized—talking politics was "like drinking milk" in her home, Mildred Jeffrey's daughter, Sharon, recalls—they soon gravitated toward UM's tiny SLID chapter, then under the direction of Alan Haber, the son of an economics professor and UAW confidant who had been active in the late New Deal's liberal statist circles.[74]

The timing was propitious. Haber had been hoping to transform SLID from the largely moribund organization it had become in the postwar years into a center of student activism. He had changed the organization's name to Students for a Democratic Society (SDS) and had attracted some of the University of Michigan's brightest undergraduates into the group. He had neither the funds nor the connections, however, to make any significant headway. Sharon Jeffrey gave him both. Working through her mother, Sharon arranged a July 1961 meeting between Haber and Victor Reuther, at which Haber laid out his plans. Reuther was immediately impressed. "[T]his kind of program," he wrote Irving Bluestone, "would contribute to the strengthening of the democratic political activities in this country. It could also become a valuable source of leadership in the decades ahead." Bluestone agreed, and together he, Reuther, and Mildred Jeffrey secured $10,000 for SDS's organizational campaign.[75]

Over the next few years the UAW and SDS strengthened their ties. Mildred Jeffrey and Irving Bluestone corresponded regularly with the SDS leadership; Jeffrey introduced Haber, Tom Hayden, and other SDS leaders to Walter Reuther and other UAW officials; and the union paid for a range of SDS activities, from the printing of stationery to the organization's pivotal 1962 conference, held at the UAW summer camp in Port Huron, Michigan. SDS leaders, in return, did their best to shape a program that they believed would please the UAW. SDS's 1962 "Port Huron Statement," for example, clearly reflected the UAW's influence. At Sharon Jeffrey's insistence, the statement urged the federal government to supervise technological change, criticized oligopolistic industries, demanded economic planning, and decried the political deadlock that made reform impossible.[76] That is not to say that SDS saw the UAW as a model of political activism. With all the myopia of youth, SDS's leading figures actually considered the UAW to be fully integrated into the political system they wanted to change. At the same time that she was using Mildred Jeffrey's connections to bankroll SDS, Sharon believed that her mother was "quite conservative." And SDS's Todd Gitlin later claimed that, while SDS accepted the UAW's largess, it considered Reuther to be another "corporate liberal," cast in the same mold as John Kennedy and George Meany. The UAW, however, was more than happy to overlook SDS's tendency to see itself as the vanguard. SDS "may be more radical than labor," Mildred Jeffrey observed, "they may ask searching questions, they may at times be critical of labor, but that's what we need on campus today." SDS had only one drawback, in the UAW's view. Despite its collegiate enthusiasm, it remained a tiny organization in 1963: its roughly 750 members were hardly strong enough to lead the reformulation of American political life.[77]

The civil rights movement, in contrast, appeared to the UAW leadership to have everything that the liberal, labor, and student movements lacked. It had a clear moral purpose; a large number of dedicated activists who were willing to risk their lives to accomplish the movement's goals; an agenda that cut to the very heart of the political deadlock by thrusting into the public arena the issue that most deeply divided northern and southern Democrats; and a long-standing tie to the UAW. UAW leaders were particularly impressed by the ability of the civil rights movement to force federal action in a way that the union, for all its influence in the administration and segments of Congress, could not. "The most impressive action in behalf of human and civil rights in this nation," Reuther told the U.S. Commission on Civil Rights after the Greensboro sit-ins of 1960, "has come not from our elected officials but from a few children in the first grade, a small group of high school students, and from a small advance guard of college students who have sat down at the lunch counters and walked in picket lines. . . ."[78]

The UAW thus threw itself into the freedom struggle. "The labor movement," Reuther told the IEB in 1963, "[is] morally obligated to be in the forefront of this great effort. After all, the labor movement is about the struggle of the people who are denied their measure of justice, and if the labor movement is not in the front rank then I think the labor movement begins to forfeit the loyalty of the people whom I profess to represent and lead."[79] The UAW insisted, however, that equality before the law was only a first step in the fight for equal rights. If the civil rights movement were to fulfill its potential as an agent of sweeping reform, the UAW leadership believed, the movement had to be directed toward an even broader social vision. In 1963, the UAW attempted to supply that vision.

[7]

The Coalition of Conscience

W hen Walter Reuther strode to the podium during the March on Washington in August 1963, he knew he would be speaking not simply to the quarter of a million marchers arrayed before him. He was speaking also to the nation as a whole: to John Kennedy, watching the proceedings on television at the White House, less than a mile away; to the representatives in whose hands comprehensive civil rights legislation now lay; to the hundreds of thousands of clergy, college students, and liberal activists who had rallied to the cause of civil rights; and to the millions of African-Americans, south and north, who in the swirling events of spring and summer had come to see the promise of equality before the law. He spoke directly to those disparate groups, pleading with them to build on the fervor that the freedom struggle had created. "Let this be the beginning of that crusade to mobilize the moral conscience of America," he said, "so that we can win freedom and justice and equality and first class citizenship for every American, not just certain Americans—not only in certain parts of America, but in every part of America, from Boston to Birmingham, from New York to New Orleans, from Michigan to Mississippi."[1]

A few days later, Reuther issued his annual Labor Day message. The contrast could not have been more stark. Each year since the 1940s the UAW had staged a massive Labor Day parade and rally in downtown Detroit, the culminating point of which was Reuther's address. By the early 1960s, Labor Day had lost much of the political meaning it had once enjoyed, and few rank and filers were willing to sacrifice their holiday afternoon to hear the labor leader speak. The UAW therefore canceled the march in 1963, and Reuther simply distributed his speech to the press. The message he delivered, however, was in many ways more militant that the one he had offered on the steps of the Lincoln Memorial. The UAW would do all it could to ensure the final destruction of Jim Crow, he said, but that alone "would be a largely abstract and empty victory." If African-Americans were to win real equality, civil rights must be coupled with fundamental economic change. "Without a job and a regular paycheck," he said, "the right to sit at a restaurant counter is a mocking mirage."[2]

Together, Reuther's two speeches that week illustrate the complex nature of the UAW's civil rights advocacy in 1963. The civil rights movement was the culmination of a long and bitter battle to destroy the American caste system. In the union's view, though, it had the potential to be much more than that. For years the UAW had hoped to build a broad political coalition dedicated to transforming the American political structure. Now that coalition had come together in support of the freedom struggle. The UAW leadership therefore threw itself into the civil rights crusade of 1963, using the union's resources and political expertise to become an integral part of the coalition it had always hoped to lead. In that role, the UAW pushed the coalition to extend its attack, to move beyond the assault on racial inequality to confront the more basic and even more explosive question of economic injustice. The UAW thus hoped to use the fire of the freedom struggle to revivify the social democratic agenda that had seemed moribund only the year before. It was a sophisticated and audacious strategy, and in early 1964 it seemed to work.

In many ways, the early 1960s was an inauspicious time for the UAW to pin its hopes on the civil rights movement. In the late 1940s and 1950s, the UAW and the traditional centers of black political activism, particularly the national NAACP, had forged a close alliance that pursued a gradual, legislative approach to racial change. In 1961 and 1962 that alliance appeared ready to crumble as African-American organizations grew increasingly critical of the racial practices within both the AFL-CIO and the UAW itself. The African-American organizations forced into public view the structural constraints within which the UAW's civil rights activism had operated throughout the 1950s. Unwilling or unable to confront those constraints, the UAW tried to sidestep the criticisms of its long-time allies, first by lashing out at those who leveled the charges, then by taking a series of small corrective steps similar to those it had taken in the 1950s. It was not enough.

The storm first broke in January 1961, when Herbert Hill, the NAACP's labor secretary, published *Racism within Organized Labor: A Report of Five Years of the AFL-CIO, 1955–1960*. Hill charged that five years after the merger of the AFL and the CIO, many trade unions still maintained an "institutionalized pattern of anti-Negro employment practices." A. Philip Randolph followed up on Hill's report by submitting a proposal to the AFL-CIO Executive Council calling for a concerted assault on affiliates that discriminated against African-Americans. The council at first stalled, but then in October 1961 not only rejected Randolph's plan but also censured him for widening "the gap that has developed between organized labor and the Negro community." The gap widened even more a year later, when Hill blasted one of the nation's most liberal unions, the International Ladies Garment Workers Union (ILGWU), for keeping its black and Puerto Rican members in low-paying, unskilled jobs and out of positions of authority in the union.[3]

At least some UAW staff members privately admitted that the NAACP was justified in criticizing the labor movement. Many African-Americans had become alienated from organized labor, Brendan Sexton and Nat Weinberg wrote Reuther, in part because of "exploitation of their plight by corrupt unions and, in other cases, from the failure of non-corrupt unions to achieve any significant improvement in the outrageous conditions under which they work." The UAW leadership, however, responded with ferocity to the public criticism. Emil Mazey, who generally took black criticism of organized labor as a personal insult, led the UAW counterattack, charging on several occasions in 1961 and 1962 that the NAACP was blaming labor for the sins of management, which, after all, controlled the hiring gate. Reuther likewise condemned Hill's charges against the ILGWU as "unfair, unfounded, [and] indiscriminate." And, in perhaps the union's least circumspect move, the UAW president acquiesced in, though he did not vote for, the AFL-CIO Executive Council's censure of Randolph.[4] The UAW also brought institutional pressure to bear against the NAACP. The UAW's officers encouraged Reuther to withhold the union's substantial annual contribution to the NAACP unless the organization reigned in its labor secretary. It was widely rumored that the UAW president would withdraw from the NAACP's board of directors, a post he had held since 1948, and William Oliver tried to persuade the NAACP's executive secretary, Roy Wilkins, to pledge that his organization would not make any public charges against UAW locals without first giving the union time to correct the problem privately.[5]

Behind the scenes, the NAACP was conciliatory. The director of the NAACP Legal Defense Fund, for example, assured Reuther that Hill had acted without the organization's approval. In public, however, black activists refused to back down under the UAW's pressure. They condemned Reuther's lack of support for Randolph within the AFL-CIO. "Where was Walter Reuther?" one African-American unionist asked. "Where were all those liberals on the [AFL-CIO Executive] Council when the vote [to censure Randolph] was taken?" Herbert Hill claimed that in attacking the NAACP, Emil Mazey was "giving comfort to the most backward anti-Negro elements of the old-line A.F.of L. craft unions as well as the avowed racists operating inside and out of the labor movement." In the cruelest cut of all, Hill turned his sights on the UAW itself, charging that UAW locals in Atlanta and Kansas City discriminated against African-Americans.[6]

Hill was right. In the early 1960s, the UAW International still had not been able to persuade most of the union's southern locals to abandon Jim Crow. As late as 1962, Atlanta Local 34, a Chevrolet and Fisher Body local, forced black workers to follow much more stringent procedures than whites when they applied for promotion. The local also maintained segregated seating in its union hall, and the plant segregated the workers' dressing rooms, restrooms, and water fountains. Ford locals 737, in Nashville, and 919, in Norfolk, likewise maintained separate seniority lists for black and white members. Although Atlanta Local 10's contract did not differentiate between black and white workers, local officials still refused to support a black worker with twenty-three years' seniority when he asked to be upgraded from his janitorial position. As a result of such intransigence, African-Americans remained dramatically underrepresented in the southern auto workforce. As of 1963, blacks made up 8.9 percent of production workers in the UAW's southern region, far below the union average of 14.2 percent.[7]

The elimination of racial barriers in northern auto plants in the 1950s, by contrast, had greatly expanded the number of black UAW members in the region. By 1960, African-Americans accounted for 21 percent of production workers in Illinois UAW plants, 20 percent in Michigan plants, and 19 percent in New Jersey plants. Even in the heart of UAW country, however, blacks still could not penetrate the citadel of skilled work. According to local records, although 65 percent of the production workers at the Ford Rouge plant in 1960 were black, only 3.5 percent of the skilled workers were black. The difference was even more pronounced at the Detroit Dodge Main plant, where blacks accounted for 45 percent of the production work force but for none of the plant's 1,500 skilled workers. Nationwide, blacks made up 1.5 percent of the union's skilled members in late 1963.[8]

Even on integrated jobs, blacks continued to experience discrimination and harassment. Officials of Detroit Dodge Main Local 3, for instance, refused to correct management's practice of promoting white workers with little or no seniority ahead of black workers with up to twenty-two years in the plant. When a manager at the GM plant in St. Louis promoted two black workers to the loading dock, the white workers walked off the job. The black workers filed a grievance, which the local then pigeonholed. A handful of white workers at the Ford Ypsilanti plant, just west of Detroit and a stronghold of white southern migrants, burned a cross on the plant lawn. "I'm so tired of being treated like a dog, I don't know what to do," an African-American worker at the North American Aviation plant in Los Angeles complained after he was repeatedly harassed by a white co-worker. "My nerves are just about shot, but this is America and I know that some how Right will outdo wrong every time."[9]

Despite the growing frustration within the black community, the Reutherites offered only token resistance to the persistent racial tension in the union's ranks. The International did make one aggressive move in the South: after years of fruitless negotiation and compromise, in 1960 the International seized control of Memphis Local 988, a bastion of white supremacy throughout the 1950s. Largely a symbolic gesture, the seizure was intended to impress on other southern locals that the International did have the will to enforce union policy. For the most part, though, the International, still fearing that white southerners might revolt if the UAW pushed too hard, preferred to chip away slowly at Jim Crow in its southern locals. The UAW Fair Practices Department therefore continued gently to prod the union's southern leadership to process African-Americans' grievances, eliminate discriminatory contract clauses, and upgrade blacks into previously all-white departments.[10]

As in the 1950s, southern UAW officials generally resisted the International's pressure. When a Fair Practices Department official asked the officers of General Motors Local 319 in Charlotte, North Carolina, why the local had no African-American members, he was told that the local opposed "socialization." The officers of Hayes Aircraft Local 1155 in Birmingham, Alabama, rejected the UAW International's demand that the local support black demands for upgrading by arguing that the community would not accept an integrated workforce. When southern locals did take action, they generally did so in the smallest of ways. In 1961 the Atlanta Chevrolet plant integrated its lunchroom; in early 1962 Atlanta Local 10 promoted one African-American janitor to the assembly line; and Birmingham Local 1155 promised to appoint a black member to a local position after city elections in 1963.[11]

Still stung by the skilled workers' revolt of the late 1950s, the International took an even more cautious approach to their racial practices. After several years of "study," the UAW established a pre-apprenticeship training program for minority high school students in the summer of 1964. The students received 120 hours of training in shop theory, drafting, tool and die work, and blueprint reading, all in preparation for entry into formal apprenticeship programs. The training, however, did not ensure access to the programs themselves. The result was predictable: the vast majority of youngsters who went through the pre-apprenticeship program could not secure apprenticeships. The International recognized the program's shortcomings. "I am sure our pre-apprenticeship program is worthwhile," a staffer wrote in late 1966, after the program had been running for two years. "[But] it will take far more than piecemeal programs . . . if we are to overcome the problem [of racial discrimination in the skilled trades]." Given the craftsmen's powerful position within the UAW, the International did not dare to offer anything more.[12]

Reuther was no more decisive in addressing the highly charged question of black representation on the UAW Executive Board than he was in confronting shop-floor discrimination. After Horace Sheffield, Willoughby Abner, and other black activists had staged their highly publicized challenge to the all-white board at the UAW convention in 1959, most observers believed that the Reuther caucus would finally add an African-American candidate to its slate at the 1962 convention. Some of the union's most powerful officers, however, urged Reuther to resist the pressure. Emil Mazey wanted Reuther to fire, rather than reward, Sheffield and Abner for violating caucus rules, and at least two board members—Vice-President Pat Greathouse and Detroit regional director Norman Matthews—firmly opposed the addition of any African-American to the board.[13]

Eager to maintain a consensus within the caucus, Reuther took a middle path. He would agree to add an African-American candidate to the slate, but he would also assert the power of the caucus by personally interviewing all prospective candidates, a procedure no white candidate had ever undergone. Reuther finally settled on four choices for the position: Sheffield, Abner, Reuther's administrative assistant Nelson Jack Edwards, and Bill Oliver. Sheffield concluded that he and Abner had been added to the list to please the black community; having violated caucus rules in 1959, he later explained, "we had about as much chance as the snowball on the proverbial hotplate." When Reuther seemed to be favoring Oliver over Edwards, Sheffield and Abner asked for a meeting with the UAW president, at which time they informed him that the person who got the board seat "at least had to have some guts." If Reuther promoted Oliver to the board, they said, they would resign from the International, an action sure to create a furor in the black community. Reuther subsequently backed Edwards, who won election at the 1962 convention.[14]

If anything, such small gestures brought the UAW under even greater attack from its traditional allies. "Negroes are tired of the 'poppa knows best' attitude [of organized labor]," the NAACP's Washington counsel said. Herbert Hill agreed. "We have altered the terms of the argument," he told *Time* magazine. "The old phony tokenism just doesn't work anymore." Rather than trust the UAW to clean its own house, Hill demanded that the President's Committee on Equal Employment Opportunity investigate the Atlanta and Kansas City locals. And in late 1962 he threatened to bring charges against the labor movement in federal court. "The opposition of Meany [and] Reuther . . . will not deter us in the slightest," he insisted. "From now on they will have to answer for their discriminatory practices." By early 1963, relations between the UAW and the traditional black political structure had reached their lowest point since the alliance had been forged in the late 1930s.[15]

The conflict with the NAACP was, in fact, an ominous portent for the UAW. By pointing to the gap between the union's promise and its performance, the NAACP had exposed the central dilemma of the auto workers' civil rights program, a dilemma that, in the late 1960s, would help to destroy Reuther's dreams of political change. In the early 1960s, however, charges of union hypocrisy seemed largely irrelevant to the civil rights struggle, the focus of which had shifted from the formal, organizational conflict to mass action by thousands of ordinary African-Americans. Across the deep South, blacks confronted the American caste system at its strongest points—at lunch counters, in bus terminals, and on the steps of city halls—and as they did so, the system gave way. In 1963 the UAW joined this sweeping movement, in the process playing a pivotal part in the second American revolution.

In form and tactics, the civil rights movement of the early 1960s bore virtually no relation to the postwar UAW. It was, first and foremost, a product of southern black life, its structure, symbols, and moral force grounded in the nexus of church, community, and family. Though it was obviously a political movement, it operated outside mainstream political structures, its power base resting primarily on the people whom the system had disenfranchised, secondarily on such political neophytes as white student and religious activists. Though it continually negotiated with the political structure, it was, in the end, absolutist, determined to topple the existing racial system, not to adjust it. And though its spokesmen at times talked of the economic plight of African-Americans, its primary goal was social, not economic, change.[16]

It was precisely those differences that brought the southern civil rights movement and the UAW into alliance. Because it relied on the least power-ful Americans for support, the movement was continually underfunded. Its lack of political connections, moreover, left the movement ill prepared to shift from the streets of the South to the halls of Congress, where its de-mands would be translated into legislation. The UAW helped to solve these problems by offering the movement the funds and the expertise it needed. In return, the UAW tapped into the moral and political force that the movement had created. In the process, it earned the right to help direct that force beyond the advocacy of racial reform.[17]

The UAW leadership had gradually become more and more supportive of direct action in the South in the late 1950s and early 1960s. The union raised some funds for the 1955–56 Montgomery bus boycott, joined the national boycott of Woolworth stores in support of the 1960 lunch counter sit-ins, contributed $5,000 to bail out the freedom riders arrested in 1961 (four of whom were UAW members), and helped to underwrite and staff grass-roots voter registration drives during 1961 and 1962. The UAW also provided movement speakers with public platforms in the North. E. D. Nixon, one of the organizers of the Montgomery campaign, spoke at UAW locals during the bus boycott; representatives of the Southern Christian Leadership Conference (SCLC), the movement's leading organization, ap-peared on the UAW's radio program in the late 1950s; and SCLC's chair-man, Martin Luther King Jr., and Walter Reuther slowly formed a personal relationship as they shared an increasing number of engagements, including the 1962 UAW convention, which King addressed.[18]

During the first two years of the Kennedy administration, the UAW had consistently urged the White House to support the growing revolt in the South. At the height of the freedom riders crisis, Roy Reuther had called on Attorney General Robert Kennedy to use federal authority to desegregate interstate transportation. When Senator James Eastland of Mississippi publicly opposed James Meredith's attempt to desegregate the University of Mississippi in 1962, Reuther urged John Kennedy to purge the senator from the Democratic Party. The UAW also strongly endorsed Martin Luther King's 1962 demand that the White House issue a "Second Emancipation Proclamation" that would cut off all federal funds from states that main-tained Jim Crow facilities.[19]

Temperamentally and politically committed to maintaining consensus, Kennedy had no intention of pursuing such an aggressive policy, which he knew would destroy the Democratic Party's delicate balance of southern conservatives and northern liberals. Throughout 1961 and 1962, therefore, he appeased the party's southern wing by failing to propose any major civil rights legislation. He was willing to take strong executive action only when civil rights activists in the South left him no choice. The administration banned segregation in bus terminals only after the freedom riders had been beaten and arrested, and it enforced a court order admitting James Meredith to Ole Miss only after a white mob had turned him away from the campus. By early 1963 the civil right activists had gotten the message. If they wanted federal action to break the back of Jim Crow once and for all, they would have to force Kennedy's hand.[20]

In early 1963 Martin Luther King and the SCLC decided to do just that. On April 3 the SCLC launched a massive campaign of civil disobedience in the heart of the segregated South, in Birmingham, Alabama, a city "so raw in its emotion and so grim in its segregation," in Arthur Schlesinger Jr.'s words, that even its white residents thought of it as "a city in fear." The resulting clash, with its riveting scenes of African-American courage in the face of white brutality, won the civil rights movement widespread sympathy and support. Days after the worst violence had been televised around the world, the long-dormant Americans for Democratic Action condemned Kennedy's inaction on the civil rights front; the National Council of Churches (NCC), the umbrella organization for American Protestantism, threw its support behind the protesters; African-Americans staged marches in thirty-three southern and ten northern cities; and college students across the country pledged their support to the cause.[21] The UAW joined the chorus. "The century-long patience of Negro Americans who have been deprived of their constitutional rights . . . is at an end," Reuther wrote JFK. ". . . [T]hey have announced to all the world that they will no longer tolerate or endure the indignities, the humiliations, and the barbaric treatment that accompany second-class citizenship." The UAW's Washington office offered the civil rights movement the union's greatest compliment. "The . . . events of the past week," the office's newsletter proclaimed, "are much like the sitdown strikes of the thirties. . . . Demands for justice by the Negro grandchildren of the slaves Lincoln thought he freed are gathering the same revolutionary momentum the sitdown strikers launched a generation ago."[22]

The UAW's most substantive contribution to the campaign was not rhetorical but financial. During the first week of May the Justice Department's Burke Marshall fashioned an agreement between Birmingham's moderate white business representatives and SCLC. The agreement met most of SCLC's demands, but a final settlement foundered on a thorny point: the businessmen refused to grant amnesty to the hundreds of black protesters still in Birmingham jail cells, and SCLC refused to put up the $160,000 in bail bonds required to gain their release. Robert Kennedy, eager to bring negotiations to a successful conclusion, phoned Jack Conway, then the director of the AFL-CIO's Industrial Union Department, explaining that the administration could think of nowhere else to turn for the funds. Conway contacted Joseph Rauh, the UAW's general counsel, and the two talked to Walter Reuther, who contributed $40,000 from the UAW and $40,000 from IUD. The UAW then asked the United Steelworkers and the AFL-CIO to pledge another $40,000 each. George Meany was hesitant, but when Reuther promised that the UAW money would be used to bail out the worst risks, the AFL-CIO went along. When the $160,000 was raised, Sheriff Bull Connor of Birmingham insisted that it be paid in cash, so Irving Bluestone and William Oliver hand-delivered the money, hidden in money belts strapped under their shirts. The next day King announced that an agreement had been reached with the business community of Birmingham.[23]

Birmingham was much more than a local victory for the Southern Christian Leadership Conference. Even as an uneasy peace settled back over the city, it was clear that the campaign had been a watershed event in American political life. After decades of struggle and sacrifice, African-American activists had created a broad national coalition in support of equal rights, a coalition that wanted nothing less than the destruction of Jim Crow. Martin Luther King recognized the change that had occurred. "The sound of the explosion in Birmingham reached all the way to Washington," he wrote late in the year. "The task of turning [civil rights] into law still lies ahead . . . and the task of conforming custom to law must follow. But the surest guarantee that both will be achieved in the end is found in the massive alliance for civil rights that was formed in the summer of 1963." The UAW likewise knew that Birmingham had opened the door to dramatic social change. "[T]he wonderful thing about the new feeling in Washington," a union spokesman declared in June 1963, "is that Negroes by their bare hands have turned the civil rights climate upside down in less than a few months." Of greater importance, John Kennedy knew that the political climate had been transformed. "The president became convinced," an aide recalls, that he "had to deal with what was clearly an explosion in the racial problem that could not, would not go away."[24]

Administration officials realized that the Birmingham campaign had scrambled the congressional calculus that had defined and circumscribed policy making since the 1940s. Any civil rights legislation JFK might propose was sure to rip the Democratic Party in two, shattering the consensus that party leaders had worked to maintain for a decade and a half. The Democratic liberals in Congress would back a strong bill, whereas even a weak proposal would lose Kennedy the support of southern Democrats and possibly the southern vote in the 1964 election as well. The Republican Party meanwhile seemed to have much to gain from the administration's dilemma. Kennedy desperately needed the support of the Republican congressional delegation if he were to overcome the inevitable southern resistance to an administration civil rights package, while the GOP's presidential candidate stood to pick up the votes of southern whites determined to punish JFK in the upcoming election.[25] Even after Birmingham, JFK refused to abandon consensus politics completely. On June 19, 1963, he sent a comprehensive civil rights bill to Capitol Hill. It was a hybrid proposal, the most sweeping ever proposed by an American president yet carefully circumscribed to minimize the southern backlash against the administration. The bill banned discrimination in public accommodations that had "a substantial effect" on interstate commerce, rather than in all accommodations. It gave the administration discretionary power to stop federal aid to segregated school districts, rather than requiring all such aid cut off. It allowed the attorney general to sue on behalf of individuals who had been denied access to schools, but only after they had filed a written complaint and had proved that they could not afford to bring suit on their own. And it made no mention whatsoever of fair employment practices or voting rights. Rather than defuse the civil rights revolt, the administration's proposal simply shifted the locus of activism from the deep South to Washington, D.C. By so doing, it dramatically increased the UAW's power within the emerging civil rights coalition.[26]

In the early summer of 1963, Walter Reuther took to calling the civil rights forces the "coalition of conscience." He meant it as a compliment, of course, a reflection of the moral righteousness that the freedom struggle embodied. But the phrase also captured the movement's greatest weakness in the days after the administration sent its bill to Capitol Hill. Congress was not moved by moral fervor alone. It was moved by pressure politics, by the intricate maneuvering of lobbyists and the handful of concerned constituents who knew the byzantine world of congressional rules. Most of the coalition's partners—the southern activists, the religious groups, college students—were without experience in that world. The UAW, by contrast, had spent a quarter of a century lobbying Congress. It maintained an elaborate and sophisticated political apparatus, and it had a substantial reserve of union funds earmarked for political action. Throughout the rest of 1963 the union leadership used those resources to try to move the coalition in the direction the UAW wanted it to go.

The Reutherites had argued since the 1940s that any attack on racial injustice had to be coupled with an assault on economic inequality. In early 1963 the union leadership once again fused the two issues. They did so, most immediately, in response to the growing rift between the UAW and its long-time allies in the black community. In January 1963, three months before the Birmingham campaign, Nat Weinberg and Brendan Sexton wrote Walter Reuther an urgent memo arguing that the UAW could not afford to lose the support of African-Americans, who in years to come would make up an increasing percentage of the working class. The best way to heal the rift, Weinberg and Sexton insisted, was to "spearhead the fight for a better life for America's dispossessed and disinherited."[27]

Though they presented their case in racial terms, Weinberg and Sexton's proposal grew out of other concerns as well. It is likely that they knew, through Jack Conway, that Robert Kennedy's staff was discussing the possibility of a federal initiative against poverty. Weinberg, moreover, had long been concerned about the persistent pockets of unemployment in the UAW's rank and file; as early as 1959, he and Roy Reuther had raised the possibility of organizing the unemployed. Weinberg also had recently read Michael Harrington's moving study of the American underclass, *The Other America,* and had been impressed by it, in part at least because it reinforced his view that the United States was not the affluent society that many liberals proclaimed it to be. Days after drafting the first memo, Weinberg sent Reuther Dwight McDonald's extended review of Harrington's book in the *New Yorker.* The UAW president also must have been moved, since he distributed copies of the review to all International officers and board members. More important, in early February Reuther called a high-level staff meeting to lay plans for "a concerted effort" to win African-Americans both political and economic equality. The centerpiece of that effort, he informed the staffers, was to be a "concerted assault" on poverty in the United States.[28]

No minutes of that meeting have survived, so it is impossible to know precisely what course Reuther thought a "concerted assault" on poverty should take. His public statements in the summer and fall of 1963 indicate, though, that he had no new departures in mind, that he believed poverty could be eliminated by the economic agenda he had long advocated: full employment, an expansion of the welfare state, and economic planning. It also seems clear that neither Reuther nor his staffers had any plan for forcing an already gridlocked federal government to take up such a heavy burden. The dramatic events of spring changed that. As civil rights activists reshaped the national agenda, the UAW leadership increasingly began to see the movement as the means through which the nation's economy could be transformed. Civil rights "is only a beginning . . . and a means," Weinberg wrote to Reuther shortly after the Birmingham campaign, ". . . the real end is basic social reform. . . . Equality of access to jobs, housing, etc. must move on the provision of enough jobs and homes for all. This should give liberals and the labor movement more leverage in their efforts to persuade the [Kennedy] administration to move more vigorously on the domestic front."[29]

Throughout the summer and fall, the UAW worked to build the link between civil rights and economic change. Most immediately, the Reutherites wanted to be sure that Congress passed a law that would end the scourge of Jim Crow. As soon as the Kennedy bill reached the Congress, the union committed itself to a lobbying campaign, using its full resources to help transform the coalition of conscience from a moral crusade into a powerful and efficient political bloc. As that transformation took place, UAW spokesmen continually urged their coalition partners to push beyond civil rights, to become the vanguard of sweeping social change.

The UAW's first goal was to strengthen the administration's civil rights bill, which, the coalition partners agreed, fell short of their minimum expectations. As early as May 1963, a month before Kennedy had sent his proposal to Congress, the UAW had called on the administration to embrace the civil rights movement. "[T]he present administration investment of talent, manpower and attention to civil rights and Negro needs is inadequate," Rauh wrote in a scathing memo to the White House drafted at the UAW's request. ". . . [T]he recent Birmingham incident . . . demonstrates that . . . the administration must fashion a new approach to the inevitably recurring sit-ins and community protests." In early June the UAW and its coalition partners laid out precisely what they wanted that new approach to be. Any civil rights bill, they announced, should eliminate segregation in all public accommodations, have a fair employment practices provision, prohibit federal aid to any discriminatory organization, provide for the appointment of federal registrars empowered to register black voters on a mass scale, reduce congressional representation in states that denied blacks the vote; and empower the attorney general to bring suit on behalf of victims of discrimination, regardless of their circumstances.[30]

Coalition spokesmen, including Walter Reuther and Rauh, took their case to the White House on June 22, when they met with the president, vice-president, and attorney general to discuss the administration's package. JFK made an impassioned plea for the administration's more limited bill, insisting that it went as far as was possible, given the alignment of forces in Congress. After the president left the meeting, Rauh informed Attorney General Robert Kennedy that the administration's proposal was inadequate and that the coalition would throw its weight behind its more far-reaching measure. As he listened, RFK paled.[31]

The differences between the White House and the UAW over the civil rights bill were in part tactical. Knowing that southern Democrats would oppose even the mildest of proposals, the administration shaped its bill to appeal to the moderate Republicans who would hold the swing vote. Kennedy therefore studiously avoided those provisions, such as fair employment practices, that the GOP was most likely to find objectionable. "The president wanted a law, not an issue," the president's aide Theodore Sorensen later explained. The UAW and other civil rights organizations, in contrast, wanted to submit the strongest civil rights bill possible at the outset, and then, by aggressive lobbying, to retain as much of the original as possible and to trade away the rest. "All-out fights," Roy Reuther told the press, "are made on all-out measures." The tactical disagreement reflected the more fundamental difference between the White House and the UAW on civil rights: Kennedy wanted to work within the existing political alignment; the UAW wanted to shatter it.[32]

In the weeks after the White House conference, the coalition members formalized their congressional strategy. The coalition would substitute its bill for the administration's proposal, thus redefining the terms of debate in its favor. The civil rights groups then were to focus their lobbying on the Republican representatives whom the administration had identified as the key votes. Since many of these people represented rural districts without substantial black or working-class populations, the religious groups would have to carry the burden of that effort. The coalition partners agreed to coordinate their day-to-day activities on Capitol Hill through the Leadership Conference on Civil Rights, (LCCR), the umbrella organization that the UAW had help found in the 1950s. By midsummer the UAW had made itself central to the implementation of the coalition's strategy.[33]

On Reuther's order, the AFL-CIO Industrial Union Department provided the LCCR with office space and assigned it two of its staffers, the only full-time help the conference had. The IUD's director, Jack Conway, gained control of LCCR's five-man emergency steering committee, which the conference had authorized to plan daily tactics. Since both Conway and Rauh were appointed to the committee, the UAW held two of the five votes from the outset. Conway then secured a third vote, the NAACP's Clarence Mitchell. "I met Clarence Mitchell privately," he recalls,

> and I said to him, "Do you have any trouble with Joe Rauh?" And he said, "No, Joe and I can always reach agreement." And I said, "Okay, you've got two members of this steering committee that you can count on, yourself and Joe Rauh; so I am making a commitment to you that there never will be a decision made against you, because I will cast my vote with you and Joe Rauh even though I might disagree with you." . . . What actually happened was that we never had a disagreement because it was clearly

known by Mitchell that he had the majority of the five-member committee so we were always able to work out our differences.[34]

UAW representatives and their LCCR allies next moved to replace the
administration's bill, then before a subcommittee of the House Judiciary
Committee, with the coalition's proposal. Rauh, Conway, and the AFL-
CIO lobbyist Andrew Biemiller visited the subcommittee's chairman, New
York's Emanuel Celler, and persuaded him to add the desired provisions to
the subcommittee's version of the bill. It was not a hard sell, according to
Rauh, "because it was the goddammed most liberal [sub]committee
ever. . . . Oh, we could have put through that the Kremlin should be moved
to New York City."[35]

Once the coalition's bill was before Congress, the UAW turned its full
attention to the lobbying campaign. The UAW made extensive use of its
own members in the fight. During the summer the Fair Practices Department brought over a hundred local union officials and rank and filers to the
capital to meet with their representatives. Such meetings were not crucial,
however, since most representatives from industrialized districts already
supported the bill. The UAW focused most of its energy, therefore, on the
efforts of the coalition's religious groups, who, all sides agreed, would make
or break the LCCR's campaign. In June the National Council of Churches
established a Commission of Religion and Race to coordinate the church
groups' efforts on behalf of the bill. The commission placed day-to-day
planning in the hands of a subcommittee under the direction of Victor
Reuther, who quickly began to shape the council's efforts in the UAW's
image. He persuaded the NCC to conduct all its lobbying through the
LCCR, a move that placed the council at the UAW's disposal. Reuther also
proposed that the NCC hold a series of training sessions for potential
lobbyists throughout the Midwest. The UAW assigned Mildred Jeffrey to
lead the classes, titled "The Necessity for a Coalition of Conscience." When
the newly trained activists arrived in Washington, the UAW Washington
office, working through the LCCR, made sure that they were employed to
good effect.[36]

The UAW's approach to George Meader, the only Michigan representative on the Judiciary Committee, illustrates the union's technique. Meader,
a Republican, represented Michigan's Second Congressional District, a pre-
dominantly rural, conservative area that also included the University of
Michigan. The UAW never contacted the congressman directly, but rather
arranged for him to be visited by people from the Michigan Council of
Churches, the Episcopal and Catholic churches of his district, Ann Arbor
Jewish leaders, members of the Ann Arbor NAACP, several University of

Michigan deans, and Edward Cushman, vice-president of American Motors and a close friend of Michigan's Republican governor, George
Romney. "We know that we have to have one thousand pounds of steam to
get one pound of pressure," Jeffrey reported.[37]

The UAW leadership did not limit its role in the coalition simply to
activating members with little lobbying experience. The union also
was more than willing to rein in its partners when their activism threatened
to disrupt the political bloc the UAW was trying to build, as the UAW's
response to the signal event of the summer of 1963, the March on Washington, demonstrates. The march was the idea of the grand old man of the
civil rights movement, A. Philip Randolph, the sixty-four-year-old president of the Brotherhood of Sleeping Car Porters. In January 1963 two of
Randolph's aides, Bayard Rustin and Tom Kahn, had suggested that the
nation's leading African-American organizations stage a mass two-day
demonstration in Washington to protest both racial injustice and "the economic subordination of the American Negro." Rustin and Kahn envisioned
the event as a radical display of African-American anger. On the first day,
black protesters would stage sit-ins on Capitol Hill, stopping all legislative
business, while their spokesmen presented a list of demands to the White
House. On the second day, the protesters would attend a massive public
rally. Randolph, whose March on Washington Movement in 1941 had
forced Franklin Roosevelt to bar discrimination in wartime industry, embraced the idea, but other civil rights leaders, including Martin Luther
King, showed little interest. After the Birmingham campaign, however,
King, eager to sustain the momentum the SCLC had built, committed
himself to the march. On June 20 he announced that it would take place in
late August.[38]

In theory, the march was precisely the kind of event the UAW hoped to
see. A carefully orchestrated mass mobilization—Randolph and King were
predicting that the march would draw 100,000 to 250,000 participants—
would undoubtedly impress uncommitted representatives while further so-
lidifying the coalition. From the start, the protest, now called the March on
Washington for Jobs and Freedom, also explicitly linked civil rights and
economic equality. Some of the march's details, however, left the UAW
leadership deeply troubled. Civil disobedience on Capitol Hill, Reuther
feared, would frighten more people in Congress than it would impress and
might lose the coalition valuable votes. More important, the march was to
be sponsored by the six major black organizations—the Brotherhood of
Sleeping Car Porters, the SCLC, the NAACP, the National Urban League,
the Congress on Racial Equality (CORE), and the Student Nonviolent

Coordinating Committee (SNCC)—rather than by the coalition of conscience as a whole.[39]

At a June 22 working lunch with civil rights leaders, Reuther urged the march organizers to abandon the idea of civil disobedience in favor of a one-day protest rally and to expand their base to include white groups such as the UAW. Whitney Young of the NAACP thought the suggestions reasonable, but the representatives of the movement's militant wing, CORE and SNCC, suspected that the UAW president was acting as a front man for John Kennedy, who opposed the very idea of the march. For the most part, though, the civil rights leaders were more than willing to cooperate. King, already convinced that a Capitol Hill sit-in was not feasible, quickly agreed to Reuther's suggestion that such an action be scrapped in favor of a rally at the Lincoln Memorial. The African-Americans proposed a reasonable compromise on the question of representation: the six black organizations would retain complete control of the march, but they would add four white activists—Reuther, a representative of the NCC, one of the nation's best known rabbis, and a highly respected Catholic layman—as co-chairs without voting power.[40]

Once the UAW was integrated into the march leadership, Reuther and his staff committed the union's resources and personnel to maximizing the event's effectiveness. The UAW paid for the march's sound system, a total of almost $19,000. The union flooded the march with prepared picket signs, each emblazoned with a slogan stressing the tie between civil rights and economic change, such as "Civil Rights Plus Full Employment Equals Freedom," "Freedom is a Lie for America's Not So Invisible Poor," and "Corporations Plan for Profits; Let the People Plan for Full Employment." It likewise flooded the march with UAW members, providing bus transportation to the capital for 5,000 rank and filers, the largest contingent from any one organization. The International placed each participant under strict orders to avoid any kind of confrontation. To ensure compliance, Reuther assigned the International's leading staffers—Victor and Roy Reuther, Horace Sheffield, Irving Bluestone, Brendan Sexton, Mildred Jeffrey, and William Oliver—as marshals. By late August the march seemed to be the highly controlled and coordinated event that the UAW hoped it would be.[41]

The night before the march was to take place, however, it threatened to unravel. Late in the evening of August 27, SNCC's representative, John Lewis, released the text of the remarks he planned to give the next day. Since SNCC's founding in 1960, its members had served as the civil rights movement's shock troops, registering voters and integrating facilities in the small towns and rural areas of the deep South. It was dangerous work, and it had left the SNCC leadership convinced that racism was far more en-

8. UAW participants in the March on Washington, August 28, 1963. (Archives of Labor and Urban Affairs, Wayne State University)

trenched and far more brutal than Martin Luther King's uplifting rhetoric acknowledged. Lewis's planned speech pulled no punches. The pending civil rights bill, he intended to say, was "too little and too late. . . . The revolution is at hand. . . . We will march through the South, through the heart of Dixie, the way Sherman did." When he read the text, Archbishop Patrick O'Boyle, who was scheduled to deliver an invocation, informed the march organizers that unless Lewis changed his speech, he would withdraw the Catholic Church's imprimatur from the event. The coalition of conscience was about to collapse before its most public event could occur.[42]

The UAW had never been particularly close to the SNCC leadership. The union had provided moral support and a small degree of financing for SNCC's grass-roots efforts and SNCC had entertained hopes of more extensive ties with the union, but they had never developed. Indeed, in late July, Reuther and SNCC had clashed over the pending civil rights bill. SNCC spokesmen had insisted that the LCCR support an amendment to the bill requiring the immediate transfer of all pending voting rights cases from state courts to the nearest federal court. Joseph Rauh knew that the Justice Department would be horrified by the idea and that the resulting controversy would damage the bill's chances of enactment. He recalls: "I said to Walter, 'God, we can't do that. You'd better be here. These crazies might put it over. . . . ' The people who proposed it were little fish, and Walter spoke and the thing was over." Now Reuther took the group on once again. At the request of the Justice Department's Burke Marshall, Reuther immediately contacted the archbishop, who agreed not to issue his statement until the morning. Reuther then tried to persuade the SNCC leadership to change Lewis's text. They refused. "[W]hen I talked to them . . . they pounded on my chest with great emotion and deep feeling," Reuther recalled a few weeks later. "They said: 'Do you realize that five of our leaders are in prison in the South charged with sedition? They could be executed.' " By morning Lewis's speech was still intact.[43]

The UAW president had hoped to make another attempt during the next day's luncheon session but the march had begun early and the speakers had to go straight to the Lincoln Memorial. When Reuther arrived, a call came for him from the White House: the archbishop, he was told, would wait no longer. Reuther quickly called the march leaders together and, with no time left for negotiation, simply browbeat Lewis. "Six weeks ago we formed a coalition," he said. "Now John Lewis has written a speech. . . . We have no right to tell him what he has a right to say in America, but we have a right to say that if you want to use the platform which this coalition made possible, you are morally obligated to speak within the policy framework around which the coalition came into being. . . . If John Lewis feels strongly that he wants to make this speech, he can go someplace else and make it, but he has no right to make it here because if he tries it he destroys the integrity of our coalition." Lewis said nothing as Randolph polled the speakers, who voted unanimously to deny SNCC the platform unless Lewis changed his remarks. King, Randolph, and Eugene Carson Blake of the NCC then took Lewis aside to help him redraft the text while Reuther phoned the archbishop, who arrived fifteen minutes later under Secret Service escort. The coalition had been preserved and the march was a triumph, a high-profile celebration of the new national agenda.[44]

As the UAW's power within the coalition expanded, so did its insistence that the movement broaden its definition of civil rights. Walter Reuther took the lead in the effort, delivering the UAW's message to as many groups in as many different ways as he could. In June he told administration officials that only by tackling the "gut issues" of employment and housing could Kennedy be sure of winning African-American votes in 1964. Speaking to a youth rally in August, he appealed to idealism. "[W]e shall be meeting only part of our responsibility if we pass the civil rights act of 1963 [sic]," he said, "yet fail to take action designed to achieve an economy of full employment, for our Negro citizens [have] . . . the most urgent need for an economy in which there are jobs for all." He also took the high road in his brief remarks to the March on Washington. "The job question is crucial," he told the massive crowd, "because we will not solve education nor housing or public accommodations as long as millions of Americans, Negroes, are treated as second class economic citizens. . . . Our slogan has got to be fair employment, but fair employment within the framework of full employment." Reuther's message took on an ominous tone when he addressed the IUD convention in November. "Does anybody in his right mind believe we can solve the civil rights revolution in the framework of mass unemployment?" he asked. "We will tear asunder the fabric of American democracy if the contest is going to be whether a white worker is going to walk the streets unemployed or a black worker is going to walk the streets unemployed."[45]

Other UAW spokespersons joined Reuther in making the union's case. "The civil rights struggle," the July 1963 issue of the UAW newspaper read, "starkly underlines the fact that along with equality there must come full employment so that ALL—white or Negro—may work without fear of joblessness or discrimination. . . ." Victor Reuther delivered the same message to the National Council of Churches. "Equality before the law," he wrote in the NCC's national magazine, "becomes a mockery for the unemployed worker or the hopeless occupant of a slum tenement, whatever the color of his skin. The coalition of Negroes, many churches, a large segment of the labor movement and the liberals . . . must channel its full energies into the fight for full employment. For without jobs, even the essential protection of a strong civil rights law will prove to be, for millions of Negroes, little more than ashes in the mouth." Jack Conway, similarly, linked racial and economic change in an address to the 1963 SNCC convention. "Wage earners, minority groups, middle- and low-income city people," he said, "have a broad interest . . . in justice, in full employment, in social security . . . in a community where there is no exploitation of one group by another."[46]

As fall faded into winter, though, the UAW's exhortations seemed to be making very little difference. To be sure, the coalition's efforts on behalf of the civil rights bill appeared to be helping: in late October the House Judiciary Committee reported to the Rules Committee a bill containing many of the strengthening changes that the LCCR had proposed early in the summer. Progress was painfully slow, however, and a month later the bill had yet to find its way out of the Rules Committee. Of all the coalition members, moreover, only the tiny Students for a Democratic Society had linked civil rights and economic change in a concrete way. In September 1963 SDS launched its experimental Economic Research and Action Project (ERAP), in which SDS members lived in and attempted to organize northern ghettos. The UAW enthusiastically supported the initiative: Mildred Jeffrey and Irving Bluestone continued to offer their counsel, UAW regional directors lent SDS members organizational support, and UAW funds underwrote the program. For the most part, however, civil rights activism remained focused on racial injustice, and particularly on the civil rights bill. Then, on November 22, 1963, John Kennedy was assassinated, and suddenly everything changed.[47]

Lyndon Johnson's accession to the presidency left the UAW leadership shocked and concerned. Johnson had been the champion of consensus politics, after all, the master of congressional procedure who had used his skills to block progressive legislation throughout the 1950s. Conway remembered sitting in Reuther's Washington hotel room the weekend of Kennedy's funeral discussing the new president. "I was saying . . . that Lyndon Johnson was a different breed, that there was no way that I could work with him," he remembered. ". . . I just kind of withdrew from everything: Reuther and the funeral and everything."[48]

For his part, LBJ knew that his administration would quickly become mired in distrust unless he allayed the fears of the liberals. In the weeks after the assassination, he turned his considerable political talents to the task, wooing liberal and labor support with a barrage of personal and policy initiatives. Reuther was one of the first to receive the "Johnson treatment." On the afternoon of November 23 LBJ phoned the UAW president, who had just returned to his hotel after viewing Kennedy's body, and pleaded for his help in the trying days ahead. "My friend, I need your friendship and support now more than ever," Reuther recalled the president saying. Johnson then asked Reuther to list his priorities for the nation. Johnson's appeal, coming at a moment of profound national crisis, touched Reuther deeply. "Everybody was pretty set up about the fact that the new president wanted advice from Walter and wanted his help," Rauh told an interviewer in 1969. "We all thought that was great."[49]

Reuther immediately took advantage of the invitation Johnson had proffered. After hanging up the phone, he dashed off a memo to the president, telling him that the coalition's civil rights bill had to receive the highest priority. The president, Reuther wrote, "must state that he supports fully the broad Kennedy civil rights program and will actively work to enact the pending civil rights legislation at the earliest possible date." A week and a half later, Reuther again wrote LBJ, calling on him to appoint "a presidential committee, to be called the National Coalition of Conscience," to "mobilize the full moral force of an aroused and awakened public and help America find its way out of bitterness and hatred into the way of understanding and brotherhood."[50]

Johnson's response was all the UAW could have hoped for. He announced on November 27 that civil rights was at the top of his legislative agenda and that he wanted the bill passed as it stood. He then began a string of meetings with the coalition leaders, each of whom received the Johnson treatment in a one-on-one session in the Oval Office. Joseph Rauh took his turn on December 19. The two men had been bitter foes for years. They had battled repeatedly in the 1950s, when Rauh considered Johnson "an enemy of the people," and Rauh had led the opposition to LBJ's nomination as vice-president in 1960. Now Johnson was the soul of reconciliation. "If I've done anything wrong in the past, I want you to know that's nothing now," he told Rauh as soon as the meeting started. "We're going to work together." Rauh left the meeting convinced, as he wrote shortly thereafter, that "the president wanted the [civil rights] bill just as badly as we do." Johnson followed up the discussion by sending the UAW counsel a photograph, personally inscribed, "To Joe Rauh—A Fighter," hardly the attribute Johnson found most attractive in Rauh.[51]

Johnson's courting of the UAW did not end there. In late December he phoned Reuther and asked if the UAW had any suggestions for the president's upcoming State of the Union message. Reuther, Conway, and Weinberg set to work on a set of proposals that Reuther transmitted to the White

House on January 4, 1964. The six-page memorandum, written by Weinberg, was a compendium of UAW policies, all grouped around a single concept. Johnson, Weinberg wrote, should dedicate his administration to creating "an economy of opportunity" that would allow "the young, the old, members of minority groups, the impoverished, the unemployed, the people of depressed areas . . . to contribute constructively, to the maximum of their respective capacities, to the progress of the nation and to share equitably in the abundance which their contribution can help to create."[52]

The memo went on to detail how the needs of each of the groups mentioned should be met. The administration should provide African-Americans with "equal access to jobs, housing, education, the ballot box, public facilities, and accommodations." It should launch "a massive national effort to provide a better life for America's submerged third, to improve their capacities to help themselves" through more public assistance, special education for underprivileged children, and greatly expanded public housing. The unemployed should receive retraining and relocation assistance. Distressed areas should receive more carefully targeted federal aid, the young should receive greater educational assistance, and the aged should receive higher social security payments and better health care. Weinberg concluded the memo by linking the entire package to national economic planning. If these wide-ranging goals were to be met, he wrote, the administration had to consider creating some planning mechanism, the first step of which should be a presidential commission on automation.[53]

By the time LBJ received the UAW's memo, he had already decided to commit his administration to the kind of program that the union was suggesting. He opened his January 8 address, delivered before a national television audience, by reiterating his desire to see the civil rights bill passed into law. Johnson then challenged Congress to meet the nation's other unmet needs. "Unfortunately," LBJ said, "many Americans live on the outskirts of hope, some because of their poverty and some because of their color, and all too many because of both. Our task is to help replace their despair with opportunity." He went on to declare an "unconditional war on poverty," the primary weapon of which would be a cooperative effort by federal, state, and local governments to provide "better schools and better health and better homes and better training and better job opportunities to help more Americans . . . escape from squalor and misery and unemployment rolls." Although Johnson made no mention of planning, he did call for a national commission on automation.[54]

It was an extraordinary moment for the UAW leaders. For years they had struggled unsuccessfully to break the deadlock that blocked reform. In the spring and summer of 1963, the civil rights movement had done what the

UAW alone could not do: it had pushed into the center of public debate the crucial question of racial inequality. But still the UAW wanted more. It wanted a grand reform coalition, dedicated to remaking the very fabric of American society. Now Lyndon Johnson seemed to be offering such a movement. The forces of change had been unleashed at last.

[8]

Building the Great Society

Throughout the darkest days of the 1950s, Brendan Sexton had remained a true believer in labor's power to transform the nation. In the early 1960s, even he had begun to lose faith; so much so, in fact, he had seriously considered leaving the UAW to become director of the more pristine, and powerless, League for Industrial Democracy. By early 1965, however, his confidence had been so far restored that he felt "very hopeful about the system. The thing looks malleable. It can be changed, and fast. I wouldn't say that happy days are here again but I will say that it looks possible now to do several essential things simultaneously— help yourself . . . , lead a good life, and move collectively toward collective and human goals, political and spiritual."[1]

Sexton's optimism was wholly justified. In 1964 and 1965, the political system was indeed malleable, as the Johnson administration, responding to the demands of newly empowered grass-roots activists, launched a wave of reform initiatives unparalleled in the postwar era. The UAW leadership embraced these initiatives, believing that they could serve as a step toward a social democratic transformation of national social policy. To that end, the union attempted to mediate between the administration and the activists, as it had done during the civil rights crisis of 1963, prodding the federal government to expand its programs while channeling grass-roots discontent in directions acceptable to the national state. For two extraordinary years the strategy seemed to work. Political power had its price, however, and for the UAW leadership that price was very high indeed.[2]

Throughout the winter and spring of 1964, the White House and the civil rights coalition moved in tandem, simultaneously pushing through Congress the pending civil rights bill and Johnson's War on Poverty. From the UAW leadership's perspective, Lyndon Johnson's handling of the civil rights bill was a revelation. The new president, Joseph Rauh later declared, "was close to perfect on that." By February LBJ had forced the coalition's strengthened bill through the House of Representatives, masterfully orchestrating the lobbying efforts of the Leadership Conference on Civil Rights with his own brand of pressure politics. Rauh recalled the day the House approved the bill. He was sitting in the gallery watching the vote when a page informed him that the president wanted to speak to him. Rauh rushed to the nearest pay phone and was immediately put through to Johnson, who barked, "What have you done to get the bill on the floor of the Senate?" In the Senate, LBJ again followed the strategy that the LCCR had urged on Kennedy the previous summer. Refusing to weaken the bill to avoid a southern filibuster, he instead pressured Republicans to join with Democratic liberals in voting for cloture. In May 1964 the Republicans agreed, thus shattering the Dixiecrat-Republican coalition that had blocked liberal reforms since the late 1930s. "A year ago, we had just passed through the ordeal of Birmingham," the UAW *Washington Report* exulted shortly afterward. "Today . . . there is an entirely different atmosphere throughout the country. . . . The struggle is not over, but it has passed an historic point of no return."[3]

The War on Poverty, by contrast, did not meet all of the UAW leadership's expectations. Cobbled together from a host of long-pending programs and proposals— job training for the chronically unemployed, college work programs, federal loans for small businesses and poor farmers, a domestic Peace Corps— the initiative differed from previous liberal policies only in its scope, not in its shape. It made no attempt to reshuffle existing power relationships, and it redistributed wealth not from the wealthy to the working class but rather from the middle and working classes to the poor. It offered no challenge to "free enterprise," much less to the sanctity of corporate decision making. Its welfare programs, moreover, were designed to address the needs of a plethora of special-interest groups rather than broadly defined economic classes. They were presented in piecemeal fashion, and they were no more coherent in their purpose or coverage than the patchwork of agencies created by the New Deal.[4]

Such an approach was perfectly in keeping with Johnson's view of the nation's political life. As a young man in the Texas hill country of the 1930s, he had been witness to the federal government's power to transform the lives of ordinary Americans, and he had never forgotten the lesson. As a national political figure in the 1950s, he had been convinced that American society had to rest on a broad-based consensus. He had helped to maintain that consensus by keeping divisive issues off the national agenda. Now that the civil rights revolution had made that approach impossible, Johnson combined the New Deal he loved with the basic premise of the postwar liberalism he had derided as Senate majority leader, concluding that the federal government could best refashion the national consensus by using its power to meet the specific demands of narrowly defined interest groups while studiously avoiding divisive appeals to class politics. "The biggest danger to American stability is the politics of principle, which brings out the masses . . . ," he told his biographer Doris Kearns, "for once the masses begin to move, then the whole thing begins to explode. Thus it is for the sake of nothing less than stability that I consider myself a consensus man." Johnson was wrong. As any number of critics have noted, by targeting some groups for aid, particularly urban African-Americans, while largely ignoring the needs of the urban white working class, the War on Poverty effectively split the Democrats' constituencies. Within a few years, white workers would turn against the Great Society and the president who had created it.[5]

Neither Johnson nor the UAW leadership could have predicted such an outcome in 1964. To be sure, the union disagreed with the administration's fragmented approach to combating poverty. "You can't compartmentalize the problem and say, 'We will just talk about this little piece,'" Reuther told the House committee considering the antipoverty program in April 1964. "You have to relate it to the basic, overall problems of this country." Reuther then offered the same class-based argument he had been presenting since the 1940s. "Poverty," he insisted, "essentially, is a reflection of our failure to achieve a more rational, more responsible, more equitable distribution of the abundance that is within our grasp. Therefore, we will not deal with the problem of poverty until we deal with the problem of the maldistribution of the national income."[6]

National income was skewed, Reuther continued, because "those in our economy who possess a large measure of freedom to appropriate more than their fair share of the fruits of our economy have been persistently abusing that freedom, particularly the major corporations that dominate whole industries." It followed, therefore, that poverty could be eliminated only by combining increased welfare and other public spending measures with the democratic control of industry that the UAW had long advocated. "A democratic planning agency will provide the mechanism for a rational approach to national problems," Reuther concluded, echoing an appeal he had made hundreds of times before. "Democratic planning would speed

enormously the solution of our nation's pervasive problems of poverty."
Reuther and the UAW leadership, it is clear, did not want the War on
Poverty simply to extend the New Deal order. They hoped, rather, that it
would facilitate the social democratic reconstruction of American economic life.[7]

The UAW saw the antipoverty effort much as it had seen World War II
and the Korean War, as a moment of strain and opportunity in which long-
standing policies and practices were open to question and change. Reuther
made the comparison explicit in an August 1964 article in *Saturday Review*.
"Randolph Bourne said that war is the health of the state," he wrote. "In
war, we have been capable of a high degree of unity of purpose; in war, there
has been virtually full employment. . . . We must find the common ground
of unity and purpose that we require to accomplish the complex tasks of
peace, as we found it under the pressure of war." Despite their potential,
Reuther admitted, World War II and Korea had not fostered permanent
changes in the economic order. This time, he thought, the possibilities were
greater, because reform was not linked to the demands of combat and the
innate conservatism of the military bureaucracy. The administration simply
needed to be prodded in the right direction. The UAW leadership threw
itself into the War on Poverty, determined not to let the moment pass again.
"[W]e enlist with you for the duration in the war against poverty and want
and pledge our full support and cooperation," Reuther wired Johnson in
March 1964. "[A]s commander in chief, you can count on us as you lead
America into battle against poverty and want."[8]

In its initial manifestation, at least, the organizational structure of the
War on Poverty lent itself to the experimentation the UAW envisioned.
Hoping to give the program an independent power base within the administration, Johnson created an entirely new poverty agency, the Office of
Economic Opportunity (OEO), headed by R. Sargent Shriver, director of
the Peace Corps and brother-in-law of John Kennedy. The OEO started as a
blank slate, free of long-standing bureaucratic practices and procedures.
Administration officials organized its myriad programs around a highly
innovative concept, the Community Action Program (CAP). Based on experimental programs developed by the President's Committee on Juvenile
Delinquency in the early 1960s, CAP required communities to create poverty boards that would administer federal antipoverty programs and
develop local initiatives. Each community could shape its board as it saw
fit, with one proviso: boards were to ensure the "maximum feasible participation" of the poor themselves in their deliberations. In theory, then,
CAP gave heretofore largely disenfranchised groups a formal place within
national and local power structures, precisely the political formulation that

the UAW had long advocated, albeit in social welfare rather than economic programs. It is hardly surprising, therefore, that in 1964 the UAW turned its full attention to CAP, working to make its performance match its promise.[9]

The Office of Economic Opportunity itself gave the UAW the greatest opportunity to influence CAP. In March 1964 Shriver asked Jack Conway to serve as the OEO's deputy director, responsible for the implementation of the Community Action Program. "Intrigued" by the still undefined concept, Conway accepted the appointment on the understanding that he would return to the labor movement as soon as CAP was in place. He remained deputy director for the next year and a half, during which he tried to shape CAP in the UAW's image. "I had spent so many years in the labor unions that I had a fairly good concept of how you organize people into action groups," he later explained. In particular, Conway wanted local community action organizations to follow the familiar UAW model of formalized powersharing through tripartite boards. "I developed a three-cornered stool concept," he recalled, "which was that the best community action organization had very strong representation from local government, from . . . private agencies, and from the people themselves. If you could figure out how you could get this kind of a three-cornered stool stability . . . that's what we strove for."[10]

Much has been made of CAP's confrontational political style, its desire to foment conflict between the poor and the power structure. That was not Conway's intention. The UAW's social democratic vision had always been integrationist at heart. It sought to give more Americans, be they workers or the poor, a say in national decision making and by so doing to create a new national consensus, committed to substantive reform rather than to the maintenance of social and economic inequality. Political conflict was necessary to create that new consensus, as the civil rights movement had shown, but once the consensus was in place, conflict was to give way to peaceful negotiations conducted within formal political structures. Conway saw CAP as just such a structure. He believed that his role was not to promote conflict but rather to integrate groups into the new system that CAP had created, and thus to make permanent the reform consensus that the civil rights revolution had made. "I was an institution builder," he explained. "I always felt that it was important to organize people into some kind of instrument which was capable of carrying out an effective program and achieve positive results."[11]

Reuther dovetailed the UAW's response to the War on Poverty with Conway's CAP. Sitting at the breakfast bar in his suburban Detroit home in March 1964, Reuther sketched out a proposal for a Citizens' Crusade against Poverty (CCAP), through which, he hoped, the organizations that

had constituted the previous year's coalition of conscience could be formally integrated into the poverty fight. "What we do, essentially," Reuther
told the UAW Executive Board a few weeks later, "is to call upon the forces
who are joined together in the civil rights struggle to couple the civil rights
struggle with the poverty struggle. . . . This would permit us to implement
the federal program and supplement that with private action." As Reuther
envisioned it, CCAP would act as a liaison between OEO, coalition of
conscience members— unions, civil rights groups, the churches, student
groups such as Students for a Democratic Society, and liberal groups such
as Americans for Democratic Action— and the poor themselves. Working
through CCAP, coalition members would join with the local poverty boards
to implement existing programs and propose new policies; CCAP would
work with administration officials to transform grass-roots proposals into
fully funded programs; and the Crusade would train the representatives of
the poor who sat on community boards. The result would be a "tripartite
partnership" among CCAP, the administration, and the poor.[12]

Organizationally, CCAP was very much a UAW operation. It was lavishly
funded—the 1964 UAW convention set aside $1 million dollars in union
funds for the project—and it was tightly controlled by the UAW leadership.
Although ultimate authority for the organization rested with the annual
CCAP conference, to which each member group was to send a representative, real power rested with the national chairman, who appointed CCAP's
executive director, approved all staff work, and set salaries. Not surprisingly,
Reuther was appointed CCAP's chairman, and he held the post throughout
the Crusade's existence. The poor were not even mentioned in CCAP's
original constitution.[13] Institutionally, CCAP was intimately linked to the
administration's domestic policy matrix. Reuther briefed Johnson on the
Crusade in April and found the president "very excited about what we're
doing." LBJ responded with warm praise for the concept and a promise that
OEO would provide whatever help the Crusade needed. In subsequent
months, OEO and CCAP exchanged not only ideas but also funding and
personnel. CCAP's training program for the poor, for example, received the
bulk of its funding from the Ford Foundation, which had also underwritten
the juvenile delinquency programs that had served as CAP's forerunners.
When CAP wanted to establish its own training program, Conway hired
Brendan Sexton to head the effort. Sexton did so for a year, then he left the
administration to run CCAP's training program. Similarly, when Reuther
chose CCAP's first executive director in early 1965, he named Richard
Boone, one of the architects of the Community Action Program.[14]

CCAP's policy makers likewise dovetailed their concept of poverty with
that of the Community Action Program. In particular, they accepted un-

9. Walter Reuther confers with Lyndon Johnson at the White House, probably in 1965. (Archives of Labor and Urban Affairs, Wayne State University)

critically the administration's linking of race and poverty. It is extraordinary that they should have done so. UAW officials had been arguing since the 1940s, after all, that racial issues had to be addressed within the context of class relations. In addition, the UAW leadership was painfully aware that many of the union's white rank and filers had been impoverished by the transformation of the auto industry during the previous decade. Yet only Nat Weinberg suggested that unemployed UAW members should be organized as part of the poverty fight. The idea received no serious consideration; having developed their concept of the poverty fight in relation to the civil rights movement, most UAW policy-makers assumed as a matter of course that community organizing should focus on the African-American underclass. Unemployed auto workers in such towns as South Bend, home of the recently bankrupt Studebaker corporation, Brendan Sexton argued without a trace of irony, lacked leadership and thus could not be organized effectively, whereas the urban poor, rooted in neighborhoods, were ripe for organizing.[15]

The UAW leadership's connection to the administration was not restricted to personnel and policy. Reuther also increasingly identified with Johnson on personal terms, a profound change from the 1950s. Throughout 1964, LBJ carefully cultivated Reuther's favor, wooing him with unprecedented access to the Oval Office. Between November 1963 and November 1964, Reuther spoke to Johnson by phone or met with him privately well over a dozen times. The UAW president, Hubert Humphrey later insisted, "was consulted as often as any man outside [the] government." Reuther attributed his newfound power to his affinity with the president. "[John Kennedy] and I were on the same wavelength," he told a reporter. "I think I'm equally close to Lyndon Johnson, but I approach him differently. He was poor. I too know poverty. Lyndon Johnson and I came out of the same family background." Johnson responded to such feeling by further stroking Reuther's ego. "Thank you, my old friend, for being at my side Friday evening," LBJ wrote Reuther after a June Democratic fundsraiser. "I can always count on you and for that kind of unswerving friendship, I am mighty grateful." Detroit's mayor, Jerome Cavanagh, best described the emerging relationship. "Walter Reuther, of course, liked to be close to the White House and the president wanted him close too." After years of struggle and defeat, the UAW leadership had finally made it to the center of power.[16]

The UAW's integration into the administration's antipoverty machinery obviously altered its relation to the coalition of conscience that had formed the previous year. In 1963 the UAW leadership had pushed its coalition partners to be more aggressive in demanding fundamental change; now the UAW sought to formalize the changes wrought by the coalition by bringing its members into the administration's programs. The UAW leadership thought it necessary to channel grass-roots discontent away from the movements of the streets, where it could threaten the stability of the emerging reform consensus, and toward the new federal structures the UAW was helping to build. The civil rights movement, Reuther told the UAW Executive Board, "must be converted from [a] protest movement to [a] positive movement." The need for such a conversion became even more acute as activists moved to the northern ghettos, which, the UAW leadership recognized, seethed with "cynicism" and "anger." "A new Negro leader must emerge," a CCAP staffer wrote, and it was the coalition's responsibility to "increase the chances he will emerge as an integrator and not a rebel." Brendan Sexton made the same point in somewhat more apocalyptic terms in early 1964. "I believe that [the poor] will be . . . organized," he said, "and that the open questions remaining are: who will do the organizing; how quickly will the organizations be built; how effective will they be; will they be led by demagogues, or by people of liberal persuasion?"[17]

In the UAW's view, converting the civil rights coalition to a "positive movement" was not a shift away from the freedom struggle but rather the next logical step in that struggle. Other members of the coalition, however, were moving in the opposite direction. Many African-American activists, particularly those associated with the Student Nonviolent Coordinating Committee, had found the triumphs of 1963 both liberating and sobering: liberating because the victories of that year gave them a sense of just how powerful racial solidarity could be, sobering because they realized that despite the Civil Rights Act, racial oppression remained embedded in the nation's political and social systems. White student activists, meanwhile, saw in the successes of the civil rights movement confirmation of the rejuvenating power grass-roots activism—participatory democracy, in their phrase—could have on society. For these activists, calls for integration into the system were premature at best, dangerous at worst.[18]

Given such differences, it was only a matter of time before the UAW leadership and the activists clashed. In the first half of 1964, however, it was easy for the UAW leadership to miss the activists' reservations. In fact, the UAW's dream of transforming the coalition into a broad reform consensus in support of the administration seemed to be working. Virtually the entire coalition membership, from SNCC to the National Council of Churches, from Students for a Democratic Society (SDS) to the AFL-CIO, accepted Reuther's invitation to join CCAP. In midsummer the national civil rights leadership announced a moratorium on protests until the November election. Shortly after the Republican Party chose Barry Goldwater as its presidential candidate, Martin Luther King endorsed Johnson, the first time King had given his support to a party's nominee.[19]

Though they joined in the moratorium pledge, in private the SNCC leadership opposed the movement's unqualified support for the administration, just as they had opposed the conciliatory tone of the March on Washington in 1963. Throughout the spring and early summer of 1964, SNCC fieldworkers, aided by SDS volunteers, had staged a dangerous voter registration drive in rural Mississippi, trying to build a multiracial Mississippi Freedom Democratic Party (MFDP) that would challenge the states' all-white regular party at the 1964 Democratic convention. In the tiny hamlets of the state, the fieldworkers had lived under the constant threat of violence. Virtually each day of that long and brutal summer a SNCC worker was beaten, shot at, or jailed. The terror peaked in June, when three SNCC members were murdered. That experience confirmed SNCC's view that civil rights activists had to be more, not less, militant if racism were to be exorcised from American society. Whatever the rest of the movement might promise, SNCC was determined to carry its protest to the floor of the 1964 Democratic convention.[20]

At first the UAW was supportive of SNCC's efforts, which were so clearly within the mainstream of civil rights activism. Undoubtedly thinking of her own organization's experience, SDS's Casey Hayden advised Robert Moses, the MFDP's director, to secure the UAW's backing for the convention challenge. "The UAW is critical," she explained. " . . . Reuther should be asked for [a] contribution to set up an office, etc. They might also contribute a staff person." Moses, a dedicated and dynamic activist who had left Harvard to join SNCC, took Hayden's advice to heart. In March he traveled to the UAW convention in Atlantic City, where he explained the proposed challenge to Mildred Jeffrey, Joseph Rauh, and William Dodds, the acting director of the union's Political Action Department.[21] All three responded enthusiastically to Moses's appeal. Jeffrey used her power to put the Michigan Democratic delegation on record in support of the MFDP's claim to convention seats. Rauh volunteered to serve as the MFDP's counsel for the challenge. And Dodds saw to it that the party received some UAW funds and a good deal of positive press, including a full issue of the widely circulated *UAW Washington Report*. "We have been involved in it since the very beginning," Dodds wrote a friend in June. "I think it will be a pretty good test of some people who have been giving a great deal of political lip service on the subject."[22]

Weeks before the Democratic convention, however, the UAW's position changed. The Republicans' decision to nominate Barry Goldwater convinced the UAW leadership that, for the first time in recent memory, American voters would be given a clear choice between conservatism and liberalism, and that, given that choice, the liberals were likely to sweep the election. Since early in the year, moreover, the UAW had been urging LBJ to make his ticket even more liberal by adding Hubert Humphrey as his running mate. Now Johnson, horrified by the thought of an embarrassing convention fight, was hinting that if he acceded to the MFDP's demands, he could not afford to name Humphrey to the ticket. Eager to defuse the protest, the president contacted Reuther, assuming that he could force Rauh to call off the challenge. "In early August I got a call from Walter asking me to withdraw as counsel and trying to blow up the movement," Rauh explained later. "He said . . . 'We can't have a fight at the convention, you have to get out of it.'" Rauh refused, using two of the UAW's traditional arguments to defend his role in the planned protest. The party would be better off if the southern power brokers bolted the party, he insisted, and if he withdrew as the MFDP's counsel, the leftist National Lawyers' Guild might step in to fill the void.[23]

The MFDP gained the upper hand on the first day of the convention, August 22, staging an emotional appearance before the Credentials Committee. Incensed, LBJ once again called on Reuther, who was in the midst of negotiations with Chrysler, and asked him to come to the convention immediately to work out a solution. Reuther at first demurred, but when Johnson called a second time, the UAW president agreed to fly to Atlantic City as soon as possible. Arriving at 3:00 A.M., Reuther immediately met with Humphrey, Democratic National Chairman David Lawrence, and Humphrey's aide Walter Mondale, who informed him they had drawn up a compromise package: the regular Mississippi delegation would retain its seats, the MFDP would receive two at-large seats, and the party would pledge that, beginning in 1968, no segregated delegations would be acceptable. It was a reasonable compromise and, according to Rauh, the MFDP might have accepted it if the group had been allowed to decide which two of its members would be given the at-large seats. Governor John Connally of Texas, though, insisted that the seats go to his choices, Aaron Henry, the head of the Mississippi NAACP, and Ed King, a white college chaplain, rather than to Aaron Henry and Fannie Lou Hamer, a sharecropper who symbolized the black empowerment for which SNCC workers had risked their lives. The party leaders "didn't consult me," Rauh charged, "because if they did a lot of the history might have been different. But Reuther always thinks he knows more than anyone else when he gets into a fight like this."24

The next morning, Reuther stepped up the pressure on Rauh and the MFDP. On his way to a critical Credentials Committee hearing, Rauh received word that Reuther wanted to speak to him immediately. Rauh quickly phoned the UAW suite. "Here's the decision," Rauh recalled Reuther saying. "I expect you will take it." Rauh explained that he had to consult with the MFDP before making any commitment, but the UAW president would not be put off. "I am telling you to take this deal," he responded, hinting broadly that Rauh's future with the UAW might be in jeopardy if he refused to cooperate. Reuther applied similar strong-arm tactics to the civil rights leadership that evening when he and Humphrey met with Martin Luther King, Andrew Young, Aaron Henry, and Bob Moses in a last ditch effort to break the impasse. Moses refused to change his position, and Reuther turned to King for support. When he refused to join the argument, the UAW president lashed out. "Look, Martin," he said, "we've given you all this money." King was not impressed. He had no right, he replied, to tell the MFDP what to do. In the midst of the argument, the group received word that the Credentials Committee had accepted the package that the party leaders had fashioned. Moses, outraged that he had been presented with a fait accompli when he had been led to believe there was still room for negotiation, stormed out of the hotel suite. In a private caucus the next day, the MFDP delegates voted overwhelmingly to reject the party's package despite Rauh's desperate pleas that winning two at-large seats was a "great victory for civil rights."[25]

The UAW leadership left the convention convinced that the incident was nothing more than a routine negotiation gone awry. Reuther, the *UAW Washington Report* claimed, had gone to Atlantic City "to try his hand at peacemaking" and had managed to fashion "an honorable compromise." Though he had courageously resisted Reuther's pressure throughout the convention, Rauh was harsher in his evaluation of events. "Communist influence was, of course, evident at the Convention," he wrote Hubert Humphrey in December 1964. ". . . [J]ust prior to the credentials committee hearing at which the compromise was unveiled, I spoke to the Mississippi Freedom Democratic Party delegation and staff in support of tolerance and understanding. . . . Miss Ella Baker, head of the Freedom Party Washington Office . . . cut me to ribbons as an appeaser in terms I had not heard since our debates with the Wallace people back in 1948."[26]

The SNCC membership saw their defeat as a confirmation of the lessons they had learned during the bitter summer in Mississippi. White Americans, from the most unreconstructed southern conservative to the most liberal northerner, SNCC concluded, did not want to integrate African-Americans into the power structure, and the liberals' claims to the contrary were nothing more than a smoke screen for co-optation of black political power. "We must stop playing this game of accepting token recognition for real change and of allowing the opposition to choose a few 'leaders' to represent the people at large," Moses wrote in his postconvention report to the MFDP membership, "especially if, as at the convention, the opposition is all white and the people are all Negro." The coalition of conscience had begun to crack.[27]

S NCC's anger was a very small crack indeed in 1964, hardly noticeable amid the stunning movement to the left that seemed to be sweeping through American political life. It was not a coherent movement. Some powerful groups, including the Johnson administration, clung to the verities of postwar liberalism. Others extended the politics of racial equality in new directions. Still others supported economic reform but remained suspicious of the African-American freedom movement. And, in the most surprising turn of events, a growing sector of the emerging reform coalition seemed to be pushing beyond liberalism to embrace the broad social democratic agenda that the UAW leadership had long advocated.

The movement to the left was undergirded by the Democrats' triumph in the 1964 presidential election. Facing the Republicans' most conservative candidate in decades, Johnson won a stunning victory, taking 61 percent of the popular vote and 486 electoral votes. He rolled up his huge margins, moreover, not by reconstituting the fraying New Deal coalition but rather by adding moderate swing voters to the Democrats' most liberal constituency. Johnson lost the five states of the deep South but swept the African-American, blue-collar, suburban, and farm votes. Johnson fared particularly well among auto workers, rebuilding the solid bloc of support that had been gradually slipping from the Democrats since 1952. In all, LBJ carried 85 percent of the UAW vote, a full 10 percentage points above his total among non-UAW blue-collar voters. Unlike Stevenson and Kennedy, Johnson swept virtually every subgroup within the union, polling 75 percent of the UAW vote in conservative Indiana and 93 percent in liberal Detroit; 80 percent of the skilled trade vote and 87 percent of the production workers; 85 percent of Protestant UAW members and 89 percent of Catholic rank and filers; 85 percent of male auto workers and 89 percent of female; 80 percent of white members and a staggering 100 percent of black rank and filers, who also voted in larger numbers than in previous elections.[28]

Johnson's electoral coalition also swept into office the most liberal Congress since 1936, the party's moderate and liberal wings picking up fifty seats in the House of Representatives and five seats in the Senate. The shift was more than numerical, since the Democrats' center-left vote outnumbered the Republican-Dixiecrat coalition that had dominated Congress for twenty-five years. The Democrats now had the power to make permanent the congressional realignment that Johnson and the coalition of conscience had brought together in support of the Civil Rights Act earlier in the year. "This is Goldwater's great contribution to American democracy," Reuther crowed. "In his defeat he made a much greater contribution than some presidents made when they got elected . . . he helped sharpen the issues so that . . . we have a working majority in terms of the things we have been talking about."[29]

In retrospect, Reuther's was a wildly optimistic reading of the Johnson landslide. LBJ had not fashioned a permanent shift to the left but rather had benefited from a particular confluence of events, albeit events he had skillfully manipulated to his advantage. His graceful handling of the Kennedy assassination trauma won him widespread goodwill among moderate voters, while Barry Goldwater's truculent conservatism had frightened many traditional Republicans into voting Democratic. LBJ's strenuous backing of civil rights, similarly, won him the African-American vote, which in some urban precincts topped 99 percent. That support could have cost him the votes of many northern white workers, given the racism that cut through a large segment of the white working class: polls taken shortly after the election showed that 32 percent of northern white auto workers and 41 percent of all northern whites thought that African-Americans were being too aggressive in demanding change. As long as civil rights activists focused their attack on the de jure racism of the South rather than the de facto racism of the North, however, the majority of northern whites did not oppose LBJ's actions on behalf of the movement.[30]

LBJ reinforced the tenuous alliance of northern white workers and African-Americans by presiding over a surge in the economy, which pulled the nation out of the recession it had been mired in throughout the Kennedy years. The unemployment rate had fallen to 4.2 percent by October 1964, its lowest rate in seven years. Just as it led the recession, the auto industry led the recovery. The Big Three had largely finished their decade-long transformation of the industry by the mid-1960s. They had completed construction of most of the new plants their decentralization plans had required. And the collapse of independent producers ensured the major manufacturers control of the auto market. As new car orders poured in, consequently, the Big Three recalled thousands of workers from layoffs and added thousands more to their payrolls. Even aging factories such as the Detroit Dodge Main and Ford Rouge plants, which had been cutting employees for over a decade, added new hands to meet the demand. UAW negotiators took full advantage of the boom market. Shortly before the election, the UAW and the Big Three signed their most generous agreements to date, raising wages and benefits by an average of 60 cents an hour. According to the Bureau of Labor Statistics, the typical auto worker ended the year with a net income of $6,326, up almost 6 percent from the year before. The wave of economic prosperity helped to mask the profound racial divisions embedded in Johnson's working-class constituency. The UAW leadership, however, did not see Johnson's victory in such narrow terms. "The American people have given the leadership of the Democratic party a clear mandate," Reuther said days after the election. "We can, by working together, fulfill that mandate and successfully complete the task of dealing with the unfinished work on the agenda of American democracy."[31]

The civil rights movement's 1965 voting rights campaign, its last great triumph, heightened the UAW's sense of hope by creating the possibility that even the deep South would soon join the reform coalition. The Southern Christian Leadership Conference (SCLC) launched its campaign in January, choosing as its target Selma, Alabama, where voting restrictions were so onerous and intimidation was so intense that the town's majority black population cast only 3 percent of the vote in the 1964 presidential election. The campaign reached its first crisis point on February 1, 1965, when Martin Luther King was jailed for leading a prohibited march. Reuther responded by demanding immediate federal action on voting rights, a point he reiterated during a meeting with Johnson on February 9. Johnson assured Reuther that appropriate legislation was being drafted. Before LBJ could send his proposal to Congress, violence flared in Selma. On Sunday, March 7, Alabama state troopers assaulted African-American protesters as they began a march from Selma to Montgomery. When news accounts of the incident reached the North, the coalition of conscience reacted with outrage. Clerical and lay activists poured into Selma to join King on his next march on Tuesday. That march was peaceful, but the aftermath was not. Late that night a gang of whites assaulted James Reeb, a Unitarian minister from Boston, who died two days later.[32]

Reeb's murder, the second of the Selma campaign, spurred the UAW leadership into action. The union donated $10,000 to a memorial fund for Reeb, and Reuther issued a call for all groups involved in the coalition of conscience to meet in Washington, D.C., to plan strategy for the congressional fight on the administration's still-unannounced bill. Walter and May Reuther, and his brother Roy, Nelson Jack Edwards of the Executive Board, and Mildred Jeffrey, William Oliver, and Horace Sheffield flew to Selma on March 15 to attend Reeb's memorial service. Immediately after arriving in Alabama, Reuther went to a local housing project where protesters had been staging a stand-in for almost a week. Standing on an old cane-bottom chair behind police barricades, he told the protesters to "take heart. Our cause and human justice will prevail." He then joined Martin Luther King at Brown's Chapel AME Church, the site of the memorial service, where Reuther praised Reeb as someone who understood that brotherhood "could not be tested in the hour of convenience, but in the hour of controversy and grave crisis."[33] That evening, Lyndon Johnson went before a joint session of Congress to call for a comprehensive voting rights bill. Telling the lawmakers that "outside this chamber is the outraged conscience of a nation," LBJ made himself one with the coalition, a point he drove home by invoking the civil rights movement's most sacred hymn, "We Shall Overcome." It was Johnson's finest hour. In a living room in Selma, Martin Luther King wept. Reuther, en route back to Detroit, caught snatches of the speech on the radio. After reading the text he called it "one of the great messages of an executive in this country." "Under your inspired leadership, I am certain we shall overcome," he wrote to LBJ the next day. "To this end, I pledge my heart and my hand."[34]

With the new Congress in place, the administration's voting rights bill sailed through the legislature in five months, passing the Senate in July by a

77–19 margin. The last vestiges of Jim Crow had given way, and now even the South seemed fertile ground for reform. Mississippi's obstructionist senator James Eastland, a UAW study pointed out, had won the 1960 Mississippi Democratic primary with a plurality of 128,000 votes, a margin that could easily be overcome by the state's nonwhite adult population of 422,000. "[I]nstead of . . . Dixiecrats coming out of the deep south and joining forces with the most reactionary Republicans to block social legislation," Reuther said, "you are going to have some of the most progressive congressmen coming out of the deep south. This is going to make one tremendous difference in the whole relationship of forces in the political arena of American society."[35]

The UAW leadership did not believe that this series of stunning triumphs simply marked a change in electoral alignments. On the contrary, in 1964 and 1965 the national agenda itself seemed open to a leftward shift, as some of the key sectors of the reform coalition began calling for social democratic, not liberal, change. SDS led the way with its Economic Research and Action Project (ERAP), launched with UAW funds in mid-1963. SDS members, including Sharon Jeffrey and Barry Bluestone, maintained close contact with their UAW sponsors over the next two years, meeting regularly with UAW officials, sending them copies of SDS position papers, and, in Rennie Davis's case, attending the 1964 UAW convention as a special guest of Reuther. By that time, Irving Bluestone was hailing SDS as one of the most active of "the socially progressive forces in this country."[36]

Its national reputation growing, SDS linked up in early 1964 with the remnants of the old socialist left and growing progressive forces in academia to draft a sweeping critique of the American political economy. The result was a widely publicized manifesto, "The Triple Revolution." Signed by thirty-three prominent activists and academics, the manifesto rang with themes the UAW had been sounding for years. Technology, the statement said, promised to create heretofore unimaginable abundance. Unless that abundance were managed, however, technology would also create mass unemployment, which in short order would wipe out the political and social gains African-Americans had won. The only way to avoid the problem was to build a "new consensus" committed to democratic economic planning. With the document, an SDS spokesman claimed, "the adults were only getting around to saying what SDS had long ago proclaimed." Reuther knew better. "The Triple Revolution," he told the UAW Executive Board, simply reiterated much of the UAW's agenda.[37]

In early 1965, two of the nation's leading civil rights activists, Bayard Rustin and Martin Luther King, likewise endorsed social democratic reform. Writing in *Commentary*, Rustin called on the civil rights movement to lead a "programmatic" reorganization of American political life. "We are challenged now to broaden our social vision," he argued. "We need to propose alternatives to technological unemployment, urban decay and the rest. We need to be calling for public works and training, for national economic planning. . . ." Rustin's support for such reform was hardly surprising. Like his mentor, A. Philip Randolph, he had long been active in socialist politics. King's endorsement was another matter. Though he too had doubts about the efficacy of American capitalism, he had avoided any overt support for substantive economic change. During his Nobel Prize tour of Sweden in December 1964, however, King said that he considered Scandinavia's economic structure to be a model for the United States. He was even more forthright early the next year. "Call it what you may," he told one audience, "call it democracy, or call it democratic socialism, but there must be a better distribution of wealth within this country for all of God's children."[38]

Later that year, the most conservative member of the coalition, the AFL-CIO, also went on record in support of democratic economic planning. Through the summer of 1963, Reuther and George Meany had barely been able to hide their hatred of each other. LBJ's reforms helped to heal their decade-long rift, at least temporarily, as both Meany and Reuther put aside their animosities to support the president's programs. As part of the détente between the pair, the 1965 AFL-CIO convention approved a resolution, written by Reuther, calling for mandatory congressional price hearings for major corporations, a technological clearinghouse, and a national planning agency. With that resolution, Michael Harrington wrote later, the AFL-CIO had "initiated a programmatic redefinition that had much more in common with the defeated socialist proposals of 1894 than with the voluntarism of [Samuel] Gompers."[39]

For Reuther and his staff, it was a moment of exultation. "[W]e are in the midst of a great revolutionary change of forces and people in American society," Reuther told his executive board in March 1965. "This change is of such dimensions, I think . . . that the historians will really put [it] in the category of a major social revolution." The UAW leadership knew that the revolution was far from complete—social democracy still remained an ideal, not a reality—but the coalition's activists were seemingly laying the base for a significant change in the American political economy. Among those activists, the UAW, firmly integrated into the administration's inner circle, was best positioned to build on that base.[40]

Two days after the 1964 presidential election, Nat Weinberg prepared a memo listing the UAW's legislative agenda for Walter Reuther to present to Lyndon Johnson. At its heart was Weinberg's familiar plea for social democratic change. "The Great Society will not be built by reliance on the blind forces of the market place," he wrote, using a phrase he had employed numerous times in the previous few years. "Ultimately, the United States must accept some form of democratic economic planning." This time, Weinberg hoped that his pleas would actually be heard. "It is probably too much to expect the administration to propose planning at this time," he admitted. "However, steps can and should be taken to lay the groundwork for a future planning mechanism." Early the next year, Reuther proposed such a step, extending the community action concept in a new and bold direction, the reconstruction of U.S. cities.[41]

In mid-May Reuther sent LBJ a four-page memorandum proposing "an urban TVA to stop erosions of cities and people." Reuther suggested that the federal government demonstrate its ability "to create architecturally beautiful and socially meaningful communities" by rehabilitating crumbling neighborhoods in six select cities. Reuther's plan called for the federal government to do more than repair old homes and build new ones. The demonstration neighborhoods, he argued, should be transformed into "research laboratories for the war against poverty" by becoming sites for new schools, old-age centers, social service outlets, and open spaces for community interaction. In keeping with the spirit of CAP and CCAP, neighborhood renewal plans were to be drawn up by local nonprofit rehabilitation corporations, which would draw together city officials, local business people, labor officials, other community elites, and area residents. The federal government would approve all plans, and the resulting funds would be channeled back into the community through the rehabilitation corporation. "Seven years hence," Reuther concluded, "the president could invite visitors from abroad to the six cities and show the living and inhabited testimony of what the essence of our concern in life really is."[42]

In part, Reuther envisioned his Demonstration Cities plan as an assault on what he believed to be the fulcrum of white racism in the North, housing. Drawing on his long-standing belief that economic security had made the UAW's rank and file more conservative, Reuther argued that most northern whites feared integration of their neighborhoods more than any other portion of the civil rights agenda because they believed that African-American residents drove down property values. Desperate to "protect their little investments" in their houses, whites locked African-Americans either into poorly constructed federal housing—"a new slum with new plumbing," in Reuther's view—or into "hand me down housing in neighborhoods where the whites are running away." "We will never solve these problems," Reuther concluded, until "we redevelop, rebuild the whole inner cores of our great cities and produce in those inner cores an attractive, healthy, wholesome, living environment that will be so exciting that everyone will want to live there." Reuther did not see the Demonstration Cities proposal simply as an end in itself, though. He also believed that it could serve as a test of and a wedge for social democratic experimentation in national policy. "National goals must, in the future," he explained, "be set by the people of the nation. And the means by which we plan to achieve them must spring from the people's mandate. The key to this whole problem of rebuilding and rehabilitating America's great urban centers is for us to demonstrate the practical ability to make public planning for people compatible with private planning for profit. . . . The demonstration cities program . . . is [a] new and significant step forward." Only a few years before, UAW leaders had believed that the federal government would not undertake such experimentation unless tremendous external pressure forced it to do so. Now Reuther simply took his idea to the president, who proved remarkably responsive.[43]

Reuther formally presented the Demonstration Cities plan to Johnson in an off-the-record White House meeting on May 20, 1965. If the president were interested, the UAW president suggested, he should establish a special task force to explore the idea more fully. LBJ like the concept. "The sense of home runs deep in me," he wrote in his memoirs, "and better housing would automatically appear on any list of priorities." Johnson also had strategic reasons to embrace the proposal. It promised to be a relatively inexpensive program at the start, since the first year was to be spent drawing up development plans rather than drawing on the federal treasury. The president turned Reuther's memo over to his aides Richard Goodwin and Joseph Califano, who, in consultation with Reuther, created an eight-man task force that brought together progressive policy elites from academia, business, labor, civil rights, and the public sector, precisely the technocratic constituencies that the UAW hoped to see represented on future planning boards. Goodwin and Califano chose Reuther to represent organized labor.[44]

When the task force first met in the White House on October 15, Califano informed the group that the president considered urban affairs to be "his most urgent domestic problem." Accordingly, Johnson was expanding the task force's mandate. Not only was it to develop the Demonstration Cities plan, but it was also to draw up the organizational structure of the newly formed Department of Housing and Urban Development (HUD). In essence, LBJ had given the task force responsibility for defining his administration's urban policy, "probably as difficult a job as the reorganization and unification of the armed services in 1947," according to a White House official. Reuther and the liberal businessman Edgar Kaiser, aided by Jack Conway, were put in charge of the Demonstration Cities portion of the task force's work, which was to be completed under the "utmost security" by late December, in time for the president to incorporate the group's suggestions in his 1966 budget proposals.[45] Despite the enormity of the assignment, the group attacked its job with alacrity, meeting in Califano's office every weekend from mid-October to mid-December. "This is the hardest working group of volunteers I've ever seen," the president's aide Harry McPherson reported to him. The task force's academics, Robert Wood of MIT and Harvard's Charles Haar, provided the knowledge, McPherson explained, but "Reuther has supplied the vision, drive and sometimes mere rhetoric that has kept us moving."[46]

With Reuther, Conway, and Kaiser in charge of the drafting process, Demonstration Cities emerged from the task force with only minor alterations. The scope of the program was expanded to make it more palatable to legislators representing districts without urban centers. The proposal was made more responsive to public demand, as the federal government was to select demonstration sites not by fiat but by competition. Interested cities were to submit planning proposals, and the secretary of HUD was to select the best among them, using as a basis how well they integrated the various components of the community, how extensively they proposed to employ innovative housing technology, and how directly they "contributed to closing the gap between the living and housing conditions of the disadvantaged and . . . the rest of the community."[47]

As the task force turned its attention to HUD's place within the administration, Reuther developed an even broader goal. He proposed that the Community Action Program be transferred from Sargent Shriver's OEO to HUD, where it could offset the conservatism of HUD's other major component, the Federal Housing Authority. The transfer would also benefit CAP, Reuther argued, since it would give the program the institutional backing that OEO, which was not a cabinet department, lacked. White House insiders surmised though, that Reuther had more than institutional reorganization in mind when he offered his proposal. At least some Johnson aides wanted Reuther to be named HUD's first secretary. "His appointment would certainly indicate your intention to make HUD a major social, as well as bricks-and-mortar, department," McPherson wrote Johnson in mid-December. Reuther let it be known that he would take the position if it were offered. If Reuther could engineer CAP's transfer, then, he could become the de facto head of the War on Poverty in the new year.[48]

Johnson adopted the Demonstration Cities proposal just as Reuther, Conway, and Kaiser had drafted it. The administration sent the enabling legislation—renamed Model Cities so it would not be associated with the protests sweeping the country—to Congress in January 1966, proclaiming it "an effort larger in scope, more comprehensive, more concentrated than any that has gone before." Reuther, however, failed to win control of the War on Poverty. Top administration officials blocked CAP's transfer, and LBJ named Robert Weaver, not Reuther, as HUD's first secretary, thus fulfilling a long-standing promise to place an African-American in charge of urban affairs.[49]

That Reuther could even have considered such a coup possible, though, and, more important, that he could have been able to make a proposal as innovative as Model Cities a central part of the national agenda, indicates how thouroughly the UAW president had become integrated into the administration. Reuther clearly saw himself in these terms, writing to LBJ in October that he was proud to be "a devoted member of your working crew." Some observers saw Reuther's identification with the president as simply personal. The UAW president, Joseph Rauh argued, desperately wanted to be "Lyndon Johnson's labor guy." To be sure, Reuther enjoyed the access to power that he had long craved and had never before been able to secure. His willingness to work within the administration was not simply a matter of ego, though. In a little more than two years, LBJ had presided over a vast expansion of American political life, an expansion that in late 1965 seemed to be moving toward the type of social democratic reform that had informed Walter Reuther's politics since the late 1930s. He had every reason to join the Great Society team.[50]

Reuther's newfound power did not come without cost. Johnson not only welcomed Reuther's advice; he expected his loyalty. In 1964 and 1965, as the president secured the Civil Rights Act and the Voting Rights Act, the War on Poverty and the other programs of the Great Society, the exchange seemed reasonable. In the next few years, as the reform coalition crumbled and the nation plunged deeper into war, the price of loyalty became increasingly high. "When Walter Reuther walks into the Oval Office with his hand in his pocket, telling Hubert [Humphrey] that unless he puts more money into the Detroit ghettos they'll burn the city down, Hubert will sit in this rocker listening and smiling, but thinking all the time how he can get Reuther to take his hand out of his pocket so he can shake it," LBJ, in his inimitable style, told Califano in 1968. "When Reuther comes to me . . . I'm sitting in this rocker, listening and smiling, but thinking all the time: how can I get him to take his hand out of his pocket so I can cut his balls off."[51]

[9]

The Widening Gyre

Shortly after 8 A.M. on July 25, 1967, Lyndon Johnson phoned Walter Reuther. The previous day had been one of the most difficult of Johnson's presidency. The attorney general had awakened the president at 3 A.M. on July 24 to tell him that rioting had broken out in Detroit. Johnson spent the rest of the day consulting with his top civilian and military advisers, unsure how to respond. Finally, just before midnight, the president, warned that civil order had completely broken down, committed troops to the city.[1] Now Johnson revealed his doubts and fears to Reuther. The very people who were criticizing him for killing women and children in Vietnam were just waiting to make the same charge in Detroit, he said. Desperate to avoid such accusations, the president evoked the spirit of the civil rights movement. He wanted the people of Detroit to know that the troops now on the streets of the city were the same soldiers who had been sent to Little Rock ten years before and to the University of Mississippi in 1962.[2]

Reuther must have understood the president's frustration and confusion. Just two years earlier, Johnson seemed to be presiding over a vast expansion of American political culture, his administration moving in harmony with a sweeping reform coalition that the UAW had helped to construct. The Vietnam War and the urban crisis had torn the coalition apart, and American politics was descending into a paroxysm of anger and violence. The violence had reached its apex in the UAW's own city, the city Reuther had dreamed of making a model of enlightened social change. Reuther responded to this profound crisis in national life by desperately trying to hold the reform coalition together, supporting the administration's foreign policy while continually pushing the White House to expand its domestic agenda. The center simply could not hold, however. By the end of 1967, Reuther, like Johnson, had become a target for both the left, which condemned him as a prop for the status quo, and the right, which saw him as a champion of social programs they had grown to despise. The anger cut through the UAW as well, not only on the factory floor and in working-class neighborhoods but also at the union's highest levels.

Vietnam had not even entered into the UAW leaders' political calculations in 1964. To be sure, they had evinced some concern for the United States' deepening involvement in the area. Victor Reuther had signed a petition calling for the Kennedy administration to withdraw its support from Ngo Dihn Diem, South Vietnam's president, and liberal critiques of the situation had circulated in Solidarity House. Such action was hardly surprising. Since 1950, Reuther and the UAW leadership had been among the foremost advocates of liberal internationalism, arguing against the bipolarism that dominated policy making. Instead of pursuing knee-jerk anticommunism abroad, the UAW had contended, the United States should support Third World anticolonialism, pouring economic rather than military aid into emerging nations struggling to establish democracy amid economic deprivation.[3]

American policy makers, the UAW leadership realized, were still far from embracing such a reorientation in 1964. To be sure, the Kennedy and Johnson administrations had taken a few hesitant steps toward lessening U.S.-Soviet tensions. In 1962 the Sino-Soviet schism had burst into the open, shattering the myth of a monolithic communist menace. The next year, the United States and the Soviet Union signed the Nuclear Test Ban Treaty. The UAW leadership warmly applauded the thaw in relations and urged the White House to do more. "It is becoming increasingly clear," Victor Reuther wrote in 1964, "that the Cold War view of the world is a distorted, over-simplified view which . . . gives both the United States and the Soviet Union a false sense of the degree to which either . . . can control events and forces beyond their borders." Given the general movement toward détente, Vietnam seemed a very small issue indeed.[4]

When Johnson escalated the war by bombing North Vietnam in February 1965, however, he thrust the issue into the center of national debate. The president's actions galvanized the New Left's university activists. The day the bombing began, Students for a Democratic Society announced plans for an Easter Sunday protest march in Washington, D.C. A month later, more than three thousand students and professors at the University of Michigan staged a day-long "teach-in" against the war. Activists on thirty-five other campuses followed their example within the week. The campus activists were driven in part by moral revulsion at the destruction the bombing had wrought. New Leftists also saw the mounting violence in Vietnam as symbolic of the dehumanizing effect bureaucratization had on American political life. They believed that by challenging the war they could create the grass-roots "participatory democracy" that animated SDS.[5]

UAW leaders were well aware of the New Left's actions. Mildred Jeffrey corresponded regularly with SDS's Paul Potter and Tom Hayden, and in early 1965 Irving Bluestone placed Rennie Davis on the UAW payroll. Both Walter Reuther's daughter, Linda, and Leonard Woodcock's daughter, Leslie, attended the University of Michigan teach-in. More important, key members of the UAW's old socialist wing—Jeffrey, Victor Reuther, Nat Weinberg, Secretary-Treasurer Emil Mazey, and the regional directors Martin Gerber and Paul Schrade—shared the New Left's opposition to American involvement in Vietnam. Mazey took the lead in expressing their opposition. "Deeply concerned about the developments in Vietnam," he requested that the UAW International Executive Board discuss the war at its meeting in March 1965.[6]

Reuther came to the meeting armed with a resolution carefully crafted to avoid both outright endorsement and condemnation of the administration's actions. Rejecting immediate withdrawal and further escalation as unacceptable alternatives, the statement called on the United States to begin negotiations with North Vietnam under the auspices of the United Nations, which would be asked to dispatch an international peacekeeping force to the South. Reuther's proposal placed him in the mainstream of liberal opinion, which in early 1965 was also searching for a way to avoid breaking with the administration on the war. For the board antiwar critics, however, liberalism was not enough.[7]

Mazey led the attack, using rhetoric that most New Leftists would have embraced. The United States had no right "to move into each of those areas where we have got revolutionary movements taking place, shifting from a feudal society to a new type society." Furthermore, he considered the Johnson administration's claim that bombing strengthened its negotiating position "the most ridiculous and asinine argument I've ever seen. . . . I have serious doubts about the competence of our government leaders in handling this particular situation." The East Coast regional director, Martin Gerber– who, like Mazey, had joined the Reuther political machine as a member of the militant World War II rank-and-file caucus—likewise advanced a radical analysis of the situation. "[T]he Vietnam War is a war of the people against the landholder," he argued. "The South Vietnamese peasants "accept the Viet Cong. . . . There is no political difference between South Vietnam and North Vietnam. It is all one nation. There is only an artificial division." The West Coast regional director, Paul Schrade, at forty-one the youngest member of the board, argued that the board was wrong to reject the option of immediate withdrawal from the conflict. "[B]ecause our intervention was unilateral," he maintained, "our withdrawal unilaterally is also an alternative." Despite their opposition to the war, though, none of the three board members was willing to push his criticism to the point of rebellion. After extended discussion, the board unanimously approved Reuther's resolution.[8]

Reuther thus avoided an embarrassing public break with the Johnson administration, but he did nothing to resolve the division within the UAW's high command. On the contrary, as Johnson continued to escalate the war in 1965 and 1966, more of Reuther's advisers privately took antiwar positions. A few supported the New Left's increasingly militant denunciations of the Johnson administration. During SDS's Easter march on Washington in 1965, its president, Paul Potter, denounced U.S. foreign policy as both antidemocratic and immoral. Shortly thereafter, Mildred Jeffrey congratulated Potter for a "great job." The entire event, she wrote, left her "terribly excited." A year later, after SDS had moved strongly to the left, Jeffrey was still making financial contributions to the organization. She kept her sympathies largely to herself, however. Paul Schrade did not. In a blistering memo to Reuther in mid-1966, Schrade blasted the UAW's acquiesence in the war and called on the union to make common cause with the antiwar movement. "I urge positive and courageous leadership by the UAW against the Johnson war policy," he wrote, "as our only hope . . . to bring about a policy that will end the war in Vietnam."[9]

Most UAW officials were not willing to go as far as Schrade. By 1966, however, antiwar sentiment had spread beyond the New Left and into the mainstream of liberal thought. Only a handful of liberal politicians and activists had objected to Johnson's bombing order in February 1965. Over the next year and a half, though, such liberal luminaries as Martin Luther King, Arthur Schlesinger, and John Kenneth Galbraith publicly broke with the president's war policy, as did a large number of the religious activists who had joined the liberal coalition during the 1963 civil rights campaign. Unlike the New Leftists, the liberal doves thought the war a tragic error of judgment rather than a symbol of national moral decay, and they demanded not the immediate withdrawal of American troops but an immediate end to the American bombing campaign, followed by negotiations. Here was both a political rhetoric and a programmatic appeal moderate enough for the UAW's social democrats to accept. Step by step in 1965 and 1966, some of Reuther's advisers did so.[10]

Emil Mazey and Joseph Rauh joined the fledgling liberal opposition shortly after the IEB meeting in March 1965. In May, Mazey made a joint appearance with Senator Wayne Morse of Oregon, one of the foremost congressional doves, during which the UAW secretary-treasurer condemned Johnson for following the "Goldwater policy." Over the next few months, Mazey took his antiwar message to a host of church and community protest rallies. In November he agreed to appear at a march on Washington sponsored by the Committee for a Sane Nuclear Policy (SANE), which drew 25,000 protesters. Rauh, more of a Washington insider, moved in a different direction. During the convention of Americans for Democratic Action in April 1965, Rauh and twelve other ADA leaders, including Nat Weinberg, met with Johnson to urge a halt to the bombing. The meeting went badly; Johnson was alternately defensive and belligerent. More convinced than ever that the war was a mistake, Rauh spent the rest of that year and the next working behind the scenes to intensify liberal pressure on the administration.[11] Weinberg, Victor Reuther, and, increasingly, Irving Bluestone took the same approach within the UAW, publicly supporting the union's official position while privately pushing Walter Reuther to take the doves' position. Weinberg was particularly active, peppering Reuther with newspaper articles critical of the war and a variety of liberal proposals for ending the conflict. In several of heated conversations Victor tried to persuade Walter to break with the White House. "I had some sharp disagreements with my brother on [the war]," Victor recalled. "It was a painful business."[12]

Walter Reuther not only shrugged off the pressure his staff was bringing to bear; throughout 1965 and 1966 he actively worked to contain the war's critics. He privately told Emil Mazey to tone down his criticism, saying that he did not question Mazey's patriotism but did question his judgment. Reuther hinted to Paul Schrade that he was endangering his position in the UAW high command by being so outspoken in his opposition to the war. To head off further defections in the union ranks, Reuther invited Arthur Goldberg, ambassador to the United Nations, to meet with the union's officers to describe the numerous efforts the administration had made to begin negotiations with North Vietnam. Goldberg's appearance apparently had little effect. When Secretary of Labor Willard Wirtz spoke at the 1966 UAW convention a month later, Reuther urged him not to mention Vietnam at all, because he was "having a hard time keeping elements within the union from precipitating a large-scale debate" on the war. Reuther also acted on the administration's behalf to quiet debate within the liberal community. At Hubert Humphrey's request, he asked ADA leaders to squelch a minority resolution critical of the war, and he served as the president's emissary in a futile attempt to prevent Martin Luther King from publicly calling on Johnson to halt the bombing.[13]

Reuther accepted the role of administration apologist partly because Johnson convinced him that the administration was indeed intent on negotiations. LBJ sent the UAW president a copy of his speech at Johns Hopkins University in April 1965, in which he declared the willingness of the United States to begin "unconditional discussions" with North Vietnam. The president inscribed the copy, "To Walter, with hope." More fundamentally, Reuther did not want to risk losing his standing in the administration, which was then paying such extensive dividends. The day Johnson initiated bombing, Reuther had met privately with the president to plead for his support of voting rights legislation, and the UAW president was less than two months away from proposing his Model Cities program. "Walter wanted to keep in line with Johnson," Joseph Rauh recalled years later, "[and] Johnson wanted 100 percent loyalty." Thus, when the White House, rather than seek negotiations, increased the number of troops in Vietnam by over 50,000, Reuther did not question LBJ's commitment to a quick settlement. Rather, he asked the Executive Board to redefine its position to support "necessary military action . . . in the hope that the communists will come to recognize the hopelessness of achieving military victory. . . ."[14]

By his words and actions, Reuther managed to maintain both his standing with Johnson and his union's outward support for the administration. What the UAW president intended as an act of loyalty to his president, however, struck the New Left as nothing less than an act of betrayal, a sign that, for all its brave talk of social change, the UAW was part of the bureaucratic political structure that had launched the brutal war in the first place. From its inception, SDS, strongly influenced by C. Wright Mills, had been somewhat suspicious of the labor movement's commitment to reform. In the organization's early years, however, its spokesmen had tempered their criticism: SDS's 1962 Port Huron Statement thus claimed that labor's liberalism was "often," but not inherently, "vestigial" and "self-interested," a charge that Reuther had been making for years. By late 1965, such fine distinctions had melted away as SDS embraced a sweeping condemnation of every segment of the labor-liberal coalition. "[W]e are suspicious of organized liberalism," Paul Potter wrote in November 1965, ". . . because it is closely tied to established political and corporate interests and committed to working with them."[15]

SDS' "corporate liberalism" thesis spread quickly from the organization's leadership to its rank and file, who often reacted to the message with venom, and to its allies in the univerisities, who gave it the sanction of academic truth. "[T]he next time some $3.90 an hour . . . workers go on strike for a 50 cent raise," a Berkeley activist wrote in 1967, ". . . so help me, I'll cross their fucking picket line." The historian Ronald Radosh led the academic attack in a widely cited 1966 article published in *Studies on the Left,* the leading journal of New Left scholarship. There was no real distinction between the "pure and simple" unionism of the AFL and the "social unionism of Sidney Hillman or Walter Reuther," Radosh insisted. "[B]eneath the avowed differences there is a fundamental consensus shared by both kinds of labor leaders—that a corporate society offers the best means of achieving industrial stability, order and social harmony." Over the next few years, young scholars broadened and sharpened Radosh's argument, focusing particularly on the duplicity of such labor leaders as Reuther, who in their eyes had co-opted the militant potential of industrial unionism.[16]

This was a remarkably myopic view of the American labor movement, given the UAW's unstinting support of SDS in the early 1960s. To be sure, the New Left was justified in criticizing the union leadership's public support of the Vietnam War, which clashed with its professed commitment to Third World independence, but to move from that contradiction to a general dismissal of social unionism was unwarranted and reductionist. The New Left's quick acceptance of the corporate liberal thesis, and the often vitriolic rhetoric that accompanied that acceptance, also had profound political consequences. Once embraced, the thesis shattered the New Left's most important tie to the labor movement and, ironically, undercut the doves in the UAW hierarchy. Emil Mazey, for one, recognized the tragedy of the break. The New Left, he said ruefully in 1968, "did a great deal of disservice to those of us who feel strongly about Vietnam."[17] More fundamentally, the UAW's caution and the New Left's anger together splintered the nascent social democratic coalition that had been taking shape in 1964 and 1965. By the end of 1966, the Vietnam War had claimed another casualty.

Just as Vietnam shattered the UAW–New Left alliance, the legislative triumphs of 1964 and 1965 exposed and expanded the tensions in the UAW-black coalition. Having toppled the last vestiges of Jim Crow, the civil rights revolution moved from the streets of the South to the ghettos of the North and from the halls of Congress back to the factory floor. Martin Luther King marked the shift in dramatic fashion, announcing in mid-1965 that the Southern Christian Leadership Conference would launch a non-violent protest campaign in Chicago to win open housing, school integration, and economic change. The shop-floor civil rights revolution was no less spectacular. With the passage of the 1964 Civil Rights Act, the auto plants of the deep South finally integrated their production lines, completing a process that had begun in the North almost a quarter century before. Change came swiftly. African-Americans accounted for only 3 percent of blue-collar workers, all in custodial classifications, in the Atlanta Chevrolet plant in 1960; by 1966, GM's management had erased the color line, and African-Americans accounted for 10 percent of the plant's blue-collar workforce. The auto plants of the North likewise expanded their African-American workforces, hiring an increasing number of blacks to fill new production jobs created by the mid-decade economic boom. African-Americans accounted for almost 20 percent of the UAW's northern membership by early 1967, up from approximately 12 percent in the early 1960s. The percentage of African-Americans was much larger in some of the industry's oldest plants, such as Detroit's Dodge Main, where blacks accounted for a majority of the production workforce. Only the UAW's skilled trades remained immune ot the change. By December 1966, only 531 of the union's more than 15,000 tradesmen were black, a minuscule increase from earlier years.[18]

The UAW leadership welcomed the transformation of shop-floor racial practices. By mandating the end of Jim Crow in southern plants, the federal government had freed both the UAW officers and the southern regional directors from the need to face the internal political consequences of integration. The UAW leadership also had been urging the civil rights movement since 1963 to expand its activism from the South to the ghettos of the North. In keeping with the UAW's position within the Johnson administration, however, Reuther was intent on making sure the movement shifted its tactics in the North from "protest to positive action." In practice, that meant channeling the movement into the new political structures the administration and the UAW had created.

The UAW pursued that goal on several fronts. In 1965 Reuther's Citizens' Crusade against Poverty established four regional educational centers—in Chicago, the New York/New Jersey area, Mississippi, and Delano, California—to train poor community activists in the intricacies of the poverty program. Students were to be nominated either by national civil rights organizations or by "spotters" working with almost ten thousand local organizations. The activists were then to be enrolled in a ten-week program. Brendan Sexton, who developed the program shortly after he left the Office of Economic Opportunity, was given leave from the UAW to run the centers, and he secured funding—$375,000 for the first year—from the Ford Foundation.[19]

Paul Schrade developed a parallel program in the Los Angeles ghetto of Watts. In 1965, shortly after that area was devastated by the decade's first major urban riot, Schrade and his staff assistant Ted Hawkins created the Watts Community Labor Union (WCLU). Run by UAW members who lived in Watts and staffed by neighborhood residents, the WCLU developed a broad range of programs, including a summer camp, remedial education classes for preschoolers, a youth conservation corps, a neighborhood consumer complaint office, and a gas station. Begun with a treasury of $5.30, WCLU quickly became a national model. The Labor Department provided $375,000 to cover expenses, and national political figures, including Hubert Humphrey and Robert Kennedy, toured its headquarters.[20]

Jack Conway launched a similar program in the western Chicago ghettos of Lawndale and Garfield Park in 1966, after those communities experienced two days of rioting. The UAW had been supportive of SCLC's campaign in Chicago from its inception; the region's director, Robert Johnston, at one point offered King the use of a hundred full-time UAW organizers. King and Conway formalized the relationship in early 1966, when King asked the UAW for help in organizing Lawndale and Garfield Park. Acting as director of the AFL-CIO Industrial Union Department (IUD), a job he resumed after leaving the Johnson administration in late 1965, Conway attempted to establish a community union in the area, to be run by UAW members and staffed by civil rights activists associated with SCLC and local church groups. The community union began by organizing tenant groups and rent strikes, but it planned to link the group to the Model Cities program. The Lawndale project received no federal funding, but IUD contributed $5,000 a month to the project throughout 1966.[21]

Reuther turned his primary attention to the blighted inner city of Detroit, which he considered an ideal site for the proposed Model Cities program. Immediately after the White House task force had completed its draft of the legislation in late 1965, Reuther proposed that Detroit establish a nonprofit development authority to prepare the city's proposal for the Model Cities Program, to supplement forthcoming federal funds with private money, and to oversee any resulting programs. Within months, the mayor had set up the Metropolitan Detroit Citizens Development Authority (MDCDA), with Reuther as chairman, to oversee the rehabilitation of nine square miles in the middle of the city. The MDCDA board followed precisely the multipart planning model that the UAW had long advocated: seats on the board were divided among representatives of the city's business elite, its leading public institutions, and its governmental bodies. To help launch the development authority, Reuther contributed $100,000 in UAW funds and pledged another $1 million in seed money if each of the Big Three auto makers would do the same. "All the diverse elements that make up the Detroit power structure, once divided and pitted against each other," *Fortune* magazine proclaimed, "are being welded together in a remarkable synthesis."[22]

The UAW's programs were not quite as synthetic as they were credited with being. None of the UAW's training programs attempted to organize or address the needs of white workers; three of the four focused on African-Americans, the fourth on Mexican-Americans. Except for the Watts Community Labor Union, none of the UAW's ghetto initiatives gave the poor a say in setting policy. CCAP's training school maintained strict control over its operation, including the choice of trainees, the determination of curriculum, and the distribution of funds. IUD's Chicago campaign likewise was a top-down affair, its organizers all permanent staffers from IUD. In its original formulation, the MDCDA, similarly, had no representative from the targeted area or any other Detroit grass-roots organization.[23] It is tempting to dismiss such exclusion as liberal elitism, and to some extent the charge is justified. Yet the union leadership's belief that northern ghetto dwellers were not yet ready to become effective participants in the formal power structures of the Great Society was coupled with a determination to prepare them for that responsibility. "[I]f their membership on policy-making and governing boards is to have meaning, the poor must be skilled articulators and negotiators," Brendan Sexton argued. "If the poor cannot persuasively argue for their points of view, they cannot affect the policies of community action programs, and if they cannot affect policy, their presence will serve only as misleading 'window dressing.' " Before they could be equal partners in the Great Society, ghetto activists had to be trained and developed, something that each of the UAW's ghetto programs aimed to do. "You cannot superimpose leadership upon the poverty neighborhood," Reuther explained. "This leadership has got to come from among the poor themselves. Now we have to help them . . . develop their own leadership"[24]

The UAW's attempts to train the African-American poor had embedded within them a strong strain of social control, particularly after the 1965 Watts riot. Time and again UAW representatives argued that their programs would build "constructive" leadership in the inner cities. "No one is going to speak for the people of the ghettos . . . but those people themselves and they are at war with the establishment," Vice-President Douglas Fraser declared in January 1966. ". . . [T]he only way you can bring this around is to develop leadership from among their own." The UAW also believed, though, that by giving the poor the training they needed to participate effectively in the Great Society bureaucracy the union was expanding American democracy in a new and dramatic way and thus fulfilling the promise of the War on Poverty. Reuther made the point in the most powerful terms he could. "What we have really got to do," he told the union's executive board, "is to train people in the poor neighborhoods to do . . . what we did thirty years ago. . . . We developed the guys inside the factories who organized these factories. It is true there were people from the outside who helped us, but John Lewis didn't go into a single General Motors plant and Phil Murray didn't go into a single Chrysler plant. They worked from the outside and the guys in the plant did the job and that is what has got to be done with the poverty neighborhoods."[25]

However well intentioned, the UAW's ghetto programs suffered from a profound misperception of inner-city politics. The urban African-American poor did not lack for leadership; they simply lacked the single voice that the UAW's social democrats believed necessary to participate in formal political structures. Northern ghettos, in fact, had a plethora of often competing political organizations deeply rooted in the African-American experience, from NAACP moderates to Marxist activists, Christian millenarians to Black Muslims. In the mid-1960s, the most militant of these organizations, committed to black empowerment free of white manipulation and control, were on the ascendancy. When the UAW sought to expand the Great Society into the ghettos in 1965 and 1966, the union ran head on into grassroots organizations that considered the UAW's efforts to be little more than white imperialism.[26]

Drawing on a variety of political influences, ghetto militants rejected the nonviolent tactics and integrationist goals of the southern civil rights movement. White America, they insisted, was inherently racist and thus would never acquiesce in the genuine empowerment of African-Americans. The only real way for African-Americans to secure power was to seize it themselves. Ghetto militants offered no single program for achieving that power. For some, black empowerment could be won through the celebration of African-Americans' cultural traditions. Others called for black political and economic separation from white society. Still others hinted at violent racial confrontation. No matter what the particulars of their program, the militants agreed that working through the Great Society was pointless, since it could not, by definition, give African-Americans the independent political base they needed. As they delivered that message, they found that an increasing number of ghetto dwellers, particularly young African-Americans who had gained no tangible advantages from the southern civil rights movement, agreed.[27]

Throughout 1965 and 1966, the militants and their supporters waged a frontal assault on the UAW's ghetto programs. In Chicago, a coalition of grass-roots activists, joined by white community organizers associated with Saul Alinksy, condemned the UAW's community union for trying to put a black face on the white power structure. In Detroit, neighborhood militants, led by the city's foremost black nationalist, actively opposed the MDCDA as unrepresentative of and unresponsive to the black community. The most embarrassing confrontation occurred at the April 1966 convention of the Citizens Crusade against Poverty. Held at Washington's posh International Inn, the convention was designed to be a media event highlighting the emerging social democratic coalition. Both Hubert Humphrey and R. Sargent Shriver had been invited to speak; Bayard Rustin, Michael Harrington, and Robert Nathan, one of the principal authors of the "Triple Revolution," were to run workshops; and community activists had been invited as representatives of the poor. But at the climactic moment, Shriver's keynote address, the activists rose in protest. Every time Shriver tried to sepak, he was shouted down, until he finally walked off the stage, leaving the microphone to the protesters. Jack Conway, serving as Reuther's representative, announced that CCAP could not sanction proceedings of this kind, and the convention broke up in a shambles. In the hotel hall afterward, Conway was despondent. "I don't know where we go from here," he said. "They have turned on the people who wanted to help them."[28]

The rising tide of African-American militancy was not confined simply to ghetto politics. It also spread to the auto plants in 1965 and 1966, as black workers adopted an increasingly aggressive tone to challenge the institutional and personal racism that had long characterized factory life. Lack of documentation makes it impossible to detail the development in any depth, but even scattered evidence indicates that many African-Americans were no longer willing to suffer racial slurs, petty harassment, and union indifference. As in the past, some black workers took their complaints to the UAW International: four times as many African-Americans lodged complaints of racial intimidation with the UAW Fair Practices Department in 1966 as in 1964. It is highly likely that far more simply took matters into their own hands, confronting foremen or fellow workers who called them "nigger," refusing onerous work assignments that should have been given to white workers, and the like. In a few instances, the new militancy took an organized form similar to the shop floor activism that white workers had engaged in during the 1930s. In late 1966, eighteen black workers at the North American Aviation plant in Anaheim, California, staged a walkout to protest the company's discriminatory promotion policy, and early the next year five hundred black workers at the Ford plant in Mahwah, New Jersey, shut down the line for three days after a foreman called a worker a "black bastard." "The brothers," a participant said, "aren't going to take this shit any more."[29]

African-American militancy found its most powerful voice not in the ghettos of the North but in an organization that had been central to the civil rights triumphs of the early 1960s. In the months after the 1964 Mississippi Freedom Democratic Party conflict, the Student Nonviolent Coordinating Committee underwent a painful process of reevaluation. That process peaked in early 1966, when SNCC staffers replaced the group's long-time chairman, John Lewis, with a much more militant activist, Stokely Carmichael. Under Carmichael's direction, SNCC purged its white members, renounced nonviolence, and began building an independent African-American political base in the deep South. During a highly publicized protest march across Mississippi in mid-1966, Carmichael gave the new militancy a name: black power. Appearing before a crowd of six hundred black marchers, the new SNCC chairman delivered a diatribe against gradualism. "I ain't going to jail no more," he shouted. "What we gonna start saying now is 'black power.'" The electrifying speech won SNCC national press coverage, in the process introducing millions of white Americans to the rising tide of anger among black Americans.[30]

The UAW leadership was unsure what to make of the radical ferment that seemed to be sweeping through the black communities of the North and South. Emil Mazey, the officer most committed to class-based politics, favored a swift denunciation of any black activist who tried to divide Americans along racial lines. "[S]omebody ought to really muzzle this guy Carmichael," he told the UAW Executive Board in June 1966. "He is the most vicious guy . . . I've ever seen." Mazey's bitter reaction won him the support of the Executive Board's most conservative members. The Chicago regional director, Bob Johnston, for instance, urged the UAW to dissociate itself from any activity involving black militants, who, he hinted, were being funded by the People's Republic of China. Most progressives in the UAW hierarchy, by contrast, tried to explain rather than condemn the African-Americans' swing to the left. Leonard Woodcock urged "understanding" of black power. "As the Negro develops a pride of race," he argued, "we are going to get this kind of thing. I think we have to be rather delicate in how we react." Paul Schrade saw black power as a viable political movement with a "very important role" to play in civil rights advocacy. "I don't think the NAACP or King's group have the whole truth about what we ought to be doing," he said. Mildred Jeffrey thought it was essential to share power with the militants, particularly in the UAW's ghetto initiatives, "since people these days are almost totally suspicious and unbelieving of promises made by establishments."[31]

In the final analysis, though, it did not matter whether or not the UAW leadership came to terms with the black power movement. African-American militants, it was clear, had no intention of coming to terms with the UAW or any other member of the liberal power structure, a stunning rejection of the coalition that a few years before had promised to refashion American politics. Walter Reuther simply could not understand what had happened. "Well, we know that political power is an essential part of changing the world," he said in bewilderment, "but if you are part of a minority how do you expect, if you isolate yourself from the majority, ever to get access to political power? It seems to me that just common sense would say that you would want to belong to a broad coalition." Many blacks, though, did not think that the coalition had changed the world. "I dig what Stokely Carmichael said," a young black auto worker in Detroit told an acquaintance. "[W]hites appear to be friendly by passing a few laws, but my basic situation gets worse and worse. They don't really mean to change a thing."[32]

As the coalition's militants swung to the left in late 1965 and 1966, the coalition's moderate wing moved to the right, pulling with it both Congress and the White House. George Meany and the AFL-CIO leadership served as the best symbol of the shift. Never comfortable with African-American activism, Meany vigorously attacked the rising militancy in black communities. He publicly condemned the black power movement as "the antithesis of democracy," and in late 1966 he threatened to withdraw the AFL-CIO from the Leadership Conference on Civil Rights unless SNCC were expelled, a move that would have crippled the lobbying organization. Meany's primary concern, however, was not the civil rights movement but the Vietnam War. Convinced that the United States was in Southeast Asia "because we have an obligation to be there," Meany was determined to put the AFL-CIO's considerable weight squarely behind the war.[33]

Meany first attempted to put the federation on record in support of the war at the December 1965 AFL-CIO convention. Early in the proceedings, he circulated a draft resolution criticizing the "tiny but noisy minority" opposed to the war and pledging "our unstinting support for all measures the administration might deem necessary" to defeat "Communist aggression in Vietnam." When Reuther objected to the tone of the resolution, which clashed with the UAW's more measured response, Meany backtracked slightly, adding a paragraph praising the administration's efforts to secure a negotiated settlement. The AFL-CIO president was not willing to temper his opposition to antiwar protesters, however. Late in the convention, a group of activists seated in the auditorium's balcony rose to protest the federation's support for the war. Meany ordered the sergeant at arms to remove the "kookies" from the hall. Meany hardened the AFL-CIO's position eight months later. Meeting in August 1966, the federation's executive council redrafted its position, eliminating the call for negotiations and, over Reuther's objections, condemning protesters for "aiding the Communist enemy of our country at the very moment that it is bearing the heaviest burdens in the defense of world peace and freedom."[34]

To many observers, the AFL-CIO's hawkishness fairly reflected the mood among blue-collar Americans, who were likewise shifting to the right. In fact, the growing conservatism of the white working class was rooted in a complex of factors that extended far beyond, and at times clashed with, George Meany's simplistic anticommunism. In large part, the swing against the the administration was racial. Many white workers were horrified by northern African-Americans' assertiveness, and they were incensed by what they perceived to be the rising cost of the administration's social programs. The white working class was not overwhelmingly hawkish, however. To be sure, many workers were angered by the New Left's increasingly strident rhetoric, but they were also angered by Johnson's handling of the war, which they did not uniformly support. In response, white workers lashed out at both the activists and the Democrats.[35]

The anger spread through the UAW's white rank and file with particular ferocity, fueled by a volatile mixture of racism, economic self-interest, and patriotism. Racial attitudes, long the fundamental fault line in the UAW, hardened first. As early as 1965 32 percent of white auto workers thought the civil rights movement was moving too quickly. By the late spring 1967, the sentiment had shifted upward markedly. According to an independent poll commissioned by the UAW International, half of white rank and filers opposed further integration.[36]

Since at least the 1930s, many white auto workers had feared that the advancement of blacks threatened their economic and social positions. As the pace of shop-floor integration picked up in the mid-1960s, those fears intensified. Again, evidence of such sentiment is spotty, but three incidents illustrate the mood in at least some shops. White workers in the St. Louis Chevrolet plant placed a can of shoe polish on the assembly line, next to a sign reading, "Paint your face black and you can get anything." A white worker at Dodge Main charged that his black committeeman had denied him the chance to upgrade because of his race. White workers at the Ford plant in Ypsilanti, Michigan spread racist newspapers throughout the plant and even burned a cross on the factory lawn to protest black "aggressiveness."[37] Many white rank and filers also feared that further African-American activism posed a direct threat to their homes and families. According to the 1965 study, white rank and filers were most opposed to the integration of their neighborhoods, which they believed would depress property values and disrupt "the safety and tranquility of" the area. That summer's Watts riot and the next summer's conflagrations dramatically heightened and broadened those fears. If riots continued in the summer of 1967, the UAW's pollsters warned in the spring of that year, white hostility could skyrocket far beyond the 50 percent level at which it then stood.[38]

As the white rank and file's fears of the ghetto mounted, so too did their frustration with the Vietnam War. Contrary to the popular perception, auto workers did not consistently support the war. Fifty one percent of Michigan union members polled in June 1966 favored a negotiated settlement to the conflict, and 19 percent of union families favored immediate withdrawal. The next spring, 54 percent of UAW rank and filers preferred a negotiated settlement or immediate withdrawal to the status quo. Those numbers were in marked contrast to national trends, which showed close to 60 percent of Americans favoring an escalation of the war. "On the whole," the 1967 pollsters concluded, "UAW members are considerably more dovelike today than is the electorate as a whole."[39]

The rank and file's dovishness is not particularly surprising. By the mid-1960s the working class's commitment to the Cold War had all but disappeared: only 1 percent of auto workers polled in 1967 considered communism a menace to the nation. The working class, moreover, bore the brunt of the fighting in Southeast Asia, since they did not have access to the draft deferments available to college students. To many workers, Vietnam must have seemed both unnecessary and unfair, an elite adventure whose price they were forced to pay. Auto workers' dovishness, however, did not translate into support for the antiwar movement. For the most part, a vast cultural chasm separated rank and filers from the protesters. Many auto workers, particularly those of Eastern European heritage, were appalled by the New Leftists' often strident anti-Americanism, which so clearly clashed with the workers' own profound patriotism. Many rank and filers were angered, moreover, by the protesters' rejection of the material standards workers had struggled to secure and by the privileges the protesters seemed to enjoy. "We can't understand how all those rich kids—the kids with the beads from the fancy suburbs—how they get off [military service] when my son has to go over there and maybe get his head shot off," a worker told a UAW staffer.[40]

Together, white rank and filers' positions in opposition to African-American activism, the Vietnam War, and the antiwar protesters undermined their tenuous commitment to the coalition that Johnson had fashioned in 1964, pushing them to the right. The movement first manifested itself in the 1966 midterm elections, when the Democrats' share of the UAW vote dropped by 10 percent from the 1964 totals. In some key states the drop was even more dramatic. Johnson had won 72 percent of the UAW vote in Illinois in 1964; two years later, the Democratic candidate for senator, the UAW's long-standing ally Paul Douglas, managed to win only 48 percent of the UAW vote, a drop that the UAW's pollsters believed "contributed enormously" to his defeat. The rank-and-file vote in California was in the long run more important. California UAW members had given LBJ 77 percent of their vote in 1964. In 1966, Ronald Reagan, running for governor as the champion of fiscal and cultural conservatism, carried 49 percent of the UAW vote.[41]

White auto workers were also turning against the president and his programs by the spring of 1967. Sixty-eight percent of African-American auto workers polled that year approved of Johnson's job performance, compared to 46 percent of white auto workers. LBJ's support slipped more dramatically in auto towns dominated by white rural migrants: only 38 percent of UAW members in Flint, for instance, approved of his performance. White auto workers clearly expected to express their anger with LBJ in the next year's election. Only 56 percent of auto workers polled in the spring of 1967 said they would vote for Johnson in 1968, a precipitous drop from the 85 percent of the UAW vote he had received in 1964, while 27 percent of UAW members claimed they would vote for Richard Nixon. Were the 1968 presidential race to become a three-way contest, a startling 20 percent of white rank and filers claimed they would vote for George Wallace. Auto workers were particularly incensed by the administration's taxation and spending policies, which they ranked first among their concerns in the 1967 poll. Their anger was not without some basis. As the White House introduced new social programs and, more important, escalated the war in 1965 and 1966, it gradually increased the tax burden on the working class. In 1965, a typical UAW family with two children retained 88.7 percent of their gross income after paying federal taxes. The next year, the figure dropped to 87 percent, and the year after that to 86.6 percent. At the same time, the administration's spending fueled a gradual rise in inflation, from 3.4 percent in 1965 to 5 percent in 1966. Those were small losses compared to the genuine economic fear that had cut through the rank and file in the late 1950s and early 1960s. In combination with the deep-seated racism of many white auto workers, however, the mounting tax burden dramatically weakened their thirty-year perception of the Democratic Party as the party of the "common man." By linking race and poverty in the early days of the War on Poverty, the administration had created in the Great Society a dangerous fault line that now seemed to be breaking wide open.[42]

The mounting white opposition to the administration had a profound effect on Washington, invigorating congressional conservatives who had been thoroughly cowed by the Johnson landslide in 1964. They took the offensive as early as mid-1966, slashing appropriations by nearly $150 million for the most experimental portion of the War on Poverty, the UAW's beloved Community Action Program. Late in the year, the powerful chairman of the House Ways and Means Committee, Wilbur Mills, stepped up the attack, demanding that the administration cut domestic spending further to help pay the spiraling cost of the Vietnam War.[43] Ever the consensus politician, Johnson moved to appease the resurgent right, just as he had moved to appease the coalition of conscience in 1963. Convinced that conservatives would eviscerate his programs if South Vietnam fell to communism, LBJ continued to escalate the war throughout 1966, intensifying the bombing of North Vietnam and adding over 200,000 ground troops to the South. The president also began reducing his domestic agenda. Hoping to "cool off" inflation, he proposed a 10 percent tax surcharge on individual and corporate incomes, and he announced an immediate cut of $1.5 billion in federal spending. The ax fell particularly hard on the administration's anti-poverty programs. The Office of Economic Opportunity had requested an appropriation of $3.5 billion for the 1967 fiscal year, but in his budget message to Congress, Johnson asked for only half that amount.[44]

For Walter Reuther, the administration's retreat from social reform was a brutal blow, far worse than the mounting militancy of the New Left and the black power advocates. He had invested so much in the president's initiatives—his vision of a social democratic breakthrough, his dreams of political power—and in return he had risked his moral authority as a spokesman for the left wing of American liberalism. Now Johnson seemed to be abandoning the fight to align himself with the nation's rightward shift. At first Reuther tried to deny what was happening. "[I]t is now obvious," he said in early 1966, ". . . that President Johnson is not going to use the argument that because we have a war in Vietnam . . . we ought to have a moratorium on the programs of the Great Society." By September 1966, however, the trend could not be denied. "Now some are saying we have to accept higher levels of unemployment to ease inflationary pressure," Reuther complained in private. "Now they do not suggest that we cut the budget for Vietnam. That kind of war budget they are quite willing to increase. It is the budget to wage war against poverty that they would like to slash."[45]

To offset such demands, Reuther launched a counteroffensive against the rightward shift, repeatedly calling on the White House to expand domestic spending. In April, Reuther charged that Congress was taking an "eye dropper" approach to fighting poverty. The next month he argued that the Great Society had been "applying poultices and palliatives to a deep sickness and raging contagion" in American society. Reuther also peppered the president with memos calling for more, not less, economic stimulation, and vigorously opposing any proposed tax increase, which, the UAW president insisted, would "unbalance" the economy and increase unemployment.[46] At first the Johnson administration welcomed Reuther's demands. "It is probably good for us to be exposed to this criticism from the left as a counter-balance to equally one sided attacks from the right," Gardner Ackley of the Council of Economic Advisers wrote LBJ. As the president came to feel more and more embattled in 1966, however, he increasingly bridled at the UAW's public statements. After one CCAP broadside against spending cuts, Johnson ordered Joseph Califano to contact the CCAP board "and tell them to cut this stuff out." By December, Johnson's aides were dismissing Reuther's criticisms as "misleading" and his fiscal suggestions as "unreasonable."[47]

Even as the White House turned against him, Reuther refused to blame Johnson either for the domestic retreat or for the war that had triggered it. The President "is in a very difficult position," he told the UAW Executive Board in January 1967. "No president . . . has ever waged a war of this dimension . . . and at the same time was committed to a domestic program that was as ambitious and fundamental as the Great Society program."[48] By then, though, it was no longer clear that Johnson was committed to that domestic agenda. Forced by the resurgent right to choose between guns and butter, he had chosen guns.

Already in tatters, the national fabric gave way in 1967. Early that year, more and more liberals, appalled by the polarization of American political life, broke with the president. The liberal revolt, in turn, infused the antiwar movement with a new intensity. In the course of a long, hot summer, more American cities went up in flames, and in the riots' wake, the white backlash intensified. The crisis struck the UAW in the most personal of ways. For the first time since the mid-1940s, the union leadership itself threatened to splinter, as some of Reuther's closest advisers rebelled against the UAW's support for Vietnam. Detroit, the UAW's Model City, experienced the worst of the summer violence. By year's end, the coalition of conscience was dead, destroyed by the anarchy in the streets.

Lyndon Johnson was stunned by the liberal revolt, convinced that it reflected the liberals' longstanding distrust of his leadership. It was more fundamental than that, however. Throughout his career, Johnson had been committed to maintaining consensus through the pursuit of interest group politics at home and anticommunism abroad. The Great Society and the Vietnam War followed those policy paths precisely. But instead of building consensus, the administration's domestic and foreign policy programs had widened national divisions. By 1967, consequently, some liberals began to question the premises on which the administration rested.[49]

The liberal revolt was an inchoate movement in 1967. It cut across generational lines, embracing some of those who had helped to define the post–New Deal liberal order two decades earlier, such as Arthur Schlesinger Jr., and activists who had come of age in the early 1960s, such as thirty-six-year-old Allard Lowenstein. It had no organizational expression, such as ADA had provided liberals in the late 1940s, and it was driven by anger and frustration rather than by a coherent program. Even in the revolt's early stages, however, it was possible to discern its core beliefs. For two years the liberal doves had been insisting that the administration had been mistaken to view Vietnam as a proving ground for American resolve. Now the liberal rebels increasingly argued that the Vietnam War was not simply an error but rather the "bitter heritage" of a flawed foreign policy. Containment might have made sense in the late 1940s, they said, but the world had changed. Communism was no longer the monolithic threat American policy makers had once assumed it to be, and a foreign policy that clung to that assumption wasted national resources and national will in a dangerous "universalism." As they rejected one of the fundamental premises of the postwar order, many of the liberal rebels tried to extend another of its premises. For all of the Great Society's promise, they contended, it had not gone far enough in meeting the needs of the nation's interest groups. The federal government had to do more to solve the problems of the ghetto, the liberal rebels said, and the Democratic Party had to do more to incorporate African-Americans, Hispanics, women, and the young into the political process, within policy circles and the party's inner councils.[50]

The complexity of the nascent liberal revolt was masked in early 1967 as the rebels focused their criticism on the Vietnam War. The *New York Times* launched the attack in late December 1966, when it published a blistering series of reports from the front detailing the brutality of the American bombing campaign and questioning its effectiveness. In January, Allard Lowenstein began a grass-roots campaign to "dump Johnson" as the head of the Democratic ticket in 1968. In February, LBJ's bête noir, Robert Kennedy, condemned "the horror" the United States was inflicting on Vietnam. In April, Martin Luther King Jr., already on record against the war, condemned American policy as "a sordid military undertaking" that drained federal funds from the War on Poverty. And in May, Americans for Democratic Action essentially endorsed Lowenstein's efforts by pledging to support any candidate in 1968 "who offers genuine hope of restraint" in Southeast Asia.[51]

Reuther steadfastly refused to join the liberal opposition to the war. As the dissent grew, however, he changed his justification for supporting the administration's policies. The UAW, he repeatedly told his staffers, was heading into a very tough bargaining round with the Big Three auto makers. The mid-decade boom in auto sales had led Big Three managers to increase the pace of production in their plants, and many factory hands, exhausted and demoralized, were demanding that the union win them some relief. UAW bargainers, moreover, hoped to use the 1967 negotiations to transform supplemental unemployment benefits into the guaranteed annual wage the UAW leadership had sought for over a decade. With such a broad agenda on the table, Reuther insisted, the union simply could not afford to break with the administration as long as the negotiations lasted. Reuther was undoubtedly correct on a tactical level. His loyalty paid off handsomely in June, when Johnson promised the UAW president "a green light to strike [the auto companies] for the rest of the summer" if in return Reuther would quickly settle a UAW strike against a Connecticut aircraft plant that threatened to cut the supply of helicopters going to Vietnam. Armed with the president's pledge, the UAW struck the Ford Motor Company in September, its first strike against Ford since the 1940s, winning added time away from the job and an increase in SUB that ensured laid-off workers 97 percent of their take-home pay.[52]

Reuther's pragmatism heightened the frustration of the UAW's doves, who considered it an abdication of the union's moral responsibility. Nat Weinberg captured the mounting anger in an April memo to Reuther. "The UAW has consistently opposed escalation of the war in Vietnam. But escalation continues," he wrote. "I am . . . aware of the many factors inhibiting UAW action. Nevertheless, I do feel deeply that we are obliged to search for some means whereby we can contribute, even in a small way, to avoidance of a catastrophe that could make meaningless everything to which we have devoted our lives." Jack Conway likewise attacked Reuther's caution by pointedly reminding the UAW president of his own rhetoric. The job of the labor movement, Conway argued in early 1967, "is to dissent, express dissatisfaction, to create restlessness—and out of dissent . . . to fashion an economic and social order that is better than the existing one." Paul Schrade publicly assailed Reuther's position at the Executive Board meeting in January. "[O]ur protests and our proposals," he said, "ought to be voiced in such a way that we begin reversing the Johnson administration, whose policies are having a very negative effect . . . on workers. . . . We cannot reverse the downward trend of the Democratic party, whether it is the president or the Congress, unless we begin protesting some of the things the Johnson administration is doing."[53]

The most brutal attack on Reuther came not from his advisers, but from their children. Every year Walter, Roy Reuther, and their wives attended Irving Bluestone's Passover seder. In 1967, Irving's son Barry and his girlfriend, Leonard Woodcock's daughter Leslie, used the opportunity to read antiwar poems by the World War I poet Wilfred Owen, interspersing excerpts from a Martin Luther King speech criticizing the war. When they were finished, the UAW president turned to them and said, "I take it that was aimed at me." He then explained that while he agreed that the war was wrong, he could not afford to break with the president during contract talks. "Leslie was taking all of this in," Barry Bluestone remembers.

> She turned to Walter and said, "You really said that, didn't you?" And Walter said, "What did I say?" And Leslie became just as angry as I ever saw her. Her face was flushed with anger. "You really said that. You really said that." And Walter, frustrated, asked again, "What did I say?" Leslie turned to him and said, "What are you trying to do, maybe get eighty cents an hour in the pay envelope, five cents here, five cents there? You're telling me that you are unwilling to make a statement that may save fifty thousand lives or one hundred lives or maybe a million lives because you want to get fifty cents more in your goddam fucking contract. . . . That's the most inhumane thing I have ever heard in my life."[54]

Bluestone does not report Reuther's response, but it is difficult to imagine that he was not deeply hurt. For a quarter century he had seen himself as a driving moral force in American politics, certainly attuned to pragmatism but never consumed by it. Now, in the midst of the postwar United States' greatest moral dilemma, even those closest to him were accusing him of abandoning his principles. As the pressure on him increased, Reuther found a proxy for the president, someone he could attack with all the scorn that the doves were now heaping on Johnson. He targeted his long-time rival, the AFL-CIO president, George Meany. The conflict actually began in May 1966, when Victor Reuther told a *Los Angeles Times* reporter that the AFL-CIO had been acting as a front for the CIA in developing nations. The confrontation escalated the next month, when Meany ordered the AFL-CIO to withdraw from an international labor organization that Reuther had long supported. The UAW president immediately condemned the walk-out as "unwise" and "undemocratic." Believing that the Reuther brothers had acted in concert, Meany struck back. At the August 1966 AFL-CIO Executive Board meeting, he pushed through a resolution censuring Victor for his accusations and, when Walter was out of the room, a motion on

Vietnam far more hawkish than the UAW's official position. Reuther immediately condemned the statement as "intemperate, hysterical, and jingoistic," by far his most vocal criticism of the war's advocates.[55]

Meany and Reuther had waged such bureaucratic warfare before, of
course, but this time Reuther quickly escalated the conflict. In February
1967 he resigned from the AFL-CIO Executive Council, claiming that the
federation had "lost its drive, its sense of purpose, its sense of social idealism," that it advanced few new ideas and made no effort to promote social
change. Reuther pressed the attack over the next few months, labeling
Meany a "custodian of the status quo" and charging that the federation
was "stagnant and vegetating." Those accusations could just as easily have
been leveled against the increasingly conservative Lyndon Johnson.[56]

There is no evidence to indicate that Reuther consciously intended his
criticism of Meany as a slap at LBJ, but the president's political advisers and
other observers interpreted Reuther's remarks that way. "I have been
following Walter Reuther's activities very closely in the last few months and
think I have a pretty good fix on his intentions," John Roche wrote the
president in February. "Reuther has made the decision that Bobby [Ken-
nedy] is . . . the wave of the future. And Reuther is busily setting up what
amounts to a parallel political movement which . . . will disassociate itself
from the administration and the 'labor establishment.' " It was a ludicrous
charge, more a manifestation of the administration's paranoia than a reflection of reality. LBJ took it to heart, however, and increasingly distanced
himself from Reuther. The president and Reuther had had thirteen conversations in 1966; the next year, the pair spoke five times, and only once after
midsummer. Johnson, it seemed, no longer intended to return the loyalty
that Reuther was sacrificing so much to maintain.[57]

As troubling as they were, the political conflicts of the winter and spring
paled in comparison with the summer's agonizing explosion of violence.
Many observers predicted that the rioting that had plagued the nation's
inner cities since 1965 would continue in 1967, but few expected it to take
on such intensity. Three cities experienced major disturbances in the first
six months of the year. Five days of rioting in Newark, New Jersey, in mid-
July left twenty people dead. Less than a week later, on July 23, a minor
incident in Detroit's Near West Side ghetto, a routine police raid of an after-
hours bar, triggered the worst civil disorder of the twentieth century to date.
By week's end, 43 Detroiters had been killed, over 1,000 had been injured,
5,000 left homeless, and over 7,000 arrested. Officials estimated that as
many as 1,000 buildings had been destroyed, 2,500 businesses looted, and
$134 million in property damaged. "It looks like Berlin in 1945," Mayor
Jerome Cavanagh lamented as he toured the riot scene.[58]

In retrospect, the Detroit riot was predictable. Despite the Great Society's expansive promises, many of the city's African-Americans remained locked in poverty. Detroit's largely white police force had earned a reputation for brutality in the ghetto, and the city's vocal black power advocates had fueled the flames of discontent. At the time, though, many of the nation's liberals were stunned that Detroit, the center of Great Society activism, could fall victim to such devastation. "For years," the *Washington Post* editorialized as the city burned, "Detroit has been the American model of intelligence and courage applied to the governance of a huge industrial city." Now the city's poor had rejected that model, the UAW's model, in the most violent of ways. Some UAW supporters simply shook their heads in disbelief. "What a bitter tragedy has befallen Detroit," Jacob Clayman of the AFL-CIO Industrial Union Department wrote Reuther on July 25, the same day federal troops took up positions in the city. Others were harsher in their evaluations. "Detroit is a symbol of UAW power," Evelyn Dubrow, the International Ladies Garment Workers' Washington representative and a long-time Reuther associate, told a reporter. "So you say, all right, here was a chance where the programs were Walter's and he had had a chance to make decisions. . . . Yet even with all his thinking ahead [he] is not able to conceive this would happen. . . . I'm not blaming him, but it shows there is a flaw in his program."[59]

Reuther did not see the riot in those terms. On the contrary, in the riot's wake he launched a broad-based effort to revive the coalition of conscience, convinced that it alone could meet such a profound crisis. Days after calm was restored in Detroit, the UAW joined with the National Conference of Mayors to launch the Urban Coalition, which brought together eight hundred of the nation's most powerful figures, including Henry Ford II, David Rockefeller, and other businessmen; union leaders; civil rights activists such as Martin Luther King and A. Philip Randolph; and the mayors of New York, Detroit, and other major cities. The coalition adopted a sweeping agenda, urging Congress to build one million low-cost housing units and, at Reuther's insistence, to create one million new jobs. "We have the resources to [rebuild the nation's cities]," Reuther told the coalition's inaugural meeting. "We have the technological know-how. What is lacking is the sense of national purpose."[60]

The UAW took an even more active role in trying to rebuild the reform coalition in Detroit. Immediately after the riot, Reuther grandly pledged that 60,000 UAW members would volunteer to clean up the most hard-hit areas of the city, and he threw the union's support to a Detroit version of the Urban Coalition, the New Detroit Committee. Reuther hoped that New Detroit would not simply lobby for more money for the ghetto but also channel the resources of the city's power structure into the poorest neigh-borhoods. Accordingly, he transformed the Metropolitan Detroit Com-munity Development Association into New Detroit's development wing, responsible for building low-cost housing and encouraging new housing technology. Reuther wasted no time in getting projects under way. In Au-gust 1967 the city sold a 192-acre site on Detroit's lower east side to MDCDA, and by November Reuther had secured funding, including $100,000 in UAW funds, for a 352-unit housing development, with a nur-sery school and kindergarten on each block. In October the UAW president announced a demonstration project of forty to sixty prefabricated units to showcase experimental construction methods.[61]

At the same time, the UAW and its associates in New Detroit reached out to the black community. Both MDCDA and New Detroit invited grass-roots organizations and black militant groups to participate in their deliberations, believing that they had to do so if the power structure was to have any meaningful dialogue with the disenfranchised. The UAW and the Big Three auto makers also launched a joint effort to provide factory jobs for inner-city African-Americans. Ford set aside 6,500 new jobs in its plants for the hard-core unemployed, then established recruiting centers in the inner city to process applications. Chrysler went a step further. When the auto maker found that many of its new recruits could not read, it hired fifty high school teachers to tutor them, and it provided alarm clocks to new hires who had trouble getting to work on time.[62]

Three years earlier, such innovative and vigorous programs probably would have won widespread support. In the increasingly polarized politics of mid-1967, they ran into a phalanx of opposition. The Johnson admin-istration strenuously objected to the Urban Coalition, which the president believed was setting unreasonably high goals, and he was stung by Reu-ther's criticism of the White House's lack of commitment to urban reform. George Meany, distrustful of any organization in which Reuther was ac-tive, initially refused to join the coalition. Once he had decided to do so, he threatened to withdraw when Reuther proposed that the group hold its first conclave on the fourth anniversary of the 1963 March on Washington. Some liberal activists scoffed at the UAW's attempt to rebuild American cities from the top down rather than the bottom up. Reuther "continues to live in the suburbs with the establishment," a Michigan Democrat wrote in a private memo, while his union "continues to speak out publicly on behalf of the Democratic party with which it is gradually losing touch." The coalition's corporate members objected to Reuther's call for a million new jobs, which went down to defeat on Capitol Hill in November.[63]

The UAW's efforts in Detroit, meanwhile, simply heightened the city's racial tension. Black militants, for their part, generally scoffed at the union's overtures. At one New Detroit meeting, an eighteen-year-old African-American activist, Norvel Harrington, pointed at Henry Ford II and General Motors president James Roche and said, "The trouble with you fat cats is that you don't know what's going on." Ford and Roche said nothing, but Reuther shot back, "You listen to me. We're going to need help and its going to have to come from these men you're calling 'fat cats.'" After the meeting, Harrington told the press, "Reuther doesn't dig me and I don't dig him. . . . What he says about me doesn't mean a damn thing."[64]

Many white workers, by contrast, saw the UAW leadership's efforts to revive the reform coalition as nothing less than appeasement. "Now Reuther," a white rank and filer from the Dodge Main plant complained, "all he keeps talking about is the colored. They shoot and burn down half the town, and he wants us to go clean it up. They say if they don't get jobs they're gonna riot some more, so what do the government do? It gives 'em jobs out at the [Ford] Rouge [plant] and places like that. . . . And who's gonna pay for it all? Me." Many white workers expressed their anger and fear in less vocal but more devastating ways: the pace of white flight from the city accelerated dramatically in the second half of 1967 and the sale of guns skyrocketed. By late in the year, the UAW's dilemma had become obvious. "We all know we are in trouble with whites . . . ," Mildred Jeffrey wrote an associate, "[and] with blacks on white failure to deliver."[65]

As if the polarization of its core constituencies were not troubling enough, the strain within the UAW leadership mounted as the union's doves made their opposition to the war increasingly public. Both the New Left and the liberal antiwar activists accelerated their protests in the summer and autumn. Drawing on SNCC's 1964 example, New Leftists organized a Vietnam Summer, centered on local protests and organized draft resistance. In October a broad range of activists joined in a massive March on the Pentagon, which drew over 100,000 protesters to Washington, D.C. Liberal sentiment against the war also grew, extending by autumn into the administration itself, where Secretary of Defense Robert McNamara began urging restraint. Allard Lowenstein and his supporters, meanwhile, continued to build grass-roots support for their plan to deny Lyndon Johnson the Democratic nomination in 1968.[66]

As antiwar sentiment gathered momentum, several of the UAW's strongest doves finally broke with the union's position in favor of the war, throwing their support behind a movement that the UAW still officially opposed. Again Paul Schrade adopted the most radical stand, speaking at the founding rally of The Resistance, the New Left's effort to promote draft resistance. Others chose instead to align themselves with the liberal activists.

Joseph Rauh took the lead, arguing through the summer that instead of trying to block LBJ's renomination in 1968, in his view an effort sure to be defeated, liberals should work to write a peace plank into the party's platform. Working under the name Negotiate Now! Rauh and his supporters, including Victor Reuther, persuaded Americans for Democratic Action to endorse their proposal at its September board meeting.[67]

Victor Reuther and Emil Mazey made the most dramatic break with the UAW's official position in November, when they joined five hundred other labor and liberal activists at the founding session of the Labor Assembly for Peace. Mazey, by then a well-known critic of the war, cosponsored the assembly, which attracted some of the nation's foremost doves along with representatives of the mostly left-wing unions that had come out against the war. Mazey opened the assembly with a ringing defense of dissent. "I believe the greatest patriots of our country are those who have the courage to speak out," he said. "It is not the cry for an honorable peace that endangers our boys but the steady escalation of the war." Victor Reuther followed the next day with a scathing condemnation of the AFL-CIO's "obsession with anti-communism," which, he charged, had led it into "open collaboration" with antidemocratic governments. Such remarks won the group widespread attention as evidence of the antiwar movement's growing reach. "Labor's newly organized doves," reads a typical report in the *Wall Street Journal*, "threaten to put a crack in one of the staunchest underpinnings of President Johnson's war policies." That, of course, was precisely the message the UAW doves had hoped to send.[68]

That message was quickly eclipsed by Allard Lowenstein, who, after months of fruitless searching, found a spokesman for his "dump Johnson" movement. On November 30, 1967, Senator Eugene McCarthy of Minnesota announced that he would challenge LBJ for the Democratic nomination in 1968, running as the party's peace candidate. Few in the UAW inner circle were impressed. McCarthy, they knew, was a lackluster candidate with no popular base of support. Two key UAW staffers nevertheless joined the McCarthy insurgency: Mildred Jeffrey quietly began building bridges to the senator, while Rauh, his Negotiate Now! strategy suddenly overshadowed, publicly endorsed the campaign. Rauh then joined with his fellow ADA officials in moving that organization, for so long the flagship of American liberalism, toward an endorsement that was to be issued at the group's next board meeting, in January 1968.[69]

Walter Reuther seemed stunned by the growing rebellion in his ranks, unsure whether to crush it or join it. In an appearance on *Meet the Press* in late September he made his first hesitant break with the president, calling for a unilateral halt to the U.S. bombing campaign. He immediately undercut the statement, however, by announcing that he favored Johnson over any other current candidate for the presidency in 1968. In November he informed his staff that the UAW "would have no truck with any 'dump Johnson' movement," and he threatened to withdraw the UAW from ADA if it endorsed McCarthy. He did not, however, stop Mildred Jeffrey from meeting with McCarthy, although he knew she was doing so.[70] Reuther also lashed out at his staffers for their activism. Schrade told a reporter in 1968 that he had been "on the carpet a couple of times for speeches I've made [on Vietnam]. . . . He [Reuther] warns me, 'You can't keep doing this because it's embarrassing to me. . . .' " Rauh likewise recalled Reuther's anger at his and Victor's outspokenness. "Walter was not happy with Vic's dovishness," he explained years later. "He called Vic and me a couple of ypsils one day. . . . He'd bawl me and Vic out together. . . ." At other times, Reuther seemed jealous of his staffers' moral self-assurance on the war. "Vietnam is a very complicated problem," Reuther admitted in a revealing moment. ". . . I wish God would give somebody the wisdom to say with absolute certainty, 'This is the right position.' I wish somebody had that kind of Divine wisdom."[71]

Such wisdom seemed more elusive than ever as 1967 came to a close. In two short years, Reuther's vision of a grand reform coalition dedicated to social democratic change had crumbled. The New Left that the UAW had nurtured now condemned his union as a prop for the status quo; the president he had supported unconditionally had distanced himself from the UAW; large sections of the union's rank and file had swung to the right; the city that he had hoped to make a model of urban rehabilitation had been devastated by rioting; and even some of his most trusted friends and advisers were implicitly questioning his moral courage. It was an agonizing time. And in the new year it would only get worse.

[10]

Things Fall Apart

On November 16, 1967, Walter, Victor, and Roy Reuther received word that their father, Valentine, was dying. They immediately rushed to Wheeling, West Virginia, the home they had left forty years earlier. There, with their mother, brother Ted, and sister Christine, they recreated the *Volksverein* of their youth, standing around their father's bed, softly singing German folk songs. Valentine momentarily managed a smile, Victor recalled, and then he was gone. Two months later, in the early morning of January 10, 1968, fifty-eight-year-old Roy Reuther suffered a minor heart attack. His wife, Fania, wanted to call an ambulance but he insisted that they drive to the hospital themselves. On the way he had a second, major attack. He was dead before they reached the emergency room.[1]

The deaths of his father and brother were deeply personal losses for Walter Reuther, but they were also symbolic of his political crisis in early 1968. Valentine had instilled in Walter the principles on which he had built his political career: his commitment to social democratic change, his faith in the regenerative power of the labor movement, his driving moralism. Roy had served as Walter's practical political voice, quietly constructing the UAW's political machine, cementing the union's ties to the Democratic Party, promoting the UAW's and the party's agendas. The UAW president had always balanced Valentine's idealism and Roy's practicality, never more effectively than in the heady days of the mid-1960s, when he had helped to push liberalism to the left. Now those moorings were gone.

So were the political moorings to which Reuther had tied the UAW twenty years before. By early 1968 liberalism had all but collapsed under the assault of the New Left and the resurgent right. In the face of this crisis, the liberal community itself unraveled. Lyndon Johnson and his supporters clung to the verities of the postwar era: a commitment to piecemeal reform at home and containment abroad. Under the pressure of a presidential campaign, meanwhile, the liberal revolt began to take on a coherent and powerful shape, and suddenly challenged Johnson for control of the Democratic Party.[2]

Plunged into "a state of physical shock" by the loss of Valentine and Roy, Walter responded to the liberal schism with a profound and uncharacteristic ambivalence, vacillating between the two factions. The other social democrats among the UAW leaders were determined to put the UAW behind the liberal revolt. Throughout Roy Reuther's funeral service, Jack Conway commiserated with Robert Kennedy, who was then considering challenging Johnson for the Democratic presidential nomination. "We stood side by side for about two or three hours," Conway recalled. "And we . . . talk[ed] about how bad the country was off and how there was simply no way to deal through the present institutional structure, that everything was stacked against progress and change and so on, and that what really was required was breaking the whole thing wide open." Conway decided that day that Kennedy would in fact run against Johnson and that when he did, Conway would support him.[3]

Throughout the winter and spring of 1968, Reuther and the UAW's activists struggled for control of the union's political program, at times threatening to break the leadership apart. At last, in early summer, Reuther joined the activists. By then, however, American political life had become too polarized for new initiatives to have any chance of success. In the end, all the UAW leadership could manage was a desperate rear-guard effort to prevent the collapse of the postwar liberal order. And by the close of that turbulent and tragic year, even that effort had failed.

In January 1968 the liberal revolt against Lyndon Johnson was still largely unformed. The rebels were united in their opposition to the Vietnam War, and Allard Lowenstein had found the movement a presidential candidate, Eugene McCarthy, who entered the New Hampshire primary backed by an army of young organizers. McCarthy, however, was a tepid campaigner virtually unknown on the national stage, and as he trudged through the snow of New Hampshire he had virtually nothing to say about the nation's domestic crisis. The conventional political wisdom was that Johnson, backed by the awesome power of incumbency, simply could not be defeated.[4] Then, on January 31, 1968, the North Vietnamese launched their massive Tet offensive and suddenly the liberal challenge took on new vigor. In Tet's wake, a host of national voices, from the *Wall Street Journal* to Walter Cronkite, came out against the war, and thousands of ordinary citizens committed themselves to the McCarthy campaign. On February 10 the national board of Americans for Democratic Action joined the grass-roots effort, formally endorsing McCarthy. The Democratic voters of New Hampshire capped the effort four weeks later, giving McCarthy a stunning 42 percent of the vote in the state's primary, just 7 points short of LBJ's total. The growing revolt in turn strengthened more traditional liberals' ties to Johnson. Led by Gus Tyler of the ILGWU, liberal labor leaders in ADA defended LBJ against the insurgents' attack, as did some of postwar liberal-ism's greatest figures, such as Harry Truman and Leon Keyserling, and the party's strongest bosses, including Chicago's Richard Daley and New York's Frank O'Connor.[5]

Reuther responded to the schism with the same uncertainty that had marked his actions the previous year. Publicly he remained unequivocal in his support for LBJ. In mid-February he sent word through Hubert Humphrey that "the UAW is for President Johnson all the way," and in an early March press conference he reiterated his intention to vote for LBJ in the fall. Reuther also argued against the ADA's endorsement of McCarthy, charging that by supporting a candidate "with a single string in his political bow," ADA would transform itself into a "single-purpose organization" incapable of representing the range of liberal interests.[6] At the same time, Reuther could not bring himself to break with the doves. After the ADA endorsed McCarthy, the representatives of the United Steelworkers of America, the Communications Workers of America, and the ILGWU, act-ing at the White House's request, resigned from the organization. Reuther refused to join them, explaining that while he shared their anger with ADA, he could not sever "the liberal-labor coalition." In private he seemed almost envious of the liberal antiwar activists, particularly the young. "There are the students," he told the UAW Executive Board in early March. "They are no different than we were when we were young people. They see . . . a pretty ugly world and they say, 'These are the values you taught us, you are not living up to them. Why don't you live by these values?' So there is a great alienation and a great generation gap. The labor movement . . . has got to have the student movement. It has got to have the intellectual aca-demic world . . . the kind of forces that motivated guys to go to Mississippi to start the civil rights movement. We need more of that kind of dedication and basic commitment."[7]

Even in the UAW's conflict with the AFL-CIO, Reuther vacillated. At the March meeting of the Executive Board he launched a long diatribe against the federation leadership, condemning them in terms the New Left would have found familiar. "If the labor movement . . . is not a dynamic force that is challenging the status quo, where the status quo is unacceptable, where the status quo denies millions of Americans that measure of justice to which they are entitled," he insisted, "then the labor movement is nothing more than an extension of the business community. . . . That is precisely what the labor movement is becoming—an extension of the business community. . . . I believe, and I believe this very sincerely, that the AFL-CIO structurally is historically obsolete. It has little to do with America today. It has much to do with yesterday."[8] Reuther nevertheless resisted all suggestions that he withdraw the UAW from the AFL-CIO, arguing that to split the federation would cripple labor's political organization and undermine LBJ's chances of reelection. He therefore tried to delay action by demanding that the AFL-CIO call a special convention in December 1968 to consider a lengthy list of proposed reforms. If the federation rejected the reforms, he said the UAW would then disaffiliate. "Walter is playing seven-card stud, high-low, with Mr. Meany," a suspicious White House political aide wrote to Johnson shortly after Reuther issued his call for the December convention, "the last card coming face down on election day."[9]

Reuther's pained equivocations simply fueled the frustration of the UAW's doves, who after Tet grew increasingly vociferous in their condemnation of the union president's inaction. On February 5 Nat Weinberg sent Reuther that day's *Wall Street Journal* editorial questioning the wisdom of the war. In a scathing cover letter, Weinberg noted that the clipping was "one more addition to the . . . hundreds you have already seen documenting the nightmarish, destructive and dangerous futility of U.S. policy throughout East Asia," a policy that led Americans to "kill, maim, uproot, incarcerate in concentration camps, and demoralize and degrade the men, women, and children we claim to be defending." Paul Schrade turned Reuther's charges against the AFL-CIO back onto the UAW at the Executive Board meeting in March. "I think," he said, "the UAW is bound up in inaction, not as great as the AFL-CIO [is], but to a degree that to me is a threat as well. . . . [R]ather than just focusing on what the AFL-CIO is doing or not doing . . . we should begin deciding what kind of a union we are going to be."[10] At times the doves shifted from verbal attacks on Reuther's caution to small acts of defiance. In a breach of union and family decorum, Victor Reuther bypassed his brother and directly asked the UAW Executive Board to endorse the Negotiate Now! platform that Joseph Rauh had drafted the previous year. When Walter instructed William Dodds, Roy Reuther's replacement as director of the Political Action Department, to vote against the ADA's endorsement of Eugene McCarthy, Dodds quietly refused to do so. "I can't do it," he told Rauh the evening before the vote. "I can't stand to vote for Johnson and his fucking war." The next day, he called in sick.[11]

In mid-March, defiance suddenly turned into open rebellion. The triggering event was Robert Kennedy's announcement on March 16 that he would challenge Johnson for the Democratic nomination. In the years after his brother's assassination, RFK had come to share the liberal rebels' doubts about the course of American foreign and domestic policy. From 1967 on, he had been an outspoken critic of the war that he had helped launch early in the decade. Unlike McCarthy, he had also become a strenuous advocate for the poor, particularly northern blacks and Hispanics. During his brief Senate career, Kennedy had consistently called for a substantial expansion of Great Society programs, and he had launched his own effort at ghetto rehabilitation in New York City. He was also intent on opening the Democrats' decision-making process, particularly the party convention, to African-American and Hispanic voters and their representatives. He planned to do so by taking his campaign to the ghettos and barrios, where he hoped his charisma would generate such massive support that the party's leaders could not ignore it. Even as he made himself the champion of minority voters, though, Kennedy remained popular with white workers, many of whom were attracted by his pugnacious personality and his family's grip on the national memory. Kennedy clearly enjoyed such support among UAW members. Polled in mid-1967, 63 percent of white and 93 percent of black rank and filers had said they would vote for RFK rather than for any Republican, figures comparable to those John Kennedy had secured in 1960. With RFK now in the race, the liberal insurgents had a candidate who could simultaneously maintain the Democratic coalition and redefine liberalism.[12]

RFK's candidacy tore the Democratic Party apart. To stand a chance of winning the nomination, Kennedy would have to defeat Johnson and McCarthy in the two key primaries remaining, Indiana and California. LBJ and McCarthy appeared likely to battle him every step of the way. The UAW immediately became engulfed in the struggle. Both the Johnson and Kennedy camps were eager to secure the UAW's support, in part because the union had large memberships and effective political action programs in the two primary states, in part because they assumed Reuther controlled the Michigan delegation to the party convention. They had to move quickly, since the union's executive board was scheduled to hold its next regular session on March 19, at which time the union leadership was sure to decide its policy toward the race. The administration brought its most powerful weapons to bear. Vice-President Humphrey repeatedly tried to phone Reuther in the days before the meeting, and on March 20 Johnson himself called the UAW president. Kennedy called his two closest connections in the union, Conway, whom he had known since the late 1950s, and Paul Schrade, whom he had come to know through the United Farm Workers' Cesar Chavez. "Well, I've announced it," Conway recalled Kennedy saying to him. "What are you going to do about it?"[13]

Unsure of his position, Reuther dodged the White House in the days before the board meeting and refused to return Humphrey's phone calls. Conway and Schrade, meanwhile, jumped at the opportunity to join the Kennedy campaign, Conway as a behind-the-scenes operative, Schrade as a member of the Kennedy slate in the California primary. Reuther was furious with the California regional director when the board met on March 19. In an off-the-record session that Conway remembers as "very divisive," the UAW president demanded that Schrade withdraw from the slate. The argument dragged on until 9 P.M., when a majority of the board, led by Leonard Woodcock, voted in Schrade's favor.[14]

Conway and Schrade spent the next four hours in almost constant discussion with the Kennedy camp, lining up delegates for the California primary. "So the slate was filed the next morning," Conway recalls, "and Holy Christ everything broke loose in the UAW board room because both Lyndon Johnson and Hubert Humphrey [had] called Walter Reuther and really read the riot act to him." Reuther tried to persuade the board to reverse its decision of the previous evening, but the rebellion had in fact spread. Vice-presidents Woodcock, Douglas Fraser, and Ken Bannon and regional directors Ray Berndt, Martin Gerber, and Ray Ross, the core of the Executive Board's social democratic contingent, all informed the UAW president that, like Schrade, they would support Kennedy no matter what position the union officially adopted. Reuther had no choice but to give in. Union officials, he conceded, could support any candidate they wished, but the UAW International would reserve its endorsement until after the Democratic convention. It was an extraordinary turn of events. The conservative members of the board had implicitly challenged Reuther's political program in the late 1940s and early 1950s, but Reuther had always been able to count on the absolute loyalty of the board's social democrats. Now they had defied and defeated him twice in as many days.[15]

As soon as Reuther freed the Executive Board members to back whichever candidate they wanted, some staffers threw their support to Kennedy. Mildred Jeffrey, who had already established contacts with the McCarthy insurgency, fed RFK's campaign information on the Michigan delegation. Conway likewise helped organize the senator's effort in Michigan, while he continued to lay the groundwork for the pivotal California primary. Sophie

10. The making of a revolt. Appearing at the 1968 UAW convention, Robert Kennedy is surrounded by his supporters in the union political bloc. From left to right, Sophie (Mrs. Victor) Reuther, Kennedy, Leonard Woodcock, Victor Reuther, Douglas Fraser, May (Mrs. Walter) Reuther, and Victor and Sophie's son, Eric. (Black Star photograph by Gene Daniels)

Reuther, Victor's wife, served on the Kennedy slate in the District of Columbia primary. And Nat Weinberg, acting as Walter Reuther's inner voice, urged him to join the movement.[16]

On March 31, two weeks after Kennedy declared his candidacy, Lyndon Johnson again transformed the election campaign, announcing on national television that he would not seek or accept the Democratic nomination. For a moment, it seemed as if the liberal insurgents had seized control of the party, but within days Hubert Humphrey, the quintessential postwar liberal who had loyally served Johnson in both the Senate and the vice-presidency, made it clear that he would pick up LBJ's standard. Humphrey's decision to seek the nomination heightened Reuther's uncertainty about a presidential choice. He was certainly friendly with RFK, but the UAW president had considered Humphrey a personal friend for over twenty years. Some of the Executive Board's most conservative members, moreover—Vice-President Pat Greathouse and Detroit's regional director, George Merrelli, both longtime members of the Association of Catholic Trade Unionists and hawks on the war, and Nelson Jack Edwards, among others—quickly pledged their support to the vice-president. His board thus "deeply divided" between the Humphrey and Kennedy camps, Reuther informed both sides that the UAW would remain "neutral" until the convention. The liberal schism had suddenly cut through the heart of the Reuther machine.[17]

Programmatically, Reuther had reason to waver between the Democratic Party's two liberal factions. The UAW leadership had long questioned the need for global military containment, as the liberal rebels now did, but Reuther had also long depended on the anticommunist rhetoric that the insurgents rejected. Reuther and the leaders of the liberal revolt shared the conviction that the Great Society had not gone far enough to meet the needs of the poor, but the rebels were not inherently more likely than the spokesmen for the postwar liberal order had been to foster social democratic change, since they continued to reject a class analysis of American society in favor of interest group politics. Politically, too, Reuther's caution in the spring of 1968 seemed reasonable, at least by normal calculations. By remaining neutral, he could avoid confronting one of the factions on his executive board, and he could maintain ties with both Democratic camps, thus maximizing the UAW's bargaining power at the party convention. That strategy made sense, though, only if the two camps had equal chances of winning the presidential election in November, and that was not the reality in 1968. The furies of the previous few years had robbed the postwar liberal order of its legitimacy and shattered its constituency. Only by committing itself to a candidate who could rally the party's constituencies to a reshaped liberal agenda could the party hope to defeat the Republicans in November, and thereby prevent national political life from swinging to the right.

Most of the UAW's social democrats understood what had happened. Even if Humphrey won the election, Leonard Woodcock said in a private moment, he would be unable to govern the nation six months after taking office. Reuther clearly did not see the election in such terms in early April. A few days after Johnson withdrew from the race, he suggested to reporters that the Democrats find a way to put both Humphrey and Kennedy on the ticket. Over the next few months, however, the national crisis deepened and the campaign seemed to career out of control. As it did so, Reuther slowly abandoned his neutrality. By mid-June, Reuther had joined the effort to define a new liberalism.[18]

The first shock to the nation came five days after LBJ's announcement: on April 4, Martin Luther King Jr. was murdered in Memphis, Tennessee. The assassination came as a terrible blow to Reuther. King had been the catalyst for the coalition of conscience in 1963, and his ringing calls for peaceful social change had served as a powerful, if not always persuasive, counterpoint to the black power advocates of the mid-1960s. Within a week of King's death, African-Americans in more than one hundred cities had rioted, demonstrating of just how desperately Americans, both black and white, still needed the voice that James Earl Ray had silenced.[19]

King's message had not remained static since the triumphs of Birmingham and Selma. Like Kennedy and other liberal rebels, he had been a strong critic of the Vietnam War, which he saw as both immoral and detrimental to domestic reform. He had publicly declared his opposition to Johnson's reelection as early as 1967, and he privately favored RFK in the Democratic contest. By 1968, though, King's domestic program had moved to the left of Kennedy's. He had come to believe that racism was inextricably linked to economic inequality, which was itself rooted in capitalism. He therefore favored a significant redistribution of economic resources and power through a federal guarantee of full employment and a vast expansion of the welfare state. At the time of his death, King was finalizing plans for a Poor People's Campaign that would bring thousands of marchers to Washington in the spring for weeks of protest and civil disobedience.[20]

In theory, King's agenda, so clearly social democratic in concept, matched the UAW's long-standing goals. Five years before, the union had been more than willing to support the Southern Christian Leadership Conference's direct action campaigns. In early 1968, however, the UAW kept its distance from the Poor People's March, in large part because the Johnson administration strongly opposed the campaign as disruptive and potentially dangerous. After King's death, Reuther committed the UAW to the project, although, in typical fashion, he did so on his own terms. On April 25, Jack Conway, Victor Reuther, and Bill Dodds met with the Reverend Ralph Abernathy, King's successor as head of the SCLC, and spelled out their requirements for participation: all protests had to be peaceful; the campaign had to be integrated; and Bayard Rustin had to be given full command of the June 19 rally at the Lincoln Memorial, which was to climax the march. Abernathy agreed to the UAW's terms. In return, the UAW contributed $55,000 to help underwrite Resurrection City, the tent encampment for marchers to be erected near the Washington Monument. The union pledged to mobilize its members in support of the campaign, and Reuther agreed to speak at the June 19 rally, the only labor leader who agreed to do so.[21]

There is no doubt that Reuther joined the march in part to influence its direction, much as he had supported the 1963 March on Washington to shape its agenda. More than ever, the UAW leadership believed that black anger had to be funneled into peaceful political channels if the nation was to avoid chaos. More fundamentally, King's death heightened the UAW leadership's conviction, forged after the previous summer's riot in Detroit, that the White House's domestic reform program was woefully inadequate. "There must be a massive rechanneling of resources toward housing, education, and reasonable guaranteed incomes," Nat Weinberg wrote the Council of Economic Advisers the week after the assassination. "There will be little comfort in price stability if it is gained by reducing our cities to ashes." In 1967 the UAW had tried to prod the administration to further action through a coalition of liberal elites. Now it was willing, as it had been in 1963, to support direct action by thousands of ordinary people. Reuther had made his first significant move away from the administration and the gradualism it championed.[22]

George Meany pushed Reuther even further from the White House. As soon as the UAW issued its call for a special federation convention in December, the AFL-CIO president tried to isolate Reuther from both the administration and the mainstream of the labor movement. When Johnson withdrew from the race, Meany took the lead in urging Humphrey to declare his candidacy, and as soon as the vice-president did so, Meany placed the AFL-CIO political apparatus at his disposal. At the same time, federation partisans spread rumors that Reuther privately favored Kennedy, rumors the White House was inclined to believe. In mid-May, after a series of intricate maneuvers, the AFL-CIO president suspended the UAW from the federation, an act tantamount to expulsion. Meany, it seemed, was daring Reuther to fulfill his grandiose promise of revitalizing the labor movement. "Almost sixty-one now, [Reuther] seems to forget he is of organized labor's vintage," wrote the labor columnist Victor Reisel, a Meany supporter. "He may want this image to fade away. But he of the old left may find the new left is a strange, inhospitable battleground." At least some members of the liberal revolt hoped that the UAW's newfound freedom would help their cause. Meany's action, a Kennedy operative reported, "makes it much easier for us to expect Walter Reuther's support should we be able to work out an accommodation to him."[23]

However irksome Reuther found the AFL-CIO president's maneuvering, the strongest force pushing him toward the liberal revolt was not Meany but the UAW's other social democrats, who throughout the Democratic primaries strengthened and deepened their, and thus the UAW's, links to the Kennedy campaign. The first test came in the Indiana primary on May 7. The 95,000 member Indiana UAW endorsed RFK, and Regional Director Ray Berndt worked tirelessly to mobilize the ethnic blue-collar workers of South Bend, Muncie, and Gary on Kennedy's behalf. The effort paid off.

RFK won the primary, sweeping the state's black areas and showing surprising strength in white working-class wards, some of which he carried by 2-to-1 margins, a signal achievement for a politician closely identified with civil rights.[24] The UAW's social democrats were even more active on Kennedy's behalf in the climactic California primary on June 4. Richard Boone, the director of the UAW's Citizens Crusade against Poverty, put the Kennedy campaign in contact with wealthy liberals likely to support the senator and Hispanic activists associated with the crusade's training center in Delano. At Kennedy's request, Conway and Schrade persuaded Cesar Chavez to serve on Kennedy's primary slate, a move sure to help the senator with the state's large Mexican-American population. Schrade also launched Volunteers for Kennedy, a $50,000 effort to match McCarthy's fabled army of young campaign volunteers, and secured funding for the Viva Kennedy campaign to be conducted in the Hispanic community, where the UAW's efforts on behalf of the United Farm Workers gave the union tremendous legitimacy.[25]

Reuther kept his distance from his lieutenants' efforts, maintaining the official neutrality that he had declared in March. Humphrey officials insisted, however, that Reuther's neutrality was actually helping RFK. Entering the race too late to qualify for the Indiana and California primaries, Humphrey focused his efforts in the spring on securing the support of party officials in nonprimary states. By May Humphrey had won the backing of several major delegations, but Reuther, the vice-president's strategists charged, was keeping the UAW delegates in Michigan "under a gag," whereas "outside of Michigan the UAW regional people are all busily working for Kennedy." The UAW president undoubtedly did not intend to make the distinction. He had tried, after all, to place his regional directors under a gag as well. Whatever Reuther's wishes, by early summer the UAW was moving toward the rebel camp.[26]

On June 4 the liberal insurgency came to a sudden, violent halt. Kennedy carried that day's California primary by a slim margin over McCarthy. That evening, the Kennedy entourage, including Schrade, crowded into Los Angeles' Ambassador Hotel for the victory celebration. RFK made a brief speech calling for the party to unite behind him. Moments later, as he walked through the hotel kitchen, he was mortally wounded. Schrade lay a few feet away, a bullet wound in his head.[27]

Kennedy's assassination devastated his supporters among the UAW's leadership. "His murder leaves an enormous gap in American political life," Victor Reuther's Washington office declared. "It may tragically . . . lead backwards into a long night of reaction, where tired old men will turn their backs to the stench of the slums, the cries of the bewildered, and the anguish of the poor." "My spirits are so low they are non-existent," Mildred Jeffrey wrote Edward Kennedy. " . . . I loved Robert Kennedy and believed in him fiercely. So I had no indecision about where I was. . . . One sort of goes along, but there's no life or vibrancy."[28] Kennedy's death also seemed to have a profound effect on Walter Reuther. The assassination had solved his political dilemma: the UAW now had no real choice but to support Humphrey, who was sure to win the Democratic nomination. Reuther, however, was not moved simply by political calculation. "I'm absolutely certain," Victor Reuther later claimed, "that as more friends came under the gun—Martin Luther King, Bobby Kennedy—Walter became very aware that there may not be much time left for him." Aboard RKF's funeral train, Walter talked incessantly of his own brush with death in a 1948 assassination attempt, and in subsequent weeks he came to see the election in almost apocalyptic terms. "This country is in trouble," he told the UAW Executive Board. "There were . . . German trade unionists who went through exactly this [in the 1930s]. Some of them were fortunate enough to be sent to the same concentration camps. Some others didn't get that far. They were shot down in the process. This is where we are in America. American society is coming apart. . . . I am not going to be put in a position where my own conscience—if I ultimately end up in a concentration camp—where I am going to be charged in my own mind with having twaddled and twiddled my thumbs when the real decisions were made."[29] Shaken out of the torpor that had afflicted him throughout the winter and spring, Reuther finally committed himself and his union to the new liberal agenda.

Reuther and the UAW leadership engaged in a frenzy of reform activity throughout the summer. Days after Robert Kennedy died, Reuther visited Resurrection City, the squalid camp of the Poor People's Campaign. Stripped to his shirtsleeves to combat the oppressive heat of the day, Reuther reveled in the camp's crusading spirit. That evening he met with Ralph Abernathy and reaffirmed the UAW's commitment to the march, despite the fact that Bayard Rustin had withdrawn from it. Reuther thought it particularly important that he speak at the June 19 rally because no other member of "the so-called white establishment" had agreed to do so.[30]

Eighty busloads of UAW members from throughout the nation arrived in the capital on June 19, the largest contingent from any organization. Scoring the administration for not spending as much on the War on Poverty as on the war in Vietnam, Reuther demanded the immediate reordering of national priorities. "In this time of testing," he said, "America and its free institutions cannot survive with . . . the rich getting richer and the poor falling further and further behind." The UAW Washington office took an even stronger stand. If the rich hear the demands of the poor, the office's official publication declared, "they are in luck. If they don't hear, then we're all headed for an ugly cycle of burning cities, brawling mobs, police brutality, smug and repressive government, and a deeply divided America. . . . There is still time, but time is running short."[31]

The UAW leadership backed up its newly expansive rhetoric with an extraordinary proposal for the rehabilitation of Detroit's devastated inner city. The previous fall the UAW had begun a 352-unit low-income housing project on the city's East Side, working through the Metropolitan Detroit Community Development Association, the nonprofit organization it had founded as part of the Model Cities program. Now Reuther insisted that the project be expanded to 100,000 units. Such a massive undertaking would be extremely expensive—according to MDCDA estimates, each unit would cost a minimum of $15,500, well beyond the development authority's resources—but Reuther claimed the city had no option. "The choice before the people of every major urban center is simple and clear," he said. "It is build or burn."[32] To drive construction costs down, the UAW proposed that the 100,000 units should be constructed not by building tradesmen but by inner-city residents, organized into "emergency housing teams." Though each team would be directed by a union craftsman, team members would not be required to join the appropriate building trade, nor would they be paid union scale. In return for these substantial concessions, each tradesman in the Detroit area would be guaranteed a minimum of 2,000 hours of work per year on local industrial, commercial, and governmental building projects. The UAW would also bear its share of the project's cost. The union, Reuther pledged, would contribute $350 million in seed money, to be drawn from the Ford, Chrysler, and General Motors pension funds. "The total community must be mobilized," he exhorted. "The crisis in our society is too deep and too dangerous to try to paper over with rhetoric, pious platitudes, or clever public relations. It will take nothing more than bold, affirmative action—action that will involve in a meaningful way the people of the inner city."[33]

Reuther also moved vigorously, and erratically, to restructure the American labor movement. The UAW officially withdrew from the AFL-CIO on July 1, a month and a half after its suspension. A few weeks later, Reuther announced a new labor center, the Alliance for Labor Action (ALA), a joint venture of the UAW and the most unlikely of partners, the International Brotherhood of Teamsters. The alliance struck many observers as bizarre. Profoundly corrupt, politically conservative, the embodiment of business unionism, the Teamsters had virtually nothing in common with the UAW.

The ALA was a marriage of convenience, not of commitment. With much of its leadership in prison on racketeering convictions, the Teamsters desperately needed the respectability that the alliance could bring, whereas the UAW leadership saw in the Teamsters a chance to challenge the AFL-CIO hierarchy quickly.[34]

Reuther initially envisioned the ALA as a prod to the AFL-CIO, not as a rival to it. The alliance's list of common concerns, drafted in late May, reflected that goal. The ALA, the two unions agreed, would focus its energies on organizing the unorganized, creating community unions, and rebuilding the nation's ghettos—the UAW's social justice agenda. The initial organizing meeting ended in a euphoric mood, with the Teamsters' president, Frank Fitzsimmons, predicting that within six months the AFL-CIO would be coming to the ALA for advice on how to reinvigorate the federation. "We all walked out of that session walking on air, we felt so good about it," Leonard Woodcock said a few weeks later.[35]

By June, Reuther had decided that the ALA could serve as much more than a yardstick for the AFL-CIO. It could, in fact, recreate the crusading progressivism that the CIO had embodied in the 1930s. The Alliance had the numbers for such an undertaking: together, the UAW and the Teamsters had 3.5 million members. To become a viable progressive rival to the AFL-CIO, however, the ALA would need a much broader base of support within the labor movement. Reuther therefore drafted, and in a few cases began talking to, a list of possible affiliates. Largely ignoring the nation's biggest unions, the UAW president turned instead to the AFL-CIO's liberal wing, District 65 of the Retail Workers, the Oil and Chemical Workers, the Meatcutters, the United Farm Workers, and its growing public sector unions, the American Federation of State, County, and Municipal Employees and the American Federation of Teachers. Reuther's other two choices for inclusion in the ALA, the International Longshoremen and the Electrical Workers, were more surprising. Both had been stalwarts of the CIO's left wing in the 1930s and 1940s and Reuther had helped direct their purging from the CIO in 1949. In Reuther's mind, though, the need for political change had outstripped Cold War traditions.[36]

In much the same vein, Reuther finally committed himself and the UAW to the liberal doves' position on Vietnam. In late June he joined the Negotiate Now! campaign, which Joseph Rauh had organized the year before to promote a peace plank at the Democratic convention. The group's proposed plank dovetailed almost perfectly with the proposals RFK and McCarthy had been making throughout the winter and spring: the United States should announce an immediate, unconditional cessation of bombing raids on North Vietnam, to be coupled with a call for a standstill cease-fire;

South Vietnam should hold free elections, with Vietcong participation; and sweeping land reform and economic rehabilitation programs should be initiated in the South. Showing all the verve of a new convert, Reuther signed on to Negotiate Now! as a national co-chairman and contributed $20,000 in union funds to help underwrite its convention activities.[37]

However impressive, Reuther's frantic maneuvering on behalf of the liberal revolt quickly proved futile. With Kennedy dead and McCarthy's candidacy moribund, the rebels could not win control of the party, much less control of the national agenda. Instead, the traditional Democratic leadership and their allies in the labor movement, now firmly in charge of the party, reasserted their commitment to the postwar liberal order, both at home and abroad. By the end of the summer, the traditionalists' victory was assured. And so was liberalism's ultimate defeat.

The Poor People's Campaign was the first of the summer's initiatives to fail. Days after the June 19 rally, the residents of Resurrection City were ejected from the capital by District police. A handful of SCLC activists remained behind, pleading with Congress to increase appropriations for poverty programs. The effort was pointless. Both Congress and the White House had largely abandoned the Great Society the year before and had no intention of reviving it now. On July 16, Ralph Abernathy told the remaining activists, utterly defeated, to go home.[38]

Reuther's grandiose plans for Detroit and the labor movement likewise collapsed, as the AFL-CIO and the Teamsters both asserted their innate conservatism. The building trades rejected out of hand his proposal that nonunion "emergency housing teams" rebuild the inner city. To drive the point home, the tradesmen struck the East Side construction site on which the UAW and MDCDA had begun work the previous fall. Construction costs had skyrocketed to $20,000 per unit by the end of the walkout and MDCDA faced bankruptcy. So did the Citizens Crusade against Poverty, launched with such high hopes four years before. CCAP had had no trouble securing foundation funding for special projects such as its training program, but the UAW had always counted on the AFL-CIO's Industrial Union Department to help cover the Crusade's operating expenses. George Meany withdrew the IUD's support when the UAW left the federation. Shortly thereafter, the UAW disbanded CCAP. The Teamsters, meanwhile, rejected the UAW's plans to transform the Alliance for Labor Action into a new labor federation, particularly one dominated by the movement's left wing. It was a moot point in any event, since most AFL-CIO affiliates Reuther approached indicated that they were not interested in joining the ALA.[39]

By far the most troubling defeat for Reuther came not at the hands of Congress or the AFL-CIO but rather at the hands of Lyndon Johnson. A week after Kennedy's death, Reuther set out to convince Hubert Humphrey, now assured of the Democratic nomination, that he too should endorse the liberal doves' position on Vietnam. ". . . I think [Humphrey] has been the prisoner of the administration's policy," Reuther told the UAW Executive Board without a trace of irony. "I think this is the big millstone that he carries, so if we can help him meet that problem it will be a great service to his candidacy. It will also be good for the country." Reuther made his appeal in private meetings with the vice-president on June 16 and 24. Like the party they now led, Humphrey's advisers were divided on the issue. One faction wanted to appease the party's doves by embracing their peace position, the other wanted to stand by Johnson. In his meetings with Reuther, Humphrey seemed to side with the doves. On June 24 he asked Reuther to draft a speech on the war for him to deliver around Labor Day. Irving Bluestone and Guy Nunn the UAW's public relations director, worked feverishly on the address over the next few weeks, drawing on drafts written by Tom Kahn of the social democratic journal *Dissent*. The final version, delivered to Humphrey on July 28, would have put the vice-president on record in support of Negotiate Now![40]

Buoyed by Humphrey's assurances that he would distance himself from the White House on Vietnam, Reuther and his newfound colleagues in Negotiate Now! also tried to secure the vice-president's support for the doves' peace plank at the convention, scheduled to open on August 26 in Chicago. The crux of the matter was the peace wing's insistence on a unilateral bombing halt, a demand the White House had long resisted. The week before the convention, as the platform committee finished the drafting process, Reuther spent hours on the phone with Humphrey, trying to hammer out a compromise. Finally, on Saturday evening, August 24, Humphrey's aides devised a formula seemingly acceptable to all parties: the vice-president would support an immediate bombing pause but would reserve the right to renew air attacks on North Vietnam at any time. The enterprise collapsed the next day, however. Johnson refused to endorse the proposed plank, which he saw as a repudiation of his leadership, and Humphrey, party loyalist to the end, refused to go against the president's wishes.[41]

Reuther was determined to make one last bid for the dove position. He and his colleagues in Negotiate Now! decided to present their peace position as a minority plank from the convention floor, where they hoped it would attract a groundswell of support. In some respects, it was an odd replaying of the 1948 convention, when the UAW and its allies had opposed the mainstream of the party and through sheer determination had pushed its reluctant candidate to the left. In 1968, however, determination was not enough. The UAW made its first attempt on Tuesday morning, August 27, when Douglas Fraser tried to amend the hawkish majority plank. LBJ's handpicked convention chairman, Carl Albert, easily blocked that attempt, refusing to recognize Fraser's motion from the floor. The next day, the full convention spent three hours debating the minority and majority planks, but in the end the groundswell on which Reuther had counted never developed. The convention went on record in support of Lyndon Johnson's handling of the war. That evening, Hubert Humphrey won the Democratic presidential nomination as the candidate of traditional postwar liberalism.[42]

As the Humphrey and Johnson forces finally defeated the liberal revolt, they too fell victim to the passions of the streets. As the delegates inside the hall cast their votes, thousands of protesters massed outside attempted to march on the convention. The Chicago police responded by brutally beating protesters, reporters, and bystanders in a stunning display of unbridled violence, all shown live on national television. By the time Humphrey arrived at the hall to accept the nomination, the convention was in ruins and the streets of Chicago were stained with blood. The polarization of American politics, already dangerously advanced in 1967, had reached its peak.[43]

The UAW Executive Board met to endorse a presidential candidate a week and a half after the Democratic convention. As they did so, they presented in microcosm the political dynamic that had shaped the union since the 1940s. Reuther began the discussion by arguing that although Humphrey did not embrace all of the UAW's principles, endorsing the vice-president was the only practical path to follow. "Hubert Humphrey is an honorable man. He is a man of compassion," he said. "Maybe there are times when he isn't as clear on something as we would be . . . Let's not throw stones and ask for perfection, because in human affairs sometimes one settles for something short of perfection."[44]

Most board members quickly joined Reuther, the conservatives agreeing that Humphrey was a man of principle, the social democrats admitting that, although they had wanted the party to take a new departure, they now saw no choice but to back the Democratic nominee. Only Paul Schrade, still recovering from the wounds he had suffered in June, refused to go along, insisting that the UAW had an obligation to stand by its principles. "I think the whole idea of the two party system is to give people a choice," he said. "And I don't think the choice is that clear. . . . I think the issue of morality is on the side of those who have been protesting and seeking some change." Reuther responded, as he had so often in the past, with the iron fist of party discipline. "You see, in our union we say if you want to come into our caucus, you are welcome," he said, "and in the framework of that caucus you have the right to participate in . . . shaping the decision and picking the candidate, but if you are not willing to abide by the caucus decision, then you have no right to participate in the democratic process in that caucus." Schrade took the threat seriously. Moments later, he agreed to support the UAW's endorsement of Humphrey. As they had done since the late 1940s, the UAW's social democrats had dreamed of social and political change but had not been able to achieve it.[45]

In one pivotal respect, the political dynamic was different in late 1968 than it had been in previous years. In the past, the UAW leadership had always been able to count on the union's rank and file to support even the most lackluster of Democratic candidates. To be sure, the UAW had always been beset by racial tensions, and some sections of the white rank and file, skilled workers in particular, had been drifting from the Democratic Party since the early 1950s, but the defections had been minor. Now the rank and file was deeply divided, more and more African-American auto workers convinced that the Democratic establishment was not addressing their concerns, many white workers convinced the party was placing undue burdens on them. The union's racial division had been growing since 1966. In the summer and fall of 1968 it found new institutional expressions.

Black power, never a fully coherent movement, had already begun to splinter by early 1968, one wing moving strongly toward African-American nationalism, another toward revolutionary politics. Most outside observers did not notice the divisions, believing that the movement was coalescing around the revolutionaries, commonly identified with the Black Panther Party, whose rhetoric of armed struggle against white oppression seemed to push the black power movement to a new level of militancy.[46] The black revolutionary movement, if not the Black Panther Party itself, flourished in many American cities, typically opposing such white power structures as the police and city schools. In Detroit the movement had its greatest success not in the inner city but in the auto plants, where it launched a bitter attack on the UAW. In several key respects the movement, operating as the Dodge Revolutionary Union Movement (DRUM), resembled the shop-floor protest groups that African-American auto workers had founded to combat racism in the 1950s. DRUM was initiated and led by a handful of African-American production workers at the Dodge Main plant. The leadership cadre enjoyed close ties to a segment of the Detroit African-American elite, particularly the black power movements of Wayne State University and the Reverend Albert Cleague. And they mounted their challenge to the union leadership through the UAW's institutional structure itself. DRUM's founders, though, were not the liberal integrationists that previous shop-floor activists had been. Drawing their inspiration from a variety of sources in the Detroit radical community—the Caribbean Marxist C. L. R. James, the Socialist Workers Party, black separatists—they claimed to be the "vanguard of a black revolution." DRUM spokesmen offered a scathing indictment of the UAW leadership. Despite their talk of racial equality, they charged, the union's officials were "stomp down racists" determined to maintain the oppression of black Americans.[47]

It is not particularly surprising that the DRUM movement began at Dodge Main. One of the oldest production facilities in Detroit, the plant had long been dominated by Eastern European workers. Though among the first to join the UAW in the 1930s, Dodge Main's workers clung doggedly to traditional racial practices. As late as the mid-1950s black workers still had trouble upgrading from janitorial classifications and were unwelcome in many of the bars and restaurants near the plant. Pressured by the International, the local ended these discriminatory practices in the late 1950s, and by 1968 African-Americans accounted for 60 percent of the plant's production workers. White workers with years of seniority, however, still controlled the highest paying jobs in the plant. "At Dodge Main," a white radical explained, "there's a young black work force being supervised by reactionary Polacks. Like, you've got a 63-year-old Pole bossing 25-year-old jitterbugs."[48]

DRUM began its activities in May 1968, distributing leaflets in the Dodge plant condemning both the Chrysler Corporation and the UAW for "demoralizing the integrity of the Black individual." The group staged its first protest in July, a two-day picketing of the plant to decry "racism, discrimination, and intimidation, bigotry and abuse." At first the UAW leadership dismissed DRUM as a fringe group whose attempts to "split the Dodge workers and to make their union ineffective" enjoyed no popular support. DRUM shattered that myth in September, when it placed one of its members, Ron Marsh, on the ballot in a preliminary election for a trustee position in the local. Running on a platform that called on black workers to stop paying their union dues, Marsh finished first in a field of twenty-seven candidates.[49]

At the same time that many of Dodge Main's African-American workers swung behind DRUM, white UAW members nationwide moved further and further to the right. The Republicans, desperate to avoid a repeat of the 1964 election debacle, nominated the pragmatic Richard Nixon as their candidate. Sensing the growing alienation from liberalism, Nixon built his campaign around carefully calibrated appeals to "the silent majority," the millions of ordinary Americans who received no welfare, joined no protests, and staged no riots. It was a clever approach, racially charged yet not overtly racist, patriotic yet not jingoistic, and many white workers found it attractive. But Nixon inspired little real passion among white workers. George Wallace, on the other hand, electrified blue-collar audiences.[50]

Wallace had made a name for himself as governor of Alabama in the early 1960s, when he had become the South's most vocal champion of segregation. He had first taken his message north in 1964, running in several Democratic presidential primaries and taking a substantial minority of the vote. In early 1968 he had decided to run for the presidency again, this time as a third-party candidate. Most political professionals dismissed his candidacy at first, but Wallace had honed his message since 1964. He no longer defended Jim Crow; instead, he slashed away at the federal government and the "pointy-headed intellectuals" who ran it, charging that they favored blacks over whites, condoned radical subversion, and rewarded lawlessness. It was a powerful appeal. Polls taken in May showed that Wallace had the support of 10 percent of the electorate. By July his support had risen to 16 percent; and by early September he appeared to have 19 percent.[51]

Wallace drew a substantial portion of his support from white auto workers, who heard in his message a confirmation of their fears and frustrations. A UAW poll in early September showed that 10 percent of the union's local leaders favored Wallace. The union predicted that he could take 23 percent of the union vote in Flint; 25 percent in Oakland County, north of Detroit; and 75 percent in southern Macomb County, the suburban area to which many white auto workers had moved in the 1950s and 1960s. A straw poll of five New Jersey UAW locals showed support for Wallace running from a low of 52 percent to a high of 92 percent. At the Indianapolis Ford plant, the UAW's Political Action drive netted $699, whereas the Wallace campaign received $1,900 from the night shift alone. "I wouldn't be surprised if 33 percent of the white voters in the plant[s] went for Wallace," a UAW official admitted. "There is deep sentiment among the white suburbanites for Wallace."[52]

With no new ideas to offer its members, UAW leaders tried to heal the divisions in the union's ranks by falling back on the formulas that had served the UAW in the past. After DRUM's success in the September preliminary election in the Dodge Main plant, the International launched a vigorous campaign of repression and co-optation, the combination Reuther had used to defeat the left-wing caucus two decades earlier. George Merrelli, one of the most conservative members of the Executive Board, counseled local leaders on tactics in the weeks before the October 3 runoff, and on election day the International arranged for a large bloc of the local's retirees, virtually all of them white, to vote. At the same time, the Reuther machine wooed moderate blacks by naming Marcellus Ivory, an African-

American, to replace the recently deceased Joseph McCusker, one of the caucus's original ACTU representatives, as a Detroit regional director. Ivory thus became the first African-American to hold that post in the union.[53]

At the same time, the UAW leadership tried to combat the white rank and file's swing to the right with appeals to economic self-interest. "Hubert Humphrey has fought on our side for more jobs, better paychecks, [and] higher living standards," a UAW pamphlet read. "Richard Nixon's Republicans bring big lay-offs, heavy unemployment, worsening living standards, taking away the gains we've made." A Wallace administration would be even worse for the working person, the UAW pointed out. During his tenure as governor of Alabama, a raft of union leaflets and mailings charged, Wallace had consistently supported anti-union legislation, had backed big business, had depressed wages, and had done nothing about the state's high crime rate. "Birmingham wages show what kind of 'friend' of the working man George Wallace really is," a typical UAW broadside declared. "George Wallace has lied to the working man, cheated the working man, and double crossed the working man. Some 'friend.'"[54]

The historian Robert Zieger has called such appeals the labor-liberal alliance's "last hurrah," and so they were. Since the 1930s, both black and white auto workers had largely accepted liberalism's basic tenets as their own. Black workers generally had sought a share of power and a measure of opportunity within a political structure dominated by whites, while both black and white workers had believed that the Democratic Party's liberals best defended both their economic positions and their social values. That identification had been shattered for many workers in the mid-1960s. The UAW's appeals therefore seemed somewhat shopworn in late 1968, more a relic of a fading era than a representation of political reality.[55]

The International's maneuvering in the Dodge Main election succeeded. DRUM's candidate lost the runoff, although he won 40 percent of the vote. Rather than defuse African-Americans' anger, the UAW's tactics seemed to confirm DRUM's charges that the union leadership opposed their empowerment. "The UAW bigots . . . went around the entire city . . . scraping the back streets and searching the cracks in the walls for old retired Polish pigs," DRUM officials said. "These Pollacks were stomp down racists when they worked at the plant and [will] continue to be so until they die." Many black rank and filers agreed with such invective. By year's end, the Revolutionary Union Movement had spread from Dodge Main to other Detroit-area plants.[56]

Many white workers, meanwhile, were not convinced by the UAW's claim that a Humphrey victory would ensure their continued prosperity.

The Great Society's liberalism had cost them money, they believed, both in higher taxes and in a steadily increasing inflation rate. Perhaps more important, the UAW's simple economic appeals did nothing to combat or even confront the other components of white backlash. Eager to downplay African-American activism, the UAW's campaign literature made no attempt to convince white workers that the advancement of black workers did not inherently pose a threat to their own economic and social positions. Also, as long as Humphrey remained committed to LBJ's Vietnam policy, the UAW could not address white workers' hostility to both the war and the anti-war activists. That difficulty was crippling: according to a Humphrey campaign poll in September only 10 percent of Michigan's union members favored continuing the administration's policies in Southeast Asia.[57]

Humphrey's candidacy surged in October, particularly among white workers, who defected from Wallace in large numbers. A host of political analysts have credited the labor movement's assaults on Wallace for turning the blue-collar vote back to the Democrats, and those attacks undoubtedly accounted for part of the change. It is reasonable to suggest, however, that the working class's opposition to the war also contributed to the swing. Humphrey broke with the White House on September 30, announcing that if elected he would declare an immediate halt to the bombing. Four days later Wallace chose as his running mate the ultra-hawk Curtis Le May. The UAW immediately grabbed the opening Wallace had given them, contrasting Le May, "a man who militarily would use any force that's necessary, and maybe a little bit more to make sure," with the Democratic vice-presidential nominee, the moderate Edmund Muskie, "who understands democracy, cherishes it and intends to preserve it." Finally, on October 31, LBJ ordered the bombing pause the doves had been seeking since 1967.[58]

The UAW's economic appeals and the Democrats' sudden dovishness undoubtedly helped Humphrey and the union leadership pull many auto workers back into the Democratic camp, but it was not enough. Since voting statistics are not available for the full UAW rank and file, it is impossible to say precisely for whom the rank and file cast their ballots in 1968. Returns from white working-class suburban areas with large numbers of UAW members suggest, however, that for the first time since the 1930s many white auto workers deserted the Democratic Party. Humphrey took 55.4 percent of the vote in blue-collar Macomb County, Michigan, for example, 9 percentage points below John Kennedy's total in 1960 and 19 percentage points behind Lyndon Johnson's 1964 margin. The vice-president fared even more poorly in Flint's Genessee County, long dominated by white rural migrants, where he took only 45.8 percent of the vote, 22 percentage points lower than the 1964 Democratic vote. Richard Nixon carried 30.4 percent of the vote in Macomb County and 38.8 percent in Genessee, while George Wallace won 14.2 percent of the vote in Macomb and 15.4 percent in Gennessee, far above his percentage of the northern blue-collar vote as a whole.[59]

The peculiarities of a three-way race masked the magnitude of the white working-class shift. With Nixon and Wallace splitting the conservative vote, Humphrey easily carried Michigan and came within 500,000 votes of winning a plurality nationwide, so close that in the election's wake Reuther could claim that "when you measure what we did compared to all the dire predictions . . . we can be proud of the way our people responded." That was a hopelessly optimistic reading. Half of the voters in UAW areas had cast their ballots for conservative candidates, a profound change for a union whose members had been among the Democrats' most loyal supporters. The change was not temporary. Over the next two decades, blue-collar Americans would continue to move away from the Democratic Party and from even the most modest of reform initiatives. The Democratic reform coalition, which four years earlier had seemed capable of transforming national life, had been irrevocably broken, and a conservative ascendancy had taken its place.[60]

It is tempting to blame the UAW, at least in part, for the collapse of the Democratic coalition in 1968. Perhaps, if the UAW leadership had not been willing to tie its agenda so intimately to the Great Society, the union might have served as a powerful voice in opposition to the administration's disastrous decisions in Southeast Asia. Perhaps, if Reuther had been willing to join the liberal revolt earlier, the UAW might have helped to forge a new agenda that would have appealed to blue-collar voters. Perhaps, if the union had not built its campaign appeals around the by-then tired formulas of postwar liberalism, no matter whom the Democrats nominated, it would have been able to rally its rank and file one more time. To make those arguments, though, is to credit Reuther and the UAW leadership with much more power than they actually had. As the events of 1968 had made painfully clear, the UAW operated within a political culture it could influence but could not control. The liberal coalition had collapsed on a Memphis motel balcony and in a Los Angeles hotel kitchen, in the White House and on Capitol Hill, in the streets of Detroit and Chicago and the rice paddies of Vietnam. No matter what the UAW might have done, it could not have been saved.

Epilogue:
The Limits of Liberalism

It is difficult to date the end of the Reuther era within the UAW. The simplest answer is to say that it ended on the evening of May 9, 1970, when the chartered jet carrying Walter and May Reuther crashed just short of the runway at the Pellston, Michigan, airport, instantly killing all aboard.[1] It is more tempting to argue that the Reuther era continued until 1983, when the UAW presidency finally passed out of the hands of Reuther's generation and into the hands of a new leadership bloc that had come of age politically not in the 1930s but in the postwar period. This analysis suggests, however, that the Reuther era ended a year and a half before Reuther's death and fifteen years before the UAW's sputtering torch was passed to a new generation, that it ended in 1968, when the Democratic Party coalition splintered and the postwar liberal ethos collapsed.

Hubert Humphrey's defeat revived the liberal revolt that had seemingly ended with Robert Kennedy's assassination. The liberals who had supported the McCarthy and Kennedy candidacies gained control of the Democratic Party machinery between 1969 and 1972. They committed the party to the antiwar position, remade the nominating process to give greater power to the party rank and file through a series of primaries, and rewrote the convention rules to give formal roles to representatives of African-American, Hispanic, women's, and other groups. In the eighteen months between the 1968 election and the accident that took his life, Walter Reuther increasingly tied the UAW to the liberal insurgency. He became an outspoken critic of the Vietnam War: in June 1969 he called on the United States to withdraw from Vietnam unilaterally, the UAW participated in the October 1969 Moratorium Day, and in his last official act as UAW president Reuther vigorously condemned the 1970 invasion of Cambodia as "morally repugnant." The UAW also joined the liberals in reforming the party's rules and procedures, as both Paul Schrade and Mildred Jeffrey served on the Democratic committees that developed the new nominating system. And Reuther moved closer and closer to the younger Democratic politicians, particularly Senator Fred Harris of Oklahoma and Senator George McGovern of South Dakota, who hoped to pick up RFK's standard.[2]

Reuther's successors, Leonard Woodcock and Douglas Fraser, continued the trend. Under Woodcock's leadership, the UAW strengthened its ties to both the antiwar movement and the liberal insurgents. The UAW organized Labor for Peace as a rallying point for unionists opposed to the war and helped underwrite antiwar lobbying efforts, and Woodcock strongly backed George McGovern's 1972 presidential campaign, the apex of the insurgents' drive to power within the party. When Fraser assumed the UAW presidency in 1977, he attempted to link the new liberalism to the UAW's long-standing social democratic agenda. That effort peaked in the late 1970s, when Fraser organized the Progressive Alliance, a broadened and updated version of the coalition of conscience, embracing over one hundred labor, civil rights, feminist, environmental, and other progressive organizations that by then enjoyed powerful positions in the Democratic Party's decision-making process. Fraser intended the alliance to spearhead an attack on the "misuse of corporate power," which he saw as the root cause of poverty and economic inequality. With the UAW in the lead, the alliance campaigned for national health care, public oversight of corporate plant closings, and national industrial policy planning to be conducted by representatives of business, labor, and government. "We in the UAW," Fraser declared, "intend to reforge the links with those who believe in struggle."[3]

Fraser's Progressive Alliance thus embraced the same agenda, by and large, that had been central to Reuther's political and economic vision during his twenty-four years as UAW president. Reuther's great hope was to bring into the post–World War II era the dream that the CIO's social democratic faction had created in the late 1930s. For the briefest of moments at the end of that decade, the CIO's social democrats and New Deal liberals together seemed to have both the power and the will to reshape the American political economy, to democratize economic decision making through national planning, to ease the burden of poverty and unemployment through the extension of the welfare state. The young Walter Reuther and his closest advisers, all of them little more than foot soldiers in the CIO's great surge forward, made that dream their dream, and never abandoned it.

Epilogue: The Limits of Liberalism

As Steven Fraser has shown, the CIO's social democratic agenda had serious shortcomings. It accepted the corporate concentration of power, hoping simply to counterbalance it with the public concentration of power. It rested on an unquestioning faith in the federal government's impartiality in the determination of economic policy. It assumed that broadening the influence of the labor movement's leadership was equivalent to extending democracy to the union rank and file. Reuther's own political ambition accentuated these weaknesses in his program. He wanted absolute control of the UAW, even if that meant checking worker activism, compromising with union factions that lay to his right, or suppressing internal democracy. "I have always said," he wrote two days before his death, "one should encourage enough opposition to make it interesting but not enough to make it dangerous." And he reveled in regular access to the inner circles of national power, even if he had to sacrifice some of his own principles to win it. The social democratic vision that Reuther adopted, however, also had great strengths. For all its commitment to bureaucracy, its faith in technocracy, Reuther's agenda promised to create a more just, more egalitarian social order that would give organizations created by and for working people equal standing with those created by and for the nation's economic elite.[4]

Reuther's agenda always rested somewhat uneasily alongside the postwar liberal ethos. Postwar liberals typically rejected the class analysis and rhetoric of the late 1930s in favor of the pluralist notion that the United States was divided into a host of special-interest groups. They distrusted the centralization of federal responsibility on which Reuther's agenda rested, preferring a fragmented welfare state and indirect economic controls as hedges against the abuse of state power. Most important, liberals and moderates alike believed that public servants' highest priority had to be the avoidance of fundamental political conflict and the maintenance of a broad national consensus. Both Democratic and Republican policy makers refused to consider proposals and programs that sought fundamental changes in existing power relationships.

The UAW leadership always believed that liberalism could be pushed further, that it could, in fact, be pushed back to the principles that liberals embraced in the late 1930s. Throughout the 1950s and early 1960s, that belief seemed hopelessly naive; the structural and ideological limits of consensus politics simply seemed too strong to be broken. In the mid-1960s, however, the limits suddenly seemed to fade away and for yet another brief moment Reuther seemed to have the power to bring the UAW's vision of social democratic change into the center of American political life. The moment passed as quickly as it had come. Unwilling or unable to transcend interest-group politics at home and containment abroad, the Great Society collapsed, destroying the political coalition that had sustained liberalism since the New Deal.

Liberalism's defeat in 1968 transformed the context in which the UAW promoted its political agenda. No longer did the UAW try to push the dominant political ideology to the left. When the UAW's leaders urged liberals to embrace social democratic change in the years after 1968, they were trying to transform an ideology that no longer had the power to define national politics. Reuther's support for a redefinition of the Democratic Party's convention rules, Woodcock's work on behalf of the McGovern campaign, and Fraser's organization of the Progressive Alliance were little more than hollow gestures, symbolic actions that proved both the UAW's continued commitment to the principles of the union's past and its increasing irrelevance to the new politics of the conservative era. Reuther had never believed that politics and principle could be separated. He had always thought that the two could, indeed must, move together. In the years after 1968, as American political culture swung more and more to the right, the UAW could no longer bring the two together in any meaningful way. Long before Douglas Fraser turned the UAW presidency over to Owen Bieber, long before the collapse of the domestic auto industry gutted the union that the Reutherites had helped to build, the Reuther era had come to an end.

Even in defeat, the UAW leadership's political efforts during the Reuther era suggest a different reading of postwar political history than the version currently taking form. For a quarter century historians have been revising the discipline's interpretation of American political life by demonstrating, again and again, how Americans have battled not simply over the specifics of public policy but over the very direction, the very meaning of the nation. As they traced the contours of this struggle, historians have shown how labor unions served as one of the most powerful voices for social change. The specifics of labor's vision changed over time, from the republicanism of Jacksonian trade unions to the syndicalism of the Industrial Workers of the World, but whatever the formulation, labor remained in the forefront of those forces fighting to make the nation more democratic and more egalitarian. Historians offer a very different interpretation of the post–World War II political order. After 1945, they argue, the labor movement became fully integrated into the political and economic power structure. In the process, the movement abandoned its social vision and became a defender of the status quo, while those groups that remained outside the corridors of power—African-Americans, women, homosexuals, the young—moved to the vanguard of reform. This book does not entirely refute this interpretation. There is no doubt that in the postwar era major industrial unions, including the UAW, were integrated into the national power structure; that sections of the labor movement, most notably George Meany and the AFL-CIO, accepted and even applauded existing power relationships; and that African-Americans in particular played the pivotal role in transforming public life.

The current interpretation is mistaken, however, in its dismissal of the entire postwar labor movement as an agent of social change. As this investigation has shown, even one of the most powerful, most privileged of postwar unions continued to advance a vision of a nation less tightly tied to the power of the corporations and to the incessant demands of the marketplace. Constrained by the political and structural limits of postwar American society, at times undercut by the compromises Reuther made in the pursuit of power, the UAW leadership could not transform the face of the nation. But the union's commitment to and struggle on behalf of social change were genuine, and the UAW's ultimate defeat, as the years since 1980 have shown, was a genuine loss for the nation. The political and economic alignment begun in the 1980s—the federal government's sycophantic support for the corporate structure's unbridled pursuit of profits, the government's dismantling of the welfare state, its attack on the economic position of the working class, and its abdication of responsibility for the poor—dramatizes just how desperately the nation still needs the vision that the UAW and organizations like it once provided.

Additional Abbreviations
Used in Notes

ACTUC	Association of Catholic Trade Unionists Collection, ALUA
ALUA	Archives of Labor and Urban Affairs, Wayne State University, Detroit
BLS	U.S. Department of Labor, Bureau of Labor Statistics
CAPC	UAW Community Action Program Collection, ALUA
CCAPC	Citizens' Crusade against Poverty Collection, WPR
CD	UAW Citizenship Department Collection, Roy Reuther Files, ALUA
CL	UAW Citizenship-Legislative Department Collection, ALUA (unprocessed collection)
Cormier-Eaton	Frank Cormier and William Eaton Collection, ALUA
FP	UAW Fair Practices Department Collection, ALUA
GMW	G. Mennen Williams Collection, MHC
HHH	Hubert H. Humphrey Collection, Minnesota Historical Society, St. Paul
HSTL	Harry S. Truman Presidential Library, Independence, Mo.
IAD	UAW International Affairs Department Collection, Victor Reuther—Lewis Carliner Files, ALUA
IEBC	UAW International Executive Board Collection, ALUA
Jacobs-Sifton	UAW Washington Office Collection, Paul Sifton and Samuel Jacobs Files, ALUA
JAH	*Journal of American History*
JFKL	John F. Kennedy Presidential Library, Boston
LBJL	Lyndon B. Johnson Presidential Library, Austin, Tex.
LC	Library of Congress, Washington, D.C.
LCCRC	Leadership Conference on Civil Rights Collection, LC
MHC	Michigan Historial Collection, Bentley Library, University of Michigan, Ann Arbor

Additional Abbreviations Used in Notes

MLK	Martin Luther King Jr. Center for Nonviolent Social Change, Atlanta
Montgomery	UAW Washington Office Collection, Donald Montgomery Files, ALUA
PA	UAW Political Action Department Collection, Roy Reuther Files, ALUA
PCS	Paul and Claire Sifton Collection, LC
Region 6	UAW Region 6 Collection, ALUA
Region 9A	UAW Region 9A Collection, ALUA
Reuther-Carliner	UAW Washington Office Collection, Victor Reuther and Lewis Carliner Files, ALUA
SCLCC	Southern Christian Leadership Conference Collection, MLK
SGML	Seeley G. Mudd Manuscript Library, Princeton University
SNCCC	Student Nonviolent Coordinating Committee Collection, MLK
SPD	UAW Special Projects Department Collection, ALUA
WHCF	White House Central Files, JFKL or LBJL
WPR	Walter P. Reuther Collection, ALUA

Notes

Introduction: Politics and Principle

1. Most of the work on labor's social democratic potential focuses on worker control of the shop floor. See Nelson Lichtenstein, "Auto Worker Militancy and the Structure of Factory Life, 1937–1955," *JAH* 67 (September 1980), 335–349; Lichtenstein, "Life at the Rouge: A Cycle of Workers Control," in Charles Stephenson and Robert Asher, eds., *Life and Labor: Dimensions of American Working Class History* (Albany, 1986), 237–248; Steve Jefferys, *Management and Managed: Fifty Years of Crisis at Chrysler* (Cambridge, 1986), 68–103; Bruce Nelson, *Workers on the Waterfront: Seamen, Longshoremen, and Unionism in the 1930s* (Urbana, 1988), esp. chap. 6. For a fascinating critique of this view, see David Brody, "Workplace Contractualism in Comparative Perspective," in Nelson Lichtenstein and Howell Harris, eds., *Industrial Democracy in America: The Ambiguous Promise* (Cambridge, 1993), 176–205. Only in the last few years have scholars begun to examine labor's social democratic potential in national politics. See Lichtenstein, "From Corporatism to Collective Bargaining: Organized Labor and the Eclipse of Social Democracy in the United States," in Steven Fraser and Gary Gerstle, eds., *The Rise and Fall of the New Deal Order, 1930–1980* (Princeton, 1989), 122–152; Ira Katznelson, "Was the Great Society a Lost Opportunity?" in Fraser and Gerstle, *New Deal Order*, 190. Stephen Amberg, *The Union Inspiration in American Politics: The Autoworkers and the Making of a Liberal Industrial Order* (Philadelphia, 1994), chap. 3, offers the most thorough exploration of the UAW's social democratic agenda in the 1930s and early 1940s. Gary Gerstle, *Working Class Americanism: The Politics of Labor in a Textile City, 1914–1960* (Cambridge, 1989), links shop floor and political concerns with ethnic and cultural politics. Steven Fraser, *Labor Will Rule: Sidney Hillman and the Rise of American Labor* (New York, 1991), is an extraordinary study of the origins and ambiguities of organized labor's social democratic agenda.

2. Nelson Lichtenstein, *Labor's War at Home: The CIO in World War II* (Cambridge, 1982), chap.12; Lichtenstein, "Conflict Over Workers' Control: The Automobile Industry in World War II," in Michael Frisch and Daniel Walkowitz, eds., *Working-Class America: Essays on Labor, Community, and American Society* (Urbana, 1983), 284–

311; Lichtenstein, "UAW Bargaining Strategy and Shop Floor Conflict, 1946–1970," *Industrial Relations* 24 (1985), 360–381; Lichtenstein, "Life at the Rouge," 248–259; Lichtenstein, "The Making of the Postwar Working Class: Cultural Pluralism and Social Structure in World War II," *Historian* 51 (November 1988), 42–63; Ronald W. Schatz, "Philip Murray and the Subordination of the Industrial Unions to the United States Government," in Melvyn Dubofsky and Warren Van Tine, eds., *Labor Leaders in America* (Urbana, 1987), 239–256; Lichtenstein, "Walter Reuther and the Rise of Labor-Liberalism," in Dubofsky and Van Tine, *Labor Leaders*, 291–301; Stephen Amberg, "The Triumph of Industrial Orthodoxy: The Collapse of Studebaker-Packard," in Lichtenstein and Stephen Meyer, eds., *On the Line: Essays in the History of Auto Work* (Urbana, 1989), 190–218; Amberg, *Union Inspiration*, chap. 4; Gerstle, *Working-Class Americanism*, chap. 10; Alan Dawley, "Workers, Capital, and the State in the Twentieth Century," in J. Carroll Moody and Alice Kessler-Harris, eds., *Perspectives on American Labor History: The Problems of Synthesis* (De Kalb, Ill., 1990), 166–179; Katznelson, "Was the Great Society a Lost Opportunity?" 190–191; Mike Davis, *Prisoners of the American Dream* (London, 1986), 52–101. The literature on the CIO's purge of its Communist members is voluminous. For an excellent survey, see Robert Zieger, "Toward the History of the CIO: A Bibliographic Report," *Labor History* 26 (1985), 491–500, and Zieger, "The CIO: A Bibliographic Update and Archival Guide," *Labor History* 31 (1990), 413–424. The best studies on the institutional framework for postwar collective bargaining are Christopher Tomlins, *The State and the Unions: Labor Relations, Law, and the Organized Labor Movement in America, 1880–1960* (Cambridge, 1985), and Melvyn Dubofsky, *The State and Labor in Modern America* (Chapel Hill, 1994). Also see David Plotke, "The Wagner Act, Again: Politics and Labor, 1935–37," *Studies in American Political Development: An Annual* 3 (1989), 105–153. The emerging interpretation has begun to transcend the monographic literature and work its way into textbooks. See, for instance, The American Social History Project, *Who Built America? Working People and the Nation's Economy, Politics, Culture, and Society*, vol. 2 (New York, 1992), chap. 10.

3. Lichtenstein, "From Corporatism to Collective Bargaining," 140–145; Davis, *Prisoners of the American Dream*, 82–101; Dawley, "Workers, Capital, and the State," 173–178; Amberg, *Union Inspiration*, chaps. 4–7.

4. Lichtenstein, "From Corporatism to Collective Bargaining," 140–145; Katznelson, "Was the Great Society a Lost Opportunity?" 190–192, 195.

5. John Barnard, *Walter Reuther and the Rise of the Auto Workers* (Boston, 1983), 198–199; Nelson Lichtenstein, "Introduction: The American Automobile Industry and Its Workers," in Lichtenstein and Meyer, *On the Line*, 1–2; Jack Stieber, *Governing the UAW* (New York, 1962), 127.

6. Lichtenstein, "Walter Reuther and the Rise of Labor-Liberalism," in Dubofsky and Van Tine, *Labor Leaders in America*, 292.

7. Fraser, *Labor Will Rule*; Amberg, *Union Inspiration*, chap. 7; Adam Przeworski, *Capitalism and Social Democracy* (Cambridge, 1985); Gösta Esping-Andersen, *Politics against Markets: The Social Democratic Road to Power* (Princeton, 1985).

8. Esping-Andersen, *Politics against Markets*, 314–324.

9. This argument draws on Ira Katznelson and Theda Skocpol's work on state structures and policy development. See in particular Katznelson, "Rethinking the Silences of Social and Economic Policy," *Political Science Quarterly* 101 (1986), 307–325; Skocpol, "Bringing the State Back In: Strategies of Analysis in Current Research," in Peter Evans, Dietrich Rueschemeyer, and Theda Skocpol, eds., *Bringing the State Back In* (Cambridge, 1985), 3–43. On the Democratic Party's configuration, see Margaret Weir, Ann

Shola Orloff, and Theda Skocpol, "Understanding American Social Politics," in Weir, Orloff, and Skocpol, *The Politics of Social Policy in the United States* (Princeton, 1988), 20–24.

10. See, for instance, Edwin Amenta and Theda Skocpol, "Redefining the New Deal: World War II and the Development of Social Provisions in the United States," in Weir, Orloff, and Skocpol, *Politics of Social Policy*, 81–122; and Margaret Weir, *Politics and Jobs: The Boundaries of Employment Policy in the United States* (Princeton, 1992), esp. chaps. 1–2.

11. Alan Brinkley, "The New Deal and the Idea of the State," in Fraser and Gerstle, *New Deal Order*, 85–121. Also see Robert M. Collins, *The Business Response to Keynes, 1929–1964* (New York, 1981), chaps. 5–6; Richard H. Pells, *The Liberal Mind in a Conservative Age: American Intellectuals in the 1940s and 1950s* (New York, 1985).

12. For a comprehensive history of the CIO, see Robert Zieger, *The CIO, 1935–1955* (Chapel Hill, 1995). There is no comprehensive study of the postwar AFL-CIO. Art Preis, *Labor's Giant Step: Twenty Years of the CIO* (New York, 1964); Zieger, *American Workers, American Unions, 1920–1985* (Baltimore, 1986), chaps. 5–6; and Zieger, "George Meany: Labor's Organization Man," in Dubofsky and Van Tine, *Labor Leaders*, 324–349, are instructive. On the Reuther machine, see Stieber, *Governing the UAW*, and Martin Halpern, *UAW Politics in the Cold War Era* (Albany, 1988), 121–131, 223–263.

13. Katznelson, "Was the Great Society a Lost Opportunity?" 195–205; Jonathan Rieder, "The Rise of the 'Silent Majority,' " in Fraser and Gerstle, *New Deal Order*, 243–268.

1. Building the Vanguard

1. On organized labor's postwar troubles, see R. Alton Lee, *Truman and Taft-Hartley: A Question of Mandate* (Lexington, Ky., 1966), 22–48; Arthur McClure, *The Truman Administration and the Problem of Postwar Labor, 1945–1948* (Rutherford, N.J., 1969); Alonzo L. Hamby, *Beyond the New Deal: Harry S. Truman and American Liberalism* (New York, 1973), 53–85; Nelson Lichtenstein, *Labor's War at Home: The CIO in World War II* (Cambridge, 1982), 203–221; and Howell John Harris, *The Right to Manage: Industrial Relations Policies of American Business in the 1940s* (Madison, 1982), 105–204. The literature on UAW factionalism is voluminous. See, for example, Jack Skeels, "The Development of Political Stability Within the United Automobile Workers Union" (Ph.D. diss., University of Wisconsin, 1957); Bert Cochran, *Labor and Communism: The Conflict That Shaped American Unions* (Princeton, 1977), 214–220, 250–251; Roger Keeran, *The Communist Party and the Auto Workers Unions* (Bloomington, 1980), 186–289; and Martin Halpern, *UAW Politics in the Cold War Era* (Albany, 1988).

2. Victor Reuther, "Look Forward Labor," *Common Sense* 14 (December 1945), 8.

3. David A. Hounshell, *From the American System to Mass Production, 1800–1932* (Baltimore, 1984), chaps. 6–7; Alfred D. Chandler Jr., *The Visible Hand: The Managerial Revolution in American Business* (Cambridge, Mass., 1977), 280, 358–359, 456–463; Sidney Fine, *The Automobile under the Blue Eagle: Labor, Management, and the Automobile Manufacturing Code* (Ann Arbor, 1963), 13–17; Stephen Meyer III, *The Five-Dollar Day: Labor Management and Social Control in the Ford Motor Company, 1908–1921* (Albany, 1981), 9–36.

4. Nelson Lichtenstein, "Introduction: The American Automobile Industry and Its Workers," in Lichtenstein and Stephen Meyer, eds., *On the Line: Essays in the History of*

Auto Work (Urbana, 1989), 1; James Rubenstein, *The Changing U.S. Auto Industry: A Geographical Analysis* (London, 1992), 68–71; BLS, *Wage Structure of the Motor Vehicle Industry,* Bulletin 706 (Washington, D.C., 1942), 5.

5. Joyce Shaw Peterson, *American Automobile Workers, 1900–1933* (Albany, 1987), chap. 5; Fine, *Automobile under the Blue Eagle,* 14–16; BLS, *Wage Structure,* 12.

6. Fine, *Automobile under the Blue Eagle,* 13–14; Meyer, *Five-Dollar Day,* 37–65; David Gartman, *Auto Slavery: The Labor Process in the American Automobile Industry, 1897–1950* (New Brunswick, N.J., 1986), 39–257; Peterson, *American Automobile Workers,* 30–107; Studs Terkel, *Hard Times: An Oral History of the Great Depression* (New York, 1970), 129.

7. On the early history of the UAW, see Sidney Fine, *Sit-Down: The General Motors Strike of 1936–1937* (Ann Arbor, 1969); Irving Bernstein, *Turbulent Years: A History of the American Worker, 1933–1941* (Boston, 1969), 499–571; Nelson Lichtenstein, "Auto Worker Militancy and the Structure of Factory Life, 1937–1955," *JAH* 67 (September 1980), 335–340; Steve Jefferys, *Management and Managed: Fifty Years of Crisis at Chrysler* (Cambridge, 1986), 55–77; and Steve Babson, *Building the Union: Skilled Workers and Anglo-Gaelic Immigrants in the Rise of the UAW* (New Brunswick, N.J., 1991), 95–199. For two fascinating discussions of the shop-floor "rule of law," see Steven Tolliday and Jonathan Zeitlin, "Shop Floor Bargaining, Contract Unionism, and Job Control: An Anglo-American Comparison," in Lichtenstein and Meyer, *On the Line,* 219–244; and David Brody, "Workplace Contractualism in Comparative Perspective," in Nelson Lichtenstein and Howell Harris, eds., *Industrial Democracy in America: The Ambiguous Promise* (Cambridge, 1993), 176–205. Also see Carl Fersuny and Cladis Kaufman, "Seniority and the Moral Economy of U.S. Automobile Workers, 1934–1946," *Journal of Social History* 18 (Spring 1985), 463–475.

8. Kevin Boyle, "Auto Workers at War: Patriotism and Shop Floor Militancy in the American Auto Industry, 1941–1945," in Robert Asher and Ronald Edsforth, eds., *Auto Work* (Albany, forthcoming); Lichtenstein, "Auto Worker Militancy," 335–341; Lichtenstein, "Life at the Rouge: A Cycle of Workers' Control," in Charles Stephenson and Robert Asher, eds., *Life and Labor: Dimensions of American Working-Class History* (Albany, 1986), 243; Jefferys, *Management and Managed,* 83–87; Kevin Boyle, "Rite of Passage: The 1939 General Motors Tool and Die Strike," *Labor History* 27 (Spring 1986), 194.

9. Raymond Boryczka, "Militancy and Factionalism in the United Auto Workers Union, 1937–1941," *Maryland Historian* 8 (Fall 1977), 13–25; Douglas P. Seaton, *Catholics and Radicals: The Association of Catholic Trade Unionists and the American Labor Movement, from Depression to Cold War* (Lewisburg, Pa., 1981), 75–87; Irving Howe and B. J. Widick, *The UAW and Walter Reuther* (New York, 1949), 75–80; John Barnard, *Walter Reuther and the Rise of the Auto Workers* (Boston, 1983), 59–61; Keeran, *Communist Party,* 196.

10. Babson, *Building the Union,* 15–94; Peter Friedlander, *The Emergence of a UAW Local, 1936–1939: A Study in Class and Culture* (Pittsburgh, 1975); Peterson, *American Automobile Workers,* chap. 2; Ronald Edsforth, *Class Conflict and Cultural Consensus: The Making of a Mass-Consumer Society in Flint, Michigan* (New Brunswick, N.J., 1986), 79–84, 87–96, and chap. 7.

11. Meyer, *Five-Dollar Day,* chap. 3; Babson, *Building the Union,* 201–239.

12. For more information on second-generation ethnic auto workers, see Friedlander, *Emergence of a UAW Local.* The Italian-American worker is Nick DiGaetano, as quoted in Brody, "Workplace Contractualism," 205. Boyle, "Auto Workers at War," and Nelson Lichtenstein, "The Making of the Postwar Working Class: Cultural Pluralism and Social

Structure in World War II," *Historian* 51 (November 1988), 53–55, discuss the appeal of Americanism. Thomas Gobel, "Becoming American: Ethnic Workers and the Rise of the CIO," *Labor History* 29 (Spring 1988), 173–198; Gary Gerstle, *Working-Class Americanism: The Politics of Labor in a Textile City, 1914-1960* (Cambridge, 1989); and Lizabeth Cohen, *Making a New Deal: Industrial Workers in Chicago, 1919–1939,* (Cambridge, 1990), trace the second generation's Americanism in other settings. See Erdmann Doane Beynon, "The Southern White Laborer Migrants to Michigan," *American Sociological Review* 3 (June 1938), 333–343, and Alan Clive, *State of War: Michigan in World War II* (Ann Arbor, 1979), 9, 170–184, for information on southern auto workers in the North. For details on southern white working-class attitudes more generally, see Jacquelyn Dowd Hall et al., *Like a Family: The Making of a Southern Cotton Mill World* (Chapel Hill, 1987). There is very little information on northern rural migrants in the auto industry. Ely Chinoy, *Automobile Workers and the American Dream* (Boston, 1955), a study of auto workers in Lansing, Mich., is informative.

13. On the African-American migration to Detroit during and immediately after World War I see Richard Thomas, *Life for Us Is What We Make It: Building Black Community in Detroit, 1915–1945* (Bloomington, 1992), esp. chap. 2. On African-American auto workers in the pre-union era and during the UAW organizational drive, see August Meier and Elliot Rudwick, *Black Detroit and the Rise of the UAW* (New York, 1979), chaps. 1–2, and Robert Korstad and Nelson Lichtenstein, "Opportunities Found and Lost: Labor, Radicals, and the Early Civil Rights Movement," *JAH* 75 (December 1988), 791–797. The two workers are quoted in Lloyd Bailer, "Negro Labor in the American Automobile Industry" (Ph.D. diss., University of Michigan, 1943), 78–81, 252.

14. Meier and Rudwick, *Black Detroit,* chaps. 2–3; Nancy Gabin, *Feminism in the Labor Movement: Women and the United Auto Workers, 1935–1975* (Ithaca, 1990), 9–100; chaps. 1–2; Korstad and Lichtenstein, "Opportunities Found and Lost," 791–797.

15. Gabin, *Feminism in the Labor Movement;* Ruth Milkman, *Gender at Work: The Dynamics of Job Segregation by Sex during World War II* (Urbana, 1987), 12–98.

16. On the UAW's AFL roots, see Fine, *Automobile under the Blue Eagle,* 416–427. On the UAW's organizational structure, see Constitution of the International Union, and Laws Governing Local Unions, adopted in Detroit, August 1935 (amended April 1936, August 1937, and March 1939), ALUA; Jack Stieber, *Governing the UAW* (New York, 1962). For a brief period in the late 1930s the center of power in the UAW shifted from the presidency to the Executive Board, but even under that arrangement the rank and file did not have a major say in the setting of union policy.

17. Fine, *Sit-Down;* Bernstein, *Turbulent Years,* chap. 11; Lichtenstein, *Labor's War at Home,* chap. 1; David Plotke, "The Wagner Act, Again: Politics and Labor, 1935–1937," *Studies in American Political Development: An Annual* 3 (1989), 105–153; Steven Fraser, "The 'Labor Question,'" in Fraser and Gary Gerstle, eds., *The Rise and Fall of the New Deal Order, 1930–1980* (Princeton, 1989), 67–71; Christopher Tomlins, *The State and the Unions: Labor Relations, Law, and the Organized Labor Movement in America, 1880–1960* (Cambridge, 1985), esp. pt. 2; Howell Harris, "The Snares of Liberalism? Politicians, Bureaucrats, and the Shaping of Federal Labour Relations Policy in the United States, ca. 1915–47," in Steven Tolliday and Jonathan Zeitlin, eds., *Shop Floor Bargaining* (Cambridge, 1985), 168–179; Nelson Lichtenstein, "Great Expectations: The Promise of Industrial Jurisprudence and Its Demise, 1930–1960," in Lichtenstein and Harris, *Industrial Democracy in America,* 125–128.

18. Lichtenstein, *Labor's War at Home;* Barnard, *Walter Reuther,* 83.

19. Nelson Lichtenstein, "Conflict Over Workers' Control: The Automobile Industry in World War II," in Michael Frisch and Daniel Walkowitz, eds., *Working-Class America: Essays on Labor, Community, and American Society* (Urbana, 1983), 284–311; Boyle, "Auto Workers at War"; Meier and Rudwick, *Black Detroit*, 162–169; Lichtenstein, "Auto Worker Militancy and the Structure of Factory Life, 1937–1955," *JAH* 67 (September 1980), 335.

20. Joshua Freeman, "Delivering the Goods: Industrial Unionism during World War II," in Daniel Leab, ed., *The Labor History Reader* (Urbana, 1985), 394–406; Lichtenstein, *Labor's War at Home*, 221–224.

21. Barnard, *Walter Reuther,* and Nelson Lichtenstein, "Walter Reuther and the Rise of Labor-Liberalism," in Melvyn Dubofsky and Warren Van Tine, eds., *Labor Leaders in America* (Urbana, 1987), 280–302, are the best biographical treatments of Reuther. Frank Cormier and William Eaton, *Reuther* (Englewood Cliffs, N.J., 1970), is also useful. John H. M. Laslett, *Labor and the Left: A Study of Socialist and Radical Influences in the American Labor Movement, 1881–1924* (New York, 1970), chap. 2, examines the Brewery Workers' ideology, and Nick Salvatore, *Eugene V. Debs: Citizen and Socialist* (Urbana, 1982), is a wonderful treatment of Debs's political thought.

22. Bruce Levine, "In the Heat of Two Revolutions: The Forging of German-American Radicalism," in Dirk Hoerder, ed., *"Struggle a Hard Battle": Essays on Working-Class Immigrants* (De Kalb, Ill., 1986), 31–32; Barnard, *Walter Reuther,* 3–5; Victor Reuther, *The Brothers Reuther and the Story of the UAW: A Memoir* (Boston, 1976), 41.

23. Lichtenstein, "Walter Reuther," 281; Babson, *Building the Union,* 43–49.

24. Olivier Zunz, *The Changing Face of Inequality: Urbanization, Industrial Development, and Immigrants in Detroit, 1880–1920* (Chicago, 1982), 285–398; Steve Babson, *Working Detroit: The Making of a Union Town* (New York, 1984), 48–50. Lichtenstein, "Walter Reuther," 281–282, discusses Reuther's flirtation with the New Era. Babson, *Building the Union,* 83–84, provides context.

25. Babson, *Building the Union,* 63–102; Frank Marquardt, *An Auto Worker's Journal: The UAW from Crusade to One-Party Union* (University Park, Pa., 1975), chap. 2–3; Lichtenstein, "Walter Reuther," 282; Reuther, *Brothers Reuther,* 55–65.

26. Reuther, *Brothers Reuther,* 64–123; Barnard, *Walter Reuther,* 9–17; Lichtenstein, "Walter Reuther," 282–284; Vic and Wal to M and G, n.d., Box 4, WPR; Kevin Boyle, "Building the Vanguard: Walter Reuther and Radical Politics in 1936," *Labor History* 30 (Summer 1989), 447.

27. Fine, *Sit-Down,* 63–99; Babson, *Building the Union,* esp. chapt. 4; Reuther, *Brothers Reuther,* 124–127.

28. Lichtenstein, "Walter Reuther," 282–284; oral history interviews with Joseph L. Rauh, December 11, 1967, and Thomas E. Harris, December 18, 1967, both in Box 2, Cormier-Eaton; transcript of Walter Reuther interview with Mike Wallace, January 25, 1958, Box 4, SPD.

29. Lichtenstein, "Walter Reuther," 282–285; Barnard, *Walter Reuther,* 40–53; Reuther, *Brothers Reuther,* 128–182; Fine, *Sit-Down,* 327–328.

30. Lichtenstein, "Walter Reuther," 285–286; Barnard, *Walter Reuther,* chap. 4; Irving Howe and B. J. Widick, *The UAW and Walter Reuther* (New York, 1949), 195–196; Keeran, *Communist Party,* 206.

31. Frank Warren, *Alternative Vision: The Socialist Party in the 1930s* (Bloomington, 1974), 134–157; Milton Cantor, *The Divided Left: American Radicalism, 1900–1975* (New York, 1978), 112–149; Keeran, *Communist Party,* 206–225; Lichtenstein, "Wal-

ter Reuther," 285; Halpern, *UAW Politics*, 24–29; Sidney Fine, *Frank Murphy: The New Deal Years* (Chicago, 1979), 492–493; Howe and Widick, *UAW and Walter Reuther*, 195. Roy and Victor followed their older brother out of the Socialist Party a few years later.

32. Milton Derber, *The American Idea of Industrial Democracy, 1865–1965* (Urbana, 1970), secs. 1–3; David Montgomery, "Industrial Democracy or Democracy in Industry? The Theory and Practice of the Labor Movement, 1897–1925," in Lichtenstein and Harris, *Industrial Democracy in America*, 22–42; Howell Harris, "Industrial Democracy and Liberal Capitalism, 1890–1925," in Lichtenstein and Harris, 44–60; Joseph McCartin, "'An American Feeling': Workers, Managers, and the Struggle over Industrial Democracy in the World War I Era," in Lichtenstein and Harris, 67–86; David Montgomery, *The Fall of the House of Labor: The Workplace, the State, and American Labor Activism, 1865–1925* (Cambridge, 1987), chaps. 7–9; Steven Fraser, *Labor Will Rule: Sidney Hillman and the Rise of American Labor* (New York, 1991), esp. chaps. 2–8; Fraser, "'Labor Question,'" 57–62. On the intellectual background of social democracy in the Progressive era in both Germany and the United States, see James Kloppenberg, *Uncertain Victory: Social Democracy and Progressivism in European and American Thought, 1870–1920* (New York, 1986), chaps. 6–9.

33. Montgomery, "Industrial Democracy?" 35; Salvatore, *Eugene V. Debs*, 191–193. For information on the Reuther brothers' training at Brookwood, see Roy Reuther's notes, "Brookwood Labor College Economic Courses," n.d. [1933?], Box 1, Roy Reuther Files, ALUA. For examples of Walter Reuther's rhetoric, see Reuther radio transcript, n.d. [1944], Box 540, WPR; Walter P. Reuther, "Our Fear of Abundance," in his *Selected Papers*, ed. Henry Christman (New York, 1961), 13–21; "Wage Earner" clippings, n.d. [1945–46], Box 33, ACTUC; Reuther's address to the National General Motors Council, July 25, 1947, Box 3, SPD.

34. Walter Reuther's address to ADA, February 22, 1948, Box 4, FP; Victor Reuther, "Look Forward Labor," 9; Walter Reuther's address to NAACP, June 28, 1946, Box 4, FP; Walter Reuther's statement for UAW convention, n.d. [1946], Box 89, and Walter Reuther to L. B. Drach, October 19, 1945, Box 24, both in WPR; UAW press releases, September 10 and December 7, 1946, both in Box 8, FP; Walter Reuther's testimony before the Senate Committee on Labor and Public Welfare, February 21, 1947, Box 3, SPD; "Wage Earner" clippings, n.d. [1945], Box 33, ACTUC.

35. I am most grateful to William Dodds, former director of the UAW's Political Action Department, for showing me, at a very early stage in my research, Reuther's debt to Thorstein Veblen. The most important text for Reuther was Veblen's, *The Engineers and the Price System* (New York, 1921). The Reuthers themselves acknowledged the debt in the July 1949 issue of UAW *Ammunition*, 35–37. For background on the Progressive commitment to technocracy, see Kloppenberg, *Uncertain Victory*, 381–385; Fraser, *Labor Will Rule*, 128–134. UAW spokesmen condemned the corporations' "scarcity mentality" throughout the postwar era. For early examples of this rhetoric, see Roy and Fania to Walter, Mae, and Linda Reuther, October 31, 1944, Box 79, Victor Reuther Collection, ALUA; Walter Reuther, "How to Raise Wages without Increasing Prices," 1945, Box 3, SPD; Reuther, "Our Fear of Abundance," 14–15; Reuther's address to National GM Conference, July 25, 1947, Box 3, SPD; UAW press releases, June 22, 1946; July 21 and 30, 1947; August 1 and 15, 1947, all in Box 8, FP.

36. Reuther's comments on *America's Town Meeting of the Air*, October 11, 1945, and his "How to Raise Wages," both in Box 3, SPD; Reuther, "Our Fear of Abundance," 15; Walter Reuther to Harry Truman, August 20, 1947, Box 8, FP; Walter Reuther radio script, n.d. [1944], Box 540, WPR.

37. Transcript of Reuther press conference with Charles E. Wilson, March 31, 1942, Box 540, WPR; Reuther to Drach, October 19, 1945, and to J. A. Mercuson, October 20, 1945, both in Box 24, WPR; UAW press release, September 10, 1946, Box 8, FP.

38. UAW press release, September 10, 1946, Box 8, FP; Victor Reuther, "Look Forward Labor," 8; Reuther's address to National GM Council, July 25, 1947, Box 3, and to ADA, February 22, 1948, Box 4, FP; text of radio debate between Reuther and Robert Taft, April 11, 1948, Box 3, SPD.

39. Walter Reuther, *The Challenge of Peace* (American Labor Conference on International Affairs pamphlet, 1945), Box 3, SPD; UAW press releases, October 6 and December 7, 1946, Box 8, FP; Reuther to Drach, October 19, 1945, Box 24, WPR; Reuther radio script, n.d. [1944], Box 540, WPR.

40. Harris, *Right to Manage*, 71–74, traces the conservative backlash against Reuther.

41. The classic statement of Reuther's anticommunism is Walter Reuther, "How to Beat the Communists," in his *Selected Papers*, esp. 34–35. Also see Reuther to Drach, October 19, 1945, Box 24, WPR; UAW press release, September 10, 1946, Box 8, FP; Reuther address to ADA National Convention, February 22, 1948, Box 15, Jacobs-Sifton.

42. Reuther's address to NAACP, June 28, 1946, and to Midwest Workers Educational Conference, n.d. [1947?], both in Box 4, FP; UAW press release, June 28, 1946, Box 542, WPR.

43. Halpern, *UAW Politics*, 24–25, 122–123, describes the UAW's socialist faction. The former Socialist is Brendan Sexton, as quoted in Emanuel Geltman and Irving Howe, "The Tradition of Reutherism: An Interview with Brendan Sexton," *Dissent* 19 (Winter 1972), 57.

44. Seaton, *Catholics and Radicals;* Halpern, *UAW Politics*, 124–125; John Cort, "Reuther and the Auto Workers," *Commonweal* 44 (April 19, 1946); Dennis Deslippe, "'A Revolution of Its Own': The Social Doctrine of the Association of Catholic Trade Unionists in Detroit, 1939–1950," *Records of the American Catholic Historical Society of Philadelphia* 102 (Winter 1991), 31.

45. The best accounts of the rank-and-file caucus are Howe and Widick, *UAW and Walter Reuther,* chap. 5, and Lichtenstein, *Labor's War at Home,* 189–197, 214–216.

46. Halpern, *UAW Politics,* 26, 197–198; Howe and Widick, *UAW and Walter Reuther,* 289.

47. Among the best studies of the Communist Party's influence in the UAW are Cochran, *Labor and Communism;* Keeran, *Communist Party,* chaps. 10–11; and Halpern, *UAW Politics.* Christopher Johnson, *Maurice Sugar: Law, Labor, and the Left in Detroit, 1912–1950* (Detroit, 1988), 292, discusses the left-wing caucus's view of Reuther.

48. Halpern, *UAW Politics,* 126–131; Lichtenstein, *Labor's War at Home,* 144–145; Keeran, *Communist Party,* 251–257; Johnson, *Maurice Sugar,* 266.

49. Meier and Rudwick, *Black Detroit,* 208–215; Halpern, *UAW Politics,* 99–101, 126–127, 155–156; Korstad and Lichtenstein, "Opportunities Found and Lost," 792–797.

50. The interpretation combines Lichtenstein, *Labor's War at Home,* 226–227, which argues that Reuther used the GM strike to gain control of the UAW rank and file, and Halpern, *UAW Politics,* 56–57, 108, which argues that the strike was, in part, an attempt to win the support of nonaligned voters at the 1946 UAW convention.

51. Barton Bernstein, "Walter Reuther and the General Motors Strike of 1945–1946," *Michigan History* 49 (September 1965), 260–277. Nelson Lichtenstein, "From Corporatism to Collective Bargaining: Organized Labor and the Eclipse of Social

Democracy in the Postwar Era," in Fraser and Gerstle, *New Deal Order,* 132–133, and Halpern, *UAW Politics,* chaps. 4–5, place the strike in its national political and union contexts. Reuther is quoted in Barnard, *Walter Reuther,* 103.

52. Harris, *Right to Manage,* 139–149; Halpern, *UAW Politics,* 62–64; Howe and Widick, *UAW and Walter Reuther,* 198.

53. Halpern, *UAW Politics,* 71–92; Barnard, *Walter Reuther,* 105–109.

54. This interpretation of the GM strike conflicts with Lichtenstein's interpretation in a key respect. In "From Corporalism to Collective Bargaining," 133, Lichtenstein argues that after 1946 Reuther abandoned hopes of "structural change in the political economy." "[J]ust as postwar liberalism gradually reduced its commitment to national planning and eschewed issues of social and economic control," he writes, "so too did the UAW abandon the quest for labor participation in the running of the automobile industry. And just as liberalism increasingly came to define itself as largely concerned with the maintenance of economic growth and an expansion of the welfare state, so too did the UAW and the rest of the labor movement define is mission in those terms." I agree that Reuther moved away from the broad bargaining goals of 1946, but I do not believe that he abandoned broad economic change in general. Even in bargaining, moreover, Reuther remained committed to reform. In 1961, for instance, the UAW briefly renewed its call to examine GM's books. See shorthand transcript of UAW contract negotiations, June 28, 1961; Nat Weinberg to Ralph, August 5, 1961, and related documents, Box 102, Joseph Rauh Jr. Collection, LC. For an effective explanation of Reuther's bargaining philosophy in the postwar era, see oral history interview with Mildred Jeffrey, August 13, 1976, ALUA.

55. Halpern, *UAW Politics,* 106–111; Korstad and Lichtenstein, "Opportunities Found and Lost," 806; George Crockett, "Labor Looks Ahead," *Michigan Chronicle,* January 19, 1956, Box 3, FP.

56. Keeran, *Communist Party,* 256–281; Halpern, *UAW Politics,* 133–222; Barnard, *Walter Reuther,* 113–117; Johnson, *Maurice Sugar,* 288–296. Stephen Meyer, *"Stalin over Wisconsin": The Making and Unmaking of Militant Unionism, 1900–1950* (New Brunswick, N.J., 1992), 166–188, discusses the anticommunist campaign on the local level. Reuther's quote is from his "How to Beat the Communists," 35.

57. There is no study of anticommunism's patriotic appeal to the UAW's rank and file. Gerstle, *Working-Class Americanism,* chap. 9, traces the dynamic in the textile town of Woonsocket, R.I. Also see Mike Davis, *Prisoners of the American Dream* (London, 1986), 90–91. Halpern, *UAW Politics,* 204–205, 233–235, details the power of Taft-Hartley to swing the 1947 election to Reuther.

58. Oral history interviews with Jack Conway, March 27, 1963, and Frank Marquardt, February 10, 1960, both in ALUA; Michael Whitty "Emil Mazey: Radical as Liberal. The Evolution of Labor Radicalism in the UAW" (Ph.D. diss., Syracuse University, 1968); Richard Gosser typescript, November 22, 1963, Box 1, Ward M. Canaday Center, University of Toledo; George Crockett to Jack Zeller, September 24, 1945, Box 1, FP; Emmett Wheaton et al. to George Addes, March 27, 1945, and Shelton Tappes to George Crockett, both in Box 20, FP; Crockett to Charles Lawrence, October 23, 1945, Box 89, WPR; author's oral history interview with Paul Schrade, June 1992, Los Angeles; Mildred Jeffrey interview, August 13, 1976, ALUA.

59. Oral history interview with Jack Conway, March 27, 1963, ALUA; *Daily Worker,* November 26, 1947, Box 20, Victor Reuther Collection, ALUA; 1947 ACTU membership list, Box 2, ACTUC; Mazey to Joe Ferris, June 27, 1967, Box 148, UAW Secretary-Treasurer Collection, ALUA; Babson, *Building the Union,* 239, 242; oral history interviews with Pat Greathouse, May 14, 1963; with Leonard Woodcock, April 30, 1963;

with Shelton Tappes, October 27, 1967 and February 10, 1968, all in ALUA; Paul Schrade interview, June 1992. Letner and Starling came from the most powerful locals in their regions, Letner from St. Louis Local 25, Starling from Atlanta Local 34. Both locals had been pivotal in the UAW's successful organizing drive of 1936–37. See Letner and Starling vertical files, ALUA.

60. Halpern, *UAW Politics,* chaps. 15–16.

61. "Proceedings of the Eleventh Convention of the United Automobile Workers, November 9–15, 1947," ALUA, 203.

2. Craven Politics

1. Gardner Jackson to Paul Sifton, February 17, 1946, Box 29, PCS; Donald Montgomery to Walter Reuther, February 17, 1948, Box 542, WPR.

2. This impact of state and political formation on policy is explored in Peter B. Evans, Dietrick Rueschemeyer, and Theda Skocpol, eds., *Bringing the State Back In* (Cambridge, 1985). The classic study of nineteenth-century ethnocultural politics is Paul Kleppner, *The Cross of Culture: A Social Analysis of Midwestern Politics* (New York, 1970). See also Morton Keller, *Affairs of State: Public Life in Late Nineteenth-Century America* (Cambridge, Mass., 1977), esp. chap. 7. On the power of patronage, see Martin Shefter, "Trade Unions and Political Machines: The Organization and Disorganization of the American Working Class in the Late Nineteenth Century," in Ira Katznelson and Aristide R. Zolberg, eds., *Working Class Formation: Nineteenth-Century Patterns in Western Europe and the United States* (Princeton, 1986), 197–276. The twentieth-century American case is examined in Margaret Weir, Ann Shola Orloff, and Theda Skocpol, "Understanding American Social Politics," and Ann Shola Orloff, "The Political Origins of America's Belated Welfare State," both in Weir, Orloff, and Skocpol, *The Politics of Social Policy in the United States* (Princeton, 1988), 3–35, 37–65. I do not mean to imply here that the American polity remained static throughout the nineteenth and twentieth centuries. See Stephen Skowronek, *Building a New American State: The Expansion of National Administrative Capacities, 1877–1920* (Cambridge, 1982), for a sophisticated discussion of state centralization. Some scholars use the term "Dixiecrats" only in reference to those southern Democrats who bolted the Democratic Party for the States' Rights Party in the 1948 presidential election. I apply the term more broadly to encompass conservative southern Democrats in general. Not all southern Democrats were conservative, of course.

3. Margaret Weir and Theda Skocpol, "State Structures and the Possibilities for 'Keynesian' Responses to the Great Depression in Sweden, Britain, and the United States," in Evans et al., *Bringing the State Back In,* 107–168; Orloff, "Political Origins," 65–80; Richard Kirkendall, "The New Deal and American Politics," in Harvard Sitkoff, eds., *Fifty Years Later: The New Deal Evaluated* (New York, 1985), 27; Alan Brinkley, "The Idea of the State," in Steven Fraser and Gary Gerstle, eds., *The Rise and Fall of the New Deal Order, 1930–1980* (Princeton, 1989), 86. The best single volume on the New Deal remains William Leuchtenberg, *Franklin D. Roosevelt and the New Deal* (New York, 1963).

4. Kevin Boyle, "Building the Vanguard: Walter Reuther and Radical Politics in 1936," *Labor History* 30 (Summer 1989), 433–448; author's oral history interview with Victor Reuther, May 6, 1987, Washington, D.C.; Irving Howe and B. J. Widick, *The UAW and Walter Reuther* (New York, 1949), chaps. 9 and 12; Emmanuel Geltman and

Irving Howe, "The Tradition of Reutherism: An Interview with Brendan Sexton," *Dissent* 19 (Winter 1972), 57. Lizabeth Cohen, *Making a New Deal: Industrial Workers in Chicago, 1919–1939* (Cambridge, 1990), 267–289, explores the allegiance of the working class to the New Deal. During World War II, Reuther maintained a distant relationship with a third party in Michigan, the Michigan Commonwealth Federation. See Nelson Lichtenstein, *Labor's War at Home: The CIO in World War II* (Cambridge, 1982), 287, n. 60.

5. Brinkley, "Idea of the State," 85–121; Weir and Skocpol, "State Structures," 108, 137–141; Alan Brinkley, "The Antimonopoly Ideal and the Liberal State: The Case of Thurman Arnold," *JAH* 80 (September 1993), 558–571; Steven Fraser, *Labor Will Rule: Sidney Hillman and the Rise of American Labor* (New York, 1991), esp. chaps. 9–14; Stephen Amberg, *The Union Inspiration in American Politics: The Autoworkers and the Making of a Liberal Industrial Order* (Philadelphia, 1994), 97–102.

6. Amberg, *Union Inspiration;* Ellis Hawley, *The New Deal and the Problem of Monopoly: A Study in Economic Ambivalence* (Princeton, 1966); Otis Graham, *Toward a Planned Economy: From Roosevelt to Nixon* (New York, 1976), 7–17, 49–90; Robert Collins, *The Business Response to Keynes, 1929–1964* (New York, 1981), 5–12. For details on one of the clearest institutional expressions of this perspective, see Marion Clawson, *New Deal Planning: The National Resources Planning Board* (Baltimore, 1981).

7. Walter P. Reuther, "Five Hundred Planes a Day: A Program for the Utilization of the Automobile Industry for Mass Production of Defense Planes," in his *Selected Papers,* ed. Henry Cristman (New York, 1961), 1–12. Both Murray and Hillman facilitated Reuther's rise in the UAW hierarchy in the late 1930s, and Reuther attempted to shape shop-floor relations in the auto industry on the model Hillman had developed in the clothing industry. See Nelson Lichtenstein, "Great Expectations: The Promise of Industrial Jurisprudence and Its Demise, 1930–1960," in Lichtenstein and Howell Harris, eds., *Industrial Democracy in America: The Ambiguous Promise* (Cambridge, 1993), 127–129.

8. Victor Reuther, *The Brothers Reuther and the Story of the UAW: A Memoir* (Boston, 1976), 226; Fraser, *Labor Will Rule,* 474; Lichtenstein, *Labor's War at Home,* 86–89; *New York Times,* December 28, 1940; *Detroit Free Press,* December 29 and 30, 1940; I. F. Stone's series of articles in *The Nation,* December 1940.

9. On wartime economic controls, see Richard Polenberg, *War and Society: The United States, 1941–1945* (Philadelphia, 1972), chaps. 1 and 6. Nelson Lichtenstein, "From Corporatism to Collective Bargaining: Organized Labor and the Eclipse of Social Democracy in the Postwar Era," in Fraser and Gerstle, *New Deal Order,* 125–128, places the unions' hopes within the wartime context. Hansen's postwar plans are detailed in Collins, *Business Response to Keynes,* 96; Clawson, *New Deal Planning,* chap. 13.

10. Jack Stieber, *Governing the UAW* (New York, 1962), 59–61.

11. In 1945 the UAW International had approximately 400 employees on staff. Half that number worked for the regional directors, servicing local unions. The other half worked for the union's officers, primarily as functionaries of the International's various offices. UAW officers treated these positions as patronage, offering them to local officials and others who had supported the officers in convention elections. Reuther was no exception: most of the routine jobs under his control went to caucus loyalists. See Stieber, *Governing the UAW,* chap. 4.

12. Claire Sifton to Paul Sifton, Box 6, PCS; Ronald Schatz, "From Commons to Dunlop: Rethinking the Field and Theory of Industrial Relations," in Lichtenstein and

Harris, *Industrial Democracy in America*, 98–100; *Detroit Times*, June 20, 1955; *Washington Evening Star*, October 11, 1957; Donald Montgomery to S. M. Levitas, February 3, 1948, Box 13, SPD; *Labor Action*, February 22, 1943.

13. Paul Sifton to Walter Reuther, October 3, 1945, Box 29, PCS; *Washington Post*, April 7, 1972; Joseph Walsh to Paul Sifton, Box 57, PCS; *Detroit Times*, June 20, 1955; newspaper clippings, 1938, Box 37, PCS; UAW press release, December 5, 1947, Box 4, FP; Leuchtenburg, *Roosevelt and the New Deal*, 161–162. Sifton is also the only UAW member to have written a screenplay: *Midnight*, for Humphrey Bogart.

14. Paul Sifton to Claire Sifton, n.d. [1945], Box 4, PCS; Sifton testimonials, March 1963, Box 57, PCS; Martin Halpern, *UAW Politics in the Cold War Era* (Albany, 1988), 237.

15. UAW press release, January 8, 1948, Box 3, FP. On Rauh's experiences in the 1930s, see Katie Louchheim, ed., *The Making of the New Deal: The Insiders Speak* (Cambridge, Mass. 1983), 55–67, 110–114; transcript of conversation, Tom Corcoran and Ben Cohen, January 4, 1946, Box 4, Joseph L. Rauh Jr. Collection, LC. Rauh explained his impressions of Reuther in an interview with me in May 1987 in Washington, D.C. Rauh remembered thinking that the "500 planes a day" plan was "manna from heaven."

16. Reuther, *Brothers Reuther*, 136, 139; *UAW Solidarity*, January 1971; Nancy Gabin, *Feminism in the Labor Movement: Women and the United Auto Workers, 1935–1975* (Ithaca, 1990), 93; oral history interviews with Jack Conway, March 27, 1963, Brendan Sexton, November 6, 1978, Box 10, Brendan Sexton Collection, both in ALUA.

17. Reuther, *Brothers Reuther*, 136; oral history interview with Mildred Jeffrey, August 13, 1976; Jack Conway interview, March 27, 1963; Brookwood student lists, 1934, 1935–1936, Box 1, Roy Reuther Files; Brendan Sexton interview, November 6, 1978, all in ALUA. On Brookwood, see Fraser, *Labor Will Rule*, 221, 332. I have not been able to find information on Frank Winn's family background. He was born in Dallas, Texas, graduated from Southern Methodist University, and wrote for several Texas newspapers before attending Brookwood as a representative of the Newspaper Guild. From Brookwood he joined the Reuthers' Local 174, then moved to the International staff as director of public relations.

18. Mildred Jeffrey to Marj, March 28, 1941, Box 47, Mildred Jeffrey Collection, ALUA; Geltman and Howe, "Tradition of Reutherism," 53–57; Sidney Fine, *Sit-Down: The General Motors Strike of 1936–1937* (Ann Arbor, 1969), 113–119, 199, 267–269; Reuther, *Brothers Reuther*, 136, 139; *Detroit Free Press*, January 18, 1988; Sexton interview, November 6, 1978; Jeffrey Interview, August 13, 1976; Conway interview, March 27, 1963; all in ALUA.

19. Reuther, *Brothers Reuther*, 136; Jeffrey interview, August 13, 1976; Sexton interview, November 6, 1978; Conway interview, March 27, 1963, all in ALUA.

20. Oral history interviews with George Reedy, January 11, 1968, and Evelyn Dubrow, February 24, 1968, both in Box 2, Cormier-Eaton; Reuther, *Brothers Reuther*, 136, 333, 428–429; *Detroit Free Press*, January 18, 1988; Jeffrey interview, August 13, 1976, and Conway interview, March 27, 1963, both in ALUA.

21. Oral history interviews with Nat Weinberg, March 20 and April 30, 1963, ALUA; Brendan Sexton's speech notes, March 6, 1979, Box 10, Sexton Collection, Weinberg to Montgomery, December 31, 1952, Box 13, SPD; *New York Times*, September 11, 1967.

22. August Meier and Elliot Rudwick, *Black Detroit and the Rise of the UAW* (New York, 1979), 213–215; oral history interview with William Oliver, May 5, 1963, ALUA; *Michigan Chronicle*, May 11, 1946; oral history interviews with George Crockett, February 2, 1968, and Shelton Tappes, October 27, 1967, and February 10, 1968, all in

ALUA. Reuther recognized Oliver's shortcomings. Rather than give Oliver full control of the Fair Practices Department, Reuther named himself codirector, and he never included Oliver in his inner circle of political advisers.

23. Leuchtenberg, *Roosevelt and the New Deal*, 252-274; Edwin Amenta and Theda Skocpol, "Redefining the New Deal: World War II and the Development of Social Provisions in the United States," in Weir, et al., *Politics of Social Policy*, 86-94, 104-119.

24. The literature on Harry Truman's background and politics is voluminous. See, for example, Bert Cochran, *Harry Truman and the Crisis Presidency* (New York, 1973), 22-115; Donald McCoy, *The Presidency of Harry S Truman* (Lawrence, Kans., 1984), 1-13; and, most important, Alonzo Hamby, *Beyond the New Deal: Harry S. Truman and American Liberalism* (New York, 1973), chap. 2.

25. Among the best works on the early Cold War are John L. Gaddis, *The United States and the Origins of the Cold War, 1941-1947* (New York, 1972); and Daniel Yergin, *Shattered Peace: The Origins of the Cold War and the National Security State* (Boston, 1977).

26. Brinkley, "Idea of the State," 100-109; Richard Pells, *The Liberal Mind in a Conservative Age: American Intellectuals in the 1940s and 1950s* (New York, 1985), chaps. 1-2; Hamby, *Beyond the New Deal;* Ira Katznelson, "Was the Great Society a Lost Opportunity?" in Fraser and Gerstle, *New Deal Order*, 189-195; Alan Wolfe, *America's Impasse: The Rise and Fall of the Politics of Growth* (Boston, 1981), 13-26; Arthur Schlesinger Jr., *The Vital Center: The Politics of Freedom* (Boston, 1949), 183.

27. Mary Sperling McAuliffe, *Crisis on the Left: Cold War Politics and American Liberalism, 1947-1954* (Amherst, Mass., 1978), 3-32; Steven Gillon, *Politics and Vision: The ADA and American Liberalism, 1947-1985* (New York, 1985), 12-13; Hamby, *Beyond the New Deal*, esp. chap. 6; Pells, *Liberal Mind*, chap. 2.

28. Hamby, *Beyond the New Deal*, 8; Mark Tushnet, *The NAACP's Legal Strategy against Segregated Education, 1925-1950* (Chapel Hill, 1987), chaps. 1-6; Harvard Sitkoff, *A New Deal for Blacks: The Emergence of Civil Rights as a National Issue* (New York, 1978); Robin D. G. Kelley, *Hammer and Hoe: Alabama Communists during the Great Depression* (Chapel Hill, 1990), and "We Are Not What We Seem: Rethinking Black Working-Class Opposition in the Jim Crow South," *JAH* 80 (June 1993), 75-112; Robert Korstad and Nelson Lichtenstein, "Opportunities Found and Lost: Labor, Radicals, and the Early Civil Rights Movement," *JAH* 75 (December 1988), 784-797; Bruce Nelson, "Organized Labor and the Struggle for Black Equality in Mobile during World War II," *JAH* 80 (December 1993), 952-988; Michael Honey, *Southern Labor and Black Civil Rights: Organizing Memphis Workers* (Urbana, 1993).

29. Jack Bloom, *Class, Race, and the Civil Rights Movement* (Bloomington, 1987), chaps. 1-2; Richard Bensel, *Sectionalism and American Political Development, 1880-1980* (Madison, Wisc., 1984), 222-243; Robert Garson, *The Democratic Party and the Politics of Sectionalism, 1941-1948* (Baton Rouge, 1974), chap. 5.

30. Samuel Lubell, *The Future of American Politics* (Garden City, N.Y, 1951), 10; William Berman, *The Politics of Civil Rights in the Truman Administration* (Columbus, Ohio, 1970), 23-39; Harvard Sitkoff, "Harry Truman and the Election of 1948: The Coming of Age of Civil Rights in American Politics," *Journal of Southern History* 37 (November 1971), 599; Donald McCoy and Richard Ruetten, *Quest and Response: Minority Rights in the Truman Administration* (Lawrence, Kans., 1973), 31-54; R. Alton Lee, *Truman and Taft-Hartley: A Question of Mandate* (Lexington, Ky., 1966), 34-38; Hamby, *Beyond the New Deal*, chap. 3; Stephen Bailey, *Congress Makes a Law: The Story behind the Employment Act of 1946* (New York, 1950); Collins, *Business Response to Keynes*, 99-106.

31. On the UAW's disagreement with the new liberal agenda, see Montgomery to Reuther, January 10, 1947, Box 470, WPR; Montgomery to S. M. Levitas, February 3, 1948, Box 13, SPD. On the UAW's view of civil rights, see the UAW brief submitted to the Senate Committee on Labor and Public Welfare, June 18, 1947, Box 89, WPR. For Reuther's interest in driving the Dixiecrats from the Democratic Party, see his comments at the CIO Executive Board, January 22–23, 1948, reel 4, CIO Executive Board minutes (microfilm), ALUA.

32. All too often, the literature on the postwar UAW has portrayed Reuther as an uncritical supporter of the early Cold War. See Halpern, *UAW Politics*, 141–142, and Roger Keeran, *The Communist Party and the Auto Workers Unions* (Bloomington, 1980), 263. Reuther's words appear in his article "How to Beat the Communists," *Collier's*, February 28, 1948, 44.

33. The UAW leadership was particularly incensed by the administration's position toward the 1945–46 GM strike, which the Reuthers believed had undermined the walkout. Truman believed that Reuther was staging the strike in part to advance his political standing in the union, and other administration officials, particularly John Synder, the head of the Office of Price and Wage Administration, explicitly opposed Reuther's linking of wages and prices. See Hamby, *Beyond the New Deal*, 76; Chester Bowles, *Promises to Keep: My Years in Public Life* (New York, 1971), 130–131; and Lichtenstein, "From Corporatism to Collective Bargaining," 130. Victor Reuther's quote is from his "Look Forward Labor," *Common Sense* 14 (December 1945), 9; Walter's is from Hamby, *Beyond the New Deal*, 67.

34. Brendan Sexton, untitled manuscript, n.d., Box 6, Sexton Collection, ALUA; Montgomery to Reuther, February 17, 1948, Box 542, WPR. Also see Reuther's statement before a Senate Judiciary subcommittee, March 25, 1948, Box 170, WPR; Sifton to Ben, January 11, 1947, Box 28, PCS.

35. The standard study of ADA is Steve Gillon, *Politics and Vision: The ADA and American Liberalism, 1947–1985* (New York, 1987). Also see Hamby, *Beyond the New Deal*, 147–168. Reuther's brains trust had a strong connection to UDA: Sifton had served as the organization's Washington director in the mid-1940s. See Paul Sifton vertical file, ALUA.

36. Walter Reuther speech, February 22, 1948, Box 4, FP; oral history interview with Joseph Rauh, December 11, 1967, Box 2, Cormier-Eaton; Sifton to Ben, January 11, 1947, Box 28, PCS; Montgomery to Reuther, February 16, 1948, Box 471, WPR; Montgomery to Reuther, January 26, 1948, Box 64, Montgomery, James Loeb to Reuther, December 8 and 12, 1947, both in Box 470, WPR. On Prichard, see Louchheim, *Making of the New Deal*, 325. The UAW also helped to underwrite ADA with a $10,000 donation, which accounted for approximately 5 percent of the organization's operating expenses. See Emil Mazey to ADA, May 14, 1948, Box 471, WPR; Gillon, *Politics and Vision*, 58.

37. Victor Reuther, "Look Forward Labor," 9.

38. Hamby, *Beyond the New Deal*, 138–139; National Educational Committee for a New Party, "Ideas for a New Party: Provisional Declaration of Principles," *Antioch Review* 6 (Fall 1946), 449–472; Ken Kramer to Paul Sifton, November 1, 1946, and press release, National Educational Committee for a New Party, October 23, 1946, both in Box 27, PCS; Clayton Fountain, *Union Guy* (New York, 1949), 171.

39. *Antioch Review* (Winter 1946–47), 608–615. The Reuthers also maneuvered to build a political base in Michigan for the new party. See Mary to Paul Sifton, October 23, 1946, and Paul Sifton to Vera Wiggins, October 25, 1946, both in Box 27, PCS.

40. Sifton to Montgomery, December 6, 1947, Box 29, PCS.

41. Norman Markowitz, *The Rise and Fall of the People's Century: Henry A. Wallace and American Liberalism, 1941–1948* (New York, 1973), 1–199; Walter Reuther to Roy Reuther, November 22, 1944, Box 79, Victor Reuther Collection, ALUA. On the Popular Front, see Hamby, *Beyond the New Deal,* chaps. 6–8; Curtis MacDougall, *Gideon's Army,* 3 vols. (New York, 1965), 1: chaps. 12–14.

42. Halpern, *UAW Politics,* 244–245; Fountain, *Union Guy,* 171.

43. Markowitz, *Rise and Fall,* 279; MacDougall, *Gideon's Army,* 1:316–322; proceedings of the International Executive Board, CIO, January 22–23, 1948, CIO Executive Board Collection, ALUA; Frank Emspack, "The Break-Up of the Congress of Industrial Organizations" (Ph.D. diss., University of Wisconsin, 1972), 233–234; IEB minutes, March 1–5, 1948, Box 10, IEBC.

44. *New York Times,* December 19, 1947; Montgomery to Reuther, February 17, 1948, Box 542, WPR; *UAW Ammunition,* April 1948, 2–6.

45. Reuther to all local unions, April 6, 1948, in "UAW Administrative Letters," 1:7, ALUA; Reuther, Richard Gosser, and John Livingston to members of Local 453, October 22, 1948 and list of pro-Wallace locals, both in Box 2, PA; IEB minutes, special session, January 10–11, 1949, Box 3, IEBC.

46. Fay Calkins, *The CIO and the Democratic Party* (Chicago, 1952), 112–118; Dudley Buffa, *Union Power and American Democracy: The UAW and the Democratic Party, 1935–1972* (Ann Arbor, 1984), 8–19; Reuther to Gus Scholle, March 12, 1948, Box 23, and Scholle to Victor Reisel, April 2, 1948, Box 21, both in Michigan AFL-CIO Collection, ALUA.

47. Montgomery to Reuther, February 17, 1948, Box 542, WPR, and January 26, 1948, Box 64, Montgomery.

48. Clifford memorandum, Box 21, Clark Clifford Papers, HSTL. For details on the memorandum, see Hamby, *Beyond the New Deal,* 209–212; Irwin Ross, *The Loneliest Campaign: The Truman Victory of 1948* (New York, 1968), 21–27.

49. Hamby, *Beyond the New Deal,* 212–215; draft memorandum, n.d. [early 1948], Box 430, WPR; IEB minutes, March 1–5, 1948, Box 10, IEBC; Robert Donovan, *Conflict and Crisis: The Presidency of Harry S. Truman, 1945–1948,* (New York, 1977), 389; James Loeb to Reuther, March 4, 1948, Box 471, WPR; Reuther's handwritten notes, n.d. [March 1948]; Chester Bowles to Walter Reuther, n.d. [March 1948]; draft of IEB resolution, n.d. [March 1948], all in Box 420, WPR; oral history interview with Jack Conway, November 20, 1967, Box 2, Cormier-Eaton; Sifton to Reuther, March 20, 1948, Box 430, WPR; William Batt Jr. to Clark Clifford, April 15, 1948, Box 20, Clifford Papers, HSTL; "ADA Statement on Political Policy," April 11, 1948, Box 471, WPR; Gillon, *Politics and Vision,* 44–45; Jack Kroll, "A Day to Day Account of the Activities of the CIO-PAC at the Democratic National Convention," n.d. [July 1948], Box 7, Jack Kroll Collection, LC; *United Automobile Worker,* July 1948.

50. Gillon, *Politics and Vision,* 47–50; Hamby, *Beyond the New Deal,* 243–244; Garson, *Democratic Party,* 203–277; Jack Kroll memorandum of 1948 Democratic Convention, n.d. [1948], Box 7, Kroll Collection, LC.

51. Gillon, *Politics and Vision,* 48–50; Carl Solberg, *Hubert Humphrey: A Biography* (New York, 1984), 11–19; Garson, *Democratic Party,* 279–307.

52. Hamby, *Beyond the New Deal,* 244–245; Ross, *Loneliest Campaign,* 129–130.

53. Ross, *Loneliest Campaign,* 176–243; Hamby, *Beyond the New Deal,* 247–260.

54. Clark Clifford handwritten note, n.d. [August 1948], Box 33, Clifford Papers, and Gibson to Harry Roberts, November 16, 1948, Box 16, John Gibson Collection, both in HSTL; minutes of CIO Executive Board meeting, August 30–September 1, 1948, reel 4, CIO Executive Board Collection, ALUA; IEB Minutes, November 29–December 2,

1948, Box 3, IEBC; oral history interview with Jack Conway, November 20, 1967, Cormier-Eaton; Reuther's radio address, October 31, 1948, Box 142, WPR; Conway to Mazey, October 31, 1948, Box 1, PA; *United Automobile Worker,* August 1948. The UAW did not cosponsor Harry Truman's Labor Day appearance in Detroit. The invitation came from the Michigan CIO. See John Gibson to Russell White, July 30, 1948, Box 15, Gibson Collection, HSTL.

55. Summary of PAC meeting, July 7, 1948 and Gus Scholle and Barney Hopkins to Reuther, August 17, 1948, both in Box 21, Michigan AFL-CIO Collection, ALUA; Ray Berndt to Roy Reuther, September 27, 1948, and Art Hughes to Norm Matthews, October 14, 1948, both in Box 2, PA.

56. Stieber, *Governing the UAW,* 67–72.

57. Hughes to Matthews, October 14, 1948; weekly international staff reports, Region 1 and Region 1A, October 16, and 29, 1948; Fraser to Political Action Department, November 5, 1948, all in Box 2, PA; Billie Farnum to Larry Getlinger, October 25, 1948, Box 3, PA.

58. International representative's report, Region 8, October 29, 1948, Box 5, PA; Roy Reuther to Charles Ballard, September 26, 1948, and International representative report, Region 2B, October 30, 1948, both in Box 3, PA; national PAC contributions, June 1, 1948–March 31, 1949, Box 2, PA.

59. International representatives reports, Region 8, October 29, 1948, Box 5, and Region 6, November 3, 1948, Box 4, PA; Irving Bluestone to Tony Canole, October 7, 1948, Box 2, PA; William Dodds to Mazey, October 18, 1948, Box 142, WPR.

60. Oral history interview with Jack Conway, November 20, 1967, Box 2, Cormier-Eaton; Reuther to Montgomery, July 27, 1948, Box 64, Montgomery; UAW Research Report, July 24, 1948, Box 20, SP. Sifton thought the GOP was capable of winning the election "with any candidate whose body is still warm." See *UAW CIO Fair Practices Fact Sheet,* May–June 1948; *United Auto Worker,* August 1948.

61. Minutes of the State CIO Council PAC meeting, August 15, 1948, Box 14, Gibson Collection, HSTL; *Labor Action,* August 23, 1948; Victor Reuther to Harry Becker, September 29, 1948; James Loeb to Victor Reuther, October 1, 1948; and Lewis Carliner to Sam Jacobs, December 21, 1948, all in Box 2, UAW Education Department Collection, 1948–1955, ALUA; Hamby, *Beyond the New Deal,* 265.

62. Markowitz, *Rise and Fall,* 293–295; MacDougall, *Gideon's Army* vol. 3; Hamby, *Beyond the New Deal,* 260–263; *UAW Ammunition,* October 1948, 31; Halpern, *UAW Politics,* 246; Ralph Showalter to Frank Winn, October 20, 1948, Box 20, SP; Ross, *Loneliest Campaign,* 245–266; Samuel Lubell, *The Future of American Politics* (New York, 1951), 218–227; Arthur Kornhauser, Harold Sheppard, and Albert Mayer, *When Labor Votes: A Study of Auto Workers* (New York, 1956), 41.

63. On the triumph of the new liberalism, see Hamby, *Beyond the New Deal,* 267–274. For details on the aborted 1949 UAW conference, see package of memos on UAW educational conference, Box 2, Education Department Collection, ALUA.

3. The Vital Center Shifts

1. Donald Montgomery to Nat Weinberg, September 14, 1947, and June 8, August 22, and December 20, 1949, all in Box 13, SPD.

2. On Truman's second term, see Eric Goldman, *The Crucial Decade and After: America, 1945–1960* (New York, 1960), 91–236; Bert Cochran, *Harry Truman and the Crisis Presidency* (New York, 1973), 291–391; Robert J. Donovan, *Tumultuous Years:*

The Presidency of Harry S. Truman, 1949–1953 (New York, 1982); Donald McCoy, *The Presidency of Harry S. Truman* (Lawrence, Kans., 1984), 163–310; Alonzo Hamby, *Beyond the New Deal: Harry S. Truman and American Liberalism* (New York, 1973), 277–503.

3. Hamby, *Beyond the New Deal*, chap. 10; William Berman, *The Politics of Civil Rights in the Truman Administration* (Columbus, Ohio, 1970), 133–146; Donald McCoy and Richard Ruetten, *Quest and Response: Minority Rights and the Truman Administration* (Lawrence, Kans., 1973), 154–156, 171–177.

4. UAW *Fair Practices Fact Sheet*, January–February 1949; Allan Knight to Cooperating Agencies, March 5, 1948, Box 90, WPR; Paul Sifton proposal, December 12, 1948, Box 66, Montgomery; Sifton draft paper, n.d. [early 1949], Box 11B, FP; IEB minutes, March 14–18, 1949, Box 4, IEBC; Emil Mazey to Roy Wilkins, May 26, 1949, Box 10, FP.

5. Bert Cochran, *Labor and Communism: The Conflict That Shaped American Unions* (Princeton, 1977), 305–315; Mary Sperling McAuliffe, *Crisis on the Left: Cold War Politics and American Liberals, 1947–1954* (Amherst, Mass., 1978), 51–62; Harvey Levenstein, *Communism, Anticommunism, and the CIO* (Westport, Conn., 1981); Martin Halpern, *UAW Politics in the Cold War Era* (Albany, 1988), 247–248.

6. Peter Weiler, "The United States, International Labor, and the Cold War: The Breakup of the World Federation of Trade Unions," *Diplomatic History* 5 (Winter 1980), 1–22; Anthony Carew, *Labour under the Marshall Plan: The Politics of Productivity and the Marketing of Management Science* (Detroit, 1987), 70–79; Victor Reuther, *The Brothers Reuther and the Story of the UAW: A Memoir* (Boston, 1976), 330–335; John Barnard, *Walter Reuther and the Rise of the Auto Workers Union* (Boston, 1983), 126–127.

7. Montgomery to Weinberg, August 22, 1949, Box 13, SPD. Also see Montgomery to Reuther, February 17, 1949, Box 18, Montgomery; A. H. Raskin, "Reuther Explains the 'Reuther Plan,'" *New York Times Magazine*, March 20, 1949.

8. UAW *Ammunition*, September 1949.

9. Undated [early 1949] manuscript, possibly for *Auto Worker*, Box 11B, FP; IEB minutes, June 6–10, 1949, Box 3, IEBC; Walter Reuther, "Cooperation of Industry and Social Work," speech delivered June 1949, and report to European labor, November 1949, both in Box 3, SPD; Donald Montgomery, "Labor's Aims and What They Mean to Agriculture," *Journal of Farm Economics* 31 (November 1949), 1141–1147; rough draft of Reuther speech, March 31, 1949, Box 3, SPD.

10. Stephen Amberg, *The Union Inspiration in American Politics: The Autoworkers and the Making of a Liberal Industrial Order* (Philadelphia, 1994), 163–164.

11. Richard Davies, *Housing Reform during the Truman Administration* (Columbia, Mo., 1966); Mark Gelfand, *A Nation of Cities: The Federal Government and Urban America, 1933–1965* (New York, 1975), chaps. 3–4.

12. Leo Goodman to Joseph L. Rauh Jr., November 4, 1968, Box 103, Joseph L. Rauh Jr. Papers, LC; Goodman to Reuther, November 10, 1948, Box 588, WPR; Raymond Foley to Matt Connelly, December 6, 1948, OF 63, HSTL; Goodman to Reuther, December 14, 1948, Box 588, WPR; Goodman background material, 1948–49, Box 6, CIO Housing Committee Collection, Leo Goodman Files, ALUA; Reuther's testimony before the Subcommittee on Housing of the Senate Banking Committee, February 14, 1949, Box 501, WPR; Reuther to CIO Housing Committee, January 18, 1949, Box 588, WPR.

13. Oral history interview with Victor Reuther, May 6, 1987, Washington, D.C.; Elisabeth Reuther Dickmeyer, *Reuther: A Daughter Strikes* (Southfield, Mich., 1989), 115–117; oral history interview with Mildred Jeffrey, August 13, 1976, ALUA; Alan

Clive, *State of War: Michigan in World War II* (Ann Arbor, 1979), 94, 103–112; *Detroit Free Press*, December 7, 1950.

14. Reuther's testimony before the Senate Subcommittee on Housing, February 14, 1949, Box 501, WPR.

15. Walter Reuther, "Homes for People, Jobs for Prosperity, Planes for Peace," 1949, Box 59, WPR; U.S. Congress, Senate, Committee on Banking and Currency, *Hearings*, 81st Cong., 1st Sess. (Washington, D.C., 1949), 445–511.

16. Reuther had presented the housing plan as early as 1945, as part of an effort to save the Ford Motor Company's wartime Willow Run plant from closing. See Walter Reuther, *Are War Plants Expendable?* (pamphlet published by UAW Local 50, 1945). For background on the 1949 proposal, see Harry Chester to Weinberg, January 17, 1949, Box 20, Nat Weinberg Collection, ALUA. The Reuther quote is from Senate Banking Committee, *Hearings*, 447.

17. The *New York Times*, November 7, 1948, explained that the administration could count on 32 liberal votes in the Senate and 200 liberal votes in the House. The classic study of the congressional alignment is James MacGregor Burns, *The Deadlock of Democracy: Four-Party Politics in America* (Englewood Cliffs, N.J., 1963). Also see John Frederick Martin, *Civil Rights and the Crisis of Liberalism: The Democratic Party, 1945–1976* (Boulder, Colo., 1979), 89–90.

18. Berman, *Politics of Civil Rights*, 141–156; McCoy and Ruetten, *Quest and Response*, 171–178.

19. Sifton to Reuther, March 3, 1949, Box 23, PA. Also see Weinberg to Reuther, February 14, 1949, Box 1, SPD; *United Automobile Worker*, March 1949 and April 1949; *UAW Fair Practices Fact Sheet*, January–February 1949.

20. Hamby, *Beyond the New Deal*, chaps. 14–15.

21. *United Automobile Worker*, May 1949; *UAW Fair Practices Fact Sheet*, November–December 1949; *New York Times*, May 28, 1950; Reuther to William Boyle, July 1950, Box 23, PA.

22. Samuel Lubell, *The Revolt of the Moderates* (New York, 1956); Robert Griffith, "Dwight D. Eisenhower and the Corporate Commonwealth," *American Historical Review* 87 (February 1982), 96–100; Charles Alexander, *Holding the Line: The Eisenhower Era* (Bloomington, 1975), 1–9.

23. For details on the second Red Scare, see, among other fine works, Richard Rovere, *Senator Joe McCarthy* (New York, 1959); Robert Griffith, *The Politics of Fear: Joseph R. McCarthy and the Senate* (Lexington, Ky., 1970); Robert Griffith and Athan Theoharis, eds., *The Spectre: Original Essays on the Cold War and the Origins of McCarthyism* (New York, 1974); David Oshinsky, *Senator Joseph McCarthy and the American Labor Movement* (Columbia, Mo., 1976); David Caute, *The Great Fear: The Anti-Communist Purge under Truman and Eisenhower* (New York, 1977); Thomas Reeves, *The Life and Times of Joe McCarthy: A Biography* (New York, 1982); and David Oshinsky, *A Conspiracy So Immense: The World of Joe McCarthy* (New York, 1983). It is important to note that the virulent anticommunism of Truman and the liberal community in the late 1940s laid the groundwork for McCarthy. This argument is presented in Athan Theoharis, *Seeds of Repression: Harry S. Truman and the Origins of McCarthyism* (Chicago, 1971).

24. Rovere, *Senator Joe McCarthy*, 119–170; Reeves, *Life and Times*, chaps. 11–12; Oshinsky, *Conspiracy So Immense*, 103–157; Griffith, *Politics of Fear*, chaps. 2–3.

25. *United Automobile Worker*, April 1950; Paul Sifton to Walter Reuther, March 21, 1950, and to Roy Reuther, November 10, 1950, both in Box 23, PA; Sifton to Roy Reuther, April 26, 1951, and to Walter Reuther, April 27, 1951, both in Box 372, WPR.

26. Walter Reuther's handwritten notes, "good and welfare" session, n.d. [early 1950], and Victor Reuther to Walter Reuther, n.d. [mid-1950], both in Box 103, WPR; oral history interview with Frank Marquart, February 10, 1960, ALUA. The summer school controversy arose after the *Wage Earner,* the ACTU newspaper, ran a front-page story detailing the LID's participation in the program. See *Labor Action,* September 25, 1950.

27. Halpern, *UAW Politics,* 242; Reuther's speech to ADA, January 28, 1949, Box 11, CIO Housing Committee Collection, Leo Goodman Files; ALUA; Reuther's address to ICFTU, December 1949, Walter Reuther Vertical File, 1947–49, ALUA; Reuther address to the National Convention of the American Association of School Administrators, March 1950, Box 3, SP. In 1949 Reuther expressed to his staff a strong interest in learning more about conditions in post–colonial areas. See William Oliver to Reuther, June 1, 1949, Box 8, FP. Reuther's most powerful statement in opposition to pursuing military containment in the Third World came shortly after the outbreak of the Korean War. "I believe we have lost Asia," he told the IEB. "We have lost it because of poverty and hunger, and we are fighting native troops all over the world—American boys and British boys and United Nations troops. They are fighting natives against us because the natives are hungry": IEB minutes, September 11–15, 1950, Box 5, IEBC.

28. Reuther to Truman, telegram, in *United Automobile Worker,* August 1950; Hamby, *Beyond the New Deal,* 408–409. The UAW's response to the outbreak of war was conditioned by the union's experience in World War II. In July 1950 Reuther issued a series of demands that echoed the UAW's World War II "equality of sacrifice" program. He rejected any suggestion that the UAW issue a no-strike pledge during the Korean war, a major point of interunion tension during World War II. The UAW's demands are laid out in an administrative letter to all local unions, dated July 27, 1950, in "UAW Administrative Letters" vol. 1, ALUA. On the no-strike pledge issue, see IEB minutes, September 11–15, 1950 and November 17–18, 1950, both in Box 5, IEBC.

29. Ralph Showalter to Oliver, August 9, 1950, Box 26, FP; Montgomery to Reuther, July 8, 1950, Box 371, WPR; IEB minutes, September 11–15, 1950, Box 5, IEBC; UAW press release, October 22, 1950, Box 31, Montgomery; Reuther to all automobile company presidents, July 20, 1950, Box 375, WPR; U.S. Congress, Senate, Committee on Banking and Currency, *Hearings,* 82d Cong., 1st sess. (Washington, D.C., 1951), 2186.

30. Reuther to Truman, July 14, 1950, OF 394, HSTL. Reuther arrived at the $13 billion figure by dividing the total cost of World War II by 100. Reuther argued that the United States could raise the money necessary to fund the program by raising corporate and upper-income personal income taxes to World War II levels. In September 1950 Nat Weinberg called on Reuther to follow up his "Peace Offensive" with a specific proposal to end the Korean conflict. The United States, he said, should pledge not to cross the 38th parallel; the United Nations should place the entire peninsula under a trusteeship, to be administered by India and Sweden; and the United States should contribute a "substantial" sum to the economic rehabilitation and development of both North and South Korea. See Weinberg to Reuther, September 26, 1950, Weinberg Collection, ALUA.

31. Hamby, *Beyond the New Deal,* chap. 20, is useful on the Korean War mobilization. Harry Truman to John Steelman, July 1950; Robert Denison to Steelman, July 27, 1950; David Bell and D. Lloyd to Steelman, August 1, 1950, all in OF 394, HSTL.

32. Montgomery to Reuther, August 7, 1950, Box 22, PA; Montgomery to Reuther, July 8, 1950, Box 371, WPR; IEB minutes, September 11–15, 1950, Box 5, IEBC; Harry Chester to Nat Weinberg, November 30, 1950, Box 20, Weinberg Collection, ALUA.

33. Hamby, *Beyond the New Deal,* 408–415; Griffith, *Politics of Fear,* 118–122; *New York Times,* July 25 and 26, August 1, 5, and 8, 1950; *UAW Ammunition,* August

1950. At least some of the workers expelled from the plants were subsequently expelled from the locals and fired from their jobs.

34. James C. Foster, *The Union Politic: The CIO Political Action Committee* (Columbia, Mo., 1975), 133–154; Seth Wigderson, "The UAW in the 1950s" (Ph.D. diss., Wayne State University, 1989), 133–154; Herbert Parmet, *Richard Nixon and His America* (Boston, 1990), 186–200; Samuel Lubell, *The Future of American Politics* (New York, 1951); Donovan, *Tumultuous Years*, 297–298; Oshinsky, *McCarthy and the Labor Movement*, 103–104; Sifton to Roy Reuther, November 10, 1950, Box 23, PA; Hamby, *Beyond the New Deal*, 440–446.

35. Hamby, *Beyond the New Deal*, 446–451; Jack Stieber, "Labor's Walkout from the Korean War Stabilization Board," *Labor History* 21 (Spring 1980), 246, 252–253.

36. Stephen Meyer, "The Persistence of Fordism: Workers and Technology in the American Automobile Industry, 1900–1960," in Nelson Lichtenstein and Stephen Meyer, eds., *On the Line: Essays in the History of Auto Work* (Urbana, 1989), 87–88; Thomas Sugrue, "The Structure of Urban Poverty: The Reorganization of Space and Work in Three Periods of American History," in Michael Katz, ed., *The "Underclass" Debate: Views from History* (Princeton, 1993), 102–103; Nelson Lichtenstein, "Walter Reuther and the Rise of Labor-Liberalism," in Melvyn Dubofsky and Warren Van Tine, eds., *Labor Leaders in America* (Urbana, 1987), 293; BLS, *Employment and Earnings, United States, 1909–1975*, Bulletin 1312–10 (Washington, D.C., 1976); Barnard, *Walter Reuther*, 137–141.

37. *Labor Action*, July 24 and August 14, 1950.

38. Weinberg to Reuther, November 27, 1951, Box 1, SPD; "How Michigan Solved Its Unemployment Crisis," n.d. [1952], Box 293, Adlai Stevenson Collection, SGML; material for UAW Conference on Defense Unemployment, January 13–14, 1952, and Weinberg to Montgomery, June 26, 1951, both in Box 13, SPD; *Labor Action*, August 16, 1950, and August 6, 1951.

39. IEB minutes, June 28, 1951, Box 5, IEBC; *Labor Action*, August 14, 1950, January 22, 1951, and April 21, 1951.

40. Oral history interview with Jack Conway, March 27, 1963, ALUA; Timothy Borden, "Richard T. Gosser and Comprehensive Unionism in Toledo, Ohio" (M.A. thesis, University of Toledo, 1994); *Labor Action*, September 25, 1950.

41. Nelson Lichtenstein, "Life at the Rouge: A Cycle of Workers Control," in Charles Stephenson and Robert Asher, eds., *Life and Labor: Dimensions of American Working Class History* (Albany, 1986), 237–259.

42. Robert Asher, "The 1949 Ford Speed-Up Strike and the Postwar Social Compact, 1946–1961," in Asher and Ronald Edsforth, eds., *Auto Work* (Albany, forthcoming); Lichtenstein, "Life at the Rouge," 255–256; Stieber, *Governing the UAW*, 144–145; 1950–1951 clippings from *Wage Earner*, Box 25, ACTUC.

43. "Mutiny at Ford Local 600," *Fortune*, August 1951, 43–48; *Detroit News*, November 19, 1951; "Notes of the Month," *Fortune*, November 1951, 50; and October through December 1951 issues of Local 600's weekly newspaper, *Ford Facts*. Much of Stellato's attack on the International was nothing more than gamesmanship. He invited Reuther's long-time critic John L. Lewis to be the keynote speaker at Local 600's tenth anniversary celebrations in mid-1951, for example, and late in the year he directed a highly publicized protest march on the UAW's International headquarters.

44. Minutes of the East Side Coordinators Committee, November 17, 1949, Box 62, PA; *Labor Action*, April 13, 1953.

45. Sifton to Reuther, February 6, 1951, Box 23, PA.

46. IEB minutes, special sessions, February 17 and June 28, 1951, Box 5, IEBC; Walter Reuther, "A Program to Expedite Tool Machines," June 25, 1951, Box 584, WPR; *United Automobile Worker,* July 1951; Montgomery to Weinberg, July 14, 1951, Box 584, WPR; U.S. Congress, Senate, Select Committee on Small Business, *Hearings,* 82d Cong., 1st sess. (Washington, D.C., 1951), 155–192.

47. "What Labor Wants: An Interview with Walter P. Reuther," *U.S. News & World Report,* April 6, 1951, 30; *Detroit Free Press,* January 8, 1951; Reuther's address to Economic Club of Detroit, November 30, 1953, Box 3, SPD.

48. Reuther to Alan Valentine, November 2, 1950, Box 371, WPR; IEB minutes, November 17–18, 1950, Box 5, IEB; *UAW Ammunition,* January 1951. The UAW gained substantial support in its fight for the escalator clause from the CIO and the AFL, which joined in the United Labor Policy Committee to lobby for changes in the defense mobilization. See minutes of the United Labor Policy Committee, December 14, 1950, Box 372, WPR; Stieber, "Labor's Walkout," 247–249; Reuther to James Murray, March 2, 1951, Box 381, WPR.

49. Minutes of the National Advisory Board on Mobilization Policy, July 24, 1951, Box 142, President's Secretary's Files, HSTL; Mazey to Maurice Tobin, August 14, 1951, Box 30, Montgomery; Reuther to all local unions in Detroit, August 30, 1951, Box 584, WPR; Reuther to Truman, October 10, 1951; David Stowe to Reuther; Reuther to C. E. Wilson, October 18, 1951, all in Box 584, WPR.

50. Montgomery to Reuther, December 3 and 24, 1951, WPR; *UAW Ammunition,* February 1952; series of memos and supporting material from Defense Distressed Area Task Force, 1952, Box 30, Montgomery. The official was Jack Small, chairman of the Munitions Board.

51. Harold Enarson to Mr. Steelman, October 31, 1951, OF 264, HSTL; Griffith, *Politics of Fear,* chaps. 2–3.

52. Walter Goodman, *The Committee: The Extraordinary Career of the House Committee on Un-American Activities* (New York, 1968), 317–318; *Labor Action,* March 3, 1952; *Michigan CIO News,* January 17, 1952; *Detroit Free Press,* February 23, 1952; IEB minutes, March 12, 1952, Box 5, IEBC.

53. U.S. Congress, House, Committee on Un-American Activities, *Hearings,* 82d Cong., 1st sess. (Washington, D.C. 1952), 2711–2958; *Detroit Free Press,* February 27, 1952. HUAC's hearings also had a racial dimension. Many of the witnesses called to explain their connections with the CP were African-Americans.

54. *Detroit News,* March 2, 1952; *Wage Earner,* March 1952; *Labor Action,* March 10 and 17, 1952; *Michigan CIO News,* March 6, 1952; *Detroit Free Press,* February 16, 1952. Though the International condemned the shop-floor attacks, in private Reuther thought them justifiable, since CP members were opposing a military action in which the sons and brothers of many rank and filers were engaged. See IEB minutes, special session, March 12, 1952, Box 5, IEBC.

55. IEB minutes, special session, March 12, 1952, Box 5, IEBC; HUAC, *Hearings,* 3035–3144. Walter Reuther also asked to appear before the committee, but the committee did not give him a chance to do so. See John Wood to Reuther, March 11, 1952, Box 249, WPR.

56. Reuther to Local 600 officers, March 12, 1952, Box 249, WPR. Carl Stellato responded by charging that Reuther was trying, "through unconstitutional means, to impose a dictatorship from the top" in the UAW. See Stellato to Reuther, March 13, 1952, WPR.

57. Minutes of the show-cause hearing, March 14, 1952, Box 5, IEBC; UAW press release, March 15, 1952, Box 249, WPR; *Labor Action,* March 31, 1952.

4. The Pull of Consensus

1. Transcript of phone conversation between Stevenson and Johnson, January 10, 1953, Box 1, Notes and Transcripts from Johnson Conversations, LBJL; Robert Dallek, *Lone Star Rising: Lyndon Johnson and His Times, 1908–1960* (New York, 1991), 428–429.

2. Samuel Lubell, *The Revolt of the Moderates* (New York, 1956). Also see Herbert Parmet, *The Democrats: The Years after FDR* (New York, 1976), chap. 6; John Frederick Martin, *Civil Rights and the Crisis of Liberalism: The Democratic Party, 1945–1976* (Boulder, Colo., 1979), chap. 6; Steven Gillon, *Politics and Vision: The ADA and American Liberalism, 1947–1985* (New York, 1987), chaps. 4 and 5.

3. Herbert Parmet, *Eisenhower and the American Crusades* (New York, 1972), 67–70. Eisenhower's political backers are traced in Robert Griffith, "Dwight Eisenhower and the Corporate Commonwealth," *American Historical Review* 87 (February 1982), 87–122.

4. The best analysis of Eisenhower's political ideology is Griffith, "Eisenhower and the Corporate Commonwealth," 87–122. On Eisenhower and the Republican Party in 1952, see Parmet, *Eisenhower and the American Crusades*, 83–114; Stephen Ambrose, *Eisenhower*, 2 vols. (New York, 1983–84), 1: chaps. 26–27; John Robert Greene, *The Crusade: The Presidential Election of 1952* (Lanham, Md., 1985); Chester Pach Jr. and Elmo Richardson, *The Presidency of Dwight D. Eisenhower*, rev. ed. (Lawrence, Kans., 1991), chap. 1; and Jeff Broadwater, *Eisenhower and the Anti-Communist Crusade* (Chapel Hill, 1992), chaps. 2 and 3.

5. Alonzo Hamby, *Beyond the New Deal: Harry S. Truman and American Liberalism* (New York, 1973), chap. 22; Gillon, *Politics and Vision*, 83–86; Greene, *Crusade*, 33–47.

6. John Bartlow Martin, *Adlai Stevenson of Illinois* (Garden City, N.Y., 1976); Porter McKeever, *Adlai Stevenson: His Life and Legacy* (New York, 1989); Gillon, *Politics and Vision*, 84–85.

7. Donald Montgomery to Walter Reuther, July 2, 1952, Box 430, WPR. Gillon, *Politics and Vision*, 88, argues that Reuther supported Harriman in the preconvention period, whereas Frank Cormier and William Eaton, *Reuther* (Englewood Cliffs, N.J., 1970), 286–287, contends that Reuther supported Stevenson. The confusion reflects the UAW's own uncertainty.

8. Tilford Dudley to Gus Scholle, n.d. [July 2, 1952], and Mary Goddard to Scholle, June 11, 1952, both in Box 39, Michigan AFL-CIO Collection, ALUA; notes of the Democratic convention meeting of the LCCR, n.d. [July 1952], Box 19, ser. E, LCCRC; William Oliver to Walter Reuther, June 10, 1952, Box 430, WPR; Roy Reuther to Neil Staebler, July 3, 1952, PA; Walter Reuther's statement to the Democratic Platform Committee, July 17, 1952, Box 23, FP; Paul Sifton to Claire Sifton, July 10, 1952, Box 6, PCS; Walter Johnson Daily Diary Notes, July 19, 1952, Box 2, Walter Johnson Collection, SGML.

9. Martin, *Civil Rights*, 108–112; Martin, *Adlai Stevenson*, 584–599; Greene, *Crusade*, 159–162; Walter Johnson Daily Diary notes, July 24 and 25, 1952, Box 2, Walter Johnson Collection, SGML; Blair Moody statement, July 28, 1952, Box 15, Mildred Jeffrey Collection, ALUA.

10. Martin, *Adlai Stevenson*, 606–607; Walter Johnson Daily Diary notes, July 23 and 25, 1952, Box 2, Johnson Collection, SGML; Paul Sifton to Claire Sifton, July 26, 1952, Box 6, PCS.

11. William Dodds to Roy Reuther, July 26, 1952, Box 46, PA; Donald Montgomery to Paul Sifton, August 12, 1952, Box 30, PCS. Also see John Heeter to William Oliver,

July 28, 1952, Box 19, FP; Paul Sifton to Walter Reuther, July 29, 1952, and Donald Montgomery to Walter Reuther, August 1, 1952, both in Box 430, WPR.

12. *UAW Ammunition*, August 1952; Walter Reuther's handwritten notes, n.d. [August 1952], Box 430, WPR.

13. *New York Times*, August 26, 1952; Reuther to Wilson Wyatt, Box 271, Adlai Stevenson Collection, SGML; oral history interview with Carl McGowan, March 31, 1966, Box 2, John B. Martin Collection, SGML. Reuther also did his best to claim he had backed Stevenson throughout the convention, though Stevenson's advisors knew better. In a letter to the nominee dated July 29, 1952, for example, Reuther refers to himself as "one of your many friends who plotted to get you into this [the nomination]." The letter is in Box 271, Stevenson Collection.

14. Reuther to Wyatt, August 26, 1952, Box 271, and background material on Michigan, August 27, 1952, Box 293, both in Stevenson Collection, SGML; Martin, *Adlai Stevenson*, 630. "It was on Labor Day," Stevenson's aide Newton Minnow later recalled, ". . . when, if I had any remaining hope of winning, I knew it was lost. I could tell by the people. There were plenty of people there, but there was no real enthusiasm, no real fire": oral history interview with Newton Minnow, July 8, 1966, Box 2, Martin Collection, SGML.

15. Reuther to all International staff, October 4, 1952, Box 2, FP; Richard Babcock report, n.d. [1955–56], Box 323, Stevenson Collection, SGML; *Labor Action*, November 17, 1952; *UAW Ammunition*, November 1952; *New York Times*, October 15, 1952; Emil Mazey to all International Executive Board members, October 7, 1952, Box 431, WPR; Mazey to Howard Coleman, September 25, 1952, Box 29, PA; Martin, *Adlai Stevenson*, 630. The UAW had difficulty maintaining effective liaison with the Stevenson campaign, which was never well organized. For details, see Bill Dodds to Dick Babcock, October 1, 1952, Box 325, Stevenson Collection.

16. Notes on Education Department–Political Action Department staff meeting, May 25–28, 1952, Box 54, Victor Reuther Collection, ALUA; Mazey to Coleman, September 25, 1952, Box 29, International representatives' weekly reports, October 4 and 25, 1952, Box 30; Chester Gloswki to Roy Reuther, February 1, 1952, Box 35; and John Bateman to Roy Reuther, October 6, 1953, all in Box 42, PA.

17. IEB minutes, September 15–18, 1952, Box 6, IEBC; *New York Times*, October 5, 1952; *UAW Ammunition*, September and October 1952; *United Automobile Worker*, November 1952.

18. Arthur Kornhauser, Harold Sheppard, and Albert Mayer, *When Labor Votes: A Study of Auto Workers* (New York, 1956), 42–43, 45, 54–55. Seventy-one percent of UAW members whose fathers were farmers voted for Stevenson, whereas 81 percent of those whose fathers were semi- or unskilled workers supported Stevenson. For comparisons with the electorate as a whole, see Angus Campbell, Gerald Gurin, and Warren E. Miller, *The Voter Decides* (Evanston, Il., 1954), 70–72. It is important to note that none of the characteristics that Kornhauser, et al. analyzed were "extremely influential as determinants of voting behavior."

19. Campbell et al., *Voter Decides*, 11–80; Lubell, *Revolt of the Moderates*, 40–43; Greene, *Crusade*, 223–225. The UAW was particularly disappointed in its inability to defeat Joseph McCarthy's reelection bid in Wisconsin, an effort to which the UAW had devoted considerable resources. See David Oshinsky, *Senator Joseph McCarthy and the American Labor Movement* (Columbia, Mo., 1976), 144–146; William Dodds to Roy Reuther and Edward Purdy, October 31, 1952, Box 46, PA.

20. *UAW Ammunition*, November 1952; William Dodds to Roy Reuther, July 28, 1952, Box 46, PA; Brendan Sexton's draft notes, n.d. [mid-1950s], Box 10, Brendan

Sexton Collection, ALUA; "CIO's 1953 Political Program," n.d. [late 1952], Box 7, Jack Kroll Collection, LC; Paul Sifton's report on congressional alignment, n.d. [late 1952], Box 7, CL.

21. Dallek, *Lone Star Rising*, 422–425.

22. The best study of Johnson's centrism is Dallek, *Lone Star Rising*, esp. chap. 13. Also see Rowland Evans and Robert Novak, *Lyndon B. Johnson: The Exercise of Power* (New York, 1966), chaps. 2–4; Doris Kearns, *Lyndon Johnson and the American Dream* (New York, 1976), chaps. 2–4; Ronnie Dugger, *The Politician: The Life and Times of Lyndon Johnson* (New York, 1982); Paul Conkin, *Big Daddy from the Pedernales: Lyndon Baines Johnson* (Boston, 1986), chaps. 4–6; Robert Caro, *The Years of Lyndon Johnson*, vols. 1 and 2 (New York, 1982, 1990).

23. Donald Montgomery to Monroe Sweetland, November 12, 1952, Box 22, Montgomery. On Eisenhower's domestic agenda, see Griffith, "Eisenhower and the Corporate Commonwealth," 100–109; James Sundquist, *Politics and Policy: The Eisenhower, Kennedy, and Johnson Years* (Washington, D.C., 1968), chaps. 2–3; Iwan Morgan, *Eisenhower versus "the Spenders": The Eisenhower Administration, the Democrats, and the Budget, 1953–1960* (New York, 1990); Margaret Weir, *Politics and Jobs: The Boundaries of Employment Policy in the United States* (Princeton, 1992), 55–56.

24. Dallek, *Lone Star Rising*, 431–447; Sundquist, *Politics and Policy*, 15–17; James Thinnes to CIO Executive Board, May 5, 1954, Box 286, WPR; Mark Gelfand, *A Nation of Cities: The Federal Government and Urban America, 1933–1965* (New York, 1975), 167–169.

25. Thomas Sugrue, "The Structures of Urban Poverty: The Reorganization of Space and Work in Three Periods of American History," in Michael Katz, ed., *The "Underclass" Debate: Views from History* (Princeton, 1993), 102–104; Stephen Meyer, "The Persistence of Fordism: Workers and Technology in the American Automobile Industry, 1900–1960," in Nelson Lichtenstein and Stephen Meyer, eds., *On the Line: Essays in the History of Auto Work* (Urbana, 1989), 86–91.

26. Between 1953 and 1958, the independents' market share fell from 9.2% of all auto sales to 5.5%. James R. Zetka, *Militancy, Market Dynamics, and Workplace Authority: The Struggle over Labor Process Outcomes in the U.S. Automobile Industry, 1946 to 1973* (Albany, forthcoming); Sugrue, "Structures of Urban Poverty," 104.

27. BLS, *Employment and Earnings, United States, 1909–1975*, Bulletin 1312–10 (Washington, D.C., 1976); David Noble, *Forces of Production: A Social History of Automation* (New York, 1984), chap. 4; Meyer, "Persistence of Fordism," 86–93; Sugrue, "Structures of Urban Poverty," 106; Harold L. Sheppard and James Sterin, "Impact of Automation on Workers in Supplier Plants," n.d., Box 54, Jacobs-Sifton; *Detroit Free Press*, June 7, 1960; Steve Babson, *Working Detroit: The Making of a Union Town* (New York, 1984), 162–163.

28. Reuther to Eisenhower, April 6, 1953, in "UAW Administrative Letters," vol. 1, ALUA; Reuther's address to UAW Full Employment Conference, December 6–7, 1953, Box 3, SPD; *UAW Ammunition*, October 1953; IEB minutes, January 18–21, 1954, and special session, February 22–23, 1954, both in Box 6, IEBC; *New York Times*, May 7, 1954. In a February 1953 meeting with Eisenhower, Reuther proposed a national management-labor-government conference to discuss a national collective bargaining program. Eisenhower, who had expected Reuther to propose a "socialistic" program, was impressed by the idea, which he thought quite moderate. When Ike passed the proposal on to congressional leaders, however, they strenuously objected, and Eisenhower dropped the idea. See Parmet, *Eisenhower and the American Crusade*, 326.

29. John Barnard, *Walter Reuther and the Rise of the Auto Workers* (Boston, 1983), 144–147.

30. Nat Weinberg to Reuther, March 22, 1949, Box 1, SPD, seems to be the first mention of automation. Also see Noble, *Forces of Production*, 74–76. For examples of the UAW's approach to automation in the mid-1950s, see Reuther's testimony in U.S. Congress, Joint Committee on the Economic Report, *Hearings*, 84th Cong., 1st sess., (Washington, D.C., 1955), 97–149; Reuther's addresses to International Woodworkers of America, October 1953, and the UAW's Education Conference, April 26, 1956, both in Box 3, SPD; Reuther's report on automation, November 12, 1954; Jack Conway's address, April 13, 1955; and Nat Weinberg's address, May 15, 1956, all in Box 54, Jacobs-Sifton; "Automation: A Report to the UAW-CIO Economic and Collective Bargaining Conference," November 12–13, 1954, Box 3, SPD.

31. Ellis Hawley, *The New Deal and the Problem of Monopoly: A Study in Economic Ambivalence* (Princeton, 1966), 174–175; Reuther's statement to the Senate Judiciary Committee, January 28, 1958, and his remarks on *Face the Nation*, March 23, 1958, both in Box 4, SPD; Reuther's address to UAW Education Conference, April 24, 1956, Box 3, SPD; Paul Sifton to Roy Reuther, April 22, 1957, Box 24, PA; Paul Sifton draft statement, n.d. [1957], Box 10, CD.

32. Ambrose, *Eisenhower*, vol 2:249–250; Griffith, "Eisenhower and the Corporate Commonwealth," 101–102; Morgan, *Eisenhower versus "The Spenders,"* chap. 1; Sundquist, *Politics and Policy*, 60–63.

33. Reuther's testimony before the 1955 Joint Economic Committee, *Hearings*, 106–114, 122; Reuther's address to UAW Education Conference, April 24, 1956, Box 3, SPD; Reuther's statements to the Democratic and Republican National Conventions, August 11, 1956; the Senate Judiciary Committee, January 28, 1958; and to the House Banking and Currency Committee, April 30, 1958, all in Box 4, SPD; Nat Weinberg's draft speech, May 1, 1956, Box 54, Jacobs-Sifton; Paul Sifton to Weinberg, March 20, 1957, Box 24, PA.

34. Jack Conway's address to the Michigan State University Automation Symposium, April 13, 1955, Box 4, CAPC.

35. The best account of the skilled trades revolt is Stephen Amberg, *The Union Inspiration in American Politics: The Autoworkers and the Making of a Liberal Industrial Order* (Philadelphia, 1994), chap. 5. Also see *Labor Action*, June 20 and November 7, 1955.

36. Eisenhower to Reuther, April 13, 1953, in "UAW Administrative Letters," 1:333–334, ALUA; Sherman Adams, *First Hand Report: The Story of the Eisenhower Administration* (New York, 1961), 164; Dwight Eisenhower, *Mandate for Change, 1953–1956* (Garden City, N.Y., 1963), 304–306; Eisenhower to Reuther, February 1, 1954, in *Public Papers of the Presidents of the United States: Dwight D. Eisenhower, 1954* (Washington, D.C., 1960), 25–26; Joint Economic Committee, *Hearings* (1955), 266; UAW press release, March 13, 1955, Box 54, Jacobs-Sifton; Sundquist, *Politics and Policy*, 18–19; Morgan, *Eisenhower versus "The Spenders,"* 63.

37. IEB minutes, January 5–11, 1955, Box 6, IEBC; Morgan, *Eisenhower versus "The Spenders,"* 33, 38.

38. *New York Times*, March 7 and September 5, 1953, and May 19, 1956; Reuther to John Foster Dulles, March 23, 1956, Box 65, Reuther-Carliner; Reuther's statement to the Democratic Platform Committee, 1956, Box 30, PCS; *UAW Ammunition*, May 1954. For the mainstream liberal perspective, see Gillon, *Politics and Vision*, 114–120.

39. See, for example, John Lewis Gaddis, *Strategies of Containment: A Critical Appraisal of Postwar American National Security Policy* (New York, 1982), 127–163;

Townsend Hoopes, *The Devil and John Foster Dulles* (Boston, 1973); Charles Alexander, *Holding the Line: The Eisenhower Era, 1952–1961* (Bloomington, 1975); Richard Malanson and David Mayers, eds., *Re-evaluating Eisenhower: American Foreign Policy in the 1950s* (Urbana, 1987); Henry Brands, *Cold Warriors: Eisenhower's Generation and American Foreign Policy* (New York, 1988); Richard Immerman, ed., *John Foster Dulles and the Diplomacy of the Cold War* (Princeton, 1990).

40. On McCarthy and McCarthyism in the Eisenhower years, see, among many others, Thomas Reeves, *The Life and Times of Joe McCarthy: A Biography* (New York, 1982), chaps. 18–24; David Oshinsky, *A Conspiracy So Immense: The World of Joe McCarthy* (New York, 1983), 355–502; Broadwater, *Eisenhower and the Anti-Communist Crusade*. Details on Reuther's FBI file are drawn from D. M. Ladd to J. Edgar Hoover, February 27, 1953; A. H. Belmont to Ladd, June 4, 1953; Hoover to Mr. Tolson, Mr. Ladd, and Mr. Belmont, May 29, 1953; and Hoover to Tolson, June 17, 1953, all in Box 1, WJBK-TV Collection, ALUA. The memorandum was unusually long, Ladd explained to Hoover, "because Reuther is a highly controversial figure." The centerpiece of the file was Walter and Victor's 1934 letter to Melvin Bishop, written while the brothers were in the Soviet Union.

41. Evans and Novak, *Lyndon B. Johnson,* chaps. 5–6; Carl Solberg, *Hubert Humphrey: A Biography* (New York, 1984), chaps. 16–17; Gillon, *Politics and Vision,* 107–109; Claire Sifton diary, June 14, 1949, Box 10, PCS; Montgomery to Roy Reuther, August 14, 1954, Box 22, PA; Dallek, *Lone Star Rising,* 430, 471.

42. Sexton's speech notes, n.d. [mid-1950s], Box 10, Sexton Collection, ALUA; summary of LCCR Executive Committee, July 19, 1955, Box 1, ser. B, LCCRC; Montgomery to Roy Reuther, July 5, 1955, Box 23, PA.

43. The best account of the last years of the CIO is Robert Zieger, *The CIO, 1935–1955* (Chapel Hill, 1995). Zieger, "Leadership and Bureaucracy in the Late CIO," *Labor History* 31 (Summer 1990), 253–270, is also excellent. Also see Art Preis, *Labor's Giant Step: Twenty Years of the CIO* (New York, 1964), pt. 7, and the voluminous literature on the CIO's purge of its Communist affiliates, cited in chapter 2, above.

44. Zieger, "Leadership and Bureaucracy," 269; Ronald Schatz, "Philip Murray and the Subordination of the Industrial Unions to the United States Government," in Melvyn Dubofsky and Warren Van Tine, eds., *Labor Leaders in America* (Urbana, 1987), 244–256. Steven Fraser, *Labor Will Rule: Sidney Hillman and the Rise of American Labor* (New York, 1991), offers a marvelous analysis of the CIO's internal contradictions.

45. Zieger, "Leadership and Bureaucracy," 255–256; Barnard, *Walter Reuther,* 132–133; Walter P. Reuther Selected Papers, ed. Henry Christman (New York, 1961), 55. For David McDonald's view of the conflict, see his *Union Man* (New York, 1969), 230–232.

46. Zieger, "Leadership and Bureaucracy," 256–260; Robert Zieger, *John L. Lewis: Labor Leader* (Boston, 1988), chap. 7; McDonald, *Union Man,* 241–242. Reuther took the rumors seriously. See Henry Fleisher to Reuther, January 31, 1955; Howard Lipton to Reuther, January 31, 1955; and set of newspaper clippings, all in Box 300, WPR. Sexton recalled Reuther's telling him that "McDonald had him in a bind and what he was doing was running . . . to get ahead of McDonald": oral history interview, November 6, 1978, Box 10, Sexton Collection, ALUA. Also see John Edelman, *Labor Lobbyist: The Autobiography of John Edelman,* ed. Joseph Carter (Indianapolis, 1974), 180–182.

47. Philip A. Taft, *The A.F. of L. from the Death of Gompers to the Merger* (New York, 1959), 257–460, and Robert Zieger, *American Workers, American Unions, 1920–1985* (Baltimore, 1986), chaps. 4–5, provide overviews of the later years of the AFL. It should be noted that not all AFL union officials fitted the conservative mold. Both David Dubinsky and A. Philip Randolph, for instance, served on the AFL's executive council.

48. Craig Phelan, "William Green and the Ideal of Christian Cooperation," in Dubofsky and Van Tine, *Labor Leaders in America*, 134–159; Irving Bernstein, *Turbulent Years: A History of the American Worker, 1933–1941* (Boston, 1969), chap. 9; Robert Zieger, "George Meany: Labor's Organization Man," in Dubofsky and Van Tine, *Labor Leaders in America*, 325–334; Archie Robinson, *George Meany and His Times* (New York, 1981).

49. Zieger, "George Meany," 324–338; Edelman, *Labor Lobbyist*, 184; Robinson, *George Meany*, chap. 7.

50. Reuther's notes, n.d. [probably early 1955], Box 299, WPR; IEB minutes, October 3–7, 1955, Box 7, and September 8–11, 1953, Box 6, IEBC; Reuther's remarks to the UAW convention, March 22, 1953, Box 298, WPR.

51. IEB minutes, special session, March 2, 1955, Box 6, IEBC.

52. Arthur Goldberg, *AFL-CIO: Labor United* (New York, 1956); Fact Sheets, April 6, 1953 and November 1, 1954, Box 298, WPR; Reuther to CIO Executive Board members, February 10, 1955, Box 299, WPR.

53. IEB minutes, special session, March 2, 1955, Box 6, IEBC; Robinson, *George Meany*, 173, 182; Goldberg, *AFL-CIO*, 98–102, 138. It remains an open question whether Reuther wanted to be AFL-CIO president. George Meany certainly believed that Reuther wanted to lead the federation, as did some of Reuther's closest advisers. They had good reason for that speculation. Thirteen years younger than Meany, Reuther could have assumed that he would move into the position after Meany retired. There is no doubt that Reuther was ambitious for high office. For Meany's opinion, see Robinson, *George Meany*, 251–254. Brendan Sexton, in an oral history interview, November 6, 1978 (ALUA), also claims that Reuther sought the AFL-CIO presidency. Reuther repeatedly denied any interest in the federation's presidency, however, and other close advisers have taken him at his word. Reuther never enjoyed his tenure as CIO president, and he consistently refused to leave the UAW presidency, which he would have had to do were he to be named to the federation presidency. See oral history interview with Jack Conway, November 20, 1967, Box 2, Cormier-Eaton; Victor Reuther, *The Brothers Reuther and the Story of the UAW: A Memoir* (Boston, 1976), 363. Whatever the truth of the matter, Meany's suspicion of Reuther's ambition helped to poison their relationship.

54. IEB minutes, special session, March 2, 1955, Box 6, IEBC; draft copy of AFL-CIO constitution, May 2, 1955; draft copy of Industrial Union Department constitution, October 27, 1955, both in Box 299, WPR; Goldberg, *AFL-CIO*, 87–96; *Proceedings of the Seventeenth Constitutional Convention of the Congress of Industrial Organizations, December 1–2, 1955* (Washington, D.C., 1955), 355.

55. Reuther, *Brothers Reuther*, 362; Montgomery to Roy Reuther, August 19, 1954, Box 22, and July 5, 1955, Box 23, both in PA; Sexton interview, November 6, 1978, ALUA.

56. Gaddis, *Strategies of Containment*, 153. Meany made his remarks before the National Religion and Labor Foundation on December 14, 1955; see *U.S. News & World Report*, December 23, 1955.

57. On Lovestone, see Ronald Radosh, *American Labor and United States Foreign Policy: The Cold War in the Unions from Gompers to Lovestone* (New York, 1969), 307–310; Harvey Klehr, *The Heyday of American Communism: The Depression Decade* (New York, 1984), 7–13, 245–248; Fraser Ottanelli, *The Communist Party of the United States: From the Depression to World War II* (New Brunswick, N.J., 1991), 13–15, 149–150.

58. For the Reuthers' view of Lovestone, see the numerous comments in Reuther, *Brothers Reuther*. Details of Reuther's trip to India can be found in David Burgess to

Victor Reuther, January 4 and 7, 1956, Box 104; Victor Reuther to Walter Reuther, January 23, 1956, and to Dave Burgess, February 27, 1956, Box 105, all in Reuther-Carliner.

59. *New York Times*, February 12, 1956; Norman Thomas to Victor Reuther, February 15, 1956; Walter Reuther to the Indian National Trade Union Congress, February 22, 1956; Walter Reuther's notes of a meeting with Ambassador Gaganvihari Lallubhai Mehta, March 14, 1956; Reuther's press conference, March 28, 1956, all in Box 105, Reuther-Carliner.

60. *New York Times*, April 15 and 17, 1956; Reuther's address before the Indian Council on World Affairs, April 5, 1956, in Reuther, *Selected Papers*, 129–142; IEB minutes, May 1–4, 1956, Box 7, IEBC. Reuther was harsher on Meany in private. "You can't imagine what a village in India is like—mud huts, straw roof, one room—three families in a room sometimes," he told the UAW IEB. "That's why when we talk about military pacts to them when they really need economic aid, it's meaningless. These people say, 'What do you mean? I don't want to defend this. I want to change this. . . .' Now you see where I disagree with Meany. George Meany's position really is based on the assumption that Europe is Asia and Asia is Europe. You cannot mechanically apply a foreign policy view that makes sense in Europe to Asia where, historically and economically and geographically, conditions are so different."

61. *New York Times*, April 13 and 15, 1956; Dave Burgess to Victor Reuther, April 18, 1956, Reuther-Carliner; Victor Reuther's notes for Walter Reuther, March 26, 1956, Box 304, WPR; Dave Burgess to Victor Reuther, May 16, 1956, Box 104, Reuther-Carliner; *Detroit Free Press*, April 3, 1956; *Christian Science Monitor*, April 26, 1956; *Washington Post*, April 26, 1956.

62. *New York Times*, May 2 and June 16, 1956; *Washington Post*, May 3, 1956; *U.S. News & World Report*, April 27, 1956; *Newsweek*, May 21, 1956; *New Republic*, May 14, 1956; Victor Reuther to David Burgess, June 21, 1956, Box 104, and March 21, 1957, Box 105, Reuther-Carliner.

5. The Crucible of Race

1. Harry Ross to William Oliver, May 21, 1956, Box 12, FP.

2. Robert Dallek, *Lone Star Rising: Lyndon Johnson and His Times* (New York, 1991), 497–498; J. W. Anderson, *Eisenhower, Brownell, and the Congress: The Tangled Origins of the Civil Rights Bill of 1956–1957* (University, Ala., 1964), 99–109; Rowland Evans and Robert Novak, *Lyndon B. Johnson: The Exercise of Power* (New York, 1966), 122–124; Paul Sifton to Walter Reuther, August 1, 1956, Box 23, PA.

3. Sifton to Reuther, August 1, 1956, Box 23, PA. Oliver, a product of the Texas CIO, was a Johnson intimate who often served the majority leader's interests. See Evans and Novak, *Lyndon B. Johnson*, 113.

4. The UAW leadership considered an FEPC the most important part of the civil rights agenda, since by its very nature FEPC focused on the connection between racial injustice and economic inequality. "If you are denied the right to make a living, every other right is secondary, meaning freedom of speech, freedom to worship as you please," Reuther argued. "All of these freedoms cannot be . . . realized in their fullest sense if the worker is denied the right to earn a living. And, therefore, FEPC comes to the very core of the civil rights fight." See Reuther's address to the UAW Fair Practices and Civil Rights Conference, November 17, 1951, Box 15, Jacobs-Sifton.

5. Civil rights mobilization background information, January 15–17, 1950, Box 6, FP; Oliver to Norm Matthews, March 6, 1952, Box 23, FP; Roy Wilkins and Arnold

Aronson to all sponsoring agencies, March 8, 1950, Box 4, FP; Sifton to Walter Reuther, December 7, 1951, Box 23, PA; August Meier and Elliot Rudwick, *Black Detroit and the Rise of the UAW* (New York, 1979); Wilson Record, *Race and Radicalism: The NAACP and the Communist Party in Conflict* (Ithaca, 1964), 154–156, 177–181; Bruce Nelson, "Organized Labor and the Struggle for Black Equality in Mobile during World War II," *JAH* 80 (December 1993), 962–969; Denton Watson, *Lion in the Lobby: Clarence Mitchell Jr.'s Struggle for the Passage of Civil Rights Laws* (New York, 1990); Nelson Lichtenstein and Robert Korstad, "Opportunities Found and Lost: Labor, Radicals, and the Early Civil Rights Movement," *JAH* 75 (December 1988), 808–809; Philip Foner, *Organized Labor and the Black Worker, 1619–1973* (New York, 1974), chaps. 19–20.

6. Reuther to Roy Wilkins, January 24, 1950, Box 15, PA; Oliver to Reuther, January 25, 1950, Box 8, FP; Sifton to Oliver, December 21, 1951, Box 26, FP; A. Philip Randolph to Reuther, May 2, 1950, Box 23, PA; Lichtenstein and Korstad, "Opportunities Found and Lost," 800–801; minutes of LCCR Steering Committee, January 11, 1952, and Walter White to participating organizations, January 8, 1952, both in Box 23, FP.

7. Randolph to Reuther, May 2, 1950, Box 23, PA; Oliver to all regional directors, May 10, 1950, Box 18, PA; *UAW Fair Practices Fact Sheet*, November–December 1949, March–April 1950, May-June 1950; *CIO Legis-Letter*, January–February 1950; Donald McCoy and Richard Ruetten, *Quest and Response: Minority Rights and the Truman Administration* (Lawrence, Kans., 1973), 192–199.

8. Oliver to Reuther, August 29, 1951, Box 19, PA; Lichtenstein and Korstad, "Opportunities Found and Lost," 800–801; Reuther's statement to the Senate Rules Committee, October 3, 1951, Box 171, WPR; Sifton to Reuther, June 5, 1950, Box 66, Montgomery; Sifton to Frank Winn, April 8, 1952, Box 23, PA.

9. McCoy and Ruetten, *Quest and Response*, 177; oral history interview with Joseph L. Rauh Jr., May 12, 1987, Washington, D.C.; brief and accompanying statement submitted by Reuther to the Senate Committee on Rules and Administration, October 3, 1951, Box 171, WPR.

10. Sifton to Reuther, December 7, 1951; Sifton to Oliver, October 23, 1951; Sifton to Reuther, October 24, 1951, all in Box 23, PA; IEB minutes, October 8–12, 1951, Box 7, IEBC; *UAW Fair Practices Fact Sheet*, January–February 1952.

11. Oliver to Reuther, December 23, 1952, Box 23, FP; *UAW Fair Practices Fact Sheet*, January–February 1953; James Sundquist, *Politics and Policy: The Eisenhower, Kennedy, and Johnson Years* (Washington, D.C, 1968), 231.

12. Evans and Novak, *Lyndon B. Johnson*, 120–122; Paul Conkin, *Big Daddy from the Pedernales: Lyndon Baines Johnson* (Boston, 1985), 139; Dallek, *Lone Star Rising*, 367–370, 380–381.

13. Carl Solberg, *Hubert Humphrey: A Biography* (New York, 1984), 169–170; Paul Sifton's handwritten notes, n.d. [c. 1962], Box 35, PCS. Sifton claimed that Humphrey's refusal to support the liberals in 1955 contributed to Herbert Lehman's decision not to seek reelection the next year. Lehman decided, according to Sifton, that he simply could not advance civil rights in the Senate.

14. Summary of LCCR Executive Committee meetings, July 19, 1955, and March 3, 1955, Box 1, ser. B, LCCRC; Adlai Stevenson to Hubert Humphrey, July 15, 1955, Box 414, Adlai Stevenson Collection, SGML; Solberg, *Hubert Humphrey*, 169–170; Stanford Bolz's review of the civil rights situation, n.d. [March 1955], Box 23, PA.

15. Sifton to Roy Reuther, July 26, 1955, and to Roy Reuther and William Oliver, July 6, 1955, both in Box 23, PA; Oliver to Sifton, January 25, 1955, Box 14, Jacobs-Sifton; summary of LCCR Executive Committee meeting, Box 1, ser. B, LCCRC.

16. Meier and Rudwick, *Black Detroit*, 34–107; Lloyd Bailer, "Negro Labor in the

American Automobile Industry" (Ph.D. diss., University of Michigan, 1943); Irving Howe and B. J. Widick, *The UAW and Walter Reuther* (New York, 1949), 214; David Roediger, *The Wages of Whiteness: Race and the Making of the American Working Class* (London, 1991); Hilliard Chambliss to Oliver, March 28, 1947, Box 19, FP; Oliver to Joseph Tuma and Lillian Hatcher, April 30, 1947, Box 12, FP; Crockett report, October 25, 1945, Box 93, WPR; Oliver to Alfred Campbell, February 5, 1968, Box 35, FP; George Crockett to Victor Reuther, July 21, 1944, Box 2, FP.

17. Jonas Silver and Everett Kassalow, "Seniority in the Automobile Industry," April 1944, Box 22; U.S. Employment Services, "Utilization of Negroes in War Production in the Wayne County Area," January 22, 1943, and "Utilization of Non-Whites in War Production in the Detroit Area," April 9, 1943, Box 6, all in UAW War Policy Division Collection, ALUA; George Crockett, "The Fight against Discrimination," n.d. [late 1945], Box 1, FP; Meier and Rudwick, *Black Detroit*, 162–174; Edward Hauganbook to Joseph Tuma, August 3, 1946, Box 9, FP. As late as 1948, African-American workers were restricted to the foundry, press room, and material handling and janitorial classifications. It is important to note that such blatant discrimination took place in a local with a vibrant shop steward system. See Steve Jefferys, *Management and Managed: Fifty Years of Crisis at Chrysler* (Cambridge, 1986).

18. Oral history interview with Mildred Jeffrey, August 13, 1976, ALUA; Jack Stieber, *Governing the UAW* (New York, 1962), 67–72.

19. Meier and Rudwick, *Black Detroit*, 212–215; First Annual Report of the Fair Practices Department, October 15, 1946, Box 1, FP; Crockett to Oliver, May 17, 1946, Box 3, FP; oral history interview with Shelton Tappes, October 27, 1967, and February 10, 1968, ALUA.

20. Statement of James Major, January 6, 1956, and Robert Ellis to Reuther and Oliver, November 18, 1947, both in Box 18, FP.

21. Report of Harry Ross, n.d. [May 1948], Box 12, FP; Walter Hargreaves et al. to Oliver, February 15, 1951, Box 7, FP. For other examples of the same process, see Oliver to Percy Llewellyn, December 26, 1946, Box 89, WPR; Marice Price to Oliver, December 1, 1947, Box 18, FP; Harry Ross report, October 17, 1950, Box 12, FP; André Marten et al. to Oliver, February 21, 1953, Box 19, PA.

22. Oliver to Ray Berndt, February 18, 1953, Box 18, FP; R. M. Ross to Russel Letner, March 11, 1955, Box 11A, FP; Harry Ross to Oliver, November 24, 1959, Box 12, FP; P. E. Castle to Reuther, October 23, 1950, Box 90, WPR; Korstad and Lichtenstein, "Opportunities Found and Lost," 794–797.

23. H. A. Moon to Harry Ross, n.d. [1953], Box 12; "In the Matter of Cleveland Fisher Local 31, May–June 1947," Box 5; Orville Beemer to Oliver, February 7, 1955, Box 15; Herbert Hill to Leonard Woodcock, June 3, 1957, Box 35, all in FP.

24. Edward Haugabook to Tuma, August 3, 1946; Emmett Wheaton et al. to George Addes, March 27, 1945, Box 20; Emil Mazey to William Jenkins, Box 19, all in FP.

25. Oral history interviews with Shelton Tappes, October 27, 1967, and February 10, 1968, and Mildred Jeffrey, August 13, 1976, ALUA; minutes of the UAW-CIO Advisory Council on Discrimination, April 2, 1947, Box 5, FP; Harry Ross to Oliver, February 27 and March 29, 1950, both in Box 12, FP; Ross to Oliver, April 20, 1956, Box 11B, FP; Oliver to Roy Reuther, January 3, 1956, Box 20, PA; Oliver to Marvin Meltzer, July 24, 1956, Box 19, FP; Summary of Activities, February 14, 1956, Box 12, FP.

26. Oral history interviews with Jack Conway, March 27, 1963, and Leonard Woodcock, April 30, 1963, ALUA; Stieber, *Governing the UAW*, 61–72, 137–149; Woodcock to Oliver, May 27, 1952, Box 18, FP; Nelson Edwards to Oliver, April 29, 1954; Oliver to Berndt, June 8, 1954, both in Box 15, FP.

27. Oliver to Roy Reuther, February 10, 1950, Box 20, FP; Roy Reuther to Oliver, February 28, 1950, Box 19, PA; Orville Beemer to Oliver, February 7, 1955, and Supplement B, Local 14, Seniority Agreement, July 19, 1946, both in Box 3, FP; Tuma to Oliver, September 12, 1947, Box 8, FP; Oliver to Roy Reuther, June 27, 1949, Box 90, WPR; Harry Ross to Oliver, April 20, 1956, Box 11B; Oliver to William Douthit, January 1957, Box 31; Oliver to Reuther, May 19, 1949, Box 18, all in FP.

28. Lillian Hatcher to Oliver, December 12, 1956, Box 11B; Oliver to Reuther, December 17, 1957, Box 5; Oliver to George L-P Weaver, January 10, 1958, Box 31, all in FP.

29. Harry Ross report, July 6, 1954, Box 21; Oliver to Harold Julian, July 16, 1954, Box 20; Oliver to Reuther, December 1, 1953, Box 19; Julian to Oliver, July 21, 1954, Box 17; Nelson Edwards to Oliver, March 11, 1955, Box 15; Oliver to Victor Reuther, July 25, 1956, Box 21; Oliver to Harry Ross, February 3, 1956, Box 11B, all in FP. The International's hesitancy to confront the racial practices of its skilled workers was compounded by the UAW craftsmen's increased restiveness in the 1950s.

30. Stieber, *Governing the UAW*, 64–65; Oliver to Roy Reuther, July 6, 1950, Box 18, PA; Harry Ross report, June 11, 1952, Box 12; Oliver to Mazey, October 27, 1953, Box 7; Oliver to Julius Thomas, September 14, 1954, Box 6; staff list, n.d. [c. 1958], Box 12, all in FP.

31. UAW Local 653 *Leader*, August 16, 1956, copy in Box 19, FP; Herbert Hill to Carl Shier, April 16, 1953, Box A 632, NAACP Collection, LC. Also see Morris Hood to Oliver, August 23, 1949; IEB minutes, April 28–May 1, 1953, Box 6, IEBC.

32. Mark Tushnet, *The NAACP's Legal Strategy against Segregated Education, 1925–1950* (Chapel Hill, 1987); J. Harvie Wilkinson III, *From Brown to Bakke: The Supreme Court and School Desegregation, 1954–1978* (New York, 1979), 11–57. There is a massive literature on the southern civil rights movement of the 1950s. See, among many other fine works, Aldon Morris, *The Origins of the Civil Rights Movement: Black Communities Organizing for Change* (New York, 1984); David Garrow, *Bearing the Cross: Martin Luther King, Jr., and the Southern Christian Leadership Conference* (New York, 1986), chaps. 1–2; Jack Bloom, *Class, Race, and the Civil Rights Movement* (Bloomington, 1987), 87–156; Taylor Branch, *Parting the Waters: America in the King Years, 1954–1963* (New York, 1988), chaps. 1–6; John Dittmer, *Local People: The Struggle for Civil Rights in Mississippi* (Urbana, 1994), chaps. 1–4.

33. Numan Bartley, *The Rise of Massive Resistance: Race and Politics in the South during the 1950s* (Baton Rouge, 1969); Garrow, *Bearing the Cross*, chap. 1.

34. Morris, *Origins of the Civil Rights Movement*, ix–xi; Korstad and Lichtenstein, "Opportunities Found and Lost," 811. This is not to argue that there was no economic basis to the southern civil rights movement. See Gavin Wright, *Old South, New South: Revolutions in the Southern Economy since the Civil War* (New York, 1986), 268–264, and Bloom, *Class, Race, and the Civil Rights Movement*.

35. *New York Times*, May 13, 1954; *UAW Fair Practices Fact Sheet*, November–December 1952 and May–June 1954.

36. List of yearly contributions of the Fair Practices Fund through March 1958, Box 9, CD; *UAW Fair Practices Fact Sheet*, March–April 1956; Walter P. Reuther, Selected Papers, ed. Henry Christman (New York, 1961), 141; Garrow, *Bearing the Cross*, chaps. 1–2; Oliver to Roy Reuther, February 11, 1960, Box 8, FP; Walter Reuther to Oliver, June 20, 1960, Box 9, FP.

37. Rough transcript of Walter Reuther's comments to Fair Practices Department staff meeting, n.d. [late 1956], Box 14, FP; *UAW Fair Practices Fact Sheet*, March–April 1956; Thomas Kilgore to Oliver, April 19, 1957, Box 20, FP; Horace Sheffield to Roy Reuther,

August 9, 1957, Box 32, PA; and February 18, 1958, Box 15, CD; list of contributions, October 3, 1961, Box 63, and Ralph Abernathy to SCLC Executive Board, October 11, 1960, Box 53, both in SCLCC. The FBI duly noted the UAW's support for the 1957 prayer pilgrimage in Walter Reuther's FBI file. See W. C. Sullivan to A. H. Belmont, May 8, 1957, WJBK-TV Collection, ALUA. Reuther and Martin Luther King Jr. did not meet until early 1959, when King and Abernathy came to Detroit on a fund-raising drive. See Oliver to Roy Reuther, February 11, 1960, Box 8, FP.

38. Walter Reuther and William Oliver to all local union presidents, February 7, 1956, Box 20, PA; Roy Reuther to Paul Butler, February 13, 1956, Box 30, PCS; Walter Reuther's press conference, April 26, 1956, Box 26, PA; Steven Gillon, *Politics and Vision: The ADA and American Liberalism, 1947–1985* (New York, 1987), 99.

39. Dallek, *Lone Star Rising,* 497; "The Political Problem, 1956," n.d. [September 1955], Box 415, and Harry Ashmore to Adlai Stevenson, March 30, 1956, Box 505, both in Stevenson Collection, SGML; Sundquist, *Politics and Policy,* 223–226.

40. Robert Griffith, "Dwight D. Eisenhower and the Corporate Commonwealth," *American Historical Review* 87 (February 1982), 114–116; Herbert Parmet, *Eisenhower and the American Crusades* (New York, 1972), 436–446; Stephen Ambrose, *Eisenhower,* 2 vols. (New York, 1983–84), 2:125–127; Robert Burk, *The Eisenhower Administration and Black Civil Rights* (Knoxville, Tenn., 1984), 23–67; Anderson, *Eisenhower, Brownell, and the Congress,* 1–43.

41. Roy Reuther to James Finnegan, July 13, 1956, Box 13, PA; Anderson, *Eisenhower, Brownell, and Congress,* 45–99; Sundquist, *Politics and Policy,* 229; Roy Reuther to Oliver, April 1956, Box 20, PA; Sifton to Reuther, August 1, 1956, Box 23, PA; Evans and Novak, *Lyndon B. Johnson,* 122–124.

42. Sifton to Reuther, August 1, 1956, Box 23, PA.

43. John Frederick Martin, *Civil Rights and the Crisis of Liberalism* (Boulder, Colo., 1979), 146–151; Gillon, *Politics and Vision,* 98–100; James Finnegan to Charles Guensch, January 10, 1956, Box 506, Stevenson Collection, SGML; Edward L. Greenfield and Company, "Erosion and Reclamation: Situation and Prospects of the Stevenson Candidacy," April 1956, Box 6, John B. Shea Collection, SGML; Reuther's statement to the Democratic Platform Committee, August 11, 1956, Box 30, PCS.

44. Joseph Rauh, "Memorandum on the Civil Rights Fight, Democratic Convention, 1956," Box 29, Joseph L. Rauh Jr. Collection, LC; oral history interview with Mildred Jeffrey, August 13, 1976, ALUA; Gillon, *Politics and Vision,* 100.

45. Rauh, "Memorandum on the Civil Rights Fight," Box 29, Rauh Collection, LC; minutes of the leadership meeting on civil rights, August 15, 1956, Box 2, Shea Collection, SGML; Martin, *Civil Rights,* 151; oral history interview with Jack Conway, April 10, 1972, JFKL.

46. Max Kampelman to Herb Waters, July 23, 1956; Humphrey to Reuther, July 23, 1956; Kampelman to Bill Dodds, July 25, 1956; Jack Flynn to Mike, August 13, 1956; and Bill to Herb and Mitch, August 21, 1956, all in 23-G-1-1b, Senate Files, HHH; oral history interview with Douglas Fraser, Detroit, February 24, 1987; oral history interview with Jack Conway, April 10, 1972, JFKL. Humphrey's candidacy was also undermined by LBJ, who delivered Texas's votes to Albert Gore on the first ballot and to John Kennedy on the second. Sifton, for one, reveled in the fact that Johnson had betrayed Humphrey after Humphrey had betrayed the civil rights groups a few weeks earlier. See Claire Sifton to Tony Sifton, August 23, 1956, Box 6, PCS.

47. John Bateman to Mazey, December 22, 1955, Oliver to Roy Reuther, January 3, 1956, both in Box 20, PA; Gordon Gregory to Mazey, February 5, 1957, Box 21, PA;

Oscar Cohen to Reuther, August 24, 1955, Box 5, FP; John Bateman to Mazey, September 7, 1955, Box 20, PA; H. L. Mitchell's report on White Citizens' Councils, March 12, 1956, Box 29, PA. Edwards's membership made national headlines when Walter Winchell attacked Reuther for demanding that the Democratic Party expel James Eastland when he did not expel Edwards. See transcript of Winchell's radio broadcast, May 6, 1956, Box 20, PA. In fact, the UAW leadership was eager to expel Edwards but could not find a legal basis for doing so. See Harold Cranefield to Mazey, January 10, 1956, Box 20, PA. For the context see Alan Draper, *Conflict of Interests: Organized Labor and the Civil Rights Movement in the South, 1954–1968.* (Ithaca, 1994), 19–33.

48. Series of memos from Harry Ross to Oliver, May 21, 1956, Box 12, FP; Oliver to Mazey, March 19, 1956, Box 5, FP.

49. Compliance survey analysis, February 26, 1958, Box 2, FP; Oliver to Joe Walsh, January 8, 1958, Box 11, FP; George Holloway to Oliver, November 28, 1955, Box 20, PA; Oliver to Reuther, April 18, 1962, Box 90, WPR; Earl Henderson to Oliver, May 19, 1961, Box 11B, FP; Michael Honey, *Southern Labor and Black Civil Rights: Organizing Memphis Workers* (Urbana, 1993), 155; Roscoe Coleman et al. to Oliver, October 21, 1957, Box 6, FP. It is interesting to compare this level of local activism with African-Americans' day-to-day resistance to Jim Crow. See esp. Robin D. G. Kelley, " 'We Are Not What We Seem': Rethinking Black Working-Class Opposition in the Jim Crow South," *JAH* 80 (June 1993), 75–112. The shop-floor movement belies the conclusion that the southern civil rights movement was largely a black middle-class phenomenon. For that view, see William Julius Wilson, *The Declining Significance of Race: Blacks and Changing American Institutions* (Chicago, 1978), 134–137.

50. Earl Henderson to Oliver, July 13, 1961, Box 13, FP; Oliver to Showalter, October 5, 1948, Box 25, FP; Harry Ross to Oliver, April 10, 1951, Box 12, FP; Larry Gettlinger to Roy Reuther, November 14, 1955; Oliver to Roy Reuther, January 3, 1956; Holloway to Oliver, November 28, 1955; Bateman to Mazey, December 22, 1955; Carl Moore to Norman Seaton, December 12, 1955, all in Box 20, PA; Harry Ross to Mazey, Box 5, FP. Local 988 was not free from racial strife before the *Brown* decision. In 1950, when plant management placed a black worker in the previously all-white steel department, the department's white workers walked out in protest. Trouble mounted at shift change, when the white wildcatters stoned a car carrying three African-Americans from the plant. See clippings from *Memphis Press Scimitar,* August 2, 1950, and *Chicago Tribune,* August 3, 1950, in Box 26, FP. When the regional director intervened in the hate strike, the white workers returned to work without further incident. The African-American worker stayed on the job. See Oliver to Sifton, August 31, 1950, also in Box 26. Honey, *Southern Labor and Black Civil Rights,* provides a detailed context for events in Local 988.

51. Stieber, *Governing the UAW,* 64–65; Harry Ross to Oliver, May 21, 1956, Box 12, FP.

52. Oliver to Henderson, January 15, 1958, and Henderson to Oliver, July 13, 1961, both in Box 13, FP; Oliver to Reuther, June 6, 1957; Oliver to Mazey, March 19, 1956; Harry Ross to Mazey, August 13, 1956; all in Box 5, FP; Oliver to Mazey, n.d. [February 1957], Box 2, FP; IEB minutes, February 2–5, 1958, Box 22, Region 9A; Coleman et al. to Oliver, October 21, 1957, Box 6, FP.

53. On the origins of TULC, see Horace Sheffield to Martin Luther King Jr., October 21, 1963, Box 46, Martin Luther King Jr. Collection, MLK; Stieber, *Governing the UAW,* 83–85; Foner, *Organized Labor,* 333; oral history interviews with Shelton Tappes, October 27, 1967, and February 10, 1968, ALUA. On the backgrounds of Sheffield, Tappes,

and Abner see Meier and Rudwick, *Black Detroit,* 80–81, 84, 113–114, and the Willoughby Abner vertical file at ALUA. According to Tappes, Oliver made a point of distancing himself from TULC.

54. Meier and Rudwick, *Black Detroit,* 209–212; Sheffield to Mazey, December 20, 1955, Box 32, PA.

55. Oral history interview with Horace Sheffield, July 24, 1968, ALUA; "Proceedings of the 17th Constitutional Convention, UAW AFL-CIO, October 9–16, 1959," 360–363, ALUA; Stieber, *Governing the UAW,* 41–43. The African-American staffers had good reason to fear for their jobs. According to Sheffield, Mazey urged Reuther to fire Sheffield for violating caucus rules, but Roy Reuther and Frank Winn, director of the Public Relations Department, persuaded Walter not to do it. Mazey never forgave Sheffield for his actions, and the two men clashed repeatedly throughout the next decade. The protest received widespread attention, particularly in the African-American press. For example, see *Pittsburgh Courier,* December 31, 1959.

6. Something Less Than Perfect

1. Victor Reuther's draft speech, June 15, 1961, Box 32, PCS. Reuther did not deliver the speech, in deference to the administration, which had just suffered the humiliation of the Bay of Pigs invasion.

2. Kevin Philips, *The Emerging Republican Majority* (Garden City, N.Y., 1970), 159–162, 342–343; Heinz Elau, *Class and Party in the Eisenhower Years: Class Politics and Perspectives in the 1952 and 1956 Elections* (Glencoe, Ill., 1962), 2; IEB minutes, November 10–14, 1956, Box 7, IEBC. Among the traditional Democratic voters who defected to Ike was Robert Kennedy. RFK thought Stevenson's campaign was so "ghastly," he told an interviewer in 1966, that he cast his ballot for Eisenhower. See John Bartlow Martin's interview with Kennedy, December 7, 1966, Box 1, John Bartlow Martin Collection, SGML.

3. J. W. Anderson, *Eisenhower, Brownell, and the Congress: The Tangled Origins of the Civil Rights Bill of 1956–1957* (University, Ala., 1964), chap. 3; Robert Burk, *The Eisenhower Administration and Black Civil Rights* (Knoxville, Tenn., 1984), 168–170; Rowland Evans and Robert Novak, *Lyndon B. Johnson: The Exercise of Power* (New York, 1966), 124–125; Robert Dallek, *Lone Star Rising: Lyndon Johnson and His Times* (New York, 1991), 517–520.

4. William Oliver to Roy Reuther, February 1, 1957, and Oliver to Arthur Hitzke, March 25, 1957, both in Box 21, PA; *UAW Fair Practices Fact Sheet,* January–February 1957 and May–June 1957; Fair Practices and Political Action Departments to all local union presidents, March 11, 1957, Box 24, Jacobs-Sifton; John Edelman to the field, June 3, 1957, Box 22, John Edelman Collection, ALUA; Walter Reuther to select House members, June 5, 1957, Box 24, PA; James Sundquist, *Politics and Policy: The Eisenhower, Kennedy, and Johnson Years* (Washington, D.C., 1968), 233–237; Evans and Novak, *Lyndon B. Johnson,* 125–140.

5. Oral history interview with Joseph Rauh Jr., July 30, 1969, LBJL; Monday and Tuesday drafts of LCCR statement, August 5 and 6, 1957, Box 26, Joseph L. Rauh Jr. Collection, LC; Rauh to Reuther, March 4, 1959, Box 116, WPR; Roy Wilkins, *Standing Fast: The Autobiography of Roy Wilkins* (New York, 1982), 245; Sundquist, *Politics and Policy,* 237.

6. Carl Solberg, *Hubert Humphrey: A Biography* (New York, 1984), 178–179; Howard Shuman, "Senate Rules and the Civil Rights Bill: A Case Study," *American*

Political Science Review 51 (December 1957), 955–975; Sundquist, *Politics and Policy*, 230–231, 239; Hubert Humphrey and Paul Douglas to newly elected Democratic senators, November 10, 1958; seventeen civil rights organizations to Lyndon Johnson, November 20, 1958; Victor Reuther and Paul Sifton to Ralph Koening et al., November 22, 1958, all in Box 75, Reuther-Carliner; Sifton to Reuther, December 30, 1958, Box 10, CD; Evans and Novak, *Lyndon B. Johnson*, 200–202.

7. Harold Vatter, *The U.S. Economy in the 1950s: An Economic History* (Westport, Conn., 1984), 115–120, 158–163; *New York Times*, January 31, 1958; February 22, 1958; and March 16, 1958; BLS, *Labor Force Statistics Derived From the Current Population Survey, 1948–1987*, Bulletin 2307 (Washington, D.C., 1987), 553; IEB minutes, special session, March 5–6, 1958, Box 78, Region 6; minutes of staff meeting, January 15, 1959, Box 37, CD.

8. James Zetka, *Militancy, Market Dynamics, and Workplace Authority: The Struggle Over Labor Process Outcomes in the U.S. Automobile Industry, 1946 to 1973* (Albany, forthcoming), chap. 9; Ed Purdy to John Fields, February 20, 1959, Box 33, CD.

9. Steve Jefferys, *Management and Managed: Fifty Years of Crisis at Chrysler* (Cambridge, 1986), 135–143; Zetka, *Militancy, Market Dynamics, and Workplace Authority*, tables 9.7 and 9.8.

10. Minutes of staff meeting, January 15, 1959, Box 37, and Ed Purdy to Ken Morris, May 8, 1959, Box 14, both in CD; minutes of staff meeting, January 26, 1958, Box 85, Mildred Jeffrey Collection, ALUA.

11. Reuther's address to IUD, January 7, 1959; transcript of Reuther's appearance on *Face the Nation*, February 8, 1959; Reuther's statement to Special Senate Committee on Unemployment Problems, November 12, 1959; Reuther's address, November 25, 1959, all in Box 4, SPD; UAW statement on unemployment, January 29, 1959, CAPC.

12. Sundquist, *Politics and Policy*, 22–23, 60–67; Iwan Morgan, *Eisenhower versus "the Spenders": The Eisenhower Administration, the Democrats, and the Budget* (New York, 1990), 103; Everett Kassalow to Reuther, October 3, 1957, Box 10, Nat Weinberg Collection, ALUA; IEB minutes, October 7–11, 1957, Box 7, IEBC; U.S. Congress, House, Committee on Banking and Currency, *Hearings*, 85th Cong. 2d Sess. (Washington, D.C., 1958), 490–493.

13. The Kefauver hearings are discussed in Joseph Gorman, *Kefauver: A Political Biography* (New York, 1971), chap. 18. On the UAW's successful attempt to save the hearings, see Sifton to Roy Reuther, April 22, 1957, Box 24, PA; Sifton's statement in support of the Kefauver hearings, n.d. [late 1957], Box 10, CD. The administered price issue had already become central to the Kefauver Committee by the time it turned its attention to the auto industry. In July 1957 the New Dealer Gardiner Means made national headlines by detailing the monopoly power of American corporations. See Sundquist, *Politics and Policy*, 32. I have been unable to establish a direct link between the UAW's support for Kefauver in the 1956 Democratic convention and the senator's willingness to investigate administered prices in the auto industry.

14. Evans and Novak, *Lyndon B. Johnson*, 161–163; Sundquist, *Politics and Policy*, 22–24, 77–80; Morgan, *Eisenhower versus "the Spenders,"* 103–105; *New York Times*, January 6, February 19, and February 25, 1959; IEB minutes, February 2–5, 1959, Box 22, Region 9A, and September 8–11, 1959, Box 80, Region 6; draft resolution for the AFL-CIO conference on the unemployed, March 30, 1959, Box 10, Weinberg Collection, ALUA; Sifton to Reuther, September 25, 1959, Box 76, Reuther-Carliner. The back-to-work conference garnered a great deal of publicity because it highlighted the tension between Reuther and George Meany. At the AFL-CIO Executive Council meeting in Peurto Rico in February 1959, Reuther proposed that the AFL-CIO stage a mass march

of the unemployed on Washington. Meany rejected the idea out of hand, and Eisenhower laughed off the proposal at a news conference, asking whether the unionists planned to march on the capital from the "sunny beaches" of Puerto Rico. The ascetic Reuther was appalled by both Meany's rejection and Eisenhower's criticism. "We don't have a labor movement," he told the IEB. "We have a club. It's a very exclusive club; stays in the best hotels, in the finest resorts in the western hemisphere. But it isn't doing the job." See IEB minutes, February 2–5, 1959.

15. U.S. Congress, Senate, Committee on the Judiciary, *Hearings*, 85th Cong., 2d Sess. (Washington, D.C., 1958), 2165–3317; and Joint Economic Committee, *Hearings*, 85th Cong., 2d Sess. (Washington, D.C., 1958), 768–772.

16. Sundquist, *Politics and Policy*, 32.

17. Frank McCulloch memorandum, January 15, 1959; McCulloch to Walter Reuther, January 16, 1959; Roy Reuther to Walter Reuther, January 20, 1959; FR handwritten note, n.d., all in Box 19, CD. The day after Roy confronted Baker, both Johnson and Sam Rayburn called Walter and demanded that he fire his brother. Walter politely refused.

18. Oral history interview with Jack Conway, April 10, 1972, Washington, D.C., JFKL. Also see Sifton to Victor Reuther, November 5, 1958, Box 75, Reuther-Carliner; IEB minutes, November 10–13, 1958, Box 79, Region 6; *New York Times*, October 9 and 12, 1959.

19. Jeffrey to Reuther, n.d. [1959], Box 85, Jeffrey Collection, ALUA; oral history interviews with Jack Conway, November 20, 1967, Box 2, Cormier-Eaton; Joseph Rauh, May 12, 1987, Washington, D.C.; and Leonard Woodcock, January 27, 1970, JFKL.

20. Theodore White, *The Making of the President, 1960* (New York, 1961), chap. 2. On Kennedy's congressional career, see Thomas Reeves, *A Question of Character: A Life of John F. Kennedy* (New York, 1991), 86–82, 118–124, 151–152; and Herbert Parmet, *Jack: The Struggles of John F. Kennedy* (New York, 1980). LBJ is quoted in Dallek, *Lone Star Rising*, 555. On the UAW's view of the field, see Bob Wallace memorandum, May 1959, Box 949, JFK Pre-Presidential Files, JFKL.

21. Arthur Schlesinger Jr., *A Thousand Days: John F. Kennedy in the White House* (Boston, 1965), 15–17; oral history interview with Paul Schrade, June 1992, Los Angeles; R. Alton Lee, *Eisenhower and Landrum-Griffin: A Study in Labor-Management Politics* (Lexington, Ky., 1990), chaps. 4–5; Dallek, *Lone Star Rising*, 555–557; Arthur Schlesinger Jr., *Robert F. Kennedy and His Times* (Boston, 1978), chaps. 8–9.

22. Schlesinger, *Robert Kennedy*, chap. 9; Robert Kennedy, *The Enemy Within* (New York, 1960), 266–275; Walter Uphoff, *Kohler on Strike: Thirty Years of Conflict* (Boston, 1966), 145–261; Conway interview, April 10, 1972, JFKL; memos to Robert Kennedy and others, 1957–1958, Box 19, and Rauh memo for files, March 15, 1958, Box 20, all in Victor Reuther Collection, ALUA. The Republicans on the committee, it should be noted, were aided by the FBI, which conducted an extensive investigation into the backgrounds of Reuther and his wife, May. See memos dated February 26, 1957, from Detroit SAC [special agent in charge] to J. Edgar Hoover; February 28, 1957, to Mr. Rosen; and May 8, 1957, from W. C. Sullivan to A. H. Belmont, all in WJBK-TV Collection, ALUA. For details on the UAW portion of the hearings, see U.S. Congress, Senate, Select Committee on Improper Activities in the Labor and Management Fields, *Hearings*, 85th Cong., 2d Sess. (Washington, D.C., 1958), 8902–9074, 9975–10255.

23. Schrade interview, June 1992; Conway interview, April 10, 1972, JFKL; Woodcock to Ralph Dugan, November 18, 1959, Box 948, JFK Pre-Presidential Files, JFKL; Sifton to Victor Reuther, November 7, 1958, Box 75, Reuther-Carliner; Jeffrey's notes on

November 1959 staff meeting, Box 7, Jeffrey Collection, ALUA; IEB minutes, January 18, 1960, Box 22, Region 9A.

24. Bob Wallace memorandum, May 1959, Box 949, JFK Pre-Presidential Files, JFKL; Jack Conway interview, April 10, 1972, JFKL; Jeffrey to Rauh, July 15, 1959, Box 18, Rauh Collection, LC; Mike Feldman to Rauh, October 2 and November 30, 1959; Rauh to Hubert Humphrey, April 14 and May 23, 1960, all in Box 20, Rauh Collection; John Kennedy to Woodcock, May 28, 1959, Box 948, Pre-Presidential Files, JFKL.

25. Conway interview, April 10, 1972; IEB minutes, January 18, 1960, Box 22, Region 9A; oral history interviews with Rauh, December 23, 1965, JFKL, and July 30, 1969, LBJL; memo from Jeffrey, n.d. [May 1959], and Ted Sorenson to Conway, May 29, 1959, both in Box 949, JFK Pre-Presidential Files, JFKL; Leonard Woodcock interview, January 27, 1970, JFKL.

26. Conway interview, April 10, 1972, JFKL; *New York Times*, October 13 and 16, 1959; Walter Reuther clipping file, Box 433, WPR.

27. White, *Making of the President, 1960*, chap. 4; Solberg, *Hubert Humphrey*, 80–95; oral history interview with Rauh, May 1987, Washington, D.C.; Conway interview, April 10, 1972, JFKL; Rauh interview, December 11, 1967, Box 2, Cormier-Eaton.

28. Conway interviews, April 10, 1972, JFKL, and July 30, 1969, LBJL; Rauh to Hollander, May 13, 1960, Box 18, Rauh Collection, LC; *New York Times,* May 15, 1960. Reuther's actions on behalf of JFK triggered a flurry of activity by supporters of other candidates. Eleanor Roosevelt immediately wrote Reuther asking him to remain neutral in the hope that Adlai Stevenson would capture the nomination, and LBJ informed Reuther that if the UAW came out in support of Kennedy, the majority leader would block consideration of health-care legislation that the UAW desperately wanted. See Eleanor Roosevelt to Reuther, May 25, 1960, Box 193, WPR; *New York Times,* June 27, 1960; Reuther's handwritten notes, n.d. [early 1960], Box 433, WPR.

29. "As to the future," Rauh wrote to an associate shortly after the West Virginia primary, "it seems to me it has to be Jack Kennedy. Our job is to try to persuade Jack to stay liberal even though he is now fighting the conservatives, not Hubert, and it is to that end that Arthur [Goldberg], Walter Reuther and the rest of us are now devoting ourselves": Rauh to Hollander, May 13, 1960, Box 18, Rauh Collection, LC. Also see Jeffrey's notes on Citizenship-Education Departments staff meeting, May 19, 1960, Box 7, Jeffrey Collection, ALUA; *New York Times*, July 8, 1960; Rauh interview, July 30, 1969, LBJL; Weinberg to Victor Reuther, May 26, 1960, and Weinberg to Carrol Hutton, July 1, 1960, both in Box 22, SPD; Weinberg to Jeffrey, Box 13, Jeffrey Collection.

30. Rauh interview, July 30, 1969, LBJL; John Frederick Martin, *Civil Rights and the Crisis of Liberalism* (Boulder, Colo., 1979), 169–170; Schlesinger, *Thousand Days*, 41–45; minutes of meeting, July 30, 1960, Box 11, CD; White, *Making of the President, 1960*, 158–172.

31. The literature on Kennedy has undergone a dramatic transformation since the 1960s. The classic study of JFK as a fighting liberal is Schlesinger, *Thousand Days*. More recent scholarship has tended to focus on Kennedy's commitment to consensus at home and Cold War confrontation abroad. See, for example, Richard J. Walton, *Cold War and Counter-Revolution: The Foreign Policy of John F. Kennedy* (New York, 1972); Henry Fairlie, *The Kennedy Promise: The Politics of Expectation* (Garden City, N.Y., 1973), which quotes Lippmann on p. 242; Lewis Paper, *The Promise and the Performance: The Leadership of John F. Kennedy* (New York, 1975); Bruce Miroff, *Pragmatic Illusions: The Presidential Politics of John F. Kennedy* (New York, 1976); Herbert Parmet, *JFK: The Presidency of John F. Kennedy* (New York, 1983); and Thomas Patterson, ed.,

Kennedy's Quest for Victory: American Foreign Policy, 1961–1963 (New York, 1989). A sympathetic treatment is Irving Bernstein, *Promises Kept: John F. Kennedy's New Frontier* (New York, 1991).

32. Conway interview, April 10, 1972, JFKL; Dallek, *Lone Star Rising*, 574–582.

33. Conway interview, April 10, 1972, JFKL; Dallek, *Lone Star Rising*, 579; oral history interviews with David Dubinsky, May 7, 1969; Rauh, July 30, 1969; and G. Mennen Williams, March 8, 1974, all in LBJL. Rauh believed that "the nomination of Johnson throws doubt on the sincerity of the platform pledges." See Rauh to Abram Chayes, July 25, 1960, Box 29, Rauh Collection, LC.

34. Rauh interview, December 11, 1967, Box 2, Cormier-Eaton; Paul Schrade interview, June 1992; Williams interview, March 8, 1974, LBJL; minutes of meeting, July 30, 1960, Box 11, CD.

35. *New York Times*, July 25 and 26, 1960; Roy Reuther to Robert Kennedy et al., September 7, 1960, and Roy Reuther to Frank Thompson, September 7, 1960, both in Box 52, RFK Pre-Administration Files, JFKL; Louis Harris and Associates, "A Study In-Depth of the Rank-and-File of the United Automobile Workers" (May 1961), Box 58, Vice-President Leonard Woodcock Collection, ALUA; Conway interview, April 10, 1972, JFKL.

36. Conway interview, April 10, 1970, JFKL; Weinberg to Reuther, August 1, 1960, Box 22, SPD; oral history interview with Walter Heller, Kermit Gordon, James Tobin, Gardner Ackley, and Paul Samuelson, August 1, 1964, JFKL.

37. The text of Kennedy's Labor Day speech is in Box 433, WPR. Reuther first suggested the possibility of a Peace Corps as part of his 1950 Total Peace Offensive, detailed in chapter 2. Gerard T. Rice, *The Bold Experiment: JFK's Peace Corps* (Notre Dame, Ind., 1985), 9–16.

38. Weinberg to Roy Reuther, September 6, 1960, Box 22, SPD; *New York Times*, October 4, 1960; Robert Kennedy to Victor Reuther, September 26, 1960, Box 25, RFK Pre-Administration Files, JFKL; Woodcock interview, January 27, 1970, JFKL. The voting statistics are in the 1961 Harris survey, Box 58, Woodcock Collection, ALUA.

39. Harris survey, 1961, Box 58, Woodcock Collection, ALUA.

40. The comparison is drawn from Arthur Kornhauser, Harold Sheppard, and Albert Mayer, *When Labor Votes: A Study of Auto Workers* (New York, 1956), 42–43, which details the UAW rank-and-file vote in the 1952 election, and the 1961 Harris survey, Box 58, Woodcock Collection, ALUA.

41. Conway interview, April 10, 1972, JFKL; IEB minutes, December 13, 1960, Box 17, Region 9A.

42. Conway interview, April 10, 1972, JFKL.

43. Ibid.

44. Author's oral history interview with Leonard Woodcock, September 13, 1988, Ann Arbor; oral history interview with Jack Conway, March 27, 1963, ALUA; Weinberg to Reuther, November 3, 1960, Box 22, Weinberg Collection, ALUA; oral history interview with Arthur Goldberg, February 27, 1970, Box 2, Cormier-Eaton; David Carper, "Kennedy and the Unions," *Dissent* 9 (Winter 1962), 35.

45. IEB minutes, December 13, 1960, Box 17, Region 9A; Ralph Showalter to Victor Reuther, January 25, 1961, Box 76, Reuther-Carliner; Showalter to Walter and Victor Reuther, March 20, 1961, Box 11, CD; U.S. Congress, Joint Economic Committee, *Hearings*, 87th Cong., 1st sess. (Washington D.C., 1961) I, 117–118; U.S. Congress, Senate, Committee on Banking and Currency, *Hearings*, 87th Cong., 1st sess. (Washington, D.C., 1961), 855–856; Mark Gelfand, *A Nation of Cities: The Federal Government and Urban America* (New York, 1975), 308–347; Conway interview, April 10, 1972,

JFKL; Sundquist, *Politics and Policy,* 83–85; Weinberg to Reuther, December 21, 1960, Box 22, Weinberg Collection, ALUA; Sifton to Reuther, November 7 and 11, 1960, Box 10; Victor Reuther and Sifton to all regional directors, department heads, and Citizenship-Legislative representatives, December 28, 1960, Box 14; and Ralph Showalter to Victor Reuther, January 23, 1961, Box 11, all in CD.

46. Harris rank-and-file study, Box 58, Woodcock Collection, ALUA. Parmet, *JFK,* 91; Frank Marquart, "Trouble in Auto," *Dissent* 8 (Spring 1961), 11; John Bodnar, "Power and Memory in Oral History: Workers and Managers at Studebaker," *JAH* 75 (March 1989), 1216; draft of statement for Joint Economic Committee, February 9, 1961, Box 22, SPD.

47. U.S. Congress, Joint Economic Committee, *Hearings,* 87th Cong., 1st Sess. (Washington, D.C., 1961), 106–118, 123–127; ibid., 2d sess. (Washington, D.C., 1962), 757–761; Reuther's remarks to the IUD, March 7, 1961, Box 15, SPD.

48. Weinberg's draft memo, June 1962, Box 107, SPD. Reuther first tested the idea of national economic planning in labor circles. See, for instance, his address of January 7, 1959, to the AFL-CIO IUD, Box 4, SPD.

49. On the UAW's view of Western European planning, see Weinberg to Showalter, May 31, 1961, Box 107, SPD; Reuther's statement to the Joint Economic Committee, February 7, 1962, Box 4, SPD; Weinberg to Reuther, June 8, 1962; Irving Bluestone to Woody Ginsberg, May 21, 1963; and Weinberg to Reuther, June 5, 1963, all in Box 107, SPD; and Reuther's address to the IUD constitutional convention, November 7, 1963, Box 4, SPD. For the specifics of the UAW's planning proposal, see Weinberg to Reuther, August 9, 1961, Box 22, SPD; Joint Economic Committee, *Hearings,* 1st sess., 123–127, and 2d sess., 718–720. Reuther's quote is from his address to the Center for the Study of Democratic Institutions, January 22, 1963, Box 4, SPD.

50. Sifton to Weinberg, March 10, 1961, Box 3; Weinberg to Reuther, June 3, 1961, Box 2; Reuther's statement to Joint Economic Committee, February 7, 1962, Box 4; Weinberg to Reuther, May 17, 1962, Box 2, all in SPD; Reuther to Paul Douglas, May 25, 1962, Box 22, Weinberg Collection, ALUA; Weinberg draft memo, June 1962; Reuther to Officers, Board Members, and Department Heads, June 11, 1962, both in Box 107; Reuther's address to the Center for the Study of Democratic Institutions, January 22, 1963, and his statement to the Senate Labor Committee, May 22, 1963, both in Box 4; Douglas Fraser's address at the fiftieth anniversary of the Labor Department, March 13, 1963, Box 107; and Dick Kelly to Frank Winn, August 5, 1963, Box 4, SP; *New York Times,* May 5, 1962, and November 20, 1963; Weinberg to Reuther, May 17 and June 13, 1962, both in Box 22, Weinberg Collection.

51. On Galbraith, see Richard Pells, *The Liberal Mind in a Conservative Age: American Intellectuals in the 1940s and 1950s* (New York, 1985), 162–175. The UAW objected to Galbraith's work because it attempted to shift the focus of public debate away from economic inequality and toward the quality of life. Weinberg, in particular, rejected the notion that the United States had become an "affluent society." On the UAW's fear of Galbraith's influence on the Kennedy camp, see Weinberg to Reuther, July 5 and August 1, 1960, both in Box 2, and August 8, 1960, Box 14, all in SPD. On Kennedy as an economic conservative, see Parmet, *JFK,* 91; Walter Heller, *New Dimensions of Political Economy* (Cambridge, Mass., 1966), 30; Hobart Rowan, *The Free Enterprisers: Kennedy, Johnson, and the Business Establishment* (New York, 1964), 15–60; Alan Matusow, *The Unraveling of America: A History of Liberalism in the 1960s* (New York, 1984), 32–42.

52. Rowen, *Free Enterprisers,* 34–35; Schlesinger, *Thousand Days,* pp. 628–629; *New York Times,* February 10, 1961.

53. *UAW Washington Report*, February 21, 1961; Weinberg to Reuther, June 3, 1961, Box 22, Weinberg Collection, ALUA; Sifton to Showalter, March 6, 1961, Box 76, Reuther-Carliner; Sifton memo, June 22, 1961, Box 32, and UAW press release, July 28, 1961, Box 33, both in PCS; Weinberg to Reuther, August 14, 1961, Box 22, Weinberg Collection.

54. *New York Times*, January 10, 1962; Matusow, *Unraveling of America*, 45–48; Parmet, *JFK*, 240–241.

55. Matusow, *Unraveling of America*, 49–51; Parmet, *JFK*, 244–245; Rowan, *Free Enterprisers*, 231–236.

56. Weinberg to Reuther, January 30, January 31, and August 21, 1963, all in Box 19, Weinberg Collection, ALUA; *New York Times*, February 16, 1963; Rowen, *Free Enterprisers*, 239–246. Reuther told the CEA in December 1962 that without a cut in taxes on lower incomes in 1963 "we're all in trouble." He deplored the administration's talk of mild improvement as "microscopic nonsense." See M. J. Simler to the Council, December 10, 1962, Box 35, Walter Heller Papers, JFKL.

57. Walter Heller to John Kennedy, October 17, 1962, Box 33, Heller Papers, JFKL; IEB minutes, September 24–26, 1963, Box 17, Region 9A.

58. Steven M. Gillon, *Politics and Vision: The ADA and American Liberalism, 1947-1985* (New York, 1987), 147; Robert M. Collins, *The Business Response to Keynes, 1929–1964* (New York, 1981), 183–184; Alan Wolfe, *America's Impasse: The Rise and Fall of the Politics of Growth* (Boston, 1981), 66–69; Weinberg to Reuther, June 7, 14, and 19, 1962, Box 22, Weinberg Collection, ALUA; Reuther's note, June 20, 1962, Box 302, WPR. On June 29, 1962, Reuther asked Heller how to exert more pressure on JFK. Heller proposed a meeting with key labor economists. Again Meany declared that the AFL-CIO would not sanction the meeting, and the plan collapsed. At the same time, according to Arthur Goldberg, Meany phoned Reuther on a minor patronage matter and did not even mention the tax question. See Reuther's notes, July 11, 1962, Box 38, WPR, and August 10, 1962, Box 302, WPR.

59. Rowen, *Free Enterprisers*, 206; Joint Economic Committee, *Hearings*, 2d sess., 808–809; Weinberg to Reuther, January 30, 1962, Box 22, Weinberg Collection, ALUA; Lloyd Ulman to CEA, April 5, 1962, Box 30, Heller Papers, JFKL.

60. IEB minutes, March 5–7 and September 24–26, 1963, both in Box 17, Region 9A. Reuther first raised the need for "an effective counter-force" to prod the administration in a November 1961 meeting with the CEA. See Ulman to Kermit Gordon, November 13, 1961, Box 28, Heller Papers, JFKL.

61. IEB minutes, September 24–26, 1963, Box 17, Region 9A. For criticisms of the labor movement in general and the UAW in particular, see, for example, Sidney Lens, *The Crisis of American Labor* (New York, 1959); Michael Harrington, "After the Union Ball," *Commonweal*, November 3, 1961, 142–146; Paul Jacobs, *The State of the Unions* (New York, 1963); Paul Sultan, *Disenchanted Unionist* (New York, 1963), 170–171; Harvey Swados, "The UAW—Over the Top or Over the Hill?" *Dissent* 10 (Autumn 1963), 332–334; Murray Kempton, "Reuther's Nursing Home," *New Republic*, November 23, 1963, 6–7; B. J. Widick, *Labor Today: The Triumphs and Failures of Unionism in the United States* (Boston, 1964). A backhanded defense of unions is David Carper, "Fashionable Fallacies about Trade Unions," *Dissent* 8 (Spring 1961), 106, 199–206.

62. Claire Sifton diary, April 7, 1953, Box 10, PCS; Harris survey, May 1961, 39–40, Box 58, Woodcock Collection, ALUA.

63. IEB minutes, January 31–February 3, 1967, and March 5–7, 1963, both in Box 24, Region 9A; Harris survey, 90–92, Box 58, Woodcock Collection, ALUA; Sultan,

Disenchanted Unionist, 170–171. For a contrasting view of union activism, see Joel Seidman, Jack London, Bernard Karsh, and Daisy Tagliacozzo, *The Worker Views His Union* (Chicago, 1958), 91–93.

64. *Washington Evening Star,* October 11, 1957; *Washington Post,* April 7, 1972; oral history interview with Irving Bluestone, February 1988, Detroit; Jack Conway interview, March 27, 1963, ALUA; Emanuel Geltman and Irving Howe, "The Tradition of Reutherism: An Interview with Brendan Sexton," *Dissent* 19 (Winter 1972), 54.

65. Joe Walsh to Paul Sifton, Box 34, PCS; Alan Haber to Sexton, August 13, 1961, Box 60, Jeffrey Collection, ALUA; Claire Sifton diary, September 20, 1960, Box 10, PCS.

66. Swados, "UAW—Over the Top," 330–332, 341; Carroll Hutton to Reuther, November 9, 1962, Box 114, WPR; A. H. Raskin, "Walter Reuther's Great Big Union," *Atlantic,* October 1963, 85–92; "Proceedings, Eighteenth Constitutional Convention, UAW, May 4–10, 1962, Atlantic City," ALUA. Gosser was removed from office after being convicted for defrauding the UAW.

67. Steve Babson, *Building the Union: Skilled Workers and Anglo-Gaelic Immigrants in the Rise of the UAW* (New Brunswick, N.J., 1991), 134, 242; "Douglas Andrew Fraser," in Gary M. Fink, ed., *Biographical Dictionary of American Labor* (Westport, Conn., 1984), 235–236; Schrade interview, June 1992.

68. "Proceedings, Eighteenth Constitutional Convention," 333–349, ALUA; Raskin, "Reuther's Great Big Union," 85–92.

69. Reuther to Eleanor Roosevelt, April 18, 1961, Box 193, WPR; *U.S. News & World Report,* November 25, 1963; Conway interview, April 10, 1972, JFKL; oral history interview with George Meany, March 12, 1969, Box 2, Cormier-Eaton; *New York Times,* December 7, 1961; B. J. Widick, "Labor's Divided House," *Nation,* December 23, 1961, 309–311; Reuther's notes, November 29, 1961, Box 301, WPR.

70. Reuther's notes, August 14, 1962, Box 302, WPR; Conway interview, April 10, 1972, JFKL. Reuther threatened to resign during the heated Executive Board meeting. Minutes of the Special IUD meeting, August 16, 1962, Box 302, WPR, provide details of how close the AFL-CIO came to splitting.

71. Conway interview, April 10, 1972, JFKL; Swados, "UAW—Over the Top," 341; Kempton, "Reuther's Nursing Home."

72. Kempton, "Reuther's Nursing Home"; oral history interview with David Dubinsky, February 28, 1968, Box 2, Cormier-Eaton; Raskin, "Reuther's Great Big Union," 87.

73. Raskin, "Reuther's Great Big Union," 86; Victor Reuther to Roy Reuther and Bluestone, July 31, 1961, Box 14, CD; Paul Jacobs, *Labor Looks at Itself* (Santa Barbara: Center for the Study of Democratic Institutions [196?], audio tape; Carl Westman to Bluestone, May 18, 1963, Box 10, CAPC.

74. Victor Reuther to Walter Reuther, August 16, 1957, Box 25, Victor Reuther Collection, ALUA; James Miller, *"Democracy Is in the Streets": From Port Huron to the Seige of Chicago* (New York, 1987), 28–30; Peter Levy, "SDS and Labor: The Early Years," paper presented at the North American Labor History Conference, Wayne State University, September 17, 1987, 4–7. In 1939 William Haber had chaired a National Resource Planning Board panel charged with investigating national social policy. The panel's report, "Security, Work, and Relief Policies," argued for an "American standard" of economic security as a basic right. See Edwin Amenta and Theda Skocpol, "Redefining the New Deal: World War II and the Development of Social Provisions in the United States," in Margaret Weir, Ann Shola Orloff, and Theda Skocpol, eds., *The Politics of Social Policy in the United States* (Princeton, 1988), 87–88.

75. Miller, *"Democracy Is in the Streets,"* chap. 1; Peter Levy, "SDS and Labor: A

Misunderstood Relationship" (Ph.D. diss., Columbia University, 1986), chap. 2; Victor Reuther to Roy Reuther and Bluestone, July 31, 1961, and Bluestone to Victor Reuther, August 7, 1961, both in Box 14, CD.

76. Tom Hayden to Jeffrey, n.d. [1962–63], Box 77, Jeffrey Collection, ALUA; Jeffrey to Reuther, December 22, 1962; Bluestone to Reuther, April 9, 1963; Bluestone to Ginsburg, October 2, 1963; Haber to Bluestone, August 9, 1963, all in Box 523, WPR; Miller, "*Democracy Is in the Streets,*" chap. 6.

77. Jeffrey to Family, Box 47, Jeffrey Collection, ALUA; Bluestone to Reuther, April 9, 1963, and Jeffrey to Reuther, December 22, 1962, both in Box 523, WPR; Todd Gitlin, *The Sixties: Years of Hope, Days of Rage* (New York, 1987), 120. At the Port Huron convention, the LID's Michael Harrington blasted SDS for not being tough enough on communism, but apparently the UAW leadership was not concerned about the issue. The next year the UAW contributed $10,000 to SDS. See Levy, "SDS and Labor: A Misunderstood Relationship," 66. At times, SDS members also seemed woefully uninformed about organized labor's history. In the mid-1960s a group of SDS members at the University of Wisconsin joined UAW pickets at a local body shop. The SDS official who organized his group's participation, C. Clark Kissinger, was amazed to find that the workers welcomed him, though he was a socialist, and he was "amazed by the degree of political awareness (class consciousness?) shown by some of the strikers. . . . Some spoke spontaneously about automation and unemployment." See C. Clark Kissinger, *The Bruns Strike,* SDS pamphlet, October 1963, Box 170, SNCCC.

78. Reuther's statement to the U.S. Commission on Civil Rights, December 14, 1960, Box 70, Reuther-Carliner. Also see *UAW Washington Report,* May 13 and June 10, 1963.

79. IEB minutes, September 24–26, 1963, Box 17, Region 9A.

7. The Coalition of Conscience

1. Walter Reuther's remarks to the March on Washington, August 28, 1963, Box 4, SPD. On Reuther's perception of the march, see IEB minutes, September 24–26, 1963, Box 17, Region 9A. To place Reuther's appearance in its historical context, see Scott Sandage, "A Marble House Divided: The Lincoln Memorial, the Civil Rights Movement, and the Politics of Memory, 1939–1963," *JAH* 80 (June 1993), 135–167.

2. Michael Kazin and Steven J. Ross, "America's Labor Day: The Dilemma of a Workers' Celebration," *JAH* 78 (March 1992), 1320; *Detroit Free Press,* September 1, 1963; *Detroit News,* September 2, 1963; Reuther's Labor Day message, September 2, 1963, Box 4, SPD.

3. A copy of Hill's pamphlet is in Box 32, PCS. For details on the black–labor tension, see Philip Foner, *Organized Labor and the Black Worker, 1619–1981* (New York, 1981), 332–345; Jervis Anderson, *A. Philip Randolph: A Biographical Portrait* (New York, 1972), 298–310; and William H. Harris, "A. Philip Randolph, Black Workers, and the Labor Movement," in Melvyn Dubofsky and Warren Van Tine, eds., *Labor Leaders in America* (Urbana, 1987), 275–276.

4. Brendan Sexton and Nat Weinberg to Walter Reuther, January 21, 1963, Box 19, Nat Weinberg Collection, ALUA; *NAACP Vanguard,* July 1962; Emil Mazey to Roy Wilkins, March 14, 1962, Box 504, WPR; Ray Marshall, "The Negro and the AFL-CIO," in John Bracey Jr., August Meier, and Elliott Rudwick, eds., *Black Workers and Organized Labor* (Belmont, Calif., 1971), 210.

5. Walter Reuther to William Oliver, Box 9, FP; *New York Times,* November 11,

1962; Oliver to Reuther, November 1, 1962, Box 90, WPR. Reuther quickly squelched the rumor that he was quitting the NAACP board. Oliver had worked out an arrangement with the National Urban League in the late 1950s, according to which the League privately informed the UAW of any charges against it before publicizing them.

6. NAACP memo for the files, October 23, 1962, and report of the NAACP Board of Directors, November 13, 1962, both in Box 504, WPR; Foner, *Organized Labor and the Black Worker*, 336; *NAACP Vanguard*, July 1962; *Detroit Free Press*, November 25, 1962; Oliver to Reuther, November 1, 1962, Box 90, WPR.

7. Oliver to Reuther, April 18, 1962, Box 90, WPR; Earl Henderson to Oliver, March 12, 1962, and August 18, 1961, both in Box 13, FP; Henderson to Oliver, May 19, 1961, Box 11B, FP; Harry Ross to Oliver, May 21, 1961, Box 12, FP; Henderson to Oliver, May 1, 1963, and UAW Fair Practices Department Survey, 1963, both in Box 90, WPR.

8. Norman Matthews to Francine Temko, December 12, 1960; Robert Battle III and Douglas Brothers to James Brown, December 13, 1960; and Nelson Samp to Walter Reuther, December 13, 1960, all in Box 50, WPR; UAW Fair Practices Department Survey, 1963, Box 90, WPR.

9. Lee Oliver to Local 3 officials, n.d. [early 1960s], Box 38, FP; Eddie Butler to Whom It May Concern, March 27, 1967, Box 35, FP; Bard Young to William Oliver, December 9, 1966, and Robert L. Horn to Mr. Roosevelt Jr., June 14, 1966, both in Box 37, FP.

10. On the culmination of the International's struggle with Local 988 (detailed in chapter 5) see newspaper clipping dated February 14, 1960, Box 66, Reuther-Carliner. On the Fair Practices Department's gradualism, see oral history interview with Shelton Tappes, October 27, 1967, and February 10, 1968, ALUA; William Oliver to E. T. Michael, August 17, 1961, Box 5, FP; Ralph Showalter to Oliver, October 25, 1961, Box 90, WPR.

11. Harry Ross to William Oliver, May 21, 1961, Box 12, FP; Henderson to Oliver, May 1, 1963; UAW Fair Practices Department Survey, 1963, and Oliver to Reuther, April 18 and November 1, 1962, all in Box 90, WPR; Henderson to Oliver, March 12, 1962, Box 13, FP, and May 23, 1963, Box 90, WPR.

12. Irving Bluestone to Reuther, April 7, 1965, and Reuther to Leonard Woodcock, April 15, 1965, both in Box 90, WPR; Pre-Apprenticeship Training Program to Date, June 9, 1966; William Jenkins to Bluestone, September 30, 1966; Tim Foley to Bluestone, December 6, 1966; Harold Dunne to Bluestone, April 21, 1967, all in Box 121, WPR.

13. *Detroit Courier*, April 21, 1962, clipping in Box 16, FP; oral history interviews with Horace Sheffield, July 24, 1968; Shelton Tappes, October 27, 1967, and February 10, 1968; Hodges Mason, November 28, 1967, all in ALUA. According to Mason, a long-time African-American activist in the UAW, Reuther won Matthews's and Greathouse's approval by adding two new white members to the IEB in 1962.

14. Weinberg to Reuther, June 5, 1963, Box 19, Weinberg Collection, ALUA; *New York Times*, July 31, 1963; Sheffield interview, July 24, 1968, ALUA. Data on the IEB selection process is in Box 65, WPR, and Box 130, UAW Secretary-Treasurer Collection, ALUA.

15. Clippings from *Detroit Free Press*, November 25, 1962; *Washington Afro-American*, November 24, 1962; *Time*, November 2, 1962, all in Box 504, WPR; William Oliver to Reuther, April 18, 1962, Box 90, WPR.

16. See, among many other works, August Meier and Elliot Rudwick, *CORE: A Study in the Civil Rights Movement* (New York, 1973), 101–326; William Chafe, *Civilities and Civil Rights: Greensboro, North Carolina, and the Black Struggle for Freedom* (New York, 1980); Clayborne Carson, *In Struggle: SNCC and the Black Awak-*

ening of the 1960s (Cambridge, Mass., 1981), 9–95; Aldon Morris, *The Origins of the Civil Rights Movement: Black Communities Organizing for Change* (New York, 1984); David Garrow, *Bearing the Cross: Martin Luther King, Jr., and the Southern Christian Leadership Conference* (New York, 1986), 127–355; Adam Fairclough, *To Redeem the Soul of America: The Southern Christian Leadership Conference and Martin Luther King, Jr.* (Athens, Ga., 1987), 57–191; Jack Bloom, *Class, Race, and the Civil Rights Movement* (Bloomington, 1987), 157–185; Taylor Branch, *Parting the Waters: America in the King Years, 1954–1963* (New York, 1988), 277–922.

17. Fairclough, *To Redeem the Soul,* 142; Denton Watson, *Lion in the Lobby: Clarence Mitchell Jr.'s Struggle for the Passage of Civil Rights Laws* (New York, 1990), 526–527; James Findlay, "Religion and Politics in the Sixties: The Churches and the Civil Rights Act of 1964," *JAH* 77 (June 1990), 66–75.

18. William Oliver to Roy Reuther, February 11, 1960, Box 8, FP; UAW flyer in support of Woolworth boycott, 1960, Box 16, FP; Oliver to Walter Reuther, December 5, 1960, Box 9, CD; Walter Reuther's statement to the U.S. Commission on Civil Rights, December 14, 1960, Box 70, and Oliver to Marvin Rich, June 21, 1961, Box 26, both in Reuther-Carliner; Reuther to Charles McDew, April 16, 1963, Box 127, SNCCC; UAW press release, Joseph L. Rauh Jr. Collection, LC; Martin Luther King Jr. to Reuther, August 22, 1962, Box 20, Martin Luther King Jr. Collection, MLK.

19. IEB statement, May 24, 1961, Box 70, Reuther-Carliner; Roy Reuther to John Kennedy, May 26, 1961, "Reuth" folder, WHCF name file, JFKL; Reuther to Robert Kennedy, March 12 and June 26, 1962, Box 377, WPR; Weinberg to Reuther, September 27, 1962, Box 22, Weinberg Collection, ALUA.

20. Carl Brauer, *John F. Kennedy and the Second Reconstruction* (New York, 1977), chaps. 3–7; Hugh Davis Graham, *The Civil Rights Era: Origins and Development of National Policy, 1960–1972* (New York, 1990), chaps. 1–2; and Mark Stern, *Calculating Visions: Kennedy, Johnson, and Civil Rights* (New Brunswick, N.J., 1992), chap. 2.

21. Garrow, *Bearing the Cross,* chap. 5; Fairclough, *To Redeem The Soul,* chap. 5; Arthur Schlesinger Jr., *Robert Kennedy and His Times* (Boston, 1978), 352; Brauer, *Kennedy and the Second Reconstruction,* 229–247; Stern, *Calculating Visions,* 80–89; Steven Gillon, *Politics and Vision: The ADA and American Liberalism, 1947–1985* (New York, 1987), 148–149; Findlay, "Religion and Politics," 69–71; Alan Matusow, *The Unraveling of America: A History of Liberalism in the 1960s* (New York, 1984), 89.

22. *UAW Solidarity,* June 1963; *UAW Washington Report,* June 24, 1963.

23. Garrow, *Bearing the Cross,* 254–260; Emil Mazey to Walter Reuther and James Carey, May 10, 1963, and Rauh to Reuther, May 13, 1963, Box 117, WPR; oral history interviews with Jack Conway, April 10, 1972, Washington, D.C., JFKL, and Irving Bluestone, Detroit, February 1988.

24. Matusow, *Unraveling of America,* 87–90; Garrow, *Bearing the Cross,* 250, 267–270; Martin Luther King Jr., *Why We Can't Wait* (New York, 1964), 117; *UAW Washington Report,* June 10, 1963; Stern, *Calculating Visions,* 84.

25. Brauer, *Kennedy and the Second Reconstruction,* 265–271; Charles Whalen and Barbara Whalen, *The Longest Debate: A Legislative History of the 1964 Civil Rights Act* (New York, 1985), 16–18; Stern, *Calculating Visions,* 83–93; Graham, *Civil Rights Era,* 75–87; Matusow, *Unraveling of America,* 88–89.

26. James Sundquist, *Politics and Policy: The Eisenhower, Kennedy, and Johnson Years* (Washington, D.C., 1968), 262–263; Stern, *Calculating Visions,* 91; Whalen and Whalen, *Longest Debate,* 1–2.

27. Sexton and Weinberg to Reuther, January 21, 1963, Box 19, Weinberg Collection, ALUA.

28. Daniel Knapp and Kenneth Polk, *Scouting the War on Poverty: Social Reform*

Politics in the Kennedy Administration (Lexington, Mass., 1971); Weinberg to Reuther, January 25, 1963, Box 19, Weinberg Collection, ALUA; Walter Reuther to Officers and IEB Members, May 17, 1963, Box 107, SPD; Otha Brown to Weinberg, Bluestone, Sexton, and Roy Reuther, CL. The UAW also had a personal connection with Michael Harrington: Victor Reuther, Martin Gerber, and Brendan Sexton's wife, Patricia Cayo Sexton, served with him on the board of directors of the League for Industrial Democracy. See LID Board of Directors list, 1965, Box 168, SNCCC.

29. Weinberg to Walter Reuther, July 3, 1963, CL.

30. "Confidential Memorandum on the Present Posture of Negro Adherence to the Democratic Party," n.d. [mid-1963], Box 117, WPR; Joseph Rauh to Oliver, April 29, 1963, Box 98, Rauh Collection, LC; *UAW Washington Report,* June 24, 1963; Reuther to John Kennedy, June 7, 1963, Box 563, WPR.

31. A detailed comparison of Kennedy's and the LCCR's bills is found in "Memorandum Concerning the Administration's 1963 Civil Rights Bills," n.d. [June 1963], CL. The UAW's meeting with the president, vice-president, and attorney general is recounted in Stern, *Calculating Visions,* 95–97; oral history interview with Rauh, Washington, D.C., May 12, 1987; and Rauh's draft article for *Progressive,* July 1964, Box 215, Rauh Collection, LC.

32. Whalen and Whalen, *Longest Debate,* 1–20; Brauer, *Kennedy and the Second Reconstruction,* 267–278; Theodore Sorensen, *Kennedy* (New York, 1966), 496–501; *UAW Washington Report,* June 24, 1963; Rauh interview, May 12, 1987; oral history interview with Jack Conway, Washington, D.C., April 10, 1972, JFKL; U.S. Congress, House, Committee on the Judiciary, *Hearings,* 88th Cong., 1st sess. (Washington, D.C., 1963), 1942. Roy Reuther is quoted in Sundquist, *Politics and Policy,* 263. The UAW found JFK's caution on civil rights as frustrating as his caution on economic policy. "[T]he administration has been as slow to recognize the realities of this situation as it has been in the economic sphere," Weinberg wrote Reuther on June 5, 1963. "The failure to make significant progress toward full employment will create grave danger of serious conflict between Negro and white workers (and between Negroes and the civil rights movement) over the division of an inadequate supply of jobs" (Box 98, SPD).

33. Reuther to Robert Kennedy, June 28, 1963, Box 377, WPR; "Civil Rights Bill as Background For Meeting of Pro–Civil Rights Groups on July 2, 1963," Box 11, RFK Attorney General Papers, JFKL; Rauh interview, May 12, 1987; Oliver to William Dodds, July 22, 1963, Box 10, CAPC; Whalen and Whalen, *Longest Debate,* 14–15; Findlay, "Religion and Politics," 73–74.

34. Watson, *Lion in the Lobby,* 531; Arnold Aronson to cooperating organizations, July 25, 1963, Box 1, ser. D, LCCRC; Conway interview, April 10, 1972, JFKL. The other members of the steering committee were Andrew Biemiller, the AFL-CIO's chief lobbyist, and Walter Fauntroy, the SCLC's Washington representative.

35. LCCR minutes, July 24 and July 31, 1963, both in Box 1, ser. D, LCCRC; Whalen and Whalen, *Longest Debate,* 22–24; Rauh interview, May 12, 1987. Biemiller took primary responsibility for making sure Congress inserted a fair employment practices provision in the bill, a provision that George Meany considered essential. See Biemiller to Hubert Humphrey, June 7, 1963, Box 5, ser. E, LCCRC.

36. Series of memos from UAW lobbyists, July–August 1963, Box 1, ser. G, LCCRC; Findlay, "Churches and Politics," 73–76; Victor Reuther to Martin Luther King, August 6, 1963, Box 20, King Collection, MLK; Frank Wallick to Victor Reuther, July 30, 1963, CL. According to Findlay, Victor Reuther was a "Methodist layman." He was not.

37. Jeffrey to Wallick, August 19, 1963, Box 1, ser. G, LCCRC. Though Meader still voted against the civil rights bill when it came before the full committee, he helped the bill on several crucial procedural votes. See Whalen and Whalen, *Longest Debate,* 63.

38. Milton Viorst, *Fire in the Streets: America in the 1960s* (New York, 1979), 216–223; Garrow, *Bearing the Cross*, 266–271; Fairclough, *To Redeem The Soul*, 150–151.

39. *New York Times*, June 23, 1963; *UAW Washington Report*, July 1, 1963. The UAW cosponsored a massive march in support of civil rights in downtown Detroit on June 23, at which Martin Luther King Jr. delivered a variation on his "I Have a Dream" speech. The march drew 125,000 participants, the largest gathering of its kind to date. The rally also raised $28,732.42 for the SCLC, a total surpassed only by a Los Angeles rally. See Reuther to all local union presidents, June 14, 1963, CL; William Oliver to Roy Reuther, June 19, 1963, Box 10, CAPC; Nelson Jack Edwards to Freedom Rally Staff, n.d. [Spring 1963], Box 52, and Detroit Council for Human Relations Financial Statement, July 1963, both in SCLCC.

40. *New York Times*, June 23, 1963; Schlesinger, *Robert Kennedy*, 376; Roy Wilkins, *Standing Fast: The Autobiography of Roy Wilkins* (Baltimore, 1984), 291–292; James Farmer, *Lay Bare the Heart: An Autobiography of the Civil Rights Movement* (New York, 1985), 243; William Mahoney's notes on March meeting, Box 124, SNCCC; Fairclough, *To Redeem The Soul*, 152; Garrow, *Bearing the Cross*, 280; first plan of operation for March on Washington, July 8, 1963, Box 25, King Collection, MLK; Leonard Schiller to Bluestone, July 12, 1963, Box 577, WPR. The march's leaders had hoped to add Reuther and George Meany as nonvoting cochairs, but Meany refused to participate. When Reuther lashed out at Meany's lack of courage, he triggered yet another crisis within the AFL-CIO. SNCC's attitude toward the march's change in emphasis was mixed. At first SNCC's representatives were upset that civil disobedience had been abandoned, but by late July they were arguing that the march would attract too many people to make civil disobedience feasible. See William Mahoney's reports on various meetings planning for the March on Washington, June–July 1963, Box 124, SNCCC.

41. Conway interview, April 10, 1972, JFKL; Reuther to Randolph, August 22, 1963, Box 494, WPR; Oliver to Reuther and Bluestone, August 24, 1963, Box 22, IAD; Mazey to Reuther, Woodcock and Pat Greathouse, November 1, 1963, Box 61, Vice-President Leonard Woodcock Collection, ALUA; Oliver to Bayard Rustin, August 13, 1963, Box 22, IAD; UAW instruction sheet for bus captains and participants, n.d. [August 1963], CL; agenda, Freedom March, UAW staff meeting, August 27, 1963, Box 22, IAD.

42. There are many accounts of the Lewis incident. See, for example, Carson, *In Struggle*, 93–94; Branch, *Parting the Waters*, 874–876; Garrow, *Bearing the Cross*, 281–283. A copy of Lewis's proposed speech, August 29, 1963, is in Box 16, SNCCC.

43. Oliver to Everard Franklin, April 28, 1960, Box 11A, and Oliver to Reuther, Box 8, FP; James Foreman to Emil Mazey, June 30, 1962, Box 22, SNCCC; Reuther to Charles McDew, April 16, 1963, and Mazey to Dee Wulf, May 29, 1963, both in Box 127, SNCCC; LCCR minutes, July 31, 1963, Box 1, ser. D, LCCRC; Rauh interview, May 12, 1987; Jeffrey Shulman, ed., *Robert Kennedy in His Own Words* (New York, 1988), 228–229; IEB minutes, September 24–26, 1963, Box 17, Region 9A.

44. IEB minutes, September 24–26, 1963, Box 17, Region 9A.

45. "Confidential Memorandum on the Present Posture of Negro Adherence to the Democratic Party," n.d. [mid-1963], Box 117, WPR; Dick Kelly to Frank Winn, August 5, 1963, and Reuther's addresses to the March on Washington, August 28, 1963, and the Fifth Constitutional Convention, IUD, November 7, 1963, all in Box 4, SPD. Also see Reuther's Labor Day address, September 2, 1963, Box 4, SPD; House Judiciary Committee, *Hearings*, 1943–1950.

46. *UAW Solidarity*, July 1963; draft of Victor Reuther article, December 30, 1963, Box 19, Weinberg Collection, ALUA. Conway is quoted in Tom Kahn, "Problems of the Negro Movement," *Dissent* (Winter 1964), 136.

47. Whalen and Whalen, *Longest Debate*, 44–45; *UAW Washington Report*, October

21, 1963; Conway interview, April 10, 1972, JFKL; Sundquist, *Politics and Policy,* 265. The UAW, though generally happy with the bill as it emerged from the Judiciary Committee, still insisted that it needed to be stronger. See Frank Wallick to Roy Reuther, October 30, 1963, CL. On ERAP, see Reuther to Mazey, July 8, 1963; Bluestone to Carroll Hutton, August 9, 1963; Bluestone to Reuther, January 6, 1964; and esp. Bluestone to Paul Schrade, February 11, 1964, all in Box 523, WPR. In the last memo, Bluestone wrote, "I urged [SDS's leadership] to shift the emphasis of their program from concern only for civil rights and the issue of world peace to a program in which recognition is given to the importance of resolving economic problems as the underpinning for achieving civil rights and peace." SDS activists, in turn, tried to persuade their allies in SNCC to strengthen their ties to the UAW, a move some UAW staff members encouraged. See Casey Hayden to Don McKelvey, May 10, 1963, and Don to Hayden, June 23, 1963, both in Box 68, SNCCC.
   48. Conway interview, April 10, 1972, JFKL.
   49. Doris Kearns, *Lyndon Johnson and the American Dream* (New York, 1976), 199. This is not to suggest that Johnson embraced civil rights for purely political reasons. LBJ was genuinely concerned for civil rights, but he expressed that concern within the political context that formed the centerpiece of his life. See T. Harry Williams, "Huey, Lyndon, and Southern Radicalism," *JAH* 60 (September 1973), 267–293; and Joe B. Frantz, "Opening a Curtain: The Metamorphosis of Lyndon B. Johnson," *Journal of Southern History* 45 (February 1979), 3–26. Walter to Lyndon Johnson, Walter Reuther folder, WHCF name file, and Johnson Daily Diary, reel 3 (microfilm) LBJL; Walter Reuther note for file, December 3, 1963, Box 368, WPR; oral history interview with Joseph Rauh, July 30, 1969, LBJL. Johnson had assigned Hubert Humphrey the job of tracking down key labor leaders for him. Humphrey gave Johnson the phone numbers of Reuther, James Carey, David Dubinsky, and Alex Rose, the union officials who had been the leading supporters of Kennedy in the 1960 presidential race.
   50. Reuther to Johnson, November 23 and December 3, 1963, both in Box 368, WPR.
   51. Stern, *Calculating Visions,* 160–169; *UAW Washington Report,* December 2, 1963; oral history interview with Rauh, July 30, 1969, LBJL; memo, January 29, 1964, Rauh folder, WHCF name file, LBJL. Immediately after the assassination Rauh had offered to help expedite the civil rights bill. "Such comments from great Americans like you have provided a source of strength and comfort," Johnson responded on December 11, 1963 (Rauh folder, WHCF name file, LBJL).
   52. Oral history interview with Jack Conway, August 13, 1980, Washington, D.C., LBJL; Reuther to Weinberg, December 30, 1963, Box 3, SP; draft memo, January 2, 1964, Box 19, Weinberg Collection, ALUA; Reuther to Johnson, January [4], 1964, Box 368, WPR.
   53. Reuther to Johnson, January [4], 1964, Box 368, WPR.
   54. *New York Times,* January 9, 1964. I have been unable to make a direct connection between Reuther's memo and Johnson's State of the Union address. The memo reached Johnson's desk the day he delivered the State of the Union address. See George Reedy to Johnson, January 8, 1964, Box 35, WHCF, Ex Be 5–5, LBJL.

8. Building the Great Society

   1. Alan Haber to Brendan Sexton, August 31, 1961, Box 60, Mildred Jeffrey Collection, ALUA; Sexton manuscript, n.d. [late 1950s] and Sexton book notes, 1965, both in Box 7, Brendan Sexton Collection, ALUA.
   2. Among the best studies of the Great Society are John Donovan, *The Politics of*

Poverty (New York, 1967); Daniel Moynihan, *Maximum Feasible Misunderstanding: Community Action in the War on Poverty* (New York, 1969); Sar Levitan, *The Great Society's Poor Law* (Baltimore, 1969); Frances Fox Piven and Richard Cloward, *Regulating the Poor: The Functions of Public Welfare* (New York, 1969); James Sundquist, ed., *On Fighting Poverty: Perspectives from Experience* (New York, 1969); Sar Levitan and Robert Taggert, *The Promise of Greatness: The Social Programs of the Last Decade and Their Major Achievements* (Cambridge, Mass., 1976); William Julius Wilson, *The Truly Disadvantaged: The Inner City, the Underclass, and Public Policy* (Chicago, 1987); Ira Katznelson, "Was the Great Society a Lost Opportunity?" in Steven Fraser and Gary Gerstle, eds., *The Rise and Fall of the New Deal Order, 1930–1980* (Princeton, 1989), 185–211; Thomas F. Jackson, "The State, the Movement, and the Urban Poor: The War on Poverty and Political Mobilization in the 1960s," in Michael Katz, ed., *The "Underclass" Debate: Views from History* (Princeton, 1993), 403–439; and Jill Quadrango, *The Color of Welfare: How Racism Undermined the War on Poverty* (New York, 1994). Two important studies that place the War on Poverty within a broad framework are Michael Katz, *In the Shadow of the Poorhouse: A Social History of Welfare in America* (New York, 1986), chap. 9, and Margaret Weir, *Politics and Jobs: The Boundaries of Employment Policy in the United States* (Princeton, 1992), chap. 3.

3. Oral history interview with Joseph L. Rauh Jr., July 30, 1969, LBJL; memo, January 29, 1964, Rauh folder, WHCF name file, LBJL; James Sundquist, *Politics and Policy: The Eisenhower, Kennedy, and Johnson Years* (Washington, D.C., 1968), 267–269; Neil MacNeil, *Dirksen: Portrait of a Public Man* (New York, 1970), 230–234; Mark Stern, *Calculating Visions: Kennedy, Johnson, and Civil Rights* (New Brunswick, N.J., 1992), 164–185; Hugh Davis Graham, *The Civil Rights Era: Origins and Development of National Policy, 1960–1972* (New York, 1990), chap. 5; *UAW Washington Report*, July 6, 1964. On the UAW's role in the lobbying effort, see *UAW Washington Report*, February 10 and April 20, 1964; Walter Reuther to Hubert Humphrey and Thomas Kuchel, May 6, 1964, Box 408, WPR; IEB minutes, May 5–7, 1964, Region 9A.

4. Katznelson, "Was the Great Society a Lost Opportunity?" 195–205; Jackson, "State, Movement, and the Urban Poor," 411–416; Eric Goldman, *The Tragedy of Lyndon Johnson* (New York, 1969), 51–56; Doris Kearns, *Lyndon Johnson and the American Dream* (New York, 1976), 159–165; Paul Conkin, *Big Daddy from the Pedernales: Lyndon Baines Johnson* (Boston, 1986); and, most important, Piven and Cloward, *Regulating the Poor,* 248–282.

5. Kearns, *Lyndon Johnson,* 159–161. Also see Robert Dallek, *Lone Star Rising: Lyndon Johnson and His Times, 1908–1960* (New York, 1991); Katznelson, "Was the Great Society a Lost Opportunity?" 195–196. On the racial tension resulting from the War on Poverty, see Weir, *Politics and Jobs,* 83–97; Jonathan Rieder, "The Rise of the 'Silent Majority,'" in Fraser and Gerstle, *Rise and Fall,* 253–258.

6. U.S. Congress, House, Committee on Education and Labor, *Hearings,* 88th Cong., 2d sess., 1964 (Washington, D.C., 1964), 422–469.

7. Ibid.

8. Walter Reuther, "Freedom's Time of Testing," *Saturday Review,* August 29, 1964; Reuther to Johnson, March 19, 1964, Box 378, WPR.

9. Sundquist, *Politics and Policy,* 137–150; Lilian Rubin, "Maximum Feasible Participation: The Origins, Implications, and Present Status," *Annals of the American Academy of Political and Social Science* 385 (September 1969), 14–29; Moynihan, *Maximum Feasible Misunderstanding;* Alan Matusow, *The Unraveling of America: A History of American Liberalism in the 1960s* (New York, 1984), 117–188, 244–252; Jackson, "State, Movement, and Urban Poor," 418–420.

10. Oral history interview with Jack Conway, August 13, 1980, LBJL.

11. Moynihan, *Maximum Feasible Misunderstanding,* 96–97; Matusow, *Unraveling of America,* chap. 9; Conway interview, August 13, 1980, LBJL.

12. IEB minutes, special session, March 16–26, 1964, Box 80, Region 6; Constitution of the CCAP, n.d., Box 1, CCAPC; Reuther to Martin Luther King Jr., April 17, 1964, and Richard Boone to Officers and Vice-Chairmen of CCAP, March 11, 1966, both in Box 6, Martin Luther King Jr. Collection, MLK; Reuther to Johnson, June 26, 1964, Box 368, WPR.

13. Constitution of CCAP, n.d., Box 1, CCAPC; Reuther to Johnson, June 26, 1964, Box 368, WPR; *New York Times,* November 7, 1965.

14. IEB minutes, May 5–7, 1964, Box 23, Region 9A; Johnson to Reuther, July 23, 1964, and Johnson to Vizzard, Patton, and Reuther, November 2, 1964, both in Reuther folder, WHCF name file, LBJL; Brendan Sexton's proposal for training program, April 1, 1965, Box 3, CCAPC; Sexton to Reuther, May 7, 1965, Box 378, WPR; Irving Bluestone to Reuther, August 26, 1965, Box 1, CCAPC.

15. Sexton to Reuther, January 14, 1964, Box 1, CCAPC.

16. Lyndon Johnson Daily Diary Cards, November 1963–November 1964, LBJL; notes of interview with Hubert Humphrey, c. May 15, 1970, Box 2, Cormier-Eaton; "How Tough Is Walter Reuther?" *Look,* August 10, 1965; Johnson to Reuther, June 29, 1964, Reuther folder, WHCF name file, LBJL; oral history interview with Jerome Cavanagh, March 22, 1971, Detroit, LBJL.

17. Reuther's handwritten notes, n.d. [June 1965], Box 78, WPR; Martin Timin's draft paper, September 8, 1965, and Sexton's informal proposal for training leadership in impoverished areas, April 1, 1965, Box 3; Sexton to Reuther, January 14, 1964, Box 1, all in CCAPC. The analysis presented here dovetails with the analysis presented in J. David Greenstone, *Labor in American Politics* (New York, 1969). In that excellent study, Greenstone argues that the UAW and other labor unions accepted responsibility for aggregating minority groups into the Democratic coalition. I agree, but I contend that the UAW accepted that role most fully on the national stage only in the mid-1960s.

18. Clayborne Carson, *In Struggle: SNCC and the Black Awakening of the 1960s* (Cambridge, Mass., 1981), 66–110; William L. Van Deburg, *New Day in Babylon: The Black Power Movement and American Culture, 1965–1975* (Chicago, 1992), 47–50; James Miller, *"Democracy Is in the Streets": From Port Huron to the Seige of Chicago* (New York, 1987), chaps. 8 and 11.

19. UAW press release, June 18, 1964, Box 23, IAD; Stern, *Calculating Visions,* 194–197; David Garrow, *Bearing the Cross: Martin Luther King, Jr., and the Southern Christian Leadership Conference* (New York, 1986), 340–347.

20. SNCC's Mississippi Summer Project is detailed in Carson, *In Struggle,* chaps. 8–9; Doug McAdam, *Freedom Summer* (New York, 1988); and John Dittmer, *Local People: The Struggle for Civil Rights in Mississippi* (Urbana, 1994), chaps. 10–11. For a graphic description of the terror of Freedom Summer, see Mississippi Summer Project running summary of incidents, June 16–July 16, 1964, Box 22, MFDP Collection, MLK.

21. Jeffrey to William Dodds, May 8, 1964, Box 77, Jeffrey Collection, ALUA; Casey Hayden to Robert Moses and others, April 15, 1964, Box 107, SNCCC; Moses to Roy Reuther, April 30, 1964, Box 26, MFDP Collection, MLK; Dodds to Moses, Box 1, PA; oral history interview with Joseph Rauh, December 11, 1967, Box 2, Cormier-Eaton.

22. Oral history interview with William Dodds, Washington, D.C., May 11, 1987; Jeffrey to Bluestone, Box 60, and Martha Kocel to Jeffrey, June 17, 1964, Box 40, both in Jeffrey Collection, ALUA; resolution passed at the Michigan Democratic Party State Convention, June 12–13, 1964, Box A61, GMW; *UAW Washington Report,* July 6,

1964; Dodds to William Becker, June 30, 1964, Box 1, CL. UAW staffers provided cars for SNCC volunteers in the South. See Detroit Friends of SNCC, transporation memo, n.d. [May 1964], Box 79, SNCCC. As late as August 6, 1964, some SNCC volunteers thought Reuther's support was secure. See Elizabeth Sutherland, ed., *Letters from Mississippi* (New York, 1965), 214.

23. IEB minutes, special session, August 26, 1964, Box 81, Region 6; Milton Viorst, *Fire in the Streets: America in the 1960s* (New York, 1979), 264; Bill to Hubert Humphrey, January 29, 1964, 23-G43B, Vice President/Senate/Mayor ser., and Humphrey's handwritten notes of discussion with Reuther, August 1, 1964, 23-G4.4F, Senatorial Files, both in HHH; oral history interview with Joseph Rauh, December 11, 1967, Box 2, Cormier-Eaton.

24. Lyndon Johnson Daily Diary, August 23, 1964, reel 3 (microfilm), oral history interview with Hubert Humphrey, May 15, 1970, Box 2, Cormier-Eaton; Reuther's handwritten notes, n.d. [August 23–25, 1964], Box 434, WPR; Rauh interview, December 11, 1967, Box 2, Cormier-Eaton.

25. Rauh interview, December 11, 1967, Box 2, Cormier-Eaton; Garrow, *Bearing the Cross,* 348–350; Godfrey Hodgson, *America in Our Time: From World War II to Nixon, What Happened and Why* (New York, 1976), 216; Charles Sherrod's report on MFDP challenge, n.d. [Autumn 1964], Box 107, SNCCC. While Reuther was pressuring Rauh, Jeffrey was lining up delegates in support of the MFDP challenge on the convention floor. See oral history interview with Joseph L. Rauh Jr., June 1967, Washington, D.C., Box 86, Joseph L. Rauh Jr. Collection, LC.

26. *UAW Washington Report,* August 31, 1964; confidential memorandum from Rauh to Hubert Humphrey, December 24, 1964, Box 117, WPR. For other positive reactions to the proposed compromise, see *New York Times,* August 27, 1964, and *Washington Post,* August 27, 1964.

27. MFDP to all friends of MFDP, n.d. [August–September 1964], reel 41 (microfilm) SNCCC; Charles Sherrod report, n.d. [Autumn 1964], Box 107, SNCCC; Carson, *In Struggle,* 126–129, chap. 10; Pat Watters and Reese Cleghorn, *Climbing Jacob's Ladder: The Arrival of the Negroes in Southern Politics* (New York, 1967); and esp. James Foreman, *The Making of Black Revolutionaries* (New York, 1972), 386–397. Also see Aaron Henry to Reuther, August 30, 1964, Box 18, WPR.

28. Theodore White, *The Making of the President, 1964* (New York, 1965), 405–406; and *New York Times,* November 4 and 5, 1964. UAW rank-and-file voting statistics are found in Oliver Quayle & Co., "A Study in Depth of the Rank and File of the United Automobile Workers (AFL-CIO)," 6:198–200, Box 59, Vice-President Leonard Woodcock Collection, ALUA.

29. *UAW Washington Report,* November 2 and 9, 1964; *New York Times,* November 4 and 5, 1964; Education Department typescript, n.d. [early 1965?], Box 21, IAD; IEB minutes, March 23–26, 1965, Box 23, Region 9A.

30. White, *Making of the President, 1964,* 383; Alfred O. Hero Jr. and Emil Starr, *The Reuther-Meany Foreign Policy Debate: Union Leaders and Members View World Affairs* (Dobbs Ferry, N.Y., 1970); George Gallup, *The Gallup Poll: Public Opinion, 1935–1971* (New York, 1972), 3:1939.

31. BLS, *Labor Force Statistics Derived from the Current Population Survey, 1948-1987,* Bulletin 2307 (Washington, D.C., 1987), 553; *Monthly Labor Review* 86 (November 1963), 1364, and 87 (November 1964), 1352. Also see BLS, *Employment and Earnings in the United States, 1909–1970,* Bulletin 1312-7 (Washington, D.C., 1971), 563–564. Details of the 1964 settlement are from *New York Times,* September 10, September 19, and October 6, 1964. The boom had its costs. To meet soaring

demand, the Big Three increased the pace of work, in the process heightening workplace tension. On the Johnson coalition, see Matusow, *Unraveling of America,* chap. 5; Thomas Byrne Edsall and Mary D. Edsall, *Chain Reaction: The Impact of Race, Rights, and Taxes on American Politics* (New York, 1991), chap. 2; Robert Huckfeldt and Carol Weitzel Kohfeld, *Race and the Decline of Class in American Politics* (Urbana, 1989), 9–10, chap. 2. Reuther's quote is from his letter to victorious governors and senators, November 7, 1964, Box 408, WPR.

32. David Garrow, *Protest at Selma: Martin Luther King, Jr., and the Voting Rights Act of 1965* (New Haven, 1978); Reuther to Johnson, March 9, 1965, Box 368, WPR; Wirtz to Johnson, February 9, 1965, Box 1, WHCF, Ex LA, LBJL; IEB minutes, March 23–26, 1965, Box 23, Region 9A.

33. UAW press release, March 14, 1965, Box 578, WPR; *Detroit News,* March 16, 1965. Though SNCC agreed to attend the March 17 meeting, John Lewis wrote to Reuther that times had changed since the March on Washington and "the groups invited to the meeting are no longer representative." Lewis strongly urged the inclusion of the MFDP. See Lewis to Reuther, March 17, 1965, Box 578, WPR.

34. Garrow, *Bearing the Cross,* 408–409; IEB minutes, session of March 23–26, 1965, Region 9A. For an insider's account of Johnson's speech, see Richard Goodwin, *Remembering America: A Voice from the Sixties* (Boston, 1988), chap. 17.

35. Sundquist, *Politics and Policy,* 274; Dan Bedell to Walter Reuther, February 25, 1966, Box 52, WPR; IEB minutes, March 23–26, 1965, Box 23, Region 9A.

36. Peter Levy, "The New Left and Labor: A Misunderstood Relationship" (Ph.D. diss., Columbia University, 1986); Irving Bluestone to Paul Schrade, February 11, 1964; Reuther to Mazey, July 8, 1963; Bluestone to Carroll Hutton, August 9, 1963; Bluestone to Dominic Fornaro, July 15, 1964; Bluestone to E. T. Michael, July 27, 1964; Haber to Conway, December 18, 1963; Bluestone to Todd Gitlin, January 31, 1964; Rennie Davis to Reuther, April 17, 1964, all in Box 523, WPR; Bluestone to Jeffrey, May 14, 1964, Box 60, Jeffrey Collection, ALUA.

37. Tom Hayden, *Reunion: A Memoir* (New York, 1988), 125; Donald Agger et al., "The Triple Revolution," *Liberation* 9 (April 1964), 9–15; Richard Rothstein, "A Short History of ERAP," *SDS Bulletin* 4 (December 1965). The UAW leadership was particularly surprised by the rising ferment on campus. The previous year the UAW staffer Carl Westman had spent a sabbatical year at Rutgers University and had found the experience depressing. "There are no 'revolutions' being fomented in the academy," he had written to Irving Bluestone. ". . . Indeed, the very lack of involvement helps one to see why an organization like the UAW is so damned important in our society" (May 18, 1963, Box 10, CAPC).

38. Bayard Rustin, "From Protest to Coalition Politics," in Marvin Gettleman and David Mermelstein, eds., *The Great Society Reader: The Failure of American Liberalism* (New York, 1967), 263–276. King's comments in Sweden and at the A. Philip Randolph Institute are recounted in Garrow, *Bearing the Cross,* 364 and 427. On King's economic philosophy, see Adam Fairclough, "Was Martin Luther King a Marxist?" *History Workshop* 15 (Spring 1983), 117–125.

39. *Proceedings of the Sixth Constitutional Convention of the AFL-CIO, 1965* (Washington, D.C., 1965), 296–304; oral history interview with Jack Conway, November 20, 1967, Box 2, Cormier-Eaton; *Wall Street Journal,* March 2, 1965; Michael Harrington, *Socialism* (New York, 1970), 264–265.

40. IEB minutes, March 23–26, 1965, Box 23, Region 9A.

41. Weinberg to Reuther, November 5, 1964, CL. Also see Reuther's statement to the Joint Economic Committee, March 1, 1965, Box 4, SPD.

42. Reuther to Johnson, May 13, 1965, Box 406, WPR. The idea of demonstration cities was not original with Reuther, nor did he draft the memo he sent to Johnson. Mayor Jerome Cavanagh of Detroit first proposed the concept to the White House when he served as a member of the President's Task Force on Cities in 1964, although he perceived the concept in somewhat different terms from those Reuther presented. See oral history interview with Cavanagh, LBJL. It seems likely, though I have found no documentation to confirm it, that Reuther developed his proposal in cooperation with Cavanagh and the Detroit city planner Charles Blessing, who had developed a $250 million plan to rebuild Detroit's cultural center, then as now a blighted area. For details, see *Detroit Free Press*, April 22, 1965. Reuther's memo to Johnson was drafted by Oskar Stonorov, an architect and Reuther confidant. The Johnson administration accepted the idea as Reuther's, and consistently referred to it as such.

43. IEB minutes, January 10–13, 1966, Box 24, Region 9A; Reuther's statement to the Senate Committee on Government Relations, December 5, 1966, Box 4, SPD.

44. Reuther's handwritten notes, May 20 and June 23, 1965, Box 369, WPR; Lyndon Johnson, *The Vantage Point: Perspectives on the Presidency, 1963–1969* (New York, 1971), 329; Califano to Johnson, September 16, 1965, Box 9, WHCF, Ex BE4/Automobiles, LBJL; Califano to Johnson, n.d., Box 1, Special Files, Legislative Background—Model Cities, LBJL. The task force included Reuther; Robert Wood, urban planner of the Massachusetts Institute of Technology; Charles Haar, Harvard law professor; Kermit Gordon, former director of the Bureau of the Budget; William Rafsky, former development coordinator for the City of Philadelphia; Edgar Kaiser of Kaiser Steel; Benjamin Heineman, chairman of the Chicago and Northwestern Railway; and the National Urban League's Whitney Young. Reuther proposed that Stonorov and Charles Blessing be named to the group as well, but Califano rejected them.

45. Summary of task force meeting, October 15, 1965, Box 1, Special Files, Lesgislative Background—Model Cities, LBJL; IEB minutes, January 10–13, 1966, Box 24, Region 9A; Califano to Johnson, October 9, 1965, Box 5, WHCF, Ex HS3, LBJL; *New York Times*, November 15, 1965.

46. Califano to Bill Moyers, November 4, 1965, Reuther folder, WHCF name file, LBJL; IEB minutes, January 10–13, 1966, Box 24, Region 9A; Harry McPherson to Johnson, Box 1, WHCF, Ex LG, LBJL.

47. McPherson to Jack Valenti, December 22, 1965, Box 5, WHCF, HS 3, LBJL; Stonorov to Reuther, November 15, 1965, Box 407, WPR; draft report of the Task Force on Urban Problems, December 1965, Box 407, WPR. The program was expanded to include not only six demonstration cities with populations over 500,000 but also ten cities with populations between 250,000 and 500,000 and fifty cities of less than 250,000 inhabitants.

48. McPherson to Johnson, December 9, 1965, Box 1, WHCF, Ex LG, LBJL; *Los Angeles Times*, December 1965; McPherson to Johnson, December 13, 1965, Box 252, WHCF, Ex FG 170, LBJL.

49. Final draft of Demonstration Cities proposal, December 8, 1965, Box 407, WPR; outline of Califano's presentation to Johnson, December 1965, Box 1; draft of Demonstration Cities bill, January 24, 1966; and Johnson's message to Congress on American cities, January 26, 1966, Box 2, all in Special Files, Legislative Background—Model Cities, LBJL; McPherson to Johnson, December 9, 1965, and McPherson to Califano, December 22, 1965, both in Box 1, WHCF, Ex LG, LBJL.

50. Reuther to Johnson, October 18, 1965, Box 368, WPR; oral history interview with Joseph Rauh, May 12, 1987; Rauh interview, December 11, 1967, Box 2, Cormier-Eaton.

51. Joseph Califano, *A Presidential Nation* (New York, 1975), 208.

9. The Widening Gyre

1. Lyndon Johnson Daily Diary, July 24, 1967, reel 10 (microfilm), LBJL; Lyndon Johnson, *The Vantage Point: Perspectives on the Presidency, 1963–1969* (New York, 1971), 167–171; Sidney Fine, *Violence in the Model City: The Cavanagh Administration, Race Relations, and the Detroit Riot of 1967* (Ann Arbor, 1989), 203–215.

2. Walter Reuther's note, July 31, 1967, Box 369, WPR. Johnson made similar comments to his aides and military advisers. See Fine, *Violence in the Model City,* 208, 213–214.

3. Huynh Sahn Thong to Victor Reuther, July 7, 1963; Lewis Carliner to Louise Levison, April 15, 1964; report on mission to Vietnam from George Baldanzi and Tom Altaffer, December 23, 1963, all in Box 47, IAD.

4. John Lewis Gaddis, *Strategies of Containment: A Critical Appraisal of Postwar American National Security Policy* (New York, 1982), chap. 7; IEB minutes, December 15–17, 1964, Box 24, Region 9A.

5. George Herring, *America's Longest War: The United States and Vietnam, 1950-1975* (New York, 1986); Larry Berman, *Planning a Tragedy: The Americanization of the War in Vietnam* (New York, 1982), chap. 3; Charles DeBenedetti, *An American Ordeal: The Antiwar Movement of the Vietnam Era* (Syracuse, 1990), 103–122; James Miller, *"Democracy Is in the Streets": From Port Huron to the Siege of Chicago* (New York, 1987), 227–243.

6. C. Clark Kissinger to Irving Bluestone, January 28, 1965, and Bluestone to Larry Getlinger, February 5, 1965, Box 523, WPR; Paul Potter to Mildred Jeffrey, March 2, 1965, Box 49, Mildred Jeffrey Collection, ALUA; Rennie Davis to Nat Weinberg, February 15, 1965, Box 19, Nat Weinberg Collection, ALUA; IEB minutes, March 23–25, 1965, Box 23, Region 9A; Emil Mazey to all officers and board members, March 4, 1965, Box 597, WPR.

7. IEB minutes, March 23–26, 1965, Box 23, Region 9A. For a sampling of liberal opinion, see Larry Berman, *William Fulbright and the Vietnam War: The Dissent of a Political Realist* (Kent, Ohio, 1988), 34–37; Steven Gillon, *Politics and Vision: The ADA and American Liberalism, 1947-1985* (New York, 1987), 179–185; and Melvin Small, *Johnson, Nixon, and the Doves* (New Brunswick, N.J., 1988), 40–43.

8. IEB minutes, March 23–26, 1965, Box 23, Region 9A.

9. Herring, *America's Longest War,* 144–156, 231–234; DeBenedetti, *American Ordeal,* 111–112; Miller, *"Democracy Is in the Streets,"* 231–234; Jeffrey to Paul Potter, April 23, 1965, and Rennie Davis to Jeffrey, March 7, 1966, Box 55, Jeffrey Collection, ALUA; Paul Schrade to Walter Reuther and Mazey, August 31, 1966, Box 597, WPR; oral history interview with Paul Schrade, June 1992, Los Angeles.

10. David Garrow, *Bearing the Cross: Martin Luther King, Jr., and the Southern Christian Leadership Conference* (New York, 1986), 429–430; Gillon, *Politics and Vision,* 188–196; DeBenedetti, *American Ordeal,* 141–148; Arthur Schlesinger Jr., *The Bitter Heritage: Vietnam and American Democracy* (Boston, 1966).

11. Mazey's remarks before the Unitarian-Universalist Fellowship for Social Justice, Detroit, May 15, 1965, Box 597, WPR; Frank Koscielski, "The United Automobile Workers International Executive Board and the Vietnam War," seminar paper prepared for Elizabeth Faue, Wayne State University, November 1992, 11; Report no. 1, March on Washington for Peace in Vietnam, September 28, 1965, Box 597, WPR; David Halberstam, *The Best and the Brightest* (New York, 1969), 572–573; Weinberg to Reuther, April 6, 1965, Box 19, Weinberg Collection, ULUA; Gillon, *Politics and Vision,* 194–195.

12. Weinberg to Reuther, April 6 and December 17, 1965, Box 19, and January 28 and April 13, 1966, Box 14, all in Weinberg Collection, ALUA; oral history interviews with Irving Bluestone, February 1988, Detroit, and Victor Reuther, May 6, 1987, Washington, D.C.

13. Reuther's handwritten notes, n.d. [probably December 1965], Box 597, WPR; Schrade interview, June 1992; oral history interview with Douglas Fraser, Detroit, February 24, 1987; W. Willard Wirtz to Lyndon Johnson, May 25, 1966, Box 61, WHCF confidential file, LA 7, LBJL; Reuther to Hubert Humphrey, March 31, 1965, Box 370, WPR; Reuther's handwritten note, August 1965, Box 463, WPR. Reuther also worked on the administration's behalf to rewrite a Vietnam resolution proposed by the U.S. Committee for the United Nations. See Reuther to Arthur Goldberg, November 23, 1965, and Goldberg to Reuther, November 27, 1965, both in Box 463, WPR.

14. Kathleen Turner, *Lyndon Johnson's Dual War: Vietnam and the Press* (Chicago, 1985), 111–133; Bill Moyers to Francis Bator, April 6, 1965, Reuther folder, WHCF name file, LBJL; Reuther to Johnson, April 6, 1965, Box 368, WPR; oral history interview with Joseph Rauh, May 7, 1987, Washington, D.C.; Elisabeth Reuther Dickmayer, *Reuther: A Daughter Strikes* (Southfield, Mich., 1989), 316–317; Berman, *Planning a Tragedy;* IEB minutes, October 12–14, 1965, Box 22, Region 9A.

15. Peter B. Levy, "The New Left and Labor: A Misunderstood Relationship" (Ph.D. diss., Columbia University, 1986); Miller, *"Democracy Is in the Streets,"* chaps. 4–6; Potter to Paul Jacobs, November 4, 1965, Box 55, Jeffrey Collection, ALUA; Todd Gitlin, *The Sixties: Years of Hope, Days of Rage* (New York, 1987), 120. According to Gitlin, by the mid-1960s the UAW and other social unions "had signed up for the duration of American prosperity, demanding only a fairer share."

16. Richard Polenberg, *One Nation Divisible: Class, Race, and Ethnicity in the United States since 1938* (New York, 1980), 220–231; Ronald Radosh, "The Corporate Ideology of American Labor Leaders from Gompers to Hillman," *Studies on the Left 6* (November–December 1966), 66–88; Martin Glaberman, "A Note on Walter Reuther," *Radical America 7* (November–December 1973), 117. For a brief review of early New Left labor history, see James Green, ed., *Workers' Struggles, Past and Present: A "Radical America" Reader* (Philadelphia, 1983), 4–8. For a blistering critique of Radosh's corporatist model, see David Brody, *Workers in Industrial America: Essays on the Twentieth-Century Struggle* (New York, 1980), 124–127, 147–150.

17. Levy, "New Left and Labor," chap. 9; Irving Howe, "Sweet and Sour Notes: On Workers and Intellectuals," *Dissent* 19 (Winter 1972), 264–269; IEB minutes, September 10–12, 1968, Box 24, Region 9A.

18. On the transformation of the civil rights movement after Selma, see Adam Fairclough, *To Redeem the Soul of America: The Southern Christian Leadership Conference and Martin Luther King, Jr.* (Athens, Ga., 1987), chaps. 10–11; Garrow, *Bearing the Cross,* chaps. 7–8; UAW compliance report, n.d. [early 1960s], Box 2, FP; Kenneth Holbert to Bryant DeWitt, January 5, 1967, Box 36, FP; Woody Ginsberg to Bluestone, Box 47, SPD; Oliver Quayle survey of UAW rank-and-file opinion, June 1967, Box 59, Vice-President Leonard Woodcock Collection, ALUA; Fraser to Bluestone, September 24, 1969, Box 92, WPR.

19. Proposal to train 1,000 persons for work with the poor, April 1966; CCAP Progress Report, December 5, 1965; Dick Boone to Brendan Sexton, October 16, 1967, all in Box 3, CCAPC; *CCAP Bulletin* 1 (September 1966) and press release, December 1966, both in Box 1, CCAPC; *New York Times,* August 22, 1966.

20. Schrade interview, June 1992; IEB minutes, January 10–13, 1966, Box 24, Region 9A; Watts Community Labor Action Committee, 1967 Report, March 12, 1967, Box 537, WPR.

21. Garrow, *Bearing the Cross*, chap. 8; Fairclough, *To Redeem The Soul*, 279–307; George Pickering and Allan Anderson, *Confronting the Color Line: The Broken Promise of the Civil Rights Movement in Chicago* (Athens, Ga., 1986); King to Boone, December 21, 1965, Box 6, Martin Luther King Jr. Collection, MLK; Melody Heaps to Executive Staff of CCCO[Coordinating Council of Community Organizations]–SCLC, n.d. [1966?], Box 150, SCLCC; Charles Chiakulas to Jack Conway, July 20, 1966, and Conway memo, n.d. [1967], both in Box 326, WPR.

22. The MDCDA was modeled after the Citizens Committee for Equal Opportunity (CCEO), which Reuther had founded in 1963 to bring together Detroit's most influential figures in support of racial equality. See Fine, *Violence in the Model City*, 87–90, 445. On MDCDA, see Reuther to Jerome Cavanagh, January 1966, Box 428, WPR; Reuther's handwritten notes [probably February 8, 1966] and MDCDA personnel list, n.d. [mid-1966], both in Box 501, WPR; Robert Conot, *American Odyssey* (Detroit, 1986), 501. B. J. Widick, *Detroit: City of Race and Class Violence* (Chicago, 1972), 158, quotes *Fortune*, June 1965.

23. Morris to Boone, December 28, 1966, Box 3, CCAPC; Charles Chiakulas to Conway, July 20, 1966, Box 326, WPR; Conot, *American Odyssey*, 501; Jeffrey to Bluestone, December 22, 1966, Box 54, WPR. Despite its top-down structure, Detroit's Community Action Program was one of the nation's most successful in maximizing the participation of community groups. See J. David Greenstone and Paul Peterson, *Race and Authority in Urban Politics: Community Participation and the War on Poverty* (New York, 1973), 34–39.

24. Brendan Sexton, "Realistic Vistas for the Poor," *Progressive* 29 (October 1965), 30; IEB minutes, January 10–13, 1966, Box 24, Region 9A.

25. IEB minutes, January 10–13, 1966, Box 24, Region 9A. Sexton's "Realistic Vistas" makes the same point. See also Martin Timin's draft paper, September 8, 1965, Box 3, CCAPC, which raises the specter of Black Muslims "lurking in the background," ready to fill the leadership vacuum in the ghettos.

26. The political history of the postwar northern ghetto has yet to be written. Greenstone and Peterson, *Race and Authority*, 79–95; Jack Bloom, *Class, Race, and the Civil Rights Movement* (Bloomington, 1987), 187–198; and Thomas F. Jackson, "The State, the Movement, and the Urban Poor: The War on Poverty and Political Mobilization in the 1960s," in Michael Katz, ed., *The "Underclass" Debate: Views from History* (Princeton, 1993), 422–430, are suggestive.

27. Stokely Carmichael and Charles Hamilton, *Black Power: The Politics of Liberation in America* (New York, 1967); James Foreman, *The Making of Black Revolutionaries* (New York, 1972); Clayborne Carson, *In Struggle: SNCC and the Black Awakening of the 1960s* (Cambridge, Mass., 1981); William Van Deburg, *New Day in Babylon: The Black Power Movement and American Culture, 1965–1975* (Chicago, 1992), esp. chaps. 1–2.

28. Agenda for the CCAP Annual Meeting, April 13, 1966, Box 42, SCLCC; unsigned draft proposal, January 5, 1967; Doug Still to Dudley, February 14, 1967; Curtis Foster to Brendan Sexton, June 7, 1967; Rennie Davis to Boone, n.d. [June 1967]; Boone to Davis, June 16, 1967; Boone to Sexton, June 16, 1967; Boone to Mitchell Sviridoff, June 4, 1968, all in Box 4, CCAPC; Conot, *American Odyssey*, 501; Preston Wilcox to interested observers, n.d. [April 1966], and Pamela Roby memo, n.d. [April 1966], both in Box 1, CCAPC; press accounts of convention, Box 3, CCAPC; John C. Donovan, *The Politics of Poverty* (New York, 1967), 69.

29. William Oliver to Reuther, December 30, 1968, Box 91, WPR; EEOC discrimination charge no. LA 7-4-102, March 11, 1967, Box 35, FP; Robert David to Ken Bannon, September 10, 1965; James Blair to Oliver, January 17, 1966; Isaiah McVicar and Robert

Green to Sir and Brother, February 22, 1966; Thomas Peloso to Walter Dorosh, November 15, 1966, all in Box 37, FP; James Santos to Schrade, July 27, 1967, Box 35, FP; Philip S. Foner, *Organized labor and the Black Worker, 1619-1973* (New York, 1974), 412; William Serrin, *The Company and the Union: The Civilized Relationship of the General Motors Corporation and the United Automobile Workers* (New York, 1970), 235; Charles Denby, *Indignant Heart: Testimony of a Black American Worker* (London, 1979), chap. 24.

30. Carson, *In Struggle,* chaps. 11–15; Carmichael and Hamilton, *Black Power;* Milton Viorst, *Fire in the Streets: America in the 1960s* (New York, 1979), chap. 10; Van DeBurg, *New Day in Babylon,* 31–34, 47–51; August Meier and Elliot Rudwick, *CORE: A Study in the Civil Rights Movement* (New York, 1973), 374–431.

31. IEB minutes, June 8, 1966, and January 31–February 3, 1967, Box 24, Region 9A; and Jeffrey to Bluestone, December 22, 1966, Box 54, WPR.

32. IEB minutes, June 8, 1966, Box 24, Region 9A; Denby, *Indignant Heart,* 228.

33. *New York Times,* October 18, 1966; confidential memo to Jack Conway, December 21, 1966, ser. B, Box 1, LCCRC; Philip S. Foner, *U.S. Labor and the Vietnam War* (New York, 1989), 20.

34. *John Herling's Labor Letter,* December 25, 1965; Jay Lovestone's draft of resolution, December 1965, Box 597, WPR; oral history interview with Paul Schrade, May 3, 1968, Atlantic City, Box 2, Cormier-Eaton; *Daily Proceedings of the Sixth Constitutional Convention of the AFL-CIO, San Francisco, December 9–15, 1965* (Washington, D.C., 1965); Reuther to Arthur Goldberg, December 28, 1965, Box 463, WPR. The AFL-CIO convention illustrates the polarization the war was then triggering. When Reuther's resolution reached the convention floor, Emil Mazey spoke against it. J. Edgar Hoover, in contrast, noting Reuther's conflict with Lovestone at the convention, sent a copy of Reuther's resolution to the Department of the Army, "in view of its interest in Mr. Reuther." See memo from Detroit office, December 20, 1965, and memo from Hoover to Director, Bureau of Personnel Investigations, December 23, 1965, both in WJBK-TV Collection, ALUA.

35. On the complexity of white working-class backlash, see Richard Hamilton, *Class and Politics in the United States* (New York, 1972), esp. chap. 4; Andrew Levinson, *The Working Class Majority* (New York, 1974), chap. 3; Gary Orfield, "Race and the Liberal Agenda: The Loss of the Integrationist Dream, 1965–1974," in Margaret Weir, Ann Shola Orloff, and Theda Skocpol, eds., *The Politics of Social Policy in the United States* (Princeton, 1988), 313–355; Jonathan Rieder, "The Rise of the 'Silent Majority,'" in Steven Fraser and Gary Gerstle, eds., *The Rise and Fall of the New Deal Order, 1930–1980* (Princeton, 1989), 269–293; Thomas Byrne Edsall and Mary D. Edsall, *Chain Reaction: The Impact of Race, Rights, and Taxes on American Politics* (New York, 1991), chaps. 2–3.

36. Alfred Hero and Emil Starr, *The Reuther-Meany Foreign Policy Dispute: Union Leaders and Members View World Affairs* (Dobbs Ferry, N.Y., 1970), table 4–1; Penetration Research, Inc., "A Study of the Political Climate in Michigan," vol. 2 (October 1966), Box A90, GMW; Oliver Quayle rank-and-file survey, June 1967, Box 59, Woodcock Collection, ALUA.

37. John Lopez to Oliver, August 24, 1967, Box 36, FP; Lopez to Oliver, May 9, 1966; Oliver to George Merrelli, October 4, 1966; and Virginia Hamilton to Oliver, March 21, 1967, all in Box 37, FP.

38. Hero and Starr, *Meany-Reuther Foreign Policy Dispute,* 173; Quayle survey, Box 59, Woodcock Collection, ALUA.

39. Survey of Political Climate in Michigan, June 1966, 34–37, Box A90, GMW;

Quayle survey, Box 59, Woodcock Collection, ALUA. For comparisons with national opinion on the war, see Harris poll in *Washington Post*, May 16, 1967; George Gallup, ed., *The Gallup Poll: Public Opinion, 1935–1971*, vol. 3 (Wilmington, Del., 1972); and Walter L. Lunch and Peter Sperlich, "American Public Opinion and the War in Vietnam," *Western Political Quarterly* 32 (March 1979), 30.

40. On working-class opposition to the war, see R. F. Hamilton, "A Research Note on the Mass Support for 'Tough' Military Initiatives," *American Sociological Review* 33 (June 1968), 429–445; Harlan Hahn, "Correlates of Public Sentiment about the War: Local Referenda on the Vietnam Issue," *American Political Science Review* 64 (December 1970), 1188–1198, which includes information on an antiwar referendum conducted in the heart of UAW country, Dearborn, Mich.; and Martin Patchen, "Social Class and Dimensions of Foreign Policy Attitudes," *Social Science Quarterly* 51 (December 1970), 649–667. On the class bias of the draft, see Michael Useem, *Conscription, Protest, and Social Conflict: The Life and Death of a Draft Resistance Movement* (New York, 1973), 83–91, 107–109; Lawrence Baskir and William Strauss, *Chance and Circumstance: The Draft, the War, and the Vietnam Generation* (New York, 1978), 7–10, 254. The Quayle study (Box 59, Woodcock Collection, ALUA) has the statistics on auto workers' fear of the Soviet Union as well as their frustration with the draft. The auto worker is quoted in Brendan Sexton and Patricia Cayo Sexton, *Blue Collars and Hard Hats: The Working Class and the Future of American Politics* (New York, 1971), 49–58. For a fascinating collection of rank-and-file views of student protesters, see the collection of letters to Walter Reuther and Frank Wallick, September 1968, Box 52, WPR.

41. Quayle survey, Box 59, Woodcock Collection, ALUA. In public, the UAW leadership thought the results "a disaster." See Weinberg to Guy Nunn, November 21, 1966, Box 14, Weinberg Collection, ALUA. Also see Alan Draper, "Labor and the 1966 Elections," *Labor History* 30 (Winter 1989), 76–92.

42. Quayle survey, Box 59, Woodcock Collection, ALUA; BLS, *Employment and Earnings, United States, 1909–1970* (Washington, D.C., 1971), 563–564; *New York Times*, January 18, 1966; Donald Kettl, "The Economic Education of Lyndon Johnson: Guns, Butter, and Taxes," in Robert A. Divine, ed., *The Johnson Years*, vol. 2, *Vietnam, the Environment, and Science* (Lawrence, Kans., 1987), 63.

43. Jim Heath, *Decade of Disillusionment: The Kennedy-Johnson Years* (Bloomington, 1975), 258; Boone to national organizations interested in the success of the poverty program, June 11, 1966, CL; Kettl, "Economic Education of Lyndon Johnson," 59–63.

44. Doris Kearns, *Lyndon Johnson and the American Dream* (New York, 1976), 272; Herring, *America's Longest War*, 181–185; Small, *Johnson, Nixon, and the Doves*, chap. 4; Heath, *Decade of Disillusionment*, 257–259; Kettl, "Economic Education of Lyndon Johnson," 63–67.

45. IEB minutes, January 10–13 and September 7–9, 1966, Box 24, Region 9A.

46. Reuther's statement to Joint Economic Committee, February 9, 1966, Box 4, SPD; draft resolution on Great Society, n.d. [April 1966], CL; *UAW Washington Report*, April 18, 1966; Boone memo, June 11, 1966, CL; Reuther to Johnson, March 22, 1966, Box 4, WHCF, Ex ST/MC, LBJL; Weinberg to Reuther, August 18, September 7, November 22, and November 30, 1966, all in Box 14, Weinberg Collection, ALUA; Reuther to Johnson, December 22, 1966, Box 25, WHCF, Ex BE 5, LBJL; Reuther's statement to Joint Economic Committee, February 20, 1967, Box 4, SPD.

47. Gardner Ackley to Lyndon Johnson, December 17, 1964, Box 25, and Marvin Watson to Johnson, February 27, 1968, Box 31, WHCF, Ex WE 9, LBJL; Ackley to Johnson, December 30, 1966, Box 25, WHCF Ex BE 5, LBJL.

48. IEB minutes, January 31–February 3, 1967, Box 24, Region 9A.

49. Jack Newfield, *Robert F. Kennedy: A Memoir* (New York, 1969), 55–83; Alan Matusow, *The Unraveling of America: A History of American Liberalism in the 1960s,* (New York, 1984) chap. 16; Gillon, *Politics and Vision,* chap. 8; Richard Cummings, *The Pied Piper: Allard K. Lowenstein and the Liberal Dream* (New York, 1985); Edsall and Edsall, *Chain Reaction,* 69–70.

50. Edsall and Edsall, *Chain Reaction,* 69–70; Matusow, *Unraveling of America,* chap. 13; Gillon, *Politics and Vision,* chap. 8; Cummings, *Pied Piper;* Richard Goodwin, *Remembering America: A Voice from the Sixties* (Boston, 1988), 452–467. Both "bitter heritage" and "universalism" are from Schlesinger, *Bitter Heritage.*

51. William Chafe, *Never Stop Running: Allard Lowenstein and the Struggle to Save American Liberalism* (New York, 1993), 262–266; DeBenedetti, *American Ordeal,* 168–169; Gillon, *Politics and Vision,* 191–199; Arthur Schlesinger Jr., *Robert F. Kennedy and His Times* (Boston, 1978), 830–833. On the White House's reaction to the liberal pressure, see Small, *Johnson, Nixon, and the Doves,* chap. 4.

52. Oral history interview with Paul Schrade, May 3, 1968, Box 2, Cormier-Eaton; Califano to Johnson, June 15, 1967, Box 73, Joseph Califano Papers, LBJL; Califano to Johnson, June 24, 1967, WHCF, CF LA 6/Aircraft, LBJL. According to Califano, a ten-day strike at the AVCO company would have seriously impaired the army's ability to provide air-mobile troops for domestic emergencies, and a strike of more than ten days would have impaired combat operations in Vietnam. Reuther describes his deal with Johnson in IEB minutes, March 1–2, 1968, Box 24, Region 9A. Stephen Amberg, *The Union Inspiration in American Politics: The Autoworkers and the Making of a Liberal Industrial Order* (Philadelphia, 1994), and *New York Times,* October 22, 1967, have details on the 1967 negotiating round.

53. Weinberg to Reuther, April 28, 1967, Box 165, WPR; Hobart Rowan, "The Bone in Meany's Throat," *New Republic,* May 6, 1967, 9–10; IEB minutes, January 31–February 3, 1967, Box 24, Region 9A.

54. Interview with Barry Bluestone, May 26, 1979, Cambridge, Mass., Oral History Collection, Columbia University.

55. John Windmuller, "The Foreign Policy Conflict in American Labor," *Political Science Quarterly* 82 (June 1967), 205–234; Hero and Starr, *Reuther-Meany Foreign Policy Dispute,* 66–76; *Los Angeles Times,* May 22, 1966; Reuther to Meany, June 9, 1966, Box 5, WHCF, IT 23, LBJL; oral history interview with George Meany, March 12, 1969, Box 2, Cormier-Eaton.

56. February 8, 1967, administrative letter from Walter Reuther in "UAW Administrative Letters" 2:1453, ALUA; *New York Times,* February 10 and April 23, 1967; *U.S. News & World Report,* February 20, 1967; Rowan, "Bone in Meany's Throat," 9–10; Sidney Lens, "Reuther v. Meany," *Commonweal,* February 17, 1967, 557–559; Lewis Carliner, "The Dispute That Never Was," *Labor History* 12 (Fall 1971), 605–613. Meany attributed Reuther's actions to personal motives. See Archie Robinson, *George Meany and His Times* (New York, 1981), 251–275; AFL-CIO Executive Council, *To Clear the Record* (Washington, D.C., 1969).

57. John Roche to Johnson, February 9, 1967, Box 29, Marvin Watson Collection, LBJL; LBJ Daily Diary Cards, LBJL. The White House was particularly suspicious of CCAP's ties to Robert Kennedy's ghetto rehabilitation program in the Bedford-Stuyvesant section of New York. For details, see Jack Conway memo, n.d. [1967], Box 326, WPR; Roche to Marvin Watson, January 24, 1967, Conway, J. folder, WHCF name file, LBJL.

58. The characterization of the riots as "major" is from *The Report of the National Advisory Commission on Civil Disorders, New York Times* ed. (New York, 1968), 114, 158. The definitive work on the Detroit riot is Fine, *Violence in the Model City.* Also see Hubert Locke, *The Detroit Riot of 1967* (Detroit, 1969); John Hersey, *The Algiers Motel Incident* (New York, 1968); and J. A. Lukas, "Postscript on Detroit: Whitey Hasn't Got the Message," *New York Times Magazine,* August 27, 1967. On Monday afternoon, July 25, Cavanagh phoned Reuther and requested that the UAW president intercede with Johnson to send federal troops into Detroit. Reuther at first said that he was not sufficiently apprised of the situation to take such action, but when Cavanagh tried again later in the evening, Reuther agreed to do so. He called Johnson at 11:00 P.M., and the president took the call in the Oval Office, where he was in consultation with his advisors. Johnson told Reuther there was some confusion between the White House and Governor George Romney about the proper form the state's request should take. Within the hour, however, Johnson ordered troops to the city.

59. Fine, *Violence in the Model City;* Jacob Clayman to Reuther, July 25, 1967, Box 596, WPR; oral history interview with Evelyn Dubrow, February 24, 1968, Box 2, Cormier-Eaton.

60. *IUD Agenda,* August 1967; Reuther to IEB members, August 3, 1967, Box 35, Woodcock Collection, ALUA; Walter Reuther's address to the Urban Coalition, August 24, 1967; Preamble and Statement of Urban Coalition, July 31, 1967; Arnold Aronson to Reuther, August 28, 1967, all in Box 532, WPR.

61. Joseph Hudson to Reuther, November 14, 1967; minutes of special meeting of MDCDA, July 28, 1967; Edward Robinson to Robert Knox, August 14, 1967, all in Box 496, WPR; Elmwood II progress report, December 1967, and Reuther to Raymond Perring, October 2, 1967, both in Box 497, WPR.

62. W. Hawkins Ferry to Ed Robinson, October 10, 1967, Box 496, WPR; Fine, *Violence in the Model City,* 321–322, 376–377, 441–443.

63. *New York Times,* August 24, 1967; Reuther's notes, n.d. [late July 1967], Box 40, and August 9, 1967, Box 303, WPR; *Washington Post,* November 26, 1967; Tom Shea to Eiler, May 16, 1967, 24-4-8-3B, HHH (the comments are those of Patti Knox, vice-chair of the Michigan Democratic Party in 1967); Jack Bielder to Reuther, July 31, 1967, Box 532, WPR.

64. Albert Cleague, *The Black Messiah* (New York, 1968); Conot, *American Odyssey,* 602; *Detroit News,* August 16, 1968.

65. Conot, *American Odyssey,* 550; Fine, *Violence in the Model City,* 384–385; Jeffrey to Sam Fishman, February 28, 1968, Box 60, Jeffrey Collection, ALUA. For discussions of whites' reactions to the riots, see Sexton and Sexton, *Blue Collars and Hard Hats,* 53–54, 214–229; H. Edward Ransford, "Blue Collar Anger: Reactions to Students and Blacks," *American Sociological Review* 37 (July 1972), 333–346.

66. DeBenedetti, *American Ordeal,* 174–200; Deborah Shapley, *Promise and Power: The Life and Times of Robert McNamara* (Boston, 1993), 310–349; Cummings, *Pied Piper,* 310–349.

67. Nancy Zaroulis and Gerald Sullivan, *Who Spoke Up? American Protest against the War in Vietnam, 1963–1975* (Garden City, N.Y., 1984), 114, 117–118; Gillon, *Politics and Vision,* 191–203; Rauh to Mazey, August 30, 1967, Box 30, Joseph L. Rauh Jr. Collection, LC; Victor Reuther to Colleagues, October 12, 1967, Box 40, WPR. On the White House's reaction to Negotiate Now! see John Roche to Johnson, September 25, 1967, Box 29, Watson Collection, LBJL; memo to Johnson, August 16, 1967, Box 115, WHCF, PL 5, LBJL.

68. Foner, *U.S. Labor and the Vietnam War*, 50–55; *Wall Street Journal*, November 9, 1967. Walter Reuther insisted that Mazey and Victor not use any UAW funds to pay for their trips to the conference (oral history interview with Victor Reuther, May 1987).

69. Matusow, *Unraveling of America*, 389–394; Cummings, *Pied Piper*, 349–360; Chafe, *Never Stop Running*, 267–275; Roche to Watson, November 14, 1967, Box 29, Watson Collection, LBJL; Gillon, *Politics and Vision*, 207–210.

70. Transcript of Reuther's appearance on *Meet the Press*, September 24, 1967, in *Meet the Press*, vol 11, no. 39 (Millwood, N.J, 1973), 5–8; Roche to Watson, November 14 and 27, 1967, Box 29, Watson Collection, LBJL.

71. Oral history interview with Paul Schrade, May 3, 1968, Atlantic City, Box 2, Cormier-Eaton; Rauh interview, May 7, 1987; IEB minutes, special session, March 1–2, 1968, Box 24, Region 9A. Reuther's political confidants also noticed his uncertainty. "Walter leaves me slightly puzzled," an aide to Vice-President Humphrey reported in mid-1967. "It's hard to know into what slot he fits. . . . The UAW has been playing it cool, staying somewhat in the background, and disengaging itself from active public participation": Nick Kostopulos to Hubert Humphrey, May 31, 1967, 24-D-8-3B, 1968 Campaign Files, HHH.

10. Things Fall Apart

1. Victor Reuther, *The Brothers Reuther and the Story of the UAW: A Memoir* (Boston, 1976), 453–456.

2. Lewis Chester, Godfrey Hodgson, and Bruce Page, *An American Melodrama: The Presidential Campaign of 1968* (New York, 1969), esp. secs. 3–4; Jack Newfield, *Robert F. Kennedy: A Memoir* (New York, 1969); Alan Matusow, *The Unraveling of America: A History of American Liberalism in the 1960s* (New York, 1984), 389–394; Richard Cummings, *The Pied Piper: Allard K. Lowenstein and the Liberal Dream* (New York, 1985), 336–365; Steven Gillon, *Politics and Vision: The ADA and American Liberalism, 1947–1985* (New York, 1987), chaps. 8–9.

3. John Roche to Lyndon Johnson, February 16, 1968, PL 2, WHCF confidential files, LBJL; oral history interview with Jack Conway, April 10, 1972, Washington, D.C., JFKL.

4. Theodore White, *The Making of the President, 1968* (New York, 1969), chap. 3; Jeremy Larner, *Nobody Knows: Reflections on the McCarthy Campaign of 1968* (New York, 1969), 34–43, and the works cited in n. 2, above.

5. Charles DeBenedetti, *An American Ordeal: The Antiwar Movement of the Vietnam Era* (Syracuse, 1990), 209–213; Gillon, *Politics and Vision*, 210–213; Chester et al., *American Melodrama*, 96–100; Arthur Schlesinger Jr., *Robert Kennedy and His Times* (Boston, 1978), 922–923. Subsequent studies showed that a substantial portion of McCarthy's support in New Hampshire came from hawks upset by Johnson's moderation in Vietnam, but at the time most analysts considered McCarthy's strong showing a triumph for the Democratic party's doves. See, for example, Larner, *Nobody Knows*, 41–42.

6. Hubert Humphrey to Lyndon Johnson, February 16, 1968, Box 17, WHCF, Ex FG 1, LBJL; transcript of press conference, March 12, 1968, Box 326, WPR; Victor Reuther to Walter Reuther, January 25, 1968, and enclosed statement, Box 472, WPR.

7. Gillon, *Politics and Vision*, 212; Roche to Johnson, February 16, 1968, PL 2, WHCF confidential files, LBJL; Reuther statement, n.d. [February 1968], Box 472, WPR; IEB minutes, special session March 1–2, 1968, Box 24, Region 9A.

8. IEB minutes, special session, March 1–2, 1968, Box 24, Region 9A.

9. Ibid.; Irving Bluestone's handwritten minutes of meeting between Walter Reuther and I. W. Abel, March 7, 1968, Box 39, WPR; AFL-CIO Executive Council, *To Clear the Record* (Washington, D.C., 1969), 32–33; Roche to Lyndon Johnson, March 4, 1968, LA 7, WHCF confidential files, LBJL.

10. Nat Weinberg to Walter Reuther, February 5, 1968, Box 14, Nat Weinberg Collection, ALUA; IEB minutes, special session, March 1–2, 1968, Box 24, Region 9A. After Tet, Weinberg flooded Reuther with antiwar memos. See Weinberg to Reuther, February 6, 9, 13, 14, 15, 1968, all in Box 14, Weinberg Collection. In an interview in February 1988 in Detroit, Bluestone contended the memos were part of a campaign by the UAW's doves to persuade Reuther to join the antiwar movement.

11. Victor Reuther to IEB members, International representatives, and local presidents, February 1, 1968; Victor Reuther to IEB members, February 12, 1968, both in Box 511, WPR; oral history interview with Joseph L. Rauh Jr., May 10, 1987, Washington, D.C. According to Rauh, Jack Conway, who also held Reuther's proxy, cast the UAW's vote opposing ADA's endorsement of McCarthy.

12. The standard biography of Robert Kennedy is Schlesinger, *Robert Kennedy and His Times*. Also see David Halberstam, *The Unfinished Odyssey of Robert Kennedy* (New York, 1969); Newfield, *Robert F. Kennedy;* and Jules Witcover, *85 Days: The Last Campaign of Robert Kennedy* (New York, 1969). UAW rank-and-file statistics are from Oliver Quayle survey, June 1967, Box 59, Vice-President Leonard Woodcock Collection, ALUA.

13. Chester et al., *American Melodrama,* 125–141; White, *Making of the President, 1968,* 156–166; Newfield, *Robert F. Kennedy,* 257–259; Roche to Johnson, March 18, 1968, Box 29, Marvin Watson Collection, LBJL; Intelligence Report, March 18, 1968, Box 9, RFK Presidential Campaign Files, JFKL; unknown to Marvin Watson, March 19, 1968, and Jim Rowe to [Marvin Watson], March 19, 1968, both in Box 9, Watson Collection; Lyndon Johnson Daily Diary Cards, LBJL; Conway interview, April 10, 1972, JFKL.

14. Jim J. to Lyndon Johnson, March 19, 1968, Box 31, WHCF, Ex LA 7, LBJL; Conway interview, April 10, 1967, JFKL; Paul Schrade to Robert Kennedy, March 18, 1968, Box 217, WPR; oral history interview with Schrade, June 1992, Los Angeles; Chester et al., *American Melodrama,* 315–317. It was particularly significant that Woodcock led the opposition to Reuther. Woodcock had long been Reuther's heir apparent to the UAW presidency, and he and Schrade had never been on friendly terms.

15. Conway interview, April 10, 1972, JFKL. For details on the board members' alignment in support of Kennedy, see IEB minutes, September 10–13, 1968, Box 24, Region 9A.

16. Mildred Jeffrey's typed notes, n.d. [April 1968], Box 2, Mildred Jeffrey Collection, ALUA; Conway interview, April 10, 1972, JFKL; interview with Victor Reuther, May 6, 1987, Washington, D.C.; Weinberg to Walter Reuther, March 28, 1968, Box 14, Weinberg Collection, ALUA.

17. Doris Kearns, *Lyndon Johnson and the American Dream* (New York, 1976), chap. 12; Carl Solberg, *Hubert Humphrey: A Biography* (New York, 1984), chaps. 28–29; Bill Welsh to Michigan Political Files, April 4, 1968, 24-D-8–3B, 1968 Campaign Files, HHH; Ted Sorensen to Robert Kennedy, April 19, 1968, Box 9, RFK Presidential Campaign Files, JFKL; Offield Dukes to Bill Connell and Bill Welsh, April 21, 1968, 23-C-2–6F, 1968 Campaign Files, HHH; IEB minutes, September 10–12, 1968, Box 24, Region 9A; Joseph Califano to Lyndon Johnson, April 29, 1968, Box 97, Presidential Appointment File (Diary Backup), LBJL; Walter Reuther's handwritten note, n.d. [April

1968], Box 435, WPR; David Burke to Edward Kennedy, April 15, 1968, Box 9, RFK Presidential Campaign Files.

18. Jeffrey to Burke, July 20, 1968, Box 47, Jeffrey Collection, ALUA; *UAW Washington Report*, April 8, 1968.

19. David Garrow, *Bearing the Cross: Martin Luther King, Jr., and the Southern Christian Leadership Conference* (New York, 1986), 622–624; Adam Fairclough, *To Redeem the Soul of America: The Southern Christian Leadership Conference and Martin Luther King, Jr.* (Athens, Ga., 1987), 382–383; Matusow, *Unraveling of America*, 395–396.

20. Adam Fairclough, "Was Martin Luther King a Marxist?" *History Workshop* 15 (Spring 1983), 117–125; Fairclough, *To Redeem the Soul*, chaps. 13–14; David Garrow, "From Reformer to Revolutionary," in Garrow, ed., *Martin Luther King, Jr., and the Civil Rights Movement* (Brooklyn, 1989), 427–436; Garrow, *Bearing the Cross*, 536–537, 563–564; White, *Making of the President, 1968*, 206–209.

21. Fairclough, *To Redeem the Soul*, 385–388; David Garrow, *The FBI and Martin Luther King, Jr.* (New York, 1981), 183–185, 207–208; Conway to Reuther, April 24, 1968, Box 517, WPR; Bill Dodds to Reuther, April 26, 1968, and UAW Officers' Committee to Reuther, June 3, 1968, both in Box 517, WPR.

22. IEB minutes, June 24–26, 1968, Box 24, Region 9A; *UAW Washington Report*, May 27, 1968; Weinberg to Arthur Okun, April 10, 1968, Box 14, Weinberg Collection, ALUA; Reuther to all UAW officers, board members, and regional directors, June 11, 1968, Box 517, WPR.

23. Chester et al., *American Melodrama*, 144; Solberg, *Hubert Humphrey*, 324; Roche to Marvin Watson, February 29, 1968, Box 29, Watson Collection, LBJL; Roche to Johnson, March 4, 1968, LA 7, WHCF confidential files, LBJL; Hobart Taylor to Cecil Burney, March 27, 1968, Reuther folder, WHCF name files; Victor Reisel column clippings, April 26, 1968, Box 437, and May 3 and 9, 1968, Box 435, WPR; AFL-CIO, *To Clear the Record*, 33–44; David Lebenbom to Edward Kennedy, April 8, 1968, Box 9, RFK Presidential Campaign Files, JFKL.

24. Witcover, *85 Days*, 128–182; D.W.B. to Edward Kennedy, March 30, 1968, and Ivan Nestigen to Edward Kennedy and others, April 8, 1968, both in RFK Presidential Campaign Files, JFKL; oral history interview with Ted Sorensen, March 21, 1969, New York City, JFKL; Robert Kennedy's remarks to UAW convention, in "Proceedings of the Twenty-first Constitutional Convention, UAW, May 4–10, 1968," ALUA.

25. Dave Hackett to unknown, March 21, 1968, Box 2, RFK Presidential Campaign Files, JFKL; Conway interview, April 10, 1972, JFKL; Chester et al., *American Melodrama*, 316; Fraser Barron to Dave Hackett, April 25 and May 11, 1968, both in Box 2, RFK Presidential Campaign Files.

26. Gillon, *Politics and Vision*, 216; Lew Rivlin to Michigan File, May 11, 1968, 24-D-8-3B, and Offield Dukes to Bill Connell and Bill Welsh, April 21, 1968, 23-C-2-6F, both in 1968 Campaign Files, HHH. For an example of how UAW forces hurt Humphrey's campaign in Michigan, see Rivlin to Walter Mondale and Tom Harris, June 3, 1968, 24-D-7-8F, 1968 Campaign Files, HHH.

27. Schlesinger, *Robert Kennedy*, 981–982; transcript of CBS interview with Paul Schrade, June 10, 1968, Box 217, WPR. The bullet grazed Schrade, who was not seriously wounded.

28. *UAW Washington Report*, June 10, 1968; Jeffrey to Edward Kennedy, July 21, 1968, Box 47, Jeffrey Collection, ALUA; oral history interview with Jeffrey, August 13, 1976, ALUA.

29. Elisabeth Reuther Dickmeyer, *Reuther: A Daughter Strikes* (Southfield, Mich., 1989), 311; Jean Stein and George Plimpton, eds., *American Journey: The Times of*

Robert Kennedy (New York, 1970), 290; IEB minutes, September 10–12, 1968, Box 24, Region 9A.

30. *UAW Washington Report,* June 24, 1968; Reuther to all officers, board members, and regional directors, June 11, 1968, Box 517, WPR; IEB minutes, June 24–26, 1968, Box 24, Region 9A; Fairclough, *To Redeem the Soul,* 387.

31. William Oliver to UAW Officers' Committee, May 31, 1968; UAW Officers' Committee to Reuther, June 3, 1968; typewritten notes, n.d. [June 1968]; UAW news release, all in Box 517, WPR; *UAW Washington Report,* June 24, 1968.

32. "A Proposal to Create 500,000 Jobs through Total Action to Provide Adequate and Decent Housing for Low-Income Families," draft, February 1968, Box 497; Edward J. Robinson to Reuther, April 1, 1968, Box 467; Robinson to Reuther, April 8, 1967, and Justin Weaver to Bluestone, June 17, 1968, Box 497, all in WPR.

33. "Proposal to Create 500,000 Jobs," Box 497, WPR.

34. Karl Treckel, *The Rise and Fall of the Alliance for Labor Action (1968–1972)* (Kent, Ohio, 1975); *John Herling's Labor Letter,* July 27, 1968; *Los Angeles Times,* July 29, 1968; John Barnard, *Walter Reuther and the Rise of the Auto Workers Union* (Boston, 1983), 380–381; Rauh interview, May 10, 1987.

35. IEB minutes, June 24–26, 1968, Box 24, Region 9A.

36. *Wall Street Journal,* July 19, 1968; Bluestone's handwritten notes of ALA meetings, June 27, July 17, and July 22, 1968, all in Box 340, WPR.

37. IEB minutes, June 24–26, 1968, Box 24, Region 9A; *New York Times,* June 30, 1968; Negotiate Now! peace plank, July 1968, Box 13, IAD; Reuther to Mary Temple, July 11, 1968, Box 511, WPR. When he decided to affiliate with Negotiate Now! Reuther told the IEB that he had been "sympathetic to this group for a long time."

38. Fairclough, *To Redeem the Soul,* 387–389; *UAW Washington Report,* June 24, 1968.

39. *New York Times,* June 9, 1968; Walker Cisler to Joseph L. Hudson, July 29, 1968, Box 497, WPR; Sidney Fine, *Violence in the Model City: The Cavanagh Administration, Race Relations, and the Detroit Riot of 1967* (Ann Arbor, 1989), 445; *Detroit Free Press,* November 27, 1968; IEB minutes, special session, November 20–21, 1968, Box 24, Region 9A; Richard Boone to Reuther, January 31, 1968, Box 1, CCAPC; Conway to Reuther, October 25 and November 8, 1968, Box 474, WPR; *New York Times,* April 27, 1969; minutes of the board of directors of the Center for Community Change, April 8, 1969, Box 475, WPR; director's report to the board and friends of CCAP, December 31, 1968, Box 1, CCAPC; Bluestone's notes, June 27, July 17, and July 22, 1968, all in Box 340, WPR. Rather than dissolve CCAP, Reuther, Conway, and Boone arranged to merge it with the newly formed Center for Community Change, a privately funded activist agency controlled by the Kennedy political machine.

40. IEB minutes, June 24–26, 1968, Box 24, Region 9A; oral history interview with Bluestone, February 1988, Detroit; Solberg, *Hubert Humphrey,* 344; Guy Nunn to Bluestone and Reuther, July 24 and 25, 1968, and Tom Kahn to Bluestone, July 25, 1968, all in Box 597, WPR; final draft of speech, Box 370, WPR. See also Humphrey to Reuther, July 24, 1968, Box 370, WPR.

41. Chester et al., *American Melodrama,* 524–537; oral history interview with Clark Kerr, August 12, 1985, Berkeley, LBJL; Humphrey's platform position on Vietnam, August 16, 1968, 23-B-2-5B, 1968 Campaign Files, HHH; Solberg, *Hubert Humphrey,* 347–354; Hubert Humphrey, *The Education of a Public Man: My Life and Politics* (Garden City, N.Y., 1976), 387–390.

42. Jeffrey interview, August 13, 1976, ALUA; oral history interview with Douglas Fraser, February 24, 1987, Detroit; list of delegates, n.d. [August 1968], Box 3, LeRoy Cappaert Collection, MHC; *Detroit Free Press,* September 22, 1968; IEB minutes, Sep-

tember 10–12, 1968, Box 24, Region 9A. Even the UAW delegation was divided. Jeffrey defied her union's orders and voted for McCarthy, while both Pat Patterson and George Merrelli voted for the majority plank supporting the Johnson war policy.

43. David Farber, *Chicago '68* (Chicago, 1988). Also see Matusow, *Unraveling of America*, 411–422; White, *Making of the President, 1968*, 257. The UAW leadership condemned the police violence in the most vigorous terms. "No, they weren't hippies," the *UAW Washington Report* insisted in its issue of September 2, 1968. "They were clean cut kids. The cream of the crop. And Daley's cops clubbed them over the head, beat them down, hustled them off to paddy wagons. Years from now when people ask for a definition of police brutality, they will recall the screams for mercy and blood on the streets in front of the Conrad Hilton in Chicago." Some rank and filers were outraged by the *Washington Report*'s analysis; see set of letters in Box 52, WPR.

44. IEB minutes, September 10–12, 1968, Box 24, Region 9A.

45. Ibid.

46. Clayborne Carson, *In Struggle: SNCC and the Black Awakening of the 1960s* (Cambridge, Mass., 1981), chaps. 17–18; William L. Van Deburg, *New Day in Babylon: The Black Power Movement and American Culture, 1965–1975* (Chicago, 1992), chap. 4.

47. Thomas R. Brook, "DRUMbeats in Detroit," *Dissent* 17 (January–February 1970), 16–25; Dan Georgakas and Marvin Surkin, *Detroit: I Do Mind Dying: A Study in Urban Revolution* (New York, 1975); James Geschwender, *Class, Race, and Worker Insurgency: The League of Revolutionary Black Workers* (Cambridge, 1977); and Steve Jefferys, *Management and Managed: Fifty Years of Crisis at Chrysler* (Cambridge, 1986), 168–187.

48. Kevin Boyle, "There Are No Union Sorrows That the Union Can't Heal: The Struggle for Racial Equality in the United Automobile Workers, 1945–1960," *Labor History*, forthcoming; Jefferys, *Management and Managed*, 162–167; Brooks, "DRUMbeats," 16–19.

49. Geschwender, *Class, Race, and Worker Insurgency*, chaps. 4–5; Georgakas and Surkin, *Detroit*, chap. 2.

50. Chester et al., *American Melodrama*, 607–631, 673–689; Stephen Ambrose, *Nixon: The Triumph of a Politician, 1962–1972* (New York, 1989), 102–222; Tom Wicker, *One of Us: Richard Nixon and the American Dream* (New York, 1991), chaps. 8–9; Thomas Byrne Edsall and Mary D. Edsall, *Chain Reaction: The Impact of Race, Rights, and Taxes on American Politics* (New York, 1991), 74–79; Jonathan Rieder, "The Rise of the 'Silent Majority,' " in Steven Fraser and Gary Gerstle, eds., *The Rise and Fall of the New Deal Order, 1930–1980* (Princeton, 1989), 259–261.

51. Marshall Frady, *Wallace* (New York, 1968), remains the best study of Wallace's background and character. On Wallace's campaign, see Chester et al., *American Melodrama*, 261–294, 652–658, and Jody Carlson, *George C. Wallace and the Politics of Powerlessness: The Wallace Campaigns for the Presidency, 1964–1976* (New Brunswick, N.J., 1981).

52. Straw poll returns, n.d. [August 1968], Box 436, WPR; Chester et al., *American Melodrama*, 705; *U.S. News & World Report*, October 7, 1968; Michigan situation report, October 22, 1968, 23-C-2-6F, 1968 Campaign Files, HHH; IEB minutes, September 10–12, 1968, Box 24, Region 9A.

53. Flyer from Local 3 leadership, October 2, 1968, Box 229, WPR; Geschwender, *Class, Race, and Worker Insurgency*, 103–109; Georgakas, *Detroit*, 48–51; Barnard, *Walter Reuther*, 209; package of memos on Region 1A directorship, 1968, Box 149, UAW Secretary-Treasurer Collection, Emil Mazey Files, ALUA.

54. Examples of UAW campaign literature are available in Box 52, WPR. The UAW also made a substantial contribution of money and personnel to Humphrey's campaign. The UAW spent $500,000 in Michigan alone to promote voter registration and an additional $30,000 on election day in a final push to bring African-Americans to the polls. The UAW also maintained "continuous" contact with the Humphrey campaign and established a full-time "Wallace desk" at Solidarity House. See Michigan status reports, September 19 and October 29, 1968, and Nick Kostopulos to Clair Stewart, September 24, 1968 all in 23-C-1B, 1968 Campaign Files, HHH; Chester et al., *American Melodrama*, 707; Reuther to Woodcock, October 31, 1968, Box 62, Woodcock Collection, ALUA.

55. Robert Zieger, *American Workers, American Unions, 1920–1985* (Baltimore, 1986), 187–190.

56. Geschwender, *Class, Race, and Worker Insurgency*, 103–109; Georgakas and Surkin, *Detroit*, 48–51; Jefferys, *Management and Managed*, 176–177; Barnard, *Walter Reuther*, 209. The shop-floor black revolutionary movement gained strength in 1969, but in the early 1970s it collapsed, undermined by the UAW leadership's continued efforts to co-opt black anger and by the movement's internal tensions.

57. Brendan Sexton and Patricia Cayo Sexton, *Blue Collars and Hard Hats: The Working Class and the Future of American Politics* (New York, 1971); Andrew Levinson, *The Working Class Majority* (New York, 1974); Richard Hamilton, *Class and Politics in the United States* (New York, 1972); poll of Michigan voters, September 7–15, 1968, 24-d-7–8F, 1968 Campaign Files, HHH. The UAW leadership continued to push Humphrey to distance himself from the war, and Reuther personally urged Johnson to announce a bombing halt: oral history interview with Victor Reuther, May 6, 1987; Mary Temple to Walter Reuther, October 11, 1968; Clark Kerr and Milton Sachs to Reuther, October 25, 1968; proposal from "Negotiate Now!" October 11, 1968, all in Box 511, WPR.

58. On labor's role in Wallace's defeat, see White, *Making of the President, 1968*, 364–366; Chester et al., *American Melodrama*, 707–710; and Zieger, *American Workers*, 189–190. Solberg, *Hubert Humphrey*, 375–385, and Carlson, *George C. Wallace*, 82–83, discuss the candidates and the war. The UAW's attack on Le May is from *UAW Solidarity*, November 1968.

59. Comparison of presidential election votes, January 2, 1969, Box 53, WPR. To place the rank and file's vote in a broader context, see Hamilton, *Class and Politics*, 460–467; Philip Converse, Jerrold Rusk, and Arthur Wolfe, "Continuity and Change in American Politics: Parties and Issues in the 1968 Election," *American Political Science Review* 63 (December 1969), 1083–1105; Richard Boyd, "Popular Control of Public Policy: A Normal Vote Analysis of the 1968 Election," *American Political Science Review* 66 (June 1972), 429–441; J. Michael Ross, Reeve Vanneman, and Thomas Pettigrew, "Patterns of Support for George Wallace: Implications for Racial Change," *Journal of Social Issues* 36 (November 1976), 69–91.

60. IEB minutes, special session, November 20–21, 1968, Box 24, Region 9A. The classic study of the shift of voters to the conservatives is Kevin Philips, *The Emerging Republican Majority* (Garden City, N.Y., 1969).

Epilogue: The Limits of Liberalism

1. John Barnard, *Walter Reuther and the Rise of the Auto Workers Union* (Boston, 1983), 212.

2. Charles DeBenedetti, *An American Ordeal: The Antiwar Movement of the Vietnam Era* (Syracuse, 1990), 253; Philip Foner, *U.S. Labor and the Vietnam War* (New York, 1989), 69–70, 87–88, 101; IEB minutes, special session, November 20–21, 1968, Box 24, Region 9A.

3. DeBenedetti, *American Ordeal,* 351–352; Foner, *U.S. Labor and the Vietnam Era,* 133–136, 147–150; Andrew Battista, "Labor and Coalition Politics: The Progressive Alliance," *Labor History* 32 (Summer 1991), 401–421; David Brody, *Workers in Industrial America: Essays on the Twentieth-Century Struggle* (New York, 1980), 250–251.

4. Steven Fraser, *Labor Will Rule: Sidney Hillman and the Rise of American Labor* (New York, 1991); Walter Reuther to York Langton, May 7, 1970, Box 41, Joseph L. Rauh Jr. Collection, LC.

Index

Abernathy, Ralph, 242, 245, 248
Abner, Willoughby, 129–130, 166
Ackley, Gardner, 144, 224
Addes, George, 29, 34
Albert, Carl, 250
Alinsky, Saul, 217
Alliance for Labor Action, 246–248
Allison Plant (Indianapolis), 116
Amalgamated Clothing Workers of America (ACWA), 41, 59
American Federation of Labor (AFL), 16, 18, 20, 33, 64, 101–105, 290n47
American Federation of Labor–Congress of Industrial Organizations (AFL-CIO), 6, 103–106, 108, 123–124, 144, 152–153, 156–157, 162–164, 170, 174, 193, 201, 219–220, 232, 236–237, 243, 246–247, 248, 261, 299–300n14, 304n58; Industrial Union Department (IUD) of, 103, 157–158, 170, 214–215, 248; Reuther/UAW and, 100–106, 136, 147, 152–154, 156–158, 227–228, 236–237, 243, 246–247, 290n47, 291n53, 299–300n14, 304n58, 310n40
American Federation of State, County, and Municipal Employees (AFSCME), 247
American Federation of Teachers (AFT), 247
American Jewish Conference, 112
American Motors Corp. (AMC), 93
Americans for Democratic Action (ADA),

4, 5, 48–51, 54–55, 59–60, 62, 65, 83, 86, 109, 125, 143, 154, 169, 210–211, 225–226, 232–233, 236–238
Area Redevelopment Act, 136–137, 148, 150
Arnold, Thurman, 37
Association of Catholic Trade Unionists (ACTU), 28, 33, 76, 81, 240, 254
Auto-Lite Corp. plant (Toledo), 148
Automobile industry, 11–12, 74–75, 93–94, 135–136, 146, 148, 198, 260, 314–315n31
Automobile workers, 12–15, 60, 73–78, 81, 90–91, 97, 135–136, 145–146, 148, 154–155, 197, 198, 226, 251, 254; African-American, 7, 15–16, 29, 91, 94, 113–116, 119, 127–129, 146, 164–166, 197, 213, 217–219, 222, 238, 251–254; semi- and unskilled, 14, 73, 113–114, 197; skilled, 14, 18–19, 90, 97, 113–114, 119, 146, 164–166, 197, 213; white, 7, 15–17, 81, 91, 113–114, 117–120, 146, 197, 198, 220–222, 231, 238, 252–256; women, 16, 146, 197

Baker, Bobby, 138
Baker, Ella, 196
Baldwin, Bereniece, 80–81
Ballard, Charles, 58, 114, 117–118
Bannon, Kenneth, 156, 239

Index

Index